The Lord Was Not on Trial

The Inside Story of the Supreme Court's Precedent-Setting *McCollum* Ruling

Dannel McCollum

Americans for Religious Liberty
Box 6656, Silver Spring, Maryland 20916

An Americans for Religious Liberty book

Inquiries should be addressed to:

Americans for Religious Liberty
Box 6656
Silver Spring, MD 20916
Telephone: 301-260-2988
FAX: 301-260-2989
arlinc@verizon.net
www.arlinc.org

ISBN: 13:978-0-9821254-0-3

Printed in the United States of America

Americans for Religious Liberty is a nonprofit public interest educaitonal organization, founded in 1982, dedicated to defending the constitutional principle of separation of church and state.

*For my parents John and Vashti McCollum
and all the other great pioneers of religious liberty
and separation of church and state.*

Table of Contents

Foreword

It has been 60 years since the events described in this book occurred, leading up to the Supreme Court's decision in my mother's historic mandamus action against the Champaign, Illinois, school district, regarding its hosting of Christian Sunday school classes during regular class time. But many things that occurred during that period of my life have remained with me. My dedication to the importance of what has become known as Jefferson's wall of separation between church and state—the First Amendment's prohibition of government action "respecting an establishment of religion"—has not abated.

I remember the entreaties to both my parents and myself from my fourth grade teacher, a taxpayer-supported public employee, to become involved in this religious program. I also remember the pressures exerted upon me by my peers and by my fifth grade teacher. An especially powerful memory is the fervor with which many of my classmates and others expressed their religious beliefs, apparently feeling that my family's stance would somehow threaten their own religious equilibrium.

Although I was harassed and on a few occasions had to defend myself physically, I remember one child who, because he was outed as Jewish as a result of his non-participation, was so badly beaten by an older brother of one of his classmates and his enlightened friends that his glasses were broken, despite being in a hardened case. There were, of course, other indignities and deplorable incidents, which the years have smoothed over, such as my mother's being deluged in a barrage of rotten vegetables on a Halloween evening, as well as the avalanche of hate mail we received.

In spite of the hassles we suffered, neither my brother Dan nor I ever had any doubt whatsoever of the importance of our mother's quest, nor any resentment or misgivings about her raising this important issue and taking it all the way to the United States Supreme Court. Brother Errol, of course, was too young at the time to have much of a clue as to what was transpiring in our lives and its importance—but he, too, is proud of having been a part of this family and what my mother accomplished. What we experienced during those years, beginning in the fall of 1945 and ending in 1948, took place within the context of a close-knit, supportive and healthy family. This gave my brothers and me the strength and perspicacity to come through the trials of those years as stronger individuals. We have all led successful and productive lives—Errol, the youngest, a successful engineer, businessman and entrepreneur; Dan, the middle child, an author, historian and three-term mayor of the city where all this took place; and I, with a nearly 34-year law practice and a second career as a computer jockey and college level professor, and still going strong, despite a second retirement.

Throughout my adult life I have been, and remain, heavily involved in efforts to ensure separation of church and state. My mother's case did indeed have a profound influence on my life . . . as my mother knew, as we all know, she was right. My wife, Betty Grace, a community minister and university instructor, and I are active Unitarian Universalists. We use the opportunities provided through our involvement in organizations such as Americans United for Separation of Church and State, the American Civil Liberties Union, the Freedom from Religion Foundation, Americans for Religious Liberty, and the Arkansas Democratic Party, to continue the fight for religious freedom and government neutrality.

It is important to note that in this country less than a quarter of a child's waking and productive hours are spent in school, leaving the balance available for whatever moral and religious training and indoctrination their families deem necessary. Mixing religion with public education, as many continue to attempt to do, creates a divisive and an often violent atmosphere in an institution that has as its mission the education of a diverse population to be good and productive citizens. There are enough distractions in public education without introducing the emotional element of religious differences and intolerance.

James Terry McCollum, J.D.
August, 2008

Preface

This is the story of *People of the State of Illinois ex rel. Vashti McCollum v. Board of Education of School District No. 71, Champaign County, Illinois, et al.* (333 US 203). The action arose as a challenge to a program of sectarian religious education classes held in public school buildings on school time. Today, the chief significance of the *McCollum* case is that it was the first of series of cases brought under the First and Fourteenth Amendments to the United States Constitution where a practice by a local or state governmental body was actually held to violate the First Amendment's "establishment of religion" clause.

The practice of "released time" religious education in public schools was not new when it was introduced into Champaign schools in 1940. The first program in the country was in Gary, Indiana, in 1921. While it is not known with certainty with whom the idea originated, school authorities or clergy, it seems that the latter, especially members of mainline Protestant denominations, took the lead in spreading the program around the country. Catholic clergy, though supportive, do not appear to have been a driving force, probably content with their system of parochial schools. Jews often had reservations but tended to go along with released time programs to avoid trouble.

Supporters of the practice justified the sectarian religious classes on a number of grounds. Some held that youngsters were not receiving sufficient training in morals and values. Religious classes, they argued, would likely reduce juvenile delinquency and other problems of youth. No data were ever produced to justify these claims. Others saw in the public schools a wonderful opportunity to provide religious instruction to the unchurched. Where else could the churches have such total access to young people, especially those who, for whatever reason, did not flock to churches on Sundays?

Many proponents of released time were sincere. The decade of the 1930s represented hard, even desperate, economic times. People were worried about social revolution. They feared "isms"—with respect to the *McCollum* case, communism and, for some reason, materialism were mentioned. (I have often wondered where the American economy would be without materialism.)

In 1940, little anticipating the determined challenge that would result in a legal decision of nationwide significance, local clergy and school officials instituted their released time program of sectarian religious instruction in the public schools of Champaign, Illinois, and the five-year fuse was lit.

My connections with this case are more than casual. The plaintiff, Vashti Cromwell McCollum, was my mother. The *causus belli* was James Terry

McCollum, my older brother. My grandfather, Arthur G. Cromwell, was a prominent participant. While I had no active involvement in the official events, either in
the trial or the appeals, my memories as a youngster from the ages of eight to
eleven are vivid, reflective, I am sure, of the personal trauma related to negative
reactions locally while the case was in the courts. Rereadings over the years of
my mother's book, *One Woman's Fight*, helped keep the details reasonably fresh
in my mind.

From the time my mother filed suit in June, 1945, well through the trial the
following September, the public perception was that the case represented a direct challenge to the Christian religion itself—that God was on trial. While it was
unlikely that this misconception could have been avoided entirely, it was greatly
aggravated by the tactics employed by my mother's trial attorney, Landon L.
Chapman. The aggressive approach, in both his pleadings and in his conduct in
the trial, tended to obscure the real issue: whether or not the sectarian religious
classes as they were conducted in the public schools of Champaign were legal.
Chapman's client and her backers were dismayed by the backlash.

Another factor certainly must have weighed heavily in the public response to
the suit. World War II was in its closing months. Already there were cracks developing among the victorious allies. (VE Day had occurred before the suit was filed;
VJ Day came afterwards but before the trial.) These international conflicts were
signs of what was to become, during the height of the Cold War, an almost hysteri-
cal fear of "atheistic communism." Such were hardly opportune times to pursue a
cause construed by so many as a godless campaign against religion.

From my vantage point, it was as if my family was under a constant state of
siege for the two and a half years the case was in the courts. I can remember my
mother telling my brothers and me at the time that we had to be especially careful
in what we did and how we acted because everyone in town knew who we were
and would be watching.

She also told us before the final decision in the case that there were more
people for us than against. She, however, had the advantage of frequent travel to
such cosmopolitan places as Chicago, New York City and Boston on matters
relating to the case. Away from the close, provincial atmosphere of Champaign-
Urbana, she was able to benefit from a much broader perspective than I as to the
attitudes of thinking people in the rest of the country. Despite her assurances of
support for her cause, I retained my doubts.

Just two years after the 1948 Supreme Court decision, I spent a portion of my
freshman year in high school in Gainesville, Florida. This was during a most
virulent stage of the Cold War, made ever more fearful by the related scourge of
McCarthyism. The school day opened with a Bible reading by students on a rota-
tional basis. Aware of the high degree of religious conformity in that southern city,
and its almost synonymous equation with good Americanism, I remember my
terror each day that my name would be called, forcing me either to conform or to
stand on principle. The result of the latter course would almost certainly have led
to my having to endure similar consequences to those I had experienced earlier
during the active years of the *McCollum* case. To my great relief, I was never
called upon. My mother did not recall saying anything to the school authorities,

so I assume they must have learned about the situation from an article in the local newspaper and were careful to avoid a conflict.

A more liberal climate came with the mild "thaw" in the Cold War. Among many persons with whom I came into contact during the mid to late 1950s there was an almost grudging respect for the action my mother had taken. With the growing unrest of the civil rights movement and the Vietnam War, the family connection with the case became a positive distinction among those with whom I associated.

By the early 1970s, due primarily to the burgeoning University of Illinois, Champaign had became a highly transient city. Most of the new arrivals knew little or nothing of the *McCollum* case. Even among the local population, those who had any memory at all of the case tended to confuse it with the later civil liberties cases which involved prayer and Bible reading in the public schools. Elsewhere, where there was no direct connection with the once notorious trial, the case was generally forgotten. Liberals, if they thought about the church-state issue at all, were likely to take the "wall of separation" proposition for granted; fundamentalists, and the religious right in general, were as yet too disorganized politically to successfully challenge the demarcation established by the Supreme Court of what was Caesar's and what was God's.

With the election of Richard Nixon in 1968, all of this began to change. The trend was reinforced by the subsequent ascendancy of Ronald Reagan in 1980. Both of these figures were heavily assisted by important support from the religious right. These two presidents, representing the right wing of the Republican Party, between them, with added help from George H.W. and George W. Bush, have appointed a majority of the justices on the United States Supreme Court. Already a noticeable change appears to have occurred in the court's perception of church-state relations.

Many civil libertarians, including myself, view this trend away from strict separation as alarming. Without question, my connection with the *McCollum* case is an influencing factor. The trial and its aftermath posed difficult times for my family and the thought that it may all have been for naught brings with it a strong sense of personal frustration and futility.

Of much greater importance is the threat to the constitutional principle involved: "Congress shall make no law respecting an establishment of religion, or prohibiting the free exercise thereof . . ."

This lofty statement of public policy and fundamental law is elemental to the survival of a free society. It is based upon the simple common sense notion that the best way to avoid religious strife, which has caused so much pain and suffering over the centuries, is by maintaining to the maximum extent possible governmental neutrality in the field of religious affairs.

The Founding Fathers had first-hand knowledge of the problems that occurred when there was mingling of church and state. As if European history had not provided examples enough, there were the more immediate examples of religious intolerance in many of the thirteen states just prior to the adoption of the Constitution.

The majority of our early settlers came from countries where church and state were not separated but were linked or interrelated. Many of them had suffered for their religious beliefs and many of them settled this country in religious communities. Ironically, although they were seeking religious freedom for themselves, they did not always want to extend that freedom to others of different beliefs.

Backed up by the precedents set by Roger Williams and the Virginia Declaration of Rights, James Madison and others felt that the best course was for a definite separation of church and state, affording the protection of minority rights, religious and otherwise. Accordingly the Bill of Rights was proposed and adopted, establishing definite limitations on the power of the federal government. After the passage of the Fourteenth Amendment, and through Court interpretation, similar limitations were placed on the states. In theory at least, these guarantees of individual liberty stand, irrespective of the majority will at any given time or place.

Unfortunately, a large percentage, perhaps a majority, of Americans does not understand the Constitution and the essential protections it afford minorities. This failing is well expressed in a letter received by Vashti McCollum during the progress of her case through the courts. The person wrote:

> We are a Democracy and in a Democracy the majority rules. The majority of people believe in religious education so why don't you shut your big mouth you old bag.

What the letter's author failed to realize is that a democracy can only exist where people are free to disagree, where divergent views are respected and, when necessary, protected by the power and authority of government. Without such guarantees, no individual or group would be secure from either the prejudices and persecution of a settled majority or the occasional and fleeting hysteria of the mob.

Many who were opposed to Mrs. McCollum either failed to understand the nature of the fight, or deliberately distorted the consequences in the event of her victory. Irrespective of the basis—ignorance or deception—the arguments often sounded the same, as exemplified in the words of one writer:

> What is to be said of our Christian civilization when the Psalms of David and the story of Jesus are excluded from schools that may teach Karl Marx and the origin of species every day of the year? This Supreme Court ban does not apply to the Communist Manifesto: It applies to the Golden Rule and the Sermon on the Mount.

The inclusion of Bible study as a part of a survey course in religion would not only be appropriate, but may be as essential as the reading of the Communist Manifesto in a course on economic history. Singing Christmas carols was also often mentioned as quite likely falling under the ban of the McCollum decision. Concerning this, Vashti wrote:

> Throughout my own public school attendance I enjoyed and looked forward to the annual Christmas carol sing on the last day before Christmas vacation started.

She, as her children, loved to sing Christmas carols; and caroling often occurred in the public schools her children attended. She never objected. She would have been critical of the practice only if it were part of a religious pageant.

Vashti McCollum, from start to finish, was interested only in the elimination of sectarian religious indoctrination in the public schools. The essential difference between education and indoctrination was summed up by Anton J. Carlson, noted physiologist from the University of Chicago. He was sent to Springfield, the state capital, during the witch-hunting days of the 1950s to appear before a committee of the legislature. The solons were concerned about subversive teaching at institutions of higher learning in Illinois. He was asked, "Do you teach Communism at the University of Chicago?"

The elderly scientist thoughtfully responded, "Yes, we teach about Communism at the University of Chicago ... (pause) ... we also teach about syphilis. That doesn't mean we recommend it."

The *McCollum* case represents an excellent case study in support of strict observance of the Bill of Rights in general, and the prevention of "an establishment of religion" in particular. That intrusion of religious classes into the Champaign schools was divisive. That was the experience of James Terry McCollum and his family as well. Other individuals and groups, Jews in particular, also were affected negatively, though most refrained from active protest.

It might well be asked why I am offering a new view of the McCollum case when my mother has already written on the subject. Her book, *One Woman's Fight*, composed in an intimate style within a year following the 1948 Supreme Court decision, is a revealing personal memoir. In contrast, this book presents an accumulation of research and archival material either not pursued by or unavailable to my mother. Some of the information comes from a detailed investigation into the origins of the conflict—the circumstances surrounding the establishment of the religious classes in 1940. Of even greater consequence was my discovery of a fascinating collection of documents relating to the case in the files of my maternal grandfather, Arthur Cromwell. Not only did he participate in the trial in 1945, but he had been active in church-state issues long before his daughter, and he saved everything. His files and letters proved to be most revealing. Also, in preparation of the manuscript, I actively sought out the various surviving participants in the case, regardless of their views or positions at the time, in a determined effort to include their thoughts and reflections.

I have set out to relate the events in as objective a manner as possible. It is true that I have had disproportionate access to the private papers of the plaintiff and her family, which cannot help but allow me to make her position, as well as her trials and tribulations, much clearer than those of her adversaries. Nevertheless, through interviews and other research, I have attempted to overcome that deficiency to the extent that the Champaign Board of Education and its allies are treated as fairly as the private candor of surviving principals and the public record permit.

The result, I feel, is a useful contribution both to an understanding of the dynamics of a well-known court case and to the current discussion of church-state relationships in the United States.

References

I began research on this book in the mid 1970s. The manuscript was essentially completed by 1985. After some effort to get the work published, I gave up on the project. Now, in this 60th anniversary year of the *McCollum* decision, I have moved decisively to see the effort in print. A major reference for this book is my mother's memoir, *One Woman's Fight*, published three years after the decision. I also was most fortunate in having two valuable archives. First were my mother's scrapbooks, which contained an amazing collection of news clips related to the case as well as other church-state issues. These are now in the possession of Illinois History and Lincoln Collections of the University of Illinois Library, the Urbana-Champaign Campus. They are referenced as MC-UI, Books 1-5. A second collection of some of these same news articles is deposited at the Archives of the Urbana Free Library in Urbana, Illinois. They are referenced as MA, Vols. 1 & 2.

Acknowledgments

First and foremost, the completion of this book has been largely due to the contributions and support of my wife, Jeanette A. McCollum. Without her help, the book would not have been possible. My older brother, James T. McCollum, has continued the family's efforts to maintain the separation of church and state and along with my younger brother, Errol C. McCollum, has encouraged me in my efforts to complete this book. Edd Doerr of Americans for Religious Liberty has offered invaluable encouragement and assistance in seeing this book through to publication. I am also indebted to Brian Inglassius for his technical assistance in organizing the references.

Let me also extend my gratitude to the Freedom from Religion Foundation of Madison, Wisconsin, for keeping my mother's book, *One Woman's Fight*, in print and for its work on behalf of church-state separation.

Unsung Heroes

With any significant undertaking there are usually a number of major contributors. These include a few unsung heroes. In the *McCollum* case there are two who stand out—Philip Schug and Milton T. Raynor. Philip Schug was the youthful Unitarian minister in Champaign-Urbana in 1945. He was quick to become the strongest and most vocal of Vashti McCollum's local supporters. As a newcomer to town in a complacent, go-along, get-along community, he had much to lose.

His involvement began inconspicuously enough when, in January 1945, in his church newsletter, he alerted his parishioners of possible action in the State Legislature legalizing religious instruction in the public schools (*One Woman's Fight*, OWF, p. 22). At that time, because of her son's difficulties in school related to such classes, Vashti McCollum (hereafter just Vashti) wrote to her local legislators. The replies proved to be an embarrassment to their authors later on. When her son's situation became precarious due to his failure to participate in the classes, Vashti called Schug to seek his counsel relative to legal action. He offered to contact a group in Chicago that was strongly opposed to the religious classes. The group, the Chicago Action Council, responded, indicating that it was prepared to supply an attorney and pay all legal expenses (OWF, p. 29).

As the case was being assembled, Schug accompanied Vashti and her attorney on calls to various persons who figured in the case, including: the superintendent of schools, members of the Board of Education, the school principal and the Board's attorney (OWF, pp. 33-36). Schug also accompanied the plaintiff when she served the president of the school board with a formal demand that the classes be stopped (OWF, p. 37).

After the suit had been filed, the local legislators to whom Vashti had written sponsored a bill to legalize the religious classes. The bill speedily passed the Illinois House. Schug rose to the occasion by assembling his "Hot Potato" flyer in which, among other items, he included the letters from the hypocritical legislators. He hand-carried copies of the flyer to Springfield and placed them on the desks of the senators before the session began. The Senate rejected the bill in part due to Schug's efforts (OWF, pp. 39-40).

On the evening before the trial, Schug hosted a "mass meeting" at his small church at which most of the major protagonists were present (OWF, pp. 55-57). At the trial the following week, Schug was a friendly witness for the plaintiff, providing valuable testimony helping to illustrate the sectarian nature of the religious classes (OWF, p. 75).

During this period, Schug also wrote a lengthy commentary in one of the local newspapers explaining Vashti's position. In all his actions the scholarly minister was utterly fearless. He was present when the case was presented to the Illinois Supreme Court on appeal. Schug was called to another pulpit before the final decision in the United States Supreme Court nearly three years after the original trial, but he had been there when it counted most.

Milton T. "Ted" Raynor was an attorney in Chicago and a member of the Chicago Action Council (CAC). It was a small group, but one that put its money where its mouth was. When the details of the situation in Champaign became known to them, the members offered their immediate support (see above). Some members of the CAC became quite concerned over the direction the trial was taking, particularly the apparent anti-religious overtones generated by the attorney that the group had supplied. That brought a delegation of three CAC members to Champaign during the trial. Fortunately, that group included Ted Raynor, who held CAC firm in its support of the plaintiff (OWF, pp. 63-64).

Of equal importance was the contribution made by Raynor when he produced the abstract of the trial required for an appeal to the Supreme Court of Illinois. This required a monumental effort and kept the case on track. When the trial lawyer left the case, Raynor was chiefly responsible for the appellant's brief in spite of the fact that constitutional law was not his specialty. All of Ted Raynor's efforts were provided without charge to either the CAC or to the plaintiff, Vashti McCollum.

Dannel McCollum
August, 2008

Prologue

In 1947 the United States Supreme Court, in the historic *Everson* decision, declared, in the first opportunity it had to do so, that the First Amendment, made applicable to state and local government by the Fourteenth Amendment, erected a "wall of separation between church and state." This metaphor of President Thomas Jefferson reflected the intent and thinking of the remarkable generation that produced our Constitution and Bill of Rights. Unfortunately, though all nine justices concurred on what the First Amendment means, by five to four they held that New Jersey had not overstepped the boundary between religion and government.

In 1948, in the *McCollum* ruling, the Court for the first time applied the Jefferson/*Everson* principle to find unconstitutional a practice involving religion and public education.

Americans for Religious Liberty is pleased to publish the definitive account of the groundbreaking *McCollum* case, written after exhaustive research by the son of the courageous plaintiff in the case and brother of the case's central figure, James Terry (Jim) McCollum.

I am personally gratified to have had a hand in publishing this book, not only because of its importance but also because I have had the good fortune to know or have known the principals in the case, Vashti McCollum (who preceded me by a generation as president of the American Humanist Association), Vashti's father, Arthur Cromwell, and her sons Jim and Dannel.

The McCollum story highlights the importance of individual citizens taking on the responsibility of defending constitutional principles in spite of social pressures and the possibility of failure. Vashti McCollum was a gutsy hero and model citizen.

Edd Doerr, President
Americans for Religious Liberty
August, 2008

Chapter 1

Pater Familias

While Vashti was, and remains, the best known member of her family associated with the church-state struggle, it would be unfair to begin the story without a brief account of the activities of her father, Arthur G. Cromwell, who entered the fray years before his daughter's involvement. His activities continued into the 1940s and beyond, and his participation in the trial in her case proved to be memorable. He truly can be labeled the Pater Familias of what was to become a family with a history of defending the separation of church and state. The tradition continues to this day with his grandson, James T. McCollum.

By 1934, his daughters Helen and Vashti raised, 43-year-old Arthur Cromwell had irrevocably discarded the "faith of his fathers" which he had inherited from a strict Presbyterian upbringing. Cromwell, never one to be private with his views, shared his increasingly unorthodox thoughts with the National Adjutant of the Disabled Americans Veterans:

> I am often asked if I do not believe in the orthodox God of the ancient Jews, and the three-way savior of the Christians, then what is my answer about God, the future and the eternal scheme? I reply, asking them why I, or any human, should answer these questions. Could I prove it if I did attempt an answer?[1]

At the time of this communication, Arthur Cromwell was the national historian for the DAV. His office-holding days in that organization were soon over, perhaps a fringe benefit of his excessive candor.

In 1938, Cromwell founded the Rochester Society of Freethinkers, a group of mostly middle-aged persons that included his wife Ruth.[2] The Freethinkers rejected prevailing Christian beliefs. Arthur Cromwell remained the organization's president and guiding spirit for the eleven years it was in existence. The group, with Cromwell as its chief spokesperson, was quite vocal in purveying its views and often provoked public consternation.

At the end of the decade, there was a movement in the New York legislature to authorize the voluntary dismissal of students from the public schools for classes in religion. Cromwell, who was unalterably opposed to the concept, hurriedly wrote a pamphlet which he titled, "Rationalism vs Religious Education in the Public Schools."[3] It was published in February, 1940. In spite of the Freethinkers' opposition, the measure became law.

1

In his tract, Cromwell made a forceful argument against religion in general and Christianity in particular. "We, as Rationalists," he wrote, "recommend and urge the establishment and construction of a moral code of ethics suited to the time and conditions in which we are now living."[4] He told readers to "place the old Jewish Bible on [their] library shelf along with other writings of antiquity and revere it only for the story it has to tell of an ancient people."[5]

"The Bible," Cromwell contended, "contains so much that is bad, so little that is good, and little or nothing that is true that it seems impossible that anyone who has read or studied it would recommend it as fit for our youth to read, much less use as a moral inspiration."[6] This statement along with another, "Religious worship is a chronic disease of the imagination contracted in childhood,"[7] were widely quoted during the trial in the *McCollum* case. It was hardly accidental on Cromwell's part that these statements proved infuriating to many good Christians.

Cromwell shared his pamphlet with his daughter and son-in-law in Champaign. In separate letters mailed together, the two shared their thoughts with her parents. Vashti wrote: "Also, Mac and I had both read Dad's pamphlet and enjoyed it. We each had a few criticisms, but in general it was very good. I'd like to buy about 25 of them ... you can bring them when you come out." John McCollum's comment was brief and more direct: [The pamphlet] "read well to one already convinced, but I'm not so sure that it would sway borderline cases, the ones you could expect to convert."[8]

Surprisingly, Cromwell made no mention in his pamphlet of the constitutional arguments against involvement of the public schools in sectarian religious education. This omission was addressed some months after the pamphlet appeared. In a radio address protesting the New York law allowing dismissed time religious instruction, Cromwell said that the First Amendment to the United States Constitution represented a deliberate effort by the Founding Fathers to prevent the damaging intrusion of religion into civil affairs. Among his other arguments, he pointed out possible anti-social consequences of the new law. These included rivalry between faiths, compulsion to conform by attending the religious classes, and the sorting out or identification of children by faith.[9] These points all figured prominently in the *McCollum* case just five years later.

In the spring of 1940, a plan for religious education in the public schools, similar to that in New York, was being contemplated in Champaign, Illinois. Cromwell happened to be visiting his daughter Vashti in Champaign at the time. Alerted by a newspaper article, he attended one of the early meetings held to plan the program. Vashti recalled that, "He warned them against the dangers of the hold of religion on the public school system." Even though the program under consideration called for classes only one day a week, she reported that her father said it would set a "bad precedent."[10]

One of the chief proponents of the religious classes, the Reverend Ray Cartlidge, also remembered Cromwell's presence at the meeting. "Cromwell," he said, "denounced us and said that this was against all ethics and he wasn't in favor of it." The group responded, according to Cartlidge, by inviting "any individual or group to join them by holding their own classes, teaching rationalism, atheism or whatever tenets they choose." This invitation was made subject to the individual or group joining the Champaign Ministerial Association's committee for a religious education program, and observing "the same yet-to-be-developed rules as the other cooperating groups."[11]

Upon his return to Rochester, Cromwell promptly sent copies of his pamphlet to the superintendent of Champaign schools, as well as to all the board members.[12] Cromwell later explained, "I couldn't get much publicity in the papers, so I resorted to that pamphlet. I had some 10,000 of them printed; I sent them everywhere I could think of."[13] In 1945, when Mrs. McCollum and her lawyer went to see the superintendent of Champaign schools concerning the religious education program, she was surprised to see the tract in the school chief's folder on the subject.[14]

Cromwell, not one to stand still, went on to involve himself in new controversies. In the fall of 1940, the Gideon Society of New York embarked upon a program of placing "A Bible in every schoolroom in New York State."[15] When the Gideons prepared to make distribution in Rochester, Cromwell, backed by his Society of Freethinkers, protested.[16] Cromwell, as he had in his previous church-state fights, lost. The superintendent of the Rochester schools, however, did feel pressed to say, "We are not requiring pupils to read the Bible nor are we asking that the book be read to the children."[17]

Cromwell and his Freethinkers continued their crusade for secularism during the three year period following the events of 1940, but on fronts other than that of sectarian religious intrusions into the public schools. Then, in early 1944, Cromwell protested a program held in one of Rochester's high schools which featured three military chaplains, representing the Catholic, Protestant and Jewish faiths.[18]

Some months later, an even greater transgression occurred as far as Cromwell was concerned. His granddaughter, entering the first grade in the fall of 1944, encountered sectarian religious instruction held in her public school building. Cromwell, along with three other members of the Rochester Society of Freethinkers, conducted an investigation which included visits to several offending schools in the Rochester area.[19]

A few school principals, according to Cromwell, did not like the practice, "as it caused a great deal of trouble and confusion." One building administrator "gave the excuse that he was only a hireling and had to do as he was told." The president of one school board "said he was a man of business and could not afford to antagonize any one group of local citizens." Cromwell claimed that most of the board presidents with whom he had talked "were fully aware" that they were violating the law.[20]

The program, as established in Central School District No. 1, in the Rochester area, and one of those investigated by the Freethinkers, can be taken as representative. Protestant religious classes were taught by area clergymen on the school premises to pupils in their respective classrooms. Students not participating usually remained in the rear of the room while religious instruction was conducted in the front. Catholic students were excused from school to attend classes in their church.[21]

In November 1944, probably as a consequence of his investigation, Cromwell spoke to the Freethinker group on the subject of the religious classes. The title of his address, "Bootlegging Religion into the Public Schools,"[22] was a phrase he was to use on a number of occasions thereafter.

Cromwell asked the school authorities to discontinue the classes. In December 1944, following their refusal, he filed a petition through his attorney before the New York Commissioner of Education, George D. Stoddard, demanding that the classes be stopped.[23]

Mindful of the potential for adverse publicity, Cromwell's attorney was reported by a wire service as saying he wanted to make it clear that "no religious issue was involved as related to (him) but, that it was rather an argument over the violation of religious freedom."[24]

A hearing on Cromwell's petition was held on April 8, 1945, in Albany and was attended by both Cromwell and his attorney. The former read into the record the relevant portions of a letter from his daughter Vashti, which mentioned problems his grandson, James Terry, was experiencing in school relating to the religious education classes in the Champaign schools.[25]

In early June, Stoddard acted by ordering the Board of Education of Central School District No.1 to "terminate religious instruction upon school property."[26] This left intact the practice, specifically authorized by New York law, of dismissing students for religious instruction off public school property. Stoddard, who was the president-elect of the University of Illinois (coincidentally situated in Champaign-Urbana, Illinois), was extremely terse in his comments to the press.[27] He termed the decision as "standard," and said "that the decision was made on a strictly legal basis."[28] Another press account quoted Stoddard as saying, "I have no discretion in the matter."[29] At the time he rendered his decision in New York, the commissioner was probably unaware that Cromwell's daughter was preparing to file suit to stop the same practice in Champaign, Illinois.

Coincidences to the contrary, it appears that neither father nor daughter had any definite idea of what the other was doing. Cromwell, four years after the events, recalled that the first he had heard that his daughter had filed suit was when a reporter came to him asking for comment on the Champaign case. When the reporter learned of the favorable decision in New York, according to Cromwell, "He jumped up with a great exclamation and worked up a story as to make it appear as though the Cromwell family, father and daughter, were fighting religion."[30] Cromwell did know something was in progress in Champaign, as indicated by his correspondence with Mrs. McCollum's attorney, Landon L. Chapman, some two weeks before the Champaign suit was filed.[31] In an interview published several days after she had filed suit, Vashti indicated that, "She was not surprised, just hadn't heard, when told of the action in New York by Dr. George D. Stoddard, banning religious education from the schools there."[32] Both happenings, however, were widely reported together, making national news.

In early July, Cromwell publicly reacted to the controversy that his activities, as well as those of his daughter, had aroused. In a letter to the editor of a Rochester newspaper, he discussed the situation from his perspective:

It has been said that this action I have taken is a part of a death struggle between Atheism and Christianity. Essentially it is entirely a question of whether our Constitutional laws are to mean anything or not.[33]

At another point he wrote:

Education is the act and process of acquiring knowledge through study, observation and experience. Instruction is the act and process of methodical teaching and discipline. And truth is the nearest approximation to actual facts possible with existing knowledge. Thus religious education in the public school curriculum would mean the scientific and factual history of religions that have moved the lives and destinies of men. Thus in this course, the Atheist would be as acceptable as the Christian or Buddhist...I should gladly accept this in the schools, but will the Christians?[34]

In the final paragraph he concluded in part:

It was the difference of religious faiths and creeds that caused rivers of blood to flow in the many centuries past, and the factual history of both nations and religions most eloquently prove the disaster that comes upon any people when their government and church unite to rule them and demand their financial support. It was this historical background that impelled the Founding Fathers to most clearly and emphatically state in the very First Amendment that "Congress shall make no law respecting an establishment of religion, or prohibiting the free exercise thereof..." This clearly caused the divorcement of church and state, while yet protecting (for) all individuals the right of freedom to worship or disbelief.[35]

Four months after his letter appeared, his views were seconded in a letter to the editor by his wife Ruth, which said in part:

The discerning person must believe that religious education is out of place in the public schools. It means a harmful division of schoolmates into Protestant, Jewish, irreligious and Catholic groups, because however "voluntary" the attendance in the classes, heavy social pressure and consequent frustration are felt by children whose parents' conviction forbids their conforming to the pattern. It is definitely undemocratic, and contrary to the spirit and text of the constitution, for which men battled bravely, not to keep our schools free of religious influences.[36]

Even as his victory was being reported by the press, Cromwell was planning a challenge to the practice of allowing credit toward graduation in the Rochester public schools to students taking religious classes on dismissed time. Nearly three months later, Cromwell was again in the national news as a result of his iconoclastic testimony in the trial phase of the *McCollum* case.

Chapter 2

Origins of the
'Champaign System'

In 1940, when weekly classes in religious education were introduced into the public schools of Champaign, Illinois, no one anticipated that the program would become the focus of national attention. The "Champaign System," as it was sometimes called, was neither the first such program in the country nor was it unique in any substantive way. But when a young Champaign housewife challenged the practice in 1945, the case generated heated debate that continued for nearly three years until the issue was decided by the United States Supreme Court in the spring of 1948.

In the years just prior to American involvement in World War II, Champaign was a quiet and peaceful town of approximately 23,000. The economic base was essentially agricultural, academic, and professional, without major industries of any sort. The relatively homogeneous population was distinctly Republican and overwhelmingly white and Protestant. Even the presence of the University of Illinois did little to disturb the parochial nature of Champaign and its sister city, Urbana.

At the time the classes were introduced, Vashti, wife of an associate professor at the University of Illinois and a resident of Champaign, was engaged in raising three young boys. She took only passing notice when the religious education program was first discussed—and only then as a result of the chance visit of her father, Arthur Cromwell, who attended one of the organizational meetings.[1]

When she instituted her suit in the Sixth Illinois Circuit Court a mere five years later, the facts surrounding the establishment of the religious education program had become obscured by time. The superintendent of Champaign schools at the time the program was instituted, Vernon L. Nickell, had become State Superintendent of Public Instruction. His successor in Champaign, Eugene H. Mellon, continued the program but was not familiar with its origins.[2] Even local ministers most closely associated with the introduction of religious education classes in the public schools appeared to have forgotten important details.

On September 9, 1945, the night before the trial was to begin, there was a memorable public meeting. In attendance were both defenders and opponents of the system. One of the speakers was Vashti's attorney, Landon L. Chapman, who charged that religion had been "sneaked into the schools" of Champaign five years earlier.[3] When a member of the audience inquired about the origin of the program, neither Vashti nor her chief local supporter, Rev. Philip Schug of the Unitarian Church of Urbana, were able to respond with specific information.[4]

Rev. A. Ray Cartlidge, pastor of First Presbyterian Church of Champaign, who was in attendance, disputed Chapman's assertion. "It was not put in at a secret meeting," he said. "There has been no effort to hide this from anyone." Few other details were given in the newspaper account, however, and even at the trial there was little substantive testimony on the subject.[5]

Rev. Cartlidge was nevertheless correct. The religion classes had been established openly and publicly. From early April to June 6, 1940, no fewer than twelve newspaper articles and three public meetings dealt with the proposed classes.[6] It was apparently the advance publicity that attracted Arthur Cromwell to one of the meetings.

Why Vashti and her legal counsel failed to look more thoroughly into the background of the program remains something of a mystery. They would have discovered that there had been substantial participation by public school officials— board members, administrators, and teachers—in the establishment of the classes. Such evidence, had it been introduced at the trial, seems likely to have strengthened one of Vashti's basic charges, that there had been an unconstitutional diversion of public funds and effort in support of a sectarian religious program.

The known history of the "Champaign System" began on March 7, 1940, at a regular meeting of the Champaign Board of Education. According to the local *News-Gazette*, "The program was recommended to the board by [Superintendent Vernon] Nickell." There was no indication whether or not local clergy had been involved in Nickell's initiative. The proposal outlined by Nickell would include students in all Champaign elementary, junior high, and senior high schools. Under the plan, described as "voluntary," students who so desired would be dismissed from school one hour each week in order to attend "services or other activity at the church of their choice." Students not wishing to participate would remain in school for a "study hour." According to Nickell, "similar weekly dismissals of students for church activity" operated successfully in other cities. He justified the program by saying that it would be "in keeping with the work of the new committee on child delinquency." Also he reminded his audience that the Champaign schools were already participating in the "released time" program approved by the Illinois General Assembly for catechism lessons during periods of the year when students are studying for confirmation.[7]

Board members questioned the Superintendent concerning the method for determining whether participating students actually attended the church classes— an important point because the proposal stipulated that students who did not participate in church activities would remain in school. Nickell indicated that a method for "checkups" on attendance would have to be worked out.[8]

Nickell was aware of the legally sensitive nature of the proposal. According to the *News-Gazette*, he stated: "It is certain that the youth of the community needs additional instruction on the spiritual side, which we, by law, are prohibited from giving in the school system."[9] The *Courier* quoted the superintendent as saying:

"There is a definite need for religious training, and according to law it is not within the jurisdiction of the public school system."[10]

When Nickell's presentation was over, the board directed him to "confer with members of the ministerial association ...[concerning] a program for the various age groups and to report back to the board concerning the feasibility of the program."[11]

The foregoing reports of Nickell's presentation and the resulting discussion are drawn from the two Champaign-Urbana newspapers, but for some reason were not included in the official minutes of the school board; neither is there any mention of the Board's directive to Nickell.[12]

The first publicly announced meeting regarding the proposed classes was held on April 15 at the Wesley Foundation, the Methodist center for University of Illinois students and faculty, situated in the campus area. The central location was significant, because clergymen from both Champaign and Urbana attended in the hope that school involvement in religious education would be a Twin Cities effort.[13]

A chief spokesman at the meeting was Rev. Charles L. Bromley, pastor of the Urbana Baptist Church and president of the Urbana Ministerial Association. In the *Courier* article announcing the meeting, Bromley continued the theme developed earlier by Superintendent Nickell. "Ministerial interest in religious education for school children," he said, "has arisen as a possible combatant against juvenile delinquency." He continued: "Criminal court records show that the young delinquents are not the children who go to church on Sunday...We must have training in religious education if we intend to solve the crime problem."[14]

Bromley then elaborated on the plan offered by Nickell. He suggested that teachers for the religious courses either "be pastors themselves or lay teachers trained in religious education." He indicated that salaries for such teachers would be paid by the churches.[15]

Rev. Cartlidge was detailed to "prepare a survey of the two communities, locating the churches and schools, and compiling the number of children in each denomination attending the schools.[16]

The group announced that its next meeting would be held on April 26. It was to be a dinner meeting to which, presumably, the clergymen, "school authorities, and others interested in the subject will be invited to attend," Bromley said in a follow-up report. Professor F.G. McKibben of Northwestern University and supervisor of the week-day program of religious education in the public schools of Oak Park, Illinois, was slated as the featured speaker.[17]

On April 26, again at Wesley Foundation, both afternoon and evening meetings were held to discuss and plan the religious education program. McKibben led the discussion at the afternoon meeting. It was that meeting that attracted the attention and attendance of Cromwell. Having opposed legislation in his native state, New York, he considered the plan as a part of "the whole national movement to eventually force religious training into the schools." His written recollections apparently represent the only detailed description of what transpired.[18]

According to Cromwell, the meeting was scheduled for 4:30, but when he arrived at 4:15 the room was "filled with men and... well under way." McKibben first discussed strategies for overcoming objections to the classes; he suggested that churches should "furnish all the teachers and necessary equipment," while asking the school boards for the "use of the school property." More extensive excerpts from Cromwell's recollections follow:

> At this meeting it was not determined to take the religious instruction into the schools, as they all admitted that it was illegal to do so. Then for nearly an hour it was discussed among the men present how to go about it to secure the teachers and places for the religious classes OUTSIDE the schools. One plan that was seriously considered was that a church nearest to each school would be used for the religious classes of all the various denominations and thus save walking or riding the students any great distance to their own particular church or church school.
>
> Then the question of money and teachers and like details came up. It was emphasized the importance of having teachers that would be sure to be at the schools at the appointed hour to get the children, so that when dismissed from their regular classes they would not be found wandering around...also, ways and means for raising the necessary funds etc. [were] discussed to pay for teachers and like assistants, and lay the necessary plans to start the teaching...in the fall.
>
> A young clergymen read a report he had compiled giving the number of students in the various schools; the number claiming to belong to some church and those that had no affiliation...He also noted that all the churches were in the center of the two cities...and that the public schools averaged about ten blocks away from the nearest church. This point brought up the serious question on how to overcome this difficulty.
>
> In addition...it was admitted that the Sunday school attendance had fallen off to a most alarming degree and hence the necessity of taking advantage of this released time in the hope that they could regain some of the lost ground under the guise and time of [the] public school program...
>
> I then went on to take issue with the Rev. (McKibben) of Northwestern for encouraging the violation of both State and Federal Constitutional laws, and said that even the various states voting to grant released time was contrary to the Federal Constitution. It was said that the Rev. Harry Emerson Fosdick was the national leader of this movement to bring religious instruction into the schools. I replied that it only made it the worse to think that great leaders would advocate or encourage the violation of the law. I continued on to tell them who I was and why I was interested to the extent of coming to their meeting. A very lively discussion followed and they fired questions and charges at me at a great rate.[19]

Cartlidge remembered Cromwell's presence at the meeting. "Cromwell," he said, "denounced us and said that this was against all ethics and he wasn't in favor of it." The group responded, according to Cartlidge, by inviting "any individual or group to join them by holding their own classes, teaching rationalism, atheism or whatever tenets they chose." This invitation was made subject to two conditions:

first, the individual or group must join the Champaign Ministerial Association's committee for a religious education program, and second, they had to observe "the same yet-to-be-developed rules as the other cooperating groups."[20]

Before departing, Cromwell handed out copies of his pamphlet,[21] though as events were to prove, it was no more successful with Champaign-Urbana ministers than it had been earlier in the year with the New York legislature.

At the dinner meeting, which attracted most of the attention of reporters, McKibben again addressed the group. He warned the assembled clergymen and educators: "To have a really worthwhile program, the teachers of the courses must be just as thoroughly trained as teachers of academic courses in the schools." He was most optimistic about the results. "One thing which has stood out about the program," he noted, "is the absence of 'problem children' among those who have taken the courses. It may be that this type of child just doesn't enroll in the classes, or it may be that the program actually helps along this line." It would seem important for Prof. McKibben to have attempted to determine which explanation, in fact, was the case, considering that the religious education program was being portrayed as an important tool in combatting juvenile delinquency. He also summarized the various ways of holding the classes; some cities, for example, used school classrooms, while others used church facilities.[22] This was the first recorded mention of the possibility of using space in the schools.

School officials remained in the background during the planning period, although newspaper reports noted their attendance at two of the meetings. Administrators from both the Champaign and Urbana districts cooperated with the ministerial associations in making the comprehensive survey of students' religious affiliations that was referred to in Cromwell's description of the April 26 afternoon meeting. (In Champaign, at least, the survey seems to have been conducted completely by school personnel.) Supt. Nickell announced that the final results would be "submitted to the [Champaign] ministerial association."[23]

The published results left little doubt as to the overwhelmingly Protestant religious makeup of the two towns. Urbana schools were first to release a report. Of the 2,432 children polled, 1,821, or 75 per cent, expressed a denominational preference; of those, ninety-seven per cent indicated Protestant affiliation. Approximately three percent were Catholic, and there was a total of only four Jewish students.[24]

In Champaign, the picture was only slightly different. Of students indicating a preference, ninety-three per cent were Protestant, six per cent were Catholic, and one per cent were Jewish. (The relatively small number of Catholic students, however, did not accurately reflect the number of Catholics in the population; a significant number were enrolled in Holy Cross School in Champaign.) Methodists were the largest denomination with 997, followed by Baptists with 373, Disciples of Christ with 367, and Presbyterians with 198. Twelve per cent of the total student body indicated "no church preference."[25]

The Jewish population, as recorded in the survey, was extremely small. Jews, however, were prominent in the Champaign business community. Thirty-five years after the classes were instituted Cartlidge recorded his recollection of Jewish participation. He said that the president of Champaign's Sinai Temple was "actively opposed to the idea of released time education."[26] Yet Jewish participation in the program was achieved through discussions between "Protestant lay leaders and Jewish business leaders," according to Cartlidge, who quoted Sinai's president as saying, "If we don't go along we will be blamed; we'll cooperate and do our part."[27] Cartlidge believed that Jews felt they were "damned if they did and damned if they didn't" participate in the classes.[28]

The final public meeting over the religious education program was held on May 6 at the Wesley Foundation. School officials were again reported in attendance.[29]

Cartlidge was appointed chairman of a nine-member committee for making arrangements before submitting the plan to the school board. Six of the other members represented Protestant denominations, and there was one representative each from the Catholic and Jewish faiths.[30]

Bromley, continuing as spokesman, identified the duties of the committee rather specifically. "This committee will contact the school boards [of Champaign and Urbana], be responsible for planning and financing the project, and for appointing a staff to administer it."[31] Bromley, at that point, was not optimistic that the program could be put into operation by the opening of school in the fall, approximately four months away. He thought that an additional year would be required for working out the details.[32]

The regular meeting of the Champaign Board of Education on June 6 was attended by a delegation from the Champaign Ministerial Association. Present were Cartlidge, Dr. H. Clifford Northcott of the First Methodist Church, and Fr. Clarence J. Higgins of Holy Cross Catholic Church,[33] all of whom were to figure in the court fight five years later.

After a discussion of the proposed program, school board members unanimously approved a motion calling for members to "cooperate with the Ministerial Association in promoting religious instruction in the schools."[34]

Yet, the program approved by the board differed in two important respects from that originally proposed by Superintendent Nickell. First, instructions were limited to the seventh, eighth, and ninth grades of the Champaign Junior High School. Second, and more significantly, due to "transportation difficulties and hazards in modern traffic," permission was given for use of public school classrooms instead of church buildings.[35] Cartlidge also requested that academic credit be given for the classes, "insofar as school law and organization rules permit."[36] Neither board minutes nor newspaper accounts record any action on that suggestion.[37]

The *Courier* cited a "statement of policy" respecting the proposed classes, but did not indicate whether any of the parties were bound by it. The official board minutes contain no mention whatsoever of the statement. According to the *Courier*, the statement was delivered by Cartlidge. It read as follows:

> It shall be our policy to establish weekday religious education on a par in quality with the standards existing in secular education in any school. The teaching staff must be of equal scholastic achievement with the teachers in secular education in the schools. The curriculum must be

educationally adequate.

We shall not undertake weekday education without adequate and well-assured financial support. We shall endeavor to secure this support through subscription through individual church budgets.It is understood by us that this is no attempt on the part of the churches to influence secular education in the public schools or to violate the principle of separation of church and state.[38]

The first paragraph of the statement seems to reflect McKibben's suggested teacher qualifications. The second paragraph restates what had been the understanding all along—that religious education teachers would be paid from church funds. The inclusion of the last paragraph indicates that both the board and the Ministerial Association were aware of the legally sensitive nature of the program.

John Franklin, attorney for the board, was not present at the meeting.[39] His recollection years later was that no legal opinion at the outset had been requested of him regarding the classes.[40]

On July 24, about six weeks after the authorizing meeting, representatives of the cooperating churches established the Champaign Council of Religious Education (CCRE), which was charged with planning and supervising the forthcoming classes. Cartlidge was appointed temporary chairman.[41]

Soon after, leaders of the Protestant denominations announced that they would have a single, combined program, supervised by "a competent teacher employed by the Council of Religious Education for this specific work." Classes were to consist of "a brief worship period, singing of religious hymns and a study lesson." Catholic and Jewish groups planned to offer separate classes, also under the auspices of the CCRE.[42]

By mid-August, a tentative budget of $800 had been prepared. Money was to be raised from local denominations and interested individuals.[43] One day after the budget was announced, the newspapers reported that the CCRE was looking for two part-time instructors for the combined Protestant classes. Earlier pessimism on the part of religious leaders concerning the September term had disappeared.[44]

The efforts of the CCRE were successful. Students at the junior high school were informed of the religious classes at an assembly in early September. The religious instructors hired by CCRE were introduced to students. Parent consent forms and information about the classes were subsequently distributed.[45]

For the 1940-1941 school year, religion classes were limited to the three grades of the junior high school. In subsequent years, however, religious classes were introduced successively into the lower grades. By the 1944-1945 school year, the classes reached the fourth grade and student James Terry McCollum.

Chapter 3

Enter Vashti and
James Terry McCollum

When James Terry McCollum, then called Terry, reached the fourth grade at South Side School in Champaign, Illinois, there was little to distinguish him from his nine-year-old colleagues. Most were children from middle and upper middle class families who were moving into the new and developing area on the southwest edge of town.

It was the 1943-1944 school year with World War II in full progress. While the fighting had taken a decisive turn for the Allies it was a time of deep public commitment and patriotism; it was not a climate where nonconformity of any sort was suffered lightly.

James Terry, or Jim as he is known today, brought home a permission slip to take the non-compulsory course in religious education. The permission slip also asked the parent to designate whether the child was to receive Protestant, Catholic or Jewish instruction.[1]

Jim's mother, Vashti, refused to sign the slip in spite of her son's desire to participate, objecting to the practice on principle. As far as Jim was concerned, the matter was not settled; he continued during the first semester to seek his parents' consent to take the course. In her book, Vashti cited several reasons for her son's interest: "For one thing...there was the desire to conform to the majority, but in addition, the ones who didn't take religious instruction had little to do while the others were in class. [Those who did not participate were sent from the classroom.] Besides that, the teacher in the Protestant class, who had been a missionary in China, was always bringing pictures and souvenirs to class, and Jim wanted to see them."[2]

Jim was not alone in not taking the class at South Side. There were "a half dozen others."

A fee of twenty-five cents per semester was charged those students participating to cover the cost of the materials. In her book, Vashti related an anecdote which does much to reflect the character of her husband, Jim's father and a quiet but supportive partner in the struggle to come. Jim, in anticipation of the second semester, had saved a quarter. Then a movie came to town which he wanted to see. "'Go on, go ahead to the movie,' Pappy told him, 'you've got a quarter, haven't

13

you?'" "'Yes, but I'm saving that for religious instruction,' Jim said."

"'Well,' Pappy laughed, "You'll just have to make up your mind—the movie or religious instruction. But I hear it's an awfully good movie.'"[3]

John Paschal McCollum was a modest, self-effacing man who quietly knew his worth. He was one of the oldest of eleven children raised on a farm in southwest Arkansas. As a youth he had been required to attend rural, fundamentalist Protestant churches. The inflexible, stern teaching profoundly alienated his gentle but purposeful inclinations and logical mind, and he was determined that his own children would have the opportunity to make their own decisions relating to religion in a free and open atmosphere. While he went to great lengths not to appear arbitrary, he was definitely opposed to his children receiving religious indoctrination of any sort.[4] In the trials and tribulations of the court case, John McCollum strongly supported his wife, though in two different accounts, he was noted as maintaining "a dignified silence throughout the proceedings" and "keeping very quiet about the whole thing".[5] Indeed, John McCollum made no reported public statement either during the trial or its immediate aftermath.

James Terry elected to see the movie. Vashti, feeling her husband's approach somewhat "unfair," gave Terry another quarter. When the second semester came, she "hurriedly scribbled" her consent for Jim's participation in the religious classes, even though she was still very much opposed to them.[6]

Quite soon the McCollums discovered that the religion class was very much out of step with their beliefs. Among the prime justifications for the released time program were that it would improve morals and behavior; juvenile delinquency was one of the evils the classes were supposed to address.[7] In her book, Vashti observed: "When [James Terry] began coming home with the results of his lessons I realized immediately that this wasn't a course in ethics or morals or tolerance or good behavior, as I'd been led to believe, but was a complete religious indoctrination, abounding in faith and miracles."[8] The McCollums were determined not to allow James Terry to participate in the religious classes again.[9]

For the 1944-1945 school year, the McCollums decided that their children, James Terry and Dannel, should change schools. The boys were sent to Dr. Howard School, about the same distance from their home as South Side. Again, James came home with the permission slip for the religious classes.[10] At Dr. Howard, for the first time, Jim was the only student in his class, at least during the second semester, who did not participate, and there was, according to Vashti, encouragement from the classroom teacher to reach the 100 per cent attendance figure. As at South Side, Jim was forced to leave the room, to sit by himself in the music room, a small ante-room to the teachers' toilet.[11] Religious education at the elementary level was confined to grades 4-6, as had been the case the previous year, and left Dannel, the second son, unaffected.

James experienced difficulties at Dr. Howard. There were, no doubt, problems associated with adjusting to a new school and making new friends. These were exacerbated by the fact that Jim did not take religious education. At a chance meeting with Jim's teacher, Vashti was told that her child should enter into school life more and the teacher added, "He's the only one who doesn't take religious instruction, and that segregates him from the others; it would help if he took the course too."[12]

In early January, 1945, a new figure entered the developing drama, Philip Schug, the minister of the Unitarian Church in Urbana. Schug was 29 years of age when he came to Urbana in late 1943. He was originally from east-central, small town Indiana. A questioner of established beliefs during his seminary training, Schug was asked to leave a conservative ministerial college in northern Illinois; he completed his theological work at the University of Chicago.[13]

Schug was a short, frail, bookish man, but also a man of considerable energy and steady courage.[14] One of his early projects at the church was to institute a mimeographed newsletter which he entitled "The Religious Modern." This he sent out to persons in the university community who expressed no religious preference.[15]

The January, 1945, issue contained an item which was of immediate interest to Vashti. Under the title "This is Religious Education with a Vengeance," Schug drew his readers' attention to the issue of religious education in the public schools. The first paragraph read as follows:

> It is bad enough that religious education in the average church is carried on in a divisive manner. It is almost unforgivable that such divisions should be carried into the public schools. It is an axiom of "released time" advocates that this religious education must begin in the lowest grades. "Young minds are more pliable," they say. We agree! They are! And just because they are we feel it necessary to protect them from educational methods that tend to quickly solidify religious and racial differences.[16]

At the end, Schug enjoined his readers to contact the area representatives in the state legislature to express their opposition to such a practice in Illinois.

Vashti, already very concerned about the situation confronting her son, wrote to each of her three legislators. The responses were reassuring. Rep. Charles W. Clabaugh wrote in part:

> Your letter of January 6, concerning religious education In the schools, came to my attention today. I think that you need have no fears about any bill passing, or even being seriously considered, by the legislature which would institute religious teaching in our schools. Long standing precedent and the ill affected by such instruction in the public schools, would, in my opinion prohibit such, even if the federal constitution did not. Upon either of these two reasons I would stand. I think your constitutional grounds in the above are sound, and allow me to compliment you or anyone else these days of constitutional disregard, who still regard our fundamental law as worthy of following.[17]

Sen. Everett R. Peters, in the following excerpt, was equally encouraging in his response.

> I wish to acknowledge your letter in regard to proposed legislation which would permit religious education in the public schools in the State of

Illinois or in any other place if given during the regular school hours. I have always taken the stand since I have been a member in the legislature that it is the duty of the schools to educate our children in the regular needs of education and that religious education should be secured in the churches. I know of no reason why I should change my opinion at this time.[18]

Rep. Ora D. Dillavou, the other legislator who responded, also seemed to share Vashti's concerns. His letter read in part:

I am in hearty accord with both your objections to mixing religious education with regular educational training in our public schools...However, I have not had any contact with anyone wishing to introduce legislation in the State of Illinois permitting religious education in the public schools, but I will be on the alert for such a bill.[19]

Vashti McCollum saved these letters. As she later observed in her book:

These letters later had an important and somewhat amusing bearing on events in my case, and like many gentlemen who write letters which end up in court, these distinguished representatives could well have regretted ever having written them.[20]

In February, matters at Dr. Howard School grew worse for James Terry, causing him to come home in tears; Vashti noted in her book, he was "not a boy given to crying easily." The music room, where he was usually sent, was occupied, so his teacher had him sit in the hall, a practice normally reserved for punishment. This was too much for Vashti, who promptly went to school to discuss the situation with the teacher.[21] While the hall experience was not repeated—Terry was placed in the other fifth grade during religious classes—Vashti was determined upon an appeal to higher authority.[22]

That higher authority was Dr. Eugene H. Mellon, the Superintendent of Champaign Schools. Mellon, like most of other principal figures in the *McCollum* case associated with the Board of Education, was downstate Illinois born and bred. After graduating from Illinois College in Jacksonville in 1923, he held a series of positions with smaller districts in downstate Illinois before taking the Champaign post in 1943.[23]

Mellon, a tall, courtly man, listened politely to Vashti as she outlined both her objections to the religious classes in principle as well as to the difficulties which confronted James Terry because of his non-participation. Vashti noted later:

He didn't express agreement with me in all respects, but he didn't thoroughly disagree either; and at least he did not seem to subscribe to that popular fallacy that there is any correlation between religious instruction and the elimination of juvenile delinquency.[24]

Mellon did point out that the program was in effect when he came. Further, the religious classes enjoyed the support of the Board of Education, thus any change would depend upon a change in board policy.[25] In the end, Mellon did what any prudent administrator would do in a like situation; he suggested to Mrs. McCollum that she write a letter to the Board. "Are you suggesting that I waste my time?" she remembered saying. "I'm going to do something." With that, she stalked out of his office.[26]

Vashti possessed a formidable personality. She inherited more than a little of her father's strong disinclination to suffer quietly. Her sharp intelligence and keen sense of fairness prompted her to draw quick conclusions which were usually accurate. Neither particularly humorous nor diplomatic and hardly slow to anger, her forbearance up to that point would seem somewhat out of character.[27]

The interview with the school chief swept all forbearance aside. Remembering the Unitarian minister whose newsletter had prompted her to write the state legislators, she went to see Philip Schug, as she later remembered, "prepared to file suit right away that very afternoon if he could suggest a lawyer." Schug counseled patience and suggested to Vashti that she allow him to contact, by mail, the Chicago Action Council (CAC), an organization interested in civil liberties and specifically opposed to the religious classes. The wait must have been painful to Vashti, one to whom patience was no virtue. The response time was short, by return mail: "Tell that woman to go ahead; we will hire her attorney and pay all the legal bills."[28]

Released time religious education in the public schools was a common practice in Illinois, as indeed it was across the nation. Many, including Arthur Cromwell and Philip Schug, had already protested the practice. Why, it might be asked, was her cause the one that led to the precedent-setting case on the subject? In this respect, the support of the CAC was extremely important both financially and otherwise. In an interview, Schug outlined the reasons why the council supported Vashti:

> The council preferred this case above [other] possible ones because leaders [of the group] regarded it as "a clear cut case of discrimination against the child," and because the McCollums appeared to be a family which would not waver on its principles and would not consent to an out-of-court agreement.[29]

Within a month of the occasion of James Terry's placement in the hall, the McCollums received a letter from Landon L. Chapman. He had been retained as her attorney by two groups, the CAC and the Chicago Civil Liberties Committee (CCLC). Chapman had been recommended by Ira Latimer of the latter group.[30]

Landon Lincoln Chapman was definitely one of the more complex personalities involved in the developing controversy. He had come a long way from the log cabin in Webster, West Virginia, where he was born. His parents were mountain people of the Christian Science persuasion. On his own from the age of 16, he put himself through his undergraduate studies at the University of Wisconsin, and law school at the University of Chicago. He did this by traveling about in rural communities selling school books to teachers during his summers away from school.

Chapman possessed a combative spirit; he had been a collegiate boxer at Wisconsin and had won the Big Ten championship in his weight division. While in law school, he taught boxing at a YMCA in Chicago and had even had a few professional fights. His boxing career ended when he was struck across the face with a pipe in an apparent effort at intimidation after underworld characters approached him about throwing a fight.

Shortly after he was admitted to the Illinois bar in 1930, Chapman was involved in defending persons accused of being Communists. According to his eldest son, "He developed a reputation for defending the poor or people who he felt weren't getting a fair shake."[31]

In his letter to Vashti, Chapman requested information "about teachers, board members and ministers involved." In the ensuing correspondence, Chapman made further requests for information which he would need to file suit. Chapman indicated, among other things, that he needed to know how the program operated. Accordingly, Vashti went to see Rev. H. Clifford Northcott, one of the original supporters of the program.[32]

It was not a cordial interview. Vashti, at the outset, recounted the trouble caused her family by the religious classes. Northcott inquired as to why Terry was not permitted to take the classes; he then grew "terribly angry," according to Vashti, when she informed him that she and her husband thought the classes were unconstitutional. Northcott noted that "there were many breaches of church-state separation; for example, the money that Notre Dame University received for the V-12 program." The interview concluded, Vashti recalled, when Northcott suggested to her that she was wasting his time and should leave.[33]

Schug and Chapman accompanied Vashti on her next series of calls. The first was a return visit to Supt. Mellon. As she remembered it, the main line of questioning dealt with the discretionary latitude of school officials in the administration of the religious education program. Chapman asked Mellon about how he would react to the Jehovah's Witnesses. "If some of the parents belonged to that sect, would you allow one of their teachers to form a class?" The superintendent thought yes. Chapman, pursuing this line of questioning, "Are you familiar with the tenets of that church? Do you know they don't believe in saluting the flag?"[34]

The question of teacher qualifications was also raised. According to Vashti, "Mellon said he would want those teachers to speak good English and have high educational standards." "Our point," she noted, "was that no public official should be in the position of having to judge the merits of a religious group ... and that if he did not exercise some discretion and approved all the groups that applied, it would lead to endless confusion."[35]

It was at that meeting that Chapman noticed, in Superintendent Mellon's file on religious education, the pamphlet "Rationalism vs. Religious Education in the Public Schools," in all probability one of the ones left by Cromwell during his visit to Champaign in 1940. As they left Mellon's office, she asked Chapman if he realized who wrote the pamphlet; when she told him that it was her father, he was "immediately interested" and wanted a copy. Vashti mused in her book, "I have often thought what a much quieter case it might have been had I never mentioned my father's pamphlet at all."[36]

Others included in the round of visits were "various members of the School Board," Lakie Munson, the principal at Dr. Howard School, and the Board's attorney, John Franklin. One board member, Mrs. Olivetta Kelley, said she thought that the "religious instruction was wonderful." Remembering the interview, Vashti observed, "It was obvious that she had come from a homogeneous community; in her experience all churches were pretty much alike, and she had no conception of the extremes to which creeds and cults could go."[37] Franklin "was not surprised" to see the delegation. According to Vashti afterwards, Franklin alluded to the distinct possibility that local public opinion would not be favorable to her cause.[38]

Vashti regarded John Franklin, from first to last, as a hostile antagonist.[39] He was a tall, slender man, given to speaking slowly and methodically. Further, Franklin enjoyed among his colleagues the reputation of being an able practitioner of his profession.[40] Coming originally from a rural, small town environment in Kankakee County, Illinois, he earned both his bachelor's and law degrees from the University of Illinois.[41] Franklin, therefore, knew the Champaign community well, and in the approaching trial, he was to prove a most formidable adversary.

Meanwhile, in late 1944, Cromwell had filed his petition before the New York Commissioner of Education, George D. Stoddard, to halt the nearly identical program of religious education in that state. Thus, he was vitally interested in, though not directly connected with, the developing drama in Champaign. Vashti had written to her father in early 1945 concerning James Terry's problems in school, which Cromwell read into the record at the hearing in his New York case.[42] Later Vashti contacted her father, this time at Chapman's request, noting the latter's interest in the pamphlet.[43] In what appears to have been the first of a long series of letters between these two men, Cromwell expressed appreciation for Chapman's support of his daughter's cause. He also indicated that he was sending separately "several copies" of his pamphlet. It was in this letter that Cromwell used a favorite expression of his which referred to the religion classes as "bootlegging of religious instruction in the public schools."[44] Chapman later was to appropriate this phrasing as his own.

Chapman was quick to respond to Cromwell's letter. In a handwritten note, Chapman stated that it was his "plan to use the pamphlets in my pleadings when we file our test case in the courts." Then Chapman followed with a post script which was remarkable in the degree to which it presumed Cromwell's ignorance of famous church-state controversies: "P.S. You may remember one of our Chicago attorneys, name of Clarence Darrow, a liberal, who tried the Scopes (monkey) case in Tennessee. It is too bad that he is not living today."[45]

Chapman then went on to say, "He [Darrow] would enjoy this fight immensely."[46] A student of Darrow might question the use of the word "enjoy." It is likely that the statement is much more revealing as to how Chapman himself regarded the case. The postscript ended with: "It does seem that the Champaign case has more historical possibilities than the Scopes Case had, although [it is] not [as] sensational".[47]

Chapman was to do his best in the coming pleadings and trial to correct that deficiency. Superintendent Mellon had little reason to suspect that a major legal test of the released time program of religious instruction was in the making. Until the time Vashti raised the issue, Mellon stated that he had received no complaints concerning the program.[48] Franklin, not consulted in 1940 at the outset of the program, and in the absence of complaints in the intervening years, also was caught somewhat unaware. He was, however, probably the first of the protagonists on the side of the Board to realize the serious nature of the challenge.

> I was taken by surprise at the vigor and the help that [Mrs. McCollum] was able to get and I came to, pretty fast, that this was a cause celebre that might be taken to the Supreme Court of the United States. I guess that the first recognition of that was the filing of the complaint by a Chicago lawyer [Chapman] who was given to fighting the establishment and (a supporter) of what I viewed as radical causes.[49]

Only one step remained before the suit could be tried, the serving of a demand on the Board of Education that it cease the released time program of religious instruction. The demand was signed by Vashti, who was joined by the Rev. Randell S. Hilton, secretary of the Western Unitarian Conference; the Rev. Paul J. Folino, a Congregational minister in Chicago; Rabbi Jacob J. Weinstein, of the K.A.M. Temple; Robert Greenfield, of the CAC; and Ira Latimer of the CCLC.[50]

Vashti, with Schug as a witness, personally served the demand upon Board Member Kelley and Delos Huxtable, the president of the Board. With the latter, the element of surprise was over; "Well, I guess this is it," she reported him as saying.[51] "We waited the minimum of time for the School Board to reply and then filed our petition, on Monday, June 11, 1945; my father's pamphlet was included in the petition without my being consulted."[52]

> The day we went over to file the suit, I, in my great innocence and ignorance, said to an attorney with whom we filed it, 'Do you think I should write up anything and take it to the local papers? Or will they be notified that a suit is being filed? He looked at me a little pityingly; 'I don't think you'll have to worry,' he said, 'I think they'll probably hear about it all right.'[53]

The wire services picked up the story, and the case. *State of Illinois ex rel. McCollum vs. School Board No. 71 Champaign, Illinois*, was suddenly state, then national news.

Chapter 4

The Battle is Joined

On Monday, June 11, 1945, through her attorney, Vashti filed a petition for mandamus in the Circuit Court of Champaign, County, Illinois. In her plea, she asked the court to order the Champaign Board of Education, "To immediately adopt and enforce rules and regulations prohibiting all instruction and all teaching in religious education in all public schools ... in ... said district."[1]

In this initial pleading, the plaintiff was represented as adhering to "the school of thought known as 'Rationalism,' including atheism..."[2] The petition went on to state that the plaintiff "desires that none of her children be indoctrinated with any of the numerous fallacious and controversial religious creeds, theories or dogmas, or with religious beliefs adverse to her own..." To further clarify "her views and understanding concerning religion," her lawyer included Arthur G. Cromwell's pamphlet, "Rationalism vs. Religious Education in the Public Schools."[3]

The pleading then took note of the Illinois Constitution of 1870, then in force, which called for the General Assembly to provide for an "efficient system of free schools." Further, it called the court's attention to the compulsory school attendance law in effect in Illinois. The petition thus sought to establish that not only was the plaintiff entitled to free education for her child, but compelled to enforce his attendance. Also included were recitations from both the Federal and State constitutions guaranteeing freedom of religion.[4]

Addressing the particulars of the case, Vashti's petition asserted that religious classes "do invade all, or nearly all, grade schools in said district," including that attended by her son, and that as a result of those classes, a "30-minute period of secular education lost each week is not later recovered." The petition went on to charge that the religious instruction was given "in a friendly and solicitous manner ... with the ultimate intent ... of establishing in the young and undiscriminating minds of children of such credulous age a knowledge, interest and belief in a certain religion, god and Bible as approved *and taught* by *said instructor.*"[5] Of major importance, Chapman emphasized the hardships on the child, noting that "his religious difference was noticed by his classmates and their good will and esteem for him were injured."[6]

Chapman was determined to prove that the one Protestant class could not encompass the wide range of sectarian religious beliefs which were being included in that category. Thus, the petition focused in detail upon the specific teachings included in the Protestant curriculum.

The pleading went on to assert that there were distinctly harmful side effects of the religious classes, and in effect, the program constituted "an establishment of religion" in the public schools. Chapman charged that the "schools become fields for private missionaries and for rivalry of religious sects, public revenue is diverted to private use, taxpayers are not all affected alike, and many persons are denied equal protection of the laws." More specifically, the petition maintained that, "When the plaintiff's child was not enrolled with his classmates because of the views of his parents, and of his own, his religious difference was noticed by his classmates and their good will and esteem for him were injured; he was shunned by them and denied enjoyment of their society and friendship." The petition also asserted that, "School houses and property...are not equally available to plaintiff for teaching the anti-religious tenets of atheism and rationalism.[7]

The Board of Education was quick to seek a legal opinion from its attorney, John Franklin. On June 12, he responded with "a preliminary survey of the authorities touching upon the legality of the religious education courses..." Franklin cited two Illinois cases which "deserve particular attention."[8] The first, *Nichols vs. School Directors*[9], allowed a public school to be used for religious services held outside of regular school hours. In Franklin's words: "The court held that the incidental use of a school building for such a purpose, while conceivably a diversion of an infinitely small amount of public funds, was not a constitutional prohibition."[10]

Franklin regarded the second case, *People ex rel. Ring vs. Board of Education*,[11] as the "leading case upon [the] question in this state." In its ruling, the Illinois Supreme Court held that objections raised by Catholic parents to religious exercises held in a public school on school time involving most students and using the Protestant King James version of the Bible was a violation of the Illinois Constitution. Franklin, in his opinion to the board, quoted some of the more important language contained in the *Ring* decision.

> The exclusion of a pupil from this part of the school exercises in which the rest of the school joins separates him from his fellows, puts him in a class by himself, deprives him of his equality with the other pupils, subjects him to a religious stigma and places him at a disadvantage in the school, which the law never contemplated.[12]

While acknowledging this case as a powerful precedent, Franklin pointed out that it had been rendered in 1911 and had "not since that time been referred to in any case..." In the final paragraph, the attorney concluded: "It should also be said that a majority of decisions in other states containing substantially similar constitutional provisions would appear to permit such religious education courses as we now have in our schools."[13]

Landon Chapman, for reasons unknown, had failed to cite the *Ring* case in his petition, even though the language in that opinion seemed persuasively consistent with Vashti's position. Chapman almost certainly was aware of the *Ring* case at the time, for he referred to it in a statement to a Chicago *Times* reporter, which was printed only three days after the suit was filled.[14]

On June 12, the Board of Education held a special meeting, with Franklin in attendance. Board member Olivetta Kelley asked, "What business [is it] of the Chicago [Action Council] that religious education classes are allowed in Champaign schools?"[15] Presumably with Franklin's legal memorandum in hand, the Board voted to "authorize Mr. Franklin to take such steps as necessary to defend the Board in the case of Petition for Mandamus of Vashti McCollum." The motion carried unanimously.[16] Board President Delos Huxtable was subsequently quoted as saying that the school district would "fight to the finish" for the program. Attorney Franklin, in a less dramatic manner, echoed the sentiment of the Board.[17] The Chicago *Sun* reported "that he [Franklin] believes the Illinois Supreme Court should be given an opportunity to examine, in the light of present-day public opinion, the desirability and legality of the Champaign type of religious education in. the schools." That same article stated that "Mrs. McCollum also intends to go to the Illinois Supreme Court if she loses in the Circuit Court."[18] By the time the controversy had reached that stage, there was little reason to doubt that the parties were determined upon a test case, carried to the highest judicial authority, to resolve the issue.

On the same day as the special board meeting, June 12, the suit was page-three news in both the *Courier* and the *News-Gazette*. Superintendent Mellon, while declining "to discuss legal aspects of the suit," maintained that the district had no administrative authority over the program, and paid none of the expenses; the only participation was in the granting of time and allowing the use of school rooms.[19] As Chapman must surely have expected, Cromwell's hard-hitting pamphlet attracted a great deal of attention, especially in the *News-Gazette*. That paper carried five and a quarter column inches of direct quotation beginning with the pamphlet's opening line: "Religious worship is a chronic disease of the imagination contracted in childhood."[20] The *Courier* mentioned the pamphlet, although it carried no quotes.[21]

Rev. Cartlidge reacted sharply to Chapman's pleading, Cromwell's pamphlet and related news reports. He "wagered" that "when you get to the background of the suit, you will find some political movement tied up in it, people who are interested in social revolution." In his view, the situation represented a "pattern of attacks on religious teachings" and he "pointed out that both Hitler and communists in Russia had found the church in their way and had been forced to get rid of the church."[22]

Two days later, on June 14, Cromwell made further news in Champaign-Urbana. On that day, both local newspapers reported that New York Commissioner of Education Stoddard had ruled favorably on Cromwell's petition to halt released time religious classes in the public schools of that state.[23]

A factor contributing to local interest, in addition to the relationship between Cromwell and McCollum, the similarity of their cases, and the timing, was that Stoddard was president-elect of the University of Illinois. As to the first three coincidences, Mrs. McCollum later noted: "Naturally everyone assumed the two cases were planned to break together. Actually there was little connection between them; I was not aware before that my father had filed a complaint, although … I knew the subject was dear to his heart."[24]

Also on June 14, the *News-Gazette* ran a supporting story under the headline, "785 Public School Students Studied Religion in '44-'45." Of particular interest was the denominational breakdown given for participating students, indicating that a religious census had been compiled, similar to the one taken prior to the establishment of the released-time program in 1940.[25] This would seem to indicate more than a casual involvement on the part of school officials.

The *News-Gazette* article went on to include a listing of the courses of study, presumably for the Protestant classes. Reading very much like a Sunday school curriculum, they were: "Old Testament stories for fourth graders; miracles of the New Testament for fifth graders; parables of the New Testament for sixth graders; the life of Christ for grade seven, and the life and writings of Paul for grades seven and eight."[26]

The *Courier*, in a related story on the same day, carried a lengthy interview with the plaintiff. The lead sentence gave a brief but clear indication of her reaction to the early repercussions caused by the law suit: "Vashti Cromwell McCollum is a novice at jousting with convention, but already she knows it begets stings but is not deterred." The article noted that, "Mrs. McCollum neither talked nor looked the part of a social reformer out to upset conventions." Concerning her own religious feelings, she said: "My father and my husband have always talked more about religious issues than I have. I usually have avoided discussing religion; I've found it's the best way to lose friends." The article also carried her comments relating to threats to her husband's job: "We feel that sometimes one has to follow the courage of [one's] convictions; perhaps it will be interesting to find out how free we are to have views."[27]

In an interview with a student reporter from the *Daily Illini*, Vashti attempted to further clarify her position:

> This is no dispute between atheism and religion. Some people are Catholics, others are Jews; I myself am an atheist. What difference does it make? Religious education as conducted in the Champaign schools has so clearly emphasized the differences of creed and race. These differences should not be brought out in young children.[28]

The reporter drew somewhat different conclusions than did Rev. Cartlidge. "Mrs. McCollum is not revolutionary in her thinking. She does not want to change anyone's religion; she only asks freedom to believe as she sees fit, and for her children to be granted the same freedom."[29]

During the same period, Fletcher Wilson of the Chicago *Sun* described the suddenly well-known plaintiff as looking "like a coed." She attempted, in that interview, to dispel the characterization of herself as an extremist—impressions drawn from Cromwell's pamphlet in particular and Chapman's pleading in general. "Atheist," she was quoted as saying, "does describe my position; it is a little too militant a term to describe my attitude." In spite of Vashti's efforts to appear moderate, the reporter described her as being "temperamentally vibrant."[30]

Chicago newspapers began carrying the story on the day after the complaint was filed. As in the *News-Gazette*, Cromwell's pamphlet was given considerable attention. On June 14, Chapman wrote to the plaintiff's father commenting upon the attention the latter's writings had attracted.

> The newspapers in Chicago have been making the most of the first sentence in your pamphlet ... Some of the members of the CAC who are financially supporting Mrs. McCollum's case think it was unfortunate that I included your pamphlet [in the petition] including [that] sentence. Personally, I think it is a good statement, and know of no reason why Mrs. McCollum should not be ready to say that she agrees with it. In fact, I would like to deliver a lecture on that subject. I am suggesting to her that she take up the challenge and show why she thinks such a statement is true. Will you please help me by sending me a statement of what you mean by that sentence, a page or two, and send Mrs. McCollum a carbon copy of it?[31]

Even at this early point in the proceedings, Landon Chapman had demonstrated an inclination to exploit the sensational aspects of the case. In so doing, however, he had clearly raised the concerns of Vashti and her allies. Apparently in defensive reaction, Chapman included the following statement in his letter to Cromwell:

> The church people immediately responded to the newspaper reporters by saying that this is a battle between atheism and religion. Of course, we are going to correct that by showing that it is a question of constitutional law. However we don't want anybody to think that we say things that are foolish. I am ready to sustain everything in our petition for mandamus, including your pamphlet.[32]

In an interview with the Chicago *Times*, Chapman was to phrase the issue in purely legal terms: "The nub of our argument ... is that the state has no power to collect taxes for schools and let the churches use them, within the period of the normal school day, for sectarian purposes."[33]

Philip Schug was clearly concerned over the characterization of the case as an assault upon religion. In a lengthy commentary published in the *Courier* he stated the basic nature of the case as he saw it.

> Only one main issue is at stake—the legality or illegality of sectarian religious teaching in tax supported public schools during school hours. There is no question of trying to destroy the churches as has been alleged. There is no question of atheism versus orthodoxy, as some have been led to believe by reporters seeking the sensational or by defenders of the existing system of religious education in the schools. Only one question stands out—shall we allow sectarian religious teaching in our public schools?

The Unitarian minister said he could:

> ... sympathize with the frustrations experienced by religious people who have seen their world split asunder; but [he could] not agree with the

solution, taking over public school classes, dividing the children into two, three, four, or more different groups, and instructing them separately in varying religious philosophies is a wise solution.[34]

He pointed out that religious instruction was the only class for which the children were divided.[35] Thus the public school, which normally would help to break down societal divisions, with the introduction of sectarian religious instruction "automatically teaches division and becomes an active agent in creating frictions." In conclusion, Schug stated: "Sectarian religious education does have its place in our country of many sects and religions, but that place is not in tax-supported public schools during school hours."[36]

At the same time, other local ministers were quick to show their support of the religious classes. Rev. Cartlidge released a prepared statement which was quoted, in part, in the *News-Gazette*:

This [the pending lawsuit] is a problem of education primarily and not of religion alone. Education is to fit children for life. Religion is part of life. We feel that the school board is justified in assuring the children an opportunity for training in this important phase of education.

I do not feel that the way in which we have our courses set up [that] there is any danger of union of church and state because the whole plan is voluntary, unsupported by tax funds, and open to any group which wishes to train its youth in religion.

Finally, I would admonish members of our church to view the whole matter with Christian patience and a spirit of forgiveness. Others have a right to differ with us in our free land.[37]

Rev. Charles L. Hollis, of the Foursquare Church in Urbana, in contrast to Rev. Cartlidge, was much less restrained in his statement: "I plan to defend religion and to declare myself opposed to statements in the court petition. It is a movement, not just to safeguard separation of church and state as is claimed, but a front to strike a blow at religion."[38] Hollis also announced that he would devote an entire service to "answer Mrs. McCollum and her colleagues."[39]

The Urbana Ministerial Association addressed the matter. Schug, a member, was present and recounted the debate in his newsletter:

At the meeting of the Urbana Ministerial Association, at which your editor is welcome, there was a frank discussion of the problem [the issue raised by the *McCollum* case] when a resolution was offered in support of the Champaign School Board. Had there been no opposition to the resolution it would probably have passed without discussion. In opposing it I forced its defense. The defense ran as follows:

1. In former days the church held a place of pre-eminence in society. The social, educational, and even the political life of the community revolved around the church. Today the church has been stripped of many of its functions. [Schug went on to mention examples.] Education of children, which formerly was the bulwark of the church, is now being pro-

gressively taken out of the hands of the church. Only a very small percentage of the children are now going to any church school—and even if they all went for the regular one hour a week program it would not be enough to compete with secular education.

2. Public school education is secular and pagan. It does not teach the great fundamentals of the Christian religion to children, and by its teaching of scientific method and scientific theories it is undercutting the foundations of the church.

3. The only way to combat this teaching and to reach all the children is to go where they are. They have to be in school, and if we can not get secular education to conform to the fundamentals of the Christian faith we will have to go to the school and teach these fundamentals.

4. We have a right [to be] in the public schools. They—whoever this may be—allow other philosophies to be taught in the schools, and we should have the privilege of teaching ours. As one minister aptly put it, "They teach Aristotle, Plato, Socrates and all those pagans; and we ought to have the right to teach Jesus Christ."[40]

In spite of Schug's opposition, the Urbana ministers added their moral support. The statement read in part:

We express our conviction that such religious training is necessary as a supplement to secular education for both good citizenship and well-rounded personality development. Only so can our schools avoid the excessive secularism which threatens us with a decadent "cut-flower civilization" by cutting off the religious roots from which democratic culture grows.[41]

Schug maintained in his account that:

No support is offered for the assumption that our democratic culture grows out of the church, and a very good case can be made to show that the development of our democratic culture was opposed strenuously by most of the churches. Consider the significance for democracy of the insistence of the churches that public education be tied to their specific philosophies of life!![42]

Unlike Landon Chapman, John Franklin was not a man inclined to making public statements. He did, however, offer his perception of the issues in the case. It was not a question of joining church and state by allowing the religious classes in the schools, but rather, "a question of whether or not children in public schools will be denied the right, if they choose to have religious training at its best." He continued: "I believe that availability of the course, rather than being an infraction of the rights of the petitioner and her child to worship or not to worship, raises a question also of Mrs. McCollum's denial to her son of the right to participate in these courses."[43]

Franklin noted the absence of courses in public schools dealing with morals and good behavior and suggested that this was what religion was supposed to do. In what must be considered to be a telling admission, he added: "It is unfair to limit such training only to the small part of the student body exposed to it by Sunday School."[44] It had been argued by the plaintiff that the religious education classes were an effort to utilize the compulsory school attendance law to propagate religion.

Personal support for the McCollums arrived in the form of a letter from Cromwell. It was addressed to his grandson, and in it he expressed pride in both him and his mother. Cromwell was an old hand at fighting convention, and his letter contained a brief but accurate prediction of the difficulties the family would face; he noted that there were also rewards:

> It is going to be a long and bitter hard fight and we will have to take much abuse, but it will be worth it. James, it has always been my contention that if life has any meaning or purpose at all it is that we do something in a real material way to make the lot of mankind a little better than what it was when we first found it.[45]

There seemed little question that, in Cromwell's view, the elimination of sectarian religious teaching in the public schools was certainly such a contribution.

Forces in support of the religious classes were quick to offer more tangible support in behalf of the Champaign Board of Education. Various "church interests" approached State Representative Clabaugh requesting that he introduce an amendment to the Illinois school code permitting released time programs such as that in Champaign.[46] Before actually proposing the legislation, Clabaugh reportedly discussed the measure with Franklin.[47]

Clabaugh's action came as something of a surprise to Vashti, who remembered the earlier written statements sent to her by Clabaugh and the two other local legislators. On "just some sort of a lucky hunch" she had saved the letters, which all appeared to show sympathy with her position: "Naturally I gave the press my letter from Clabaugh ... my possession of the letter served to embarrass Clabaugh and to make news at a time when we wanted favorable publicity for our case."[48]

Clabaugh's response was reported in the *News-Gazette*: "Clabaugh said that when in the letter, he referred to 'in the schools' he quite naturally meant 'by the schools;' There was no issue then and I was not aware then one must split hairs in dealing with Mrs. McCollum."[49]

Another legislator was quick to react, this time to the threat to public morality posed by atheists teaching at the University of Illinois. Rep. A.A. "Boots" Brands of Prairie de Rocher introduced a resolution designed to send a message to university officials. It read in part: "We [members of the legislature] are opposed to having persons employed by the State of Illinois who hold views such as expressed by Mrs. McCollum and we ask the Board of Trustees of the University to take steps to correct this deplorable situation."[50]

Vashti taught dancing part-time with the College of Physical Education, and her husband, who presumably shared her views, was an assistant professor in the College of Agriculture.

The resolution was tabled after Rep. Ora Dillavou told his colleagues that "Mrs. McCollum is not employed at the UI summer session and she will not be employed again." He went on to say that "the resolution was unnecessary and would only serve to gratify Mrs. McCollum's taste for publicity by further advertising her case."[51] Vashti recalled in her book: "It was the end of the semester when the suit was filed, and that summer the University did not offer the courses in square dancing that I would have taught, and by fall they had another teacher in physical education to take over the course."[52]

The controversy prompted Rep. Clabaugh's first public statements associating Vashti's supporters with subversive elements.

The unanimity which made possible the advancement without committee reference and endorsement of the bill by all faiths, seems to preclude any organized opposition, unless it comes from a small group such as the plaintiff seems to represent, or from the Communist party. The suit by Mrs McCollum, who describes herself as an atheist, was the first effect we have had in Champaign-Urbana of the coddling of the political philosophies of Godless Communists.[53]

Vashti reported other reactions of university officials which tended to show that the institution was vulnerable to the whims of the legislature and public opinion:

A representative of the university approached the Associated Press and asked that they refrain from referring to me as the "wife of a University of Illinois professor." One of my husband's bosses told him there'd been a call from the office of the President of the University to the dean of the College of Agriculture asking if there were any grounds on which they should fire Dr. McCollum. I later learned that the telephone call had been prompted by outside pressures and when the authorities were assured there could be no grounds for dismissal, the matter was dropped.[54]

An indirect confirmation of the threats to Dr. McCollum's position came in the form of an editorial in the University of Illinois student newspaper:

Sentiment has been high among students, townspeople, and some faculty members to have John P. McCollum, husband of Mrs. Vashti Cromwell McCollum, instigator of the case against religion in the Champaign public schools, removed from the faculty of the University."[55]

The writer concluded that McCollum's religious beliefs had little to do with his work at the University and that: "If a man should lose his position because of his particular religious beliefs, this would be a direct abridgement of his freedom of worship, which is guaranteed in both the federal and state constitutions."[56]

In the meantime, on June 20, Schug was in Chicago for a strategy—and damage control—session with the "heads" of the CAC. Also present was Landon Chapman. Among the items discussed was the furor raised by Chapman's pleading. Hardly in a position to repudiate their attorney, the council, in Schug's words, expressed "almost complete satisfaction" in his handling of the case. The council decided to carry the attack by soliciting funds to purchase space in newspapers statewide explaining its opposition to released time religious education programs.[57] Nothing appears to have come of the project. Downstate ministers, according to Schug, had been invited to attend the Chicago meeting so that they could participate in the discussion. None attended, prompting Schug to comment: "Of course, there was no reason why they should attempt to get the issues clarified with us; they benefit more by having people believe that the foundations of religion are being attacked."[58]

Publication of Clabaugh's letter to Vashti in the *Courier* did little to impede the progress of his bill in the House. On June 26, overwhelmingly supported by a vote of 85 to two, the bill was approved. Only one legislator spoke openly behalf of Mrs. McCollum's position. Rep. Carl Preihs of Pana was quoted as saying: "By implication it [the proposed bill] permits religion to be taught in the public schools. The moment you begin to intermingle religion with public schools you're traveling a dangerous course."[59]

Preihs, however, was careful to disassociate himself from Vashti's personal views: "He [Preihs] said of Mrs. McCollum, a professed atheist, 'I am not in sympathy with this Champaign woman but she has rights that must be protected.'"[60]

The bill was hurried off to the Senate for consideration, now under the guidance of Sen. Everett Peters. Following established procedure, the bill was referred to the Senate Committee on Education. A number of persons, independently or representing various groups, appeared before the Committee to speak against the bill. One, a member of the Chicago Board of Education, Mrs. Cora Heineman, submitted a statement to the committee which read in part: "Only in the schools can the children of Protestants, Catholics and Jews learn to work and play together, to understand one another, before they learn what separates them— different religions."[61]

Apparently the bill's backers were confident and wanted to expedite the matter, for, "No effort was made to call witnesses from church groups and other organizations which have endorsed the bill because there was apprehension they might confuse the issue."[62]

Clabaugh reacted sharply to the criticism which his bill encountered in the Senate committee. Following the hearing he was reported as returning to the communist theme: "With the exception of Dr. (John A.) Lapp (of the Chicago Citizens' School Committee), this group (objectors to his proposed bill) seems to represent organized communistic atheism."[63] The education committee, on June 28, voted the Clabaugh Bill out to the full Senate without recommendation.

There was little confidence among the McCollum forces that the Clabaugh Bill could be stopped. In a letter to Cromwell, Chapman commented: "I am not able to attend [the Senate hearing on the Clabaugh Bill], and I doubt if there will be much time to hear speakers on the bill. I feel certain that the bill will pass the Senate and probably be signed by the governor and become law next week."[64]

But no one figured into the legislative equation the determined efforts of the CAC and Philip Schug—the former to arouse opposition in Chicago, the latter to carry the fight directly to the Senate itself.

The same afternoon that the Senate committee passed the Clabaugh Bill on to the full Senate, Schug hurriedly wrote a five-page open letter; in very large script. It began: "Dear Senator, you have been handed a very hot potato!" Stretched across the second page, the letter continued:

> We believe in constitutional government! Our tradition has carefully sepa-
> rated church and state! This is indeed a hot potato!! You will never have
> to regret handling this as a statesman! Sincerely Yours, Philip Schug,
> Minister, Unitarian Church, Urbana.[65]

On the third page, Schug went into the substance of the matter. It was a direct and concise statement: "The House has sent you a bill to "legalize" sectarian religious education in tax-supported public schools during school hours. The constitutionality of such education is now being tested in the courts."[66]

Beginning at the bottom of the page and continuing on page four were quotes from applicable sections of the Federal and State Constitutions. Page five was devoted to excerpts from both Peters' and Clabaugh's letters. The former was introduced by the statement: "Senator Peters is not sure he wants to be a statesman."[67] Vashti McCollum helped mimeograph and assemble the letter.[68]

Schug, years after the events, recalled the final showdown in the state Senate.

> The next morning I took the train to Springfield before daylight and ar-
> rived on the senate floor about 8:30 a.m. It was vacant. I placed a copy of
> the "Hot Potato" letter on each desk and went to the gallery to wait. In due
> time the bill came up. Some senators had read the letter. A flustered Sen.
> Peters tried for a quick and easy passage, but a heated debate ensued
> and the bill was rejected. At an intermission I introduced myself to Sen.
> Peters. He cursed and shouted and threatened to throw me through the
> window of the Senate chamber. I stayed out of reach.[69]

Leading the fight against the bill in the Senate was Sen. Robert W. Lyons, Oakland, a Republican. Lyons, also chairman of the education committee, who said he had been "swamped" with telegrams denouncing the bill. One of the messages came from Chicago pastor and radio commentator, Dr. Preston Bradley, who declared, "We want religious education but not on school time."[70]

The Senate sponsor was prompt in offering his interpretation for the Senate's refusal to consider the bill on its substance. As summed up in the *Courier*:

> Senator Peters explained the torrent of opposition which rolled up in the
> upper chamber by pointing out the Clabaugh Bill was rammed through
> the House before its contents were fully known around the state. Oppo-
> nents did not begin waking up to the nature of the bill until it went into the
> Senate, he said.[71]

In the same report, Vashti was quoted as saying, "Many seemed to think we were just trying to start trouble," but, "now we're getting support from others who think as we do." In another account, she said: "I was glad to see it. I wasn't surprised. If such a bill were to be passed, I think it should have more deliberate consideration and several of the senators evidently felt the same way."[72]

During this period, John Franklin was also busy. He entered a motion to quash, a challenge to Vashti's right to file her suit. The hearing was scheduled for July 5, before Judge Frank B. Leonard, himself formerly both the attorney for the Champaign Board of Education and Franklin's law partner.[73]

The defense motion was brief. Franklin contended that a petition for a writ of mandamus was an assertion of a "public right" and should have been filed by either the county state's attorney or the state attorney general.[74]

> He (Franklin) declared that Mrs. McCollum has no case on a purely private right, has not established violation of any right of her own, and that if any right was violated, it was her child's right "although we don't know that James Terry McCollum supports his mother's lack of belief in religion."[75]

Vashti later described the resolution of the issue:

> On and on the arguments went, and finally Judge Leonard apparently got sick and tired of hearing [the attorneys] cite the same cases to prove different points. When it was learned that one of the cases cited, the *Bay Window* case of 1903, had been heard in Champaign, he recessed and sent for the case.
>
> The *Bay Window* case had involved a window that projected over a sidewalk and interfered with persons walking by. The window thus involved the public welfare. Had this suit carried the state official's signature? On this bulging architectural nuisance hung all my hopes.
>
> We returned from recess, during which Judge Leonard consulted the precedent. The *Bay Window* suit had not been signed by the state official. My right to file was supported.[76]

In late July, Judge Leonard set the hearing date for September 10. According to the *News-Gazette*, because the case was "regarded as a test case," Leonard decided upon the "unusual" procedure of naming the two other circuit court judges, Grover C. Watson and Martin E. Morthland, to sit with him "en banc" to hear the case.[77] On August 10, Franklin filed a lengthy answer which addressed, point by point, the issues raised by Chapman's original pleading.[78]

In early August, the released time issue attracted the attention of Prof. O.L. McCaskill of the College of Law at the University of Illinois. In a speech to the Urbana Exchange Club, he distinguished the *McCollum* case from the famous *Scopes* "Monkey" trial:

> Tennessee wanted and got dogma instead of education, and that law (the Tennessee creation law) taught its lesson. In the local suit [*McCollum* case] complaint is made that dogma is being taught, whereas the petitioner [Mrs. McCollum] wants as a substitute another type of dogma, her dogma.[79]

A month later, in a long rambling article, a *News-Gazette* writer restated the professor's assertion "that the *Scopes* and *McCollum* cases represent almost directly opposite contentions... "[80] Vashti, Landon Chapman and the plaintiff's other supporters held, in contrast, that the same principle was involved in both cases, the intrusion of religious dogma into the public schools.

Also alluded to by McCaskill in his speech was the fact that both the *Scopes* and *McCollum* cases attracted outside protagonists "seeking to try the case(s) in the forum of public opinion."[81] In the former, the knights errant took the forms of Clarence Darrow and William Jennings Bryan. While the *McCollum* case did not draw such nationally known figures, both sides received outside help. Plaintiff McCollum benefited at the outset when the CAC stepped in on her behalf by supplying her attorney. By mid-July, the Champaign Board of Education learned that it also would receive help. The Chicago Federation of Churches, joined later by the Illinois Church Council, engaged the prominent Chicago law firm of Eckert and Peterson to assist the defense. Dr. David Lindstrom, a professor at the University of Illinois and president of the Church Council, appears to have been a key organizer of the initiative.[82]

The motives for the church groups' participation in the case seem to have been related to the attitude of the Champaign Board of Education concerning legal expenses for appeals. One of several *Courier* reports on the matter stated: "It is unlikely, Franklin conceded, that the board of education will elect to bear the expense of the suit after it progresses beyond the circuit court stage en route for eventual determination in the United States Supreme Court."[83]

It would seem that the church groups wanted to be prepared to defend the released time system should the Champaign Board of Education step out of the case rather than bear the costs of appeal, a conclusion borne out by a second *Courier* article of the same date: "Apprehension that the system followed in Chicago will be jeopardized if Mrs. McCollum's plea is sustained in the courts has been voiced by some members of the federation who favor lending financial assistance to local school authorities."[84]

The offer of legal help was accepted by the Board "with the provision he (Franklin) could approve the choice of attorneys."[85]

Franklin soon thereafter went to Chicago to confer with Abe Peterson, the firm's senior partner and his associate, Owen Rall.[86] In a news report, Franklin outlined the role of the Chicagoans: "They have indicated a willingness to take part in whatever phases of the case we mutually decide is desirable and, through the representatives of interested churches and religious organizations will hope to focus the attention of the court upon the fact that this case is of importance to religious-minded persons throughout the country."[87]

It seems reasonable to assume that if the church groups were going to bear the financial costs of the inevitable appeals, their leaders, not the Board of Education, would determine the choice of counsel. They, however, were satisfied with the capabilities of the local attorney: "The [church] group went on record as commending John L. Franklin, Champaign School Board attorney, for his handling of the case to date. Although the School Board will not spend taxpayer's money for appealing the case, Franklin will remain for any appeals that may be taken, it was determined."[88]

Years later, Franklin recalled with some satisfaction an early understanding with his upstate colleagues:

> They (Peterson and Rall) didn't know me from Adam, and I suppose took the case out of the concern that I was not a competent trial attorney. One of the first things I found out, somewhat to my amazement, was that they investigated me, and appraised me, and let me take the role of chief counsel when, I am sure, ordinarily, they would have expected to assume that role themselves.[89]

The Illinois Council of Churches authorized a poll of downstate religious leaders to determine if it should form a joint committee with the Chicago church organization;[90] the proposed committee's specific concern would be to "analyze the issues and give advice to clear up the issues involved to bring the [McCollum] case to a proper solution."[91] The result was an organization variously referred to as the "Illinois Association for Religious Education on Released School Time," and the "Illinois Committee on Released School Time." The most prominent leaders of the new body were Thomas H. West, a Chicago attorney, and David Lindstrom. Its stated purposes were:

> ...to strengthen existing systems of religious education on released school time in the communities of the state; to promote the instruction of such systems in other communities; to develop standards of curriculum and teachers for the system; and in general to promote religious education on released school time as a cooperative project of all the faiths and denominations to the end that the United States of America shall continue to be— as she began—a religious nation.[92]

Another definite aim of the group was to raise money to help the Champaign Board of Education meet the challenge to its released time program.[93]

Vashti remained busy during the summer with a variety of activities incidental to her suit. Important among them were those related to public reaction to her cause. In early July, she was invited to speak to the local Kiwanis Club along with Superintendent Mellon, but the invitation was withdrawn when some of the wives objected to her presence.[94]

While formal contacts with the public, such as that offered by the ill-fated Kiwanis invitation, were few and far between, there was the telephone. Call frequency fluctuated considerably, with the high incidence periods following each "new rash of newspaper headlines."[95] "Men seldom called," Vashti remembered, "but when they did they almost always gave their names. Not a single woman who called to criticize me ever gave her name."[96]

One woman, Mrs. Ruth Tager, who did give her name, told of what happened when a thoughtless fifth grade teacher asked those students not signed up to stand and explain why they were not taking the religious classes. The foster child in the caller's care was one of those singled out. The youngster explained that he was Jewish; there were no Jewish classes then offered in his school. On the following day the boy was severely beaten by the older brother of one of the children in the class.[97] Accompanying anti-Semitic remarks strongly suggested that the two incidents were not unrelated.

There were also many tasks to be done that pertained directly to the preparation of her lawsuit.

> Phil [Schug], Chapman and I spent many hot summer afternoons running around town, hunting up witnesses, especially religious spokesmen. One of Chapman's main strategies was to try to show that there were many conflicting views among Gentiles and non-Catholics, that you couldn't have a Catholic group, a Jewish group, and then lump all the others together.[98]

As part of the effort, Chapman and Vashti visited the "head of the Jewish group" in Champaign. While unnamed in her book, he was probably Lee Reineberg, president of the Sinai Temple congregation. He greeted her enthusiastically. "So this is the little girl who started all the trouble?" While supportive, he was also "noncommittal." As Vashti recalled his position: "He said the instruction classes weren't to the advantage of the Jewish group. ... but they did not intend to fight or protest [the released time program in] the public school system."[99]

This was consistent with the Jewish attitude five years earlier when the released time program was established in Champaign.

As the trial date approached, Ira Latimer of the CCLC decided that a mass meeting should be held in Champaign-Urbana.[100] The purpose appears to have been two-fold, to explain the issues involved in the case from the plaintiff's and her backers point of view, and to organize a local civil liberties committee.[101] To help ensure attendance, advertisements were placed in the Sunday, September 9, editions of both the *News-Gazette* and *Courier*; the meeting was scheduled for that evening at the Unitarian Church. Four speakers were listed—Latimer, Chapman, Schug and Vashti.[102]

Alfred Prowitt of the *Daily News* vividly described the emotional climate in the twin cities in general, and in particular at the meeting itself. "Champaign passions on the issue, which have been boiling for weeks, reached a new high temperature in a public meeting before the trial opened. In the ivied little Unitarian Church of Urbana, at the elbow of the University's campus, both sides traded blows across hot pews."[103]

The meeting was less than a resounding success from the point of view of its organizers. Described by the *News-Gazette* as a "small mass meeting"[104]—the *Courier* set attendance at "about 50 persons"[105]—there were at least as many opponents of Vashti as there were supporters.[106] Schug, described in a report afterwards as "an intense scholarly man," acted as moderator,[107] while Chapman, Latimer and Vashti read prepared statements.[108] The Unitarian minister led off his brief, introductory remarks with a charge:

> Everywhere religious training has been tried in public schools, it has caused trouble. There is a question whether we really have religious tolerance. We have no quarrel with any church in its propagation of its faith, but let each church pay its own way.[109]

Schug, continuing on this theme, "indicated that the very small attendance at the mass meeting was due to the same social pressure and coercion which is brought upon students to attend the classes."[110]

For the most part, the speakers stressed the legal and policy aspects of the case. Somewhat sarcastically, Chapman suggested, when his turn came, that the correct way to have established the religious classes would have been to repeal the Federal Constitution and parts of the State Constitution, then hold a referendum to determine the majority will, and finally elect legislators who would enact the appropriate legislation. As it was, according to Chapman, the Champaign School Board "bootlegged" the classes into the schools.[111]

At another point in his remarks, Chapman said: "There are 256 established religions in the United States. Unless you permit the teaching of all of them, you are giving sectarian teaching.[112]" In another version, he declared: "With 256 religious denominations, each believing different things, not all can be right," and "Churches have not yet reached the point where they may be entrusted with state support."[113] Chapman called the School Board's policy "religious fascism." He went on to say:

> There is a state law against sectarian teaching. But only the King James version of the Bible is used. How about Mohammed, Buddha and Brahma? Haven't they, too, given something to world morals? Most churches are engaged in a struggle to destroy each other. Shall we let them destroy our schools in their warfare?[114]

In this same vein, the plaintiff's attorney added: "[The] churches while in control of the schools didn't do much for science or contribute much to help mankind advance in studies of evolution."[115]

This last report ended with Chapman saying: "Skeptics, agnostics and atheists ask free religion for all while churches are cutting each others' throats."[116] Returning to the broad public policy issue, Chapman stated:

> The issue involved is whether the state shall support religion in the schools. There are too many churches to be wed to one government or state and there would be rivalry in the schools if they were all taught. If the churches are going to feed out of the public trough, it would be a fight to see who gets the most.[117]

Chapman seldom denied himself the opportunity to couch his statements in a way designed to give offense to religious people. In probably a remarkable misreading of local attitudes, Chapman continued: "Why didn't you people in Champaign-Urbana vote on a ballot whether religion should be put in the schools? Because you knew it wouldn't stand the test?"[118]

Latimer deviated somewhat from the issues, using some of his time in an unsuccessful effort to recruit members for the CCLC. According to Vashti, Latimer further diverged from the subject of the meeting by taking the opportunity to criticize the community "because Negroes were discriminated against by restaurants and boarding houses."[119] The Chicagoan then returned to the case at hand:

Schoolmates say about Mrs. McCollum's boy: "He even throws a baseball like a little atheist." Would you want that said about your child? Churches are hard-pressed when they have to ram dogma down the throats of little kids.[120]

At another point, Latimer declared: "This case is to support the little people … to prove that they cannot be pushed around."[121] Before concluding, Latimer charged that: "Mrs. McCollum had to go to Chicago to get a lawyer because there was not a single attorney in Champaign-Urbana who had the guts to take her case."[122] While that may have been true, it was never put to a test by Mrs. McCollum; she never sought a willing, competent local attorney.[123]

The plaintiff, and star attraction, was described variously by reporters in attendance as a "young matron of decided views,"[124] "speaking forcefully,"[125] and displaying the "law training she has had in college."[126] She directed her comments to the issues and the local reaction to her challenge. "As the suit has developed," she said, "many have stressed the religious differences and have forgotten the legal point involved."[127] Along a similar vein, she continued: "This is a public, not a private, affair; there is no justification, under the constitution, for permitting the pressure that children bring on another child who belongs to a minority."[128]

She also spoke of the telephone calls and correspondence received as a consequence of the suit. These communications, she said, were both supportive and hostile. Many of the former, while disagreeing with her religious views, nevertheless supported her on the legal issue. Those in opposition were not nearly as kind, prompting her to observe: "If putting religion in the schools has caused so much bitterness when a legal issue is raised, I wonder if it should ever have been there."[129]

The "high spot" of the meeting was reported to have occurred during the lively discussion session following the speakers.[130] A major factor stimulating the discussion was the presence of "the ministers in full force." Someone raised the question of how the classes were installed in the schools in the first place.[131] That prompted an immediate response from Vashti, who remembered her own frustrated efforts at learning the facts.

That's just what I've been trying to find out, and that's why I filed this suit. I went to the superintendent of schools and he wouldn't tell me, and I went to one of the ministers and he was very rude.[132]

Schug, intervening, redirected the question back to the audience, presumably to the ministers. After a brief period of hesitation, Rev. Cartlidge rose in response. He admitted being "the one who had a major part in getting religious education in schools started here." He denied that the program had been established at a "secret meeting" as Chapman had charged earlier in the program. Somewhat defensively, Cartlidge said: "I don't believe it will increase religious bigotry as charged." He concluded by expressing the view that the suit was "brought by some persons to gain publicity." His remarks were followed by applause, the only such demonstration of the evening. Before the meeting was over,

Cartlidge apologized for the "publicity" remark, but he let stand his assertion that the classes had not been instituted in "secret."[133]

Two additional incidents helped highlight the meeting. One was the presence of a "surprise spectator," Mrs. Ralph Cummins, a Champaign resident who was the first teacher in the first released time religious education program in the country—in Gary, Indiana, in 1913. She said that the Gary program was not instituted at the request of the ministers but rather at the initiative of the superintendent of schools.[134] The other incident was the "stir" caused when a "representative of the Jehovah's Witnesses...charged that his faith had not been invited to join other churches in the program."[135]

At the conclusion of the meeting, in spite of Ira Latimer's initial appeal, "no effort was made to take up a collection to organize and finance a civil liberties committee in the Champaign-Urbana area, one of the primary purposes of the meeting." The reason offered by the *News-Gazette* was the "small crowd, however, financial pledges were requested at the conclusion of the meeting"[136] but the complexion of the group was such as would hardly have given the sponsors much hope in that regard.

The meeting clearly illustrated a fundamental difficulty complicating local controversies that are invested by outside interests. Vashti and Schug, although neither were natives of Champaign-Urbana, were at least residents and knew the local people. Both sought to limit the debate to the specific issues involved. From the outset, Chapman antagonized the local population, as did Latimer at the meeting. Franklin was to prove adroit in exploiting the public relations deficiencies of the Chicagoans supporting Vashti while maintaining a relatively low profile for his own legal allies from the Windy City. He later observed:

> It seemed to me that he [Chapman] took an aggravated position and that frankly he was more inclined to make headlines in the public press and to advance the cause, if you want to term it as that, of atheism versus religion, than winning the lawsuit—and I helped him along in that.[137]

Chapter 5

The Circus Begins

On Monday, September 10, 1945, the curious, the witnesses and the principals in the case assembled at the Champaign County courthouse in Urbana. One Chicago reporter, short on his history, noted that the courthouse "stands on the spot where Lincoln and Douglas held one of their famed debates."[1] There was little need for this additional misinformation; the presence of Chicago reporters alone was sufficient evidence of the sensational nature and wide interest in the "Bible Trial."[2] One of the more thoughtful reporters took the time to look up the story of Vashti in the Gideon Bible in his hotel room. After sharing it in much abbreviated form with his readers he concluded: "Thus Vashti [is] the first recorded exponent of free thinking among women."[3] (Shortly after the close of the trial, reference would again be made to the Biblical story.)

Before the proceedings began, a large man in his forties approached Supt. Mellon. "I'm here to testify for the Lord," he announced. Mellon politely directed him to John Franklin. The man repeated his purpose to the school board's attorney, who responded: "I'm sorry sir, but the Lord is not on trial here today." Years later, in recalling the incident, Mellon observed: "Many people thought it was sort of a conflict with religion itself ... to me it was not."[4]

Another reporter, noting that the courtroom was "well-filled," surmised that, "Some of the spectators obviously came to have a look at a woman atheist."[5] He described the plaintiff as "about 34, a brunette with a turned-up nose and strong opinions."[6]

The three-judge panel was headed by Judge Frank B. Leonard. A native of Metropolis in far southern Illinois, he first came to the east-central part of the state to earn his AB and JD degrees from the University of Illinois. Though he returned to Metropolis for a brief period to practice law, in 1919 he moved to Champaign, where he remained for the rest of his life, first as a lawyer and later as a judge.[7]

The judges were first called upon to decide whether or not the two Chicago attorneys who had been working with Franklin, Peterson and Rall, could officially enter the case. The legal stratagem employed was to have Elmer Bash, a local roofing contractor, his wife Alice, and daughter Wanda, petition to intervene as co-defendants on behalf of the Board of Education with the Chicagoans as their counsel. The involvement of the Bashes occurred somewhat by chance. They were acquainted socially with Franklin who, during a meeting of a bridge club of which all were members, casually asked if they would consider participating as intervenors. Elmer and Alice were agreeable to the proposition.[8]

Arguing the Bashes' legal standing on the basis that Wanda was enrolled in the religious classes and wanted to continue, Peterson and Rall used as authority one of the same provisions of the Illinois Constitution used by Vashti in her challenge of the Champaign System. The relevant section read:

> The free exercise and enjoyment of religious profession and worship, without discrimination, shall forever be guaranteed; and no person shall be denied any civil or political right, privilege or capacity on account of his religious opinions … No person shall be required to attend or support any ministry or place of worship against his consent, nor shall any preference be given by law to any religious denomination or mode of worship.[9]

This language, in the view of Peterson and Rall, guaranteed that "the said Wanda I. Bash is entitled freely to attend said course in religious education during the coming school year without interference from the relator [McCollum] or any persons whom she purports to represent."[10] Chapman did not challenge the intervention of the Bashes; he merely filed an answer to their petition, responding briefly to its factual and legal substance. After a discussion, the court allowed the Bashes to intervene.[11]

Chapman's opening statements consisted largely of a repetition of the allegations contained in his original pleadings.[12] He said he "was prepared to prove that the religious education classes represent 'proselytizing' of children by 'religious sects' and an attempt to 'unite church and state'."[13] He continued: "The private church teachers, by going to the public schools, oust secular education for a period and substitute religious education. As they teach only their own beliefs, this too is sectarian in nature."[14]

Chapman further charged that "social pressure from fellow students and from adult secular teachers is applied to those students failing to enroll in the course."[15] The petitioner's attorney felt it necessary again to deny that the suit was a challenge to religion: "This case is no contest between religion and atheism; we say neither should be taught in the public schools. … We are neutral so far as religion and atheism are concerned."[16]

Franklin, in his statement, "asserted the board was ready to prove the classes are voluntary and entirely legal."[17] He went on to charge that the suit was "an attack on an institution of American democracy existing in 46 of the 48 states, in 1,858 school districts and in more than 80 Illinois communities."[18] Illinois law was cited that empowered school boards "to have control and supervision of all public school houses in their districts, and to grant the temporary use of them, when not occupied by schools, for religious meetings and Sunday schools."[19] He contended further that, "there is no discrimination against any sect or faith."[20] Peterson, when his turn came, "termed Mrs. McCollum an 'infidel' and said the Bashes came into court to represent the opposite view."[21] The "high courts," he said, "repeatedly have asserted that this is a religious nation and that constitutional provisions supposedly violated were only formulated to protect religious beliefs."[22] Rall, after his "adoption" of Franklin's opening argument, continued along a theme similar to that pursued by Peterson: "This is a religious nation with a constitution to protect religion."[23]

Mae Chapin, superintendent of the religious education program, was the first witness called by Chapman. She was described in two press reports as "a tiny, grey-haired woman with a confident smile, "[24] and "small, pert and neat."[25] A former classroom teacher at South Side School remembered Miss Chapin as a "fine person, religious and kindly."[26]

Chapman's examination began quietly enough as he developed background material relating to her relationship to the Champaign Council of Religious Education (CCRE), duties as superintendent of the religious classes and the mechanics of the program. Miss Chapin testified that, as part of her responsibilities with the CCRE, she handled the scheduling of all classes, Protestant and Catholic, wrote curriculum for the former and taught during the 1944-1945 school year 19 of the 35 religious classes.[27]

Altering his line of questioning, Chapman became increasingly aggressive in an attempt "to find out what the children are being taught." Two newspapermen later reported that the lawyer had "quizzed Miss Chapin closely,"[28] and even indulged in "pitiless questioning."[29] This approach as well as Chapman's manner brought repeated objections from John Franklin: "I object to that [question], she is his witness and he has no right to cross-examine her." Shortly thereafter, "We object to [Chapman's] interrogating his witness as to her knowledge or belief with reference to Bible matters." Chapman countered: "The court will observe that this is a hostile witness."

The Court: "I will permit him (Chapman) to interrogate fully as to what she taught, not as to her personal belief."

At one point, Chapman attempted to show that the Protestant classes promoted religious prejudice against Jews.

Chapman: "I want to know what you teach. Don't you teach that the Jews were enemies of Christ?"

Chapin: "They were hostile to Jesus in many ways."

After an objection by Franklin, the court struck the answer when the witness said that the response indicated what she believed rather than what she taught.

Chapman: "Did you teach the children that the Jews were afraid of Jesus?"

Chapin: "Some of them were."

Chapman: "How about the others?"

The questioning was then interrupted by an objection from Franklin, but the court allowed Chapman to continue.

Chapman: "Have you during the last three years at any time been teaching that the Jews had anything to do with the crucifixion of Jesus Christ?"

Peterson objected: "I do not think anybody could answer it (the question) unless counsel says whether he means the Jews as a race or as part of an organization."

Chapman: "Anyway you want to take it."

Peterson: "Did any Jews participate? That is another question."

Chapin: "Yes."

Chapman: "Did you tell or mention this to the children?"

Chapin: "No."

When his questions failed to produce the answers he wanted, Chapman produced the course outline used by the witness and he asked her to read a specific passage from it. Chapin read, "The Jews rejected Jesus." The witness then added gratuitously that, "It does not mean as a people; it means as individuals." On a motion by Chapman, the latter statements were stricken as "not responsive."

When Chapman attempted to have the witness read further from the outline concerning the participation of Jews in the "conspiracy against Jesus," the court ruled that since the outline was in evidence she could only read it to herself and that Chapman could call her attention to it. According to a report in the *Daily Illini*, "The outline named the Jews as the executioners of Christ."[30]

In reference to this particular interchange, one reporter commented: "With determined spunk, she [Chapin] resisted all efforts by Chapman, to show that her classes instilled racial prejudice in pupils."[31]

It was a central point in the plaintiff's case that the religious classes created problems for children of religious minorities. The hostility against Jews engendered by their supposed involvement in the crucifixion of Jesus as taught in the classes was a major issue. It was not just the atheist kid who suffered.

The main thrust of Chapman's questioning, however, was directed towards establishing for the record the sectarian nature of the teaching in the Protestant classes. To this end, Chapman asked Miss Chapin what Bible she used.

Chapin: "I usually taught from the King James version or the American Revised Bible."

Chapman: "Do you use the Douay (Catholic) version?

Chapin: "No."

(The *Ring* case had, in part, hinged on the fact that the King James Bible was used in religious activities at a public school. This was held by the Illinois Supreme Court to be sectarian. The plaintiffs in that case were Catholics.)[32]

To further demonstrate the sectarian nature of the classes, Chapman embarked upon a detailed examination of what Miss Chapin taught with respect to Bible stories and religious doctrine. The witness, resisting the lawyer's approach, countered: "I do not teach those doctrinal things; I just teach the Bible story." Later in her testimony she insisted: "In my course, first I teach Bible content. I take the stories of the Bible and tell them as they are told in the Bible without any comment as to their interpretation, and I try to teach the ethical teachings."

Vashti recalled that "Chapman questioned [Chapin] in a way that was amusing to some spectators but didn't increase our popularity any."[33] Miss Chapin, however, was able to hold her own. In the words of one reporter she "fenced adroitly,"[34] in what another described as a "doctrinal sparring match."[35]

Chapman: "Did you teach that Mary and Jesus fled into Egypt?"

Chapin: "It's a Bible fact; I taught that."

Chapman: "After the death of Herod?"

Chapin: "Until the death of Herod."

Miss Chapin's correction "drew a laugh—Judge Leonard warned against demonstrations and threatened to clear the courtroom saying, 'this is a trial, not a spectacle.'"[30]

Miss Chapin ended her testimony on direct examination by again stating, "I do not teach doctrines; I teach content."

On cross-examination, Franklin worked to refute Chapman's contentions that the religious education program was sectarian, unconstitutionally tied to the public school program, unfair in its treatment of some beliefs or sects, and that it proselytized students.

Franklin: "What do you teach?"

Chapin: "I teach religious education in the public schools in the public school buildings."

Franklin: "Are Catholics included in the program?"

Chapin: "I have referred to the fact that there are classes taught by Catholic priests in the school district as part of the religious education program."

Franklin: "What is done with respect to Jewish children?"

Chapin: "I have sent the cards of the Jewish children who registered to the rabbi who has to make arrangements for them."

Franklin: "Are there any Jews in your classes?"

Chapin: "No."

Franklin: "What religious groups are members of the Champaign Council of Religious Education?"

Chapin: "In addition to the Protestant churches, the Catholic church and the Jewish churches cooperate as members."

Franklin: "With reference to the classes you teach, do you teach your own beliefs or do you teach Bible content?"

Chapin: "I teach Bible content."

Franklin: "Have you ever urged on the children in your classes any particular belief other than as stated in the Bible that you used?"

Chapin: "No."

Chapman: "Objection. It calls for a conclusion as to what she urges."

Court: "Overruled."

Franklin: "Have you ever practiced proselytizing in connection with any children coming under your care and jurisdiction, or have you ever attempted to form or change any [child's] belief from one denomination to another?"

Chapin: "No."

Franklin: "In substance, what was your intention to teach these children?"

Chapin: "The brotherhood of man, the fatherhood of God and the practical application of the ethical teaching of Christ to the pupils' everyday life."

And finally in this vein, Franklin asked: "Has your teaching been generally well received by parents?"

Chapin: "As far as I know."

When Franklin asked if the classes had an effect on the students, Miss Chapin said she did not know, but subsequently, she took the opportunity to cite two specific instances designed to illustrate her feeling that the influence was positive. Chapin:

In one class where we taught of the prodigal son, one of the boys came up after class and said he was glad he had gone [to the religious class], that he had decided to run away from home, but then decided not to. One girl came to me after class and said, "Before I came to your class I had a problem but now it is solved."

Franklin also questioned Miss Chapin concerning her background. She revealed that she had been raised in Champaign and had earned both bachelor's and master's degrees from the University of Illinois. Under further questioning she said that for most of her working career she had been involved in teaching and missionary work in the Far East (China and the Philippines). Thus, Franklin sought to prove that Miss Chapin possessed equal qualifications to those of the regular classroom teachers she replaced for the 30-minute religious class periods.

The next witness, Mrs. Lakie B. Munson, was the first of several whom Chapman called that day to show the extent of school involvement in the program. Mrs. Munson had been, the year previous to the trial, the principal at Dr. Howard and teacher of one of the sixth grades; that same year, James Terry had been a student there. She had also been interviewed during the previous spring by Vashti McCollum, Philip Schug and Chapman, at which time she had revealed information Chapman felt was valuable to the case.

Assuming, correctly as it turned out, that he had a hostile witness, Chapman aggressively launched into the substance of his examination: "What happened to the students you abandoned to Miss Chapin?"

Franklin objected and was sustained. Undaunted, Chapman pursued the actual mechanics of the religious class as well as the working relationship which existed between Mrs. Munson and Miss Chapin. During the spring interview, Mrs. Munson had been asked what she and the students not enrolled did during the religious class. According to Vashti, "She said she sat with them and graded papers while they read books." Repeated efforts by Chapman to elicit the earlier response from the teacher-principal on the witness stand were unsuccessful

Chapman: "Do you then spend 30 minutes more each week with them [students not taking the course] than with those who take religious education?"

Munson: "No. As teachers we work with children as individuals, not a mass. I have completed my individual work with those who are with me in those 30 minutes."

Also during the spring interview, Mrs. Munson had told the group that she made room in her schedule for the religious class by taking 30 minutes from arithmetic. It seems likely that Chapman used that response as a basis for his charge that "the 30-minute period of secular education [was] lost each week [and] not later recovered."

Chapman: "How long is your room used for· religious education?"
Munson: "Thirty minutes."
Chapman: "Do you teach overtime to make up for that time?"
Munson: "No."
Although Chapman pursued the topic, Mrs. Munson refused to admit that time

from secular studies was actually lost. She even "shook her finger and asserted she 'knew' he was wrong." In order to impeach her testimony, Chapman attempted, during redirect examination, to bring out statements apparently made by Mrs. Munson during the spring meeting.

Chapman: "Do you remember telling me and several others present that on Monday morning you took out 30 minutes from arithmetic—that is, you were behind 30 minutes in opening the Monday class?"

Franklin: "Objection."

Court: "Sustained. Is this an attempt to impeach your own witness?"

Chapman: "This is a hostile witness."

Court: "I will allow you to ask leading questions but I do not believe you can impeach her."

During cross-examination by Peterson, the question of singing of the "Star Spangled Banner" and "America" came up." In singing them, Mrs. Munson said, "We do not omit that part of it which says In God We Trust."

Superintendent Mellon was then called to reinforce the plaintiff's contention that the public school system was intimately involved with the religious classes.

Chapman: "Did you state in your bulletin: 'Teachers and principals will make arrangements with the religious education instructors, music supervisors, art supervisors and all other people who have work to do in the schools, other than the regular classroom teachers'?"

Mellon: "Probably."

Several questions later Chapman asked, "Before children take the course, are cards sent to parents for permission?"

Mellon: "Yes."

Chapman: "Were they distributed through your office?"

Mellon: "No."

Chapman: "Would your office mimeograph the cards?"

Mellon: "Sometimes."

Chapman: "Who paid for them?"

Mellon: "Miss Chapin."

Chapman: "Who did the mimeographing?"

Mellon: "The office clerk."

Chapman: "Was the clerk under your supervision and paid by the school board?"

Mellon: "She was."

Chapman then questioned whether the schools were open to all denominations equally.

Mellon: "I made no objection to (Miss Chapin) teaching in the school nor have I ever objected to anybody teaching in the schools. The schools are open to all denominations who want to teach in them."

Chapman then pursued detailed questioning related to whether or not Mellon would permit specific sects and beliefs in the schools.

Chapman: "Are the schools available to Christian Scientists if they want to conduct a class?"

Mellon: "Yes."

Several questions later, Mellon said he would also "permit" Jehovah's Witnesses to use the classrooms, but he indicated that the teacher had to be "qualified to teach." In one of the follow-up questions, Chapman asked: "Would the classroom be available to people who teach religion to the effect that saluting the flag is wrong?"

Mellon: "Yes, but they have never asked for it."

The lawyer then attempted to get Mellon to "designate" a classroom for Jehovah's Witnesses. After the court sustained Franklin's objection to the question, Chapman asked if the "classrooms are available to a person who believes in no religion?"

Mellon: "As far as I know."

Rev. John George Kaiser, pastor of St. John's Lutheran church of the Missouri Synod, was the next witness. He testified that he was aware of the efforts to organize the religious education program (in 1940) but he did not participate. During the past summer (1945) he had begun to meet with the CCRE. At that time he had requested that provision be made for a Lutheran class. "I was assured that if and when there were sufficient children desiring instruction according to the Lutheran faith, time would be granted us." He said he had not "as yet arranged to provide a teacher."

Chapman then sought to bring out doctrinal differences between what Miss Chapin taught and what Lutherans believe. This brought a quick objection from Franklin, who said: "This suit does not require an expression or statement of all or any of the representatives of the different faiths of what they believe in."

Chapman: "One of the chief issues of this case is whether or not this religious teaching is sectarian. The only way we can tell that, is to compare it with the doctrines and teachings of the various sects. We want to know if they are all in accord with the teaching of other denominations." The court allowed this line of questioning not only with Rev. Kaiser but with the representatives of the several faiths who followed. All this prompted one reporter to observe: "Many spectators yawned as doctrines were expounded by the witnesses, who were questioned by Chapman and cross-examined by John L. Franklin."[37]

A brief afternoon recess preceded the testimony of the next witness. In the hallway outside the courtroom there was a gathering of several of the religious leaders who had been called. Father Clarence J. Higgins of the Holy Cross Catholic Church in Champaign was heard to comment wryly: "I don't know what I'm doing here; this trial is about sectarian religion—I'm the church."[38]

Also during the break, Harold E. Barcus and T .E. Wells, both affiliated with the Jehovah's Witnesses, approached Supt. Mellon and a member of the "Religious Council" and requested permission for a time and place in the schools for children of their faith. After the break, Chapman called Barcus as his first witness. Mr. Barcus was asked about his conversation with Mellon. After an objection from Franklin, Barcus was quizzed briefly about the tenets of his faith, then excused.

Superintendent Mellon was then recalled to give testimony relating to his reaction to the request of the Jehovah's Witnesses. Mellon apparently told Barcus during their conversation that he could not grant permission on the spot, that the "regular procedure" would have to be followed.

Chapman: "What is this regular procedure through which people must go in order to obtain the use of the school house, such as Jehovah's Witnesses." After an objection by Franklin, Mellon outlined what he meant by "regular procedure."

> I would like to have the names of the pupils and the schools in which they are located, and the number of pupils; that would have to be taken care of in my office. I am a practical person. I would like to know, before I would grant permission to Jehovah's Witnesses to use the school buildings the number of persons in the school [desiring to take the class] and also to make regular arrangements.

To prove that the school district worked "in cooperation with the religious council," Chapman asked the Superintendent what the other gentleman present had said—presumably the member of the religious council.

Mellon: "He tried to explain to Mr. Barcus the orderly procedure, and that all of the groups should work together; it was hard for us as a board of education or me as a superintendent to work with a lot of different groups."

School board president Delos L. Huxtable was then called. In his brief tenure on the stand he testified as to what was contained in the minutes of the June 6, 1940 board meeting, when the board, in Huxtable's words, "agreed to cooperate with reference to teaching religious education in the schools." He also said that, "They [the religious groups] were all to be treated alike, with the understanding that the teachers they would bring into the school were approved by the superintendent."

Rev. H. Clifford Northcott was called next. The *News-Gazette* devoted nearly seven column inches to his testimony, beginning with the following:

> Spectators awarded honors for the best witness stand performance to Dr. H. Clifford Northcott, pastor of the First Methodist church. With a smile that never disappeared, Dr. Northcott frequently got ahead of Chapman's questioning as he explained how religious education classes were started in the schools.[39]

The *News-Gazette* coverage went on to mention: "The Methodist pastor drew a laugh from the galleries when he commented he guessed 'Mr. Chapman doesn't know much about churches'."[40] Northcott's performance did not seem to make the same impression on the other reporters present; the only other news report that went into any detail concerning his testimony was a terse reference in the *Courier*:

> Mrs. Munson and Rev. H.C. Northcott, both Chapman's witnesses but both hostile, resisted questioning, either by roundabout answers or by oversimplification. Rev. Mr. Northcott, who has been a Champaign minister 17 years, was asked to tell how religious education came to be in Champaign schools.[41]

Northcott testified that the CCRE "got together as good democratic organizations do." When asked if anyone had complained, Northcott responded: "My goodness, Mr. Chapman, I never heard of any parents objecting to the courses for any reason, except possibly that the schedule was crowded."[42]

Following Northcott's testimony, Chapman called two witnesses to further his case that religious diversity existed in the community. Edwin H. Reeder, a university professor and a member of the Urbana Society of Friends, testified that, "There are as many beliefs with reference to Jesus Christ and his divinity as there are Quakers." Reeder, the Saturday before the trial, had received a telephone call from a man who identified himself as "John Franklin." "I wonder," the caller said, "if you know that a record is going to be made of everything you say, and a copy will be sent to the university president."[43] Chapman attempted to prove intimidation by questioning Reeder concerning the incident. Franklin objected.

The judge then asked the witness if he had ever talked to Franklin on the phone at any other time, so he could identify his voice. He had not so the testimony was thrown out.[44]

The other witness, a minister of a fundamentalist Protestant church, testified briefly respecting the divinity of Christ, his crucifixion, resurrection and other doctrines of his group. When asked by Franklin on cross-examination if he objected to the classes, the minister "answered a resounding 'No'."[45]

The witness who, along with Miss Chapin, excited the most comment in the press during the first day of the trial was Mrs. Bessie Taylor, James Terry's teacher in the fifth grade the previous year. Under questioning by Chapman, she testified that "at times" she stayed in the room to "observe" when the religious teacher [Miss Chapin] came to teach. During the 1944-1945 school year, Mrs. Taylor said that she had two children who did not take the course—James Terry both semesters and Elwin Miller during the first semester only.

Chapman: "Where did you go when religious education was being taught?"

Taylor: "We went to the music room."

Chapman: "What did they (the students who did not participate) do?"

Taylor: "They took material they needed to work (on), maybe recreational reading or something like that."

Under follow-up questioning by Chapman, Mrs. Taylor admitted that on one occasion James "sat out in the corridor." As he had done with Mrs. Munson, Chapman probed the extent to which Mrs. Taylor participated in the religious education program. She maintained: "I distributed [the parental consent cards] and I collected them, that is all." Earlier she had indicated that she "passed [the cards] on to the religious education teacher." Bessie Taylor, as had Mrs. Munson, said she did not teach an additional half hour to make up for the time lost during the religious class.

Franklin's cross-examination was perfunctory and designed to show that utilities and janitorial services which Mrs. Taylor had admitted on direct examination were provided by the school were only nominal subsidies to the religious education program.

Rather than leaving matters there, Chapman decided to engage in a redirect examination of the witness, introducing new matters and ultimately providing the press with its best copy of the day.

Chapman: "Did you notice anything unusual with regard to Terry McCollum, any discomfort about him when he left the room and he came back again?"

Franklin: "I object to that."

Court: "She may answer."

Taylor: "I felt that he wanted to stay in the room very badly; he showed an interest in the class, he did not seem to want to leave."

Subsequently, Mrs. Taylor testified that James Terry "was poor in his work when he came to [her] class." She admitted suggesting to Mrs. McCollum that allowing her son to take the course "might help him to become a member of the group."

On re-cross-examination, Franklin took the opportunity to probe further into James Terry's problems in school. Under his questioning, she testified that her now well-known former student "never seemed to be accepted by the other youngsters from the beginning."

Franklin: "Did you ever observe anything about him or his relations with other children, or what they may have said at any time which would have indicated that the presence of religious education classes had anything whatever to do with his non-acceptance by the group?"

Taylor: "No."

Further questioning by Franklin drew from the witness yet more damaging testimony: "When they would get into trouble I would ask the other children what was the cause, and they would say James had called them names, James had kicked them and punched them and he spit in their faces."[46]

Chapman, on re-direct examination, attempted to repair the damage by asking Mrs. Taylor, "When you suggested to James' mother that if he would take the religious education course it might help him to become more acceptable to other students, what did you have in mind at that time?" The lawyer, however, was not successful in impeaching Mrs. Taylor's earlier testimony that the religious classes had nothing to do with James Terry's problems in school.

The damage had been done, and Franklin declined his opportunity for re-cross-examination. It is surprising, certainly in retrospect, that Chapman should have attempted to use Mrs. Taylor, a hostile witness, to prove that the religious classes were the cause of James Terry's problems.

Most affected by the teacher's testimony was Mrs. McCollum. Her reaction was described in the local press as follows:

> Mrs. McCollum, relaxed and silent through all the day's session, leaving to Ira Latimer ... all decisions with her attorney, exhibited indignation at Mrs. Taylor's testimony. Her dark eyes snapping, she walked to the reporter's table to declare that in previous conferences the teacher never had told her of misconduct by Terry that might have caused other children to dislike him.[47]

Without question, Mrs. Taylor's testimony had caused Vashti considerable anguish. Since the "question of Jim's general adjustment had been raised," She said later, "I wanted to bring [a psychologist-friend familiar with Jim] in as a witness." She continued, "Chapman didn't think it was very important, but I insisted that it was important to me as a mother, so he said I should call her."

Now up to this time few of our friends, except the very closest ones, had said much to us about the case. It was peculiar in a way. We had close acquaintances among the professors and their wives, who would have eagerly talked with us about a baby or a death in the family or a new house. With the case, it was different. They not only didn't mention it, they carefully avoided mentioning it. However, the psychologist was a close friend of mine and I had no qualms about calling her.

Instead of getting her on the phone, I got her husband. He said she was in Chicago, and I asked how I could get in touch with her explaining why I wanted and needed her. He spoke sharply. "Don't you try to drag us into this," he said. "If Jim's having a bad time, don't come crying around to us. You should have known what it would do to him when you filed that suit, and we don't want any part of it. You leave us out of this."

Crestfallen, I hung up. Naturally I couldn't blame my friend, who knew nothing about it. In fact, when I told her later that I had wanted to get in touch with her, she said, "If I had known, I'd have started walking toward Champaign." That's the sort of person she is. But even knowing that at the time wasn't much help. I don't cry any easier than Jim does, but that night I sat down and bawled.[48]

It had not helped that her father had been in the rear of the courtroom all day offering "to cite stories of immorality and torture from the worn and indexed Bible on his lap."[49] Of even greater concern was a report that the CAC had withdrawn its support from her cause.[50]

For the plaintiff, the first day of the trial was an ordeal of ordeals. Little did she realize how far from over her discomforts were.

Chapter 6

The Trial, Day Two

The courtroom was crowded when proceedings resumed on the second day of the trial. The *Daily News* reported: "The hundreds of spectators who overflowed Circuit Court yesterday and again today needed the overnight rest. They couldn't have taken any more of the emotional tuggings at one time."[1]

Lengthy coverage in the local press the previous evening may well have been a factor influencing the size of the crowd. There was also anticipation that Vashti herself would take the stand. A surfeit of reporters provided some indication that the outside world remained interested in the Urbana trial. As the *Daily Illini* noted: "The press table in the front of the courtroom was not large enough to accommodate all of the reporters from Chicago and local papers attending the trial. Wires to Chicago were being kept 'hot' with reports of the hearing's developments."[2]

One of those Chicago reporters, in recognition of the attention drawn by the case after the first day, noted: "The test case Mrs. McCollum inspired has turned the eyes of the nation on this red-bricked courthouse."[3]

Chapman called Mrs. Sarah Grace Jorgensen as his first witness of the day. She was Miss Chapin's associate in teaching the Protestant classes. Mrs. Jorgensen was described as "grey-haired, motherly"[4] and "rosy-cheeked."[5] Her examination, like that of her supervisor, was lengthy, taking "most of the morning court session."[6] Chapman was determined to show the sectarian nature of the classes by establishing as complete a record as possible relating to the teaching in the Protestant classes. Mrs. Jorgensen was, in the words of the Chicago *Sun* reporter, "catechized by Chapman as to what she taught and what she believed."[7] Again, as with Miss Chapin, the attorney proceeded in an aggressive manner, causing one reporter to write: "The directness of questions by Attorney Chapman on her religious beliefs caused her lips to tremble at times."[8] Mrs. Jorgensen's nervousness was also mentioned in another press report. Chapman asked her to relate one of the stories she used to tell children so that they could understand the idea of faith; "Nervously playing with her hands she looked up at Judge Leonard who directed her to 'go ahead'."[9]

As they had during Chapman's questioning of Miss Chapin, Franklin and Peterson objected repeatedly.[10] After a long and repetitive series of questions concerning what she meant by "God" and the role played by that being in people's lives, Chapman asked: "Do you teach any relationship between God and Man? Is there any connection between the Two? Is God able to help you in any way or able to help children or are they able to exercise any influence over him by praying to him or appealing to his decisions or anything of that kind?"

Peterson: "I object to that (question) as multiple."

Court: "Objection sustained, and on the ground it has already been covered; this court will take notice that the answer to that question would be yes."

Chapman: "I offer to prove that she teaches the children faith and obedience to God."

Court: "You did not ask her that question."

Chapman: "Do you teach the children obedience to God?"

Franklin: "Objection. There is no evidence upon which to base that cross-examination, if he is entitled to cross-examination. This witness has not refused to answer any of his questions. There is no reason to call her hostile."

Chapman: "Her very position makes her a hostile witness, the fact that her employment would be abolished by this law suit."

Court: "Objection sustained until it has been demonstrated she is withholding information."

Chapman, with the apparent approval of the court, then continued to pursue the "obedience" question. Mrs. Jorgensen, even under considerable pressure from the attorney, was reported to have "departed from a conversational tone only once under extended questioning. When he [Chapman, the reporter wrote,] "asked her what religion she teaches, she replied sharply: 'The Christian religion.'"

On cross-examination, Franklin delved briefly into some of the exotic and ancient religions his opponent, with questionable relevancy, had cited in his petition.

Franklin: "Have you ever taught any Mohammedan children in your class or are there any who believe in the Zoroastrian Zend-Avesta?"

Jorgensen: "No."

At this juncture, "Franklin offered to spell the latter for the benefit of the court reporter, but he replied that he was familiar with it, which gave him an advantage over the newspaper reporters."[11] Franklin continued his questioning: "Are there any students in your charge who believe in Allah or Ormuzd or Brahma?"

Jorgensen: "None."

Franklin: "Have you ever practiced proselytizing upon any atheist child or upon any of the believers in religious faiths which I have mentioned?"

Chapman: "Objection."

Court: "Sustained, she said she had not any."

Franklin: "Have you ever proselytized for any particular religion?"

Chapman: "Objection. That calls for a conclusion."

Franklin: "It is a conclusion in their own pleading."

Court: "Objection sustained."

A few questions later, Franklin made an inquiry similar to one he had addressed to Mae Chapin: "Has any child in your classes ever expressed to you a feeling or belief that you were attempting to teach them something contrary to their conscience or their own religious belief or that of their parents?"

Jorgensen: "No."

Like Miss Chapin, the Protestant teacher testified under cross-examination that the course was concerned with "the ethical teachings of the Bible, or the Bible content." In support of her interdenominational orientation she said: "I am affiliated with the Christian church. I also work in the Methodist church and I taught at the Presbyterian. I am married to a Lutheran." "The crowd laughed."[12]

Chapman pursued a redirect examination followed by a re-cross-examination by Franklin. During his second opportunity, Franklin drew from the witness, as he had from Miss Chapin, her academic qualifications, which included bachelor's and master's degrees from the University of Illinois. The CCRE had certainly lived up to its agreement with the Board of Education in providing teachers with at least comparable qualifications to those of the regular classroom teachers.

The next witness called was Reta Campbell, a teacher at Champaign's Colonel Wolfe School. Vashti later explained why this particular person was called:

> We had a feeling...that such people as the teachers and School Board officials had had so much time to think about what they were going to say that we weren't getting quite the same frank discussion that we'd had in informal conversations with them. Chapman wanted to take some teacher by surprise and ask the same questions we had asked in our pretrial interviews, so Phil got a cab—a major expense for him, since he was always broke—and set out to hunt one down.[13]

Chapman attempted to prove with the witness the point that as a result of the religious classes, teachers "simply dropped out a half hour (of regular instruction)." Objections by Franklin and Peterson blunted the effort. Chapman then probed into other official involvement by the regular classroom teachers and the district administrative personnel.

Chapman's next witness was William C. Bursk, a Christian Scientist practitioner. He was asked by Chapman to tell the meaning of the word "God" as it is used by persons of his faith.

Bursk: "If you will give me that book (*Science and Health with Key to the Scriptures* by Mary Baker Eddy), I will tell you exactly what it means."

Peterson: "Objection as immaterial to the issue."

Court: "I will let him answer."

Franklin: "There is nothing in the record in this case to indicate that any Christian Science child participates in these classes."

Court: "There may be some children with Christian Science in the schools here." (The court thus continued its policy of allowing Chapman considerable latitude in his efforts to prove religious diversity within the Protestant religious community.)

Being allowed by the court to proceed, Bursk read: "The definition of 'God' according to the textbook is: 'The great I am; the all-knowing, all-seeing, all-acting, all-wise, all-loving and eternal; Principle: mind, soul, spirit, life, truth, love, all substance, intelligence'." Chapman then pursued other tenets of the Christian Scientists which might have been in conflict with the general Protestant teachings testified to earlier by Miss Chapin and Mrs. Jorgensen.

On concluding his brief cross-examination, Peterson inquired: "Does the Christian Science church have any objection to the voluntary religious education system as conducted in some schools?"

Bursk: "I cannot answer that."

Rev. Clarence Higgins followed Bursk. He was described in the press as "a small, rotund man with a genial air."[14] He acknowledged that he had participated actively in the formation of the religious classes five years earlier. When asked how the Catholic class at South Side School worked, he indicated that it was one combined class for all three participating grade levels, fourth, fifth and sixth. Thus, each class in which Catholic children were present was offered twice each week, once for the Protestant class, once for the Catholic. Other questioning by Chapman reinforced testimony by earlier witnesses that the facilities, space and furnishings, were provided by the school authorities.

On cross-examination Franklin asked: "Do you believe in religious toleration?"

Higgins: "Yes, it is a part of the Catholic teaching that I teach in my religious education classes." The court refused to allow testimony by Higgins referring to his belief that there had been a "broadening (of) religious toleration" as a result of the classes.

Thirteen-year-old Wanda Bash, who with her parents was an intervenor in the case, was then called by Chapman. Wanda was described as "a serious, sweet, blond bobby-soxer, with an honor society pin pinned to her."[15] When Chapman asked her what religion she was studying, she responded: "The Christian Protestant religion." Responding to whether or not she wanted to study the Mohammedan religion or any other kind, she answered, "No."

Peterson, cross-examining his own client, elicited from Miss Bash that her participation was voluntary and that, in her view, the class was beneficial. She also testified that she had felt no criticism from children not taking the course, and she mentioned a number of them, her friends, by name. One of them, Mary Lou Terry, was later called as a witness by the defense.

Cartlidge's turn on the stand came next. A Chicago reporter described him as a "tall, handsome minister" with a "resonant voice."[16] He received, in the words of the *News-Gazette*, "Chapman's most vigorous grilling of the trial … on the benefits of religious education." The account went on to say:

> Even though the minister formally had been "his witness," Chapman tore into him with a line of questioning that reached the merits of Holiness Faith Healing versus Presbyterianism before Judge Leonard shut off the debate. The exchange and hair-splitting over the meaning of words went on between the minister and lawyer for more than an hour.[17]

As it had with Northcott, in contrast with other newspapers, the *News-Gazette* gave disproportionate coverage to Cartlidge's testimony. The *Courier*, though less extensive in its account, echoed the appraisal of its competitor in describing Chapman's examination: "Chapman…ragged at the nerves of … Cartlidge …

regarded as a founder of the religious education program, during prolonged testimony."[18]

Chapman's examination of Cartlidge began peacefully enough. He probed at some depth the organizational structure of the CCRE. According to Cartlidge, the "organization [had] three elements, the Protestant, Catholic and Jewish groups." All had representatives on the council. Working directly under the CCRE were three committees, finance, personnel and curriculum, on which the several faiths were also represented. "The purpose," testified Cartlidge, "is to examine personnel and curriculum so that nothing prejudicial to anyone of the groups or intolerance to anyone of the groups shall be presented through personnel or curriculum."

All of the three religious "elements," according to Cartlidge, also had their own individual organizations, including "their own curriculum committee, finance committee and personnel committee..." It is probable, however, that this was true only in theory. In practice it was the Protestant element alone, with the overwhelmingly major proportion of students in the religious classes with privately-employed teachers, that actually was organized and operated as Cartlidge indicated.

On cross-examination by Franklin, Cartlidge testified that the "interest" in organizing the CCRE came "from the whole community." "At that time," he continued, "approximately five years ago, there was quite a discussion in the newspapers and in private circles of the problem of juvenile delinquency. There was such a problem in this community at that time." According to Cartlidge, "The Council felt that the moral and ethical conduct of people is dependent upon the religious belief of people, and set forth that American democracy can only be maintained by strong character, honesty, truthfulness, dependability, and things such as that, and we believe that through the forces of religion these might be strengthened and our democracy be helped."

Franklin, sensitive to the issue of religious dissension and strife, asked: "Was it your aim to indoctrinate any child with the particular belief of any religion or religious faith or cult?"

Cartlidge: "No."

Franklin: "Was it your policy to mention the differences upon which the religious denominations deviate?"

Cartlidge: "No." He went on to comment: "We consider tolerance of other person's beliefs the objective of the whole program."

It was on redirect examination that Chapman proceeded to question one of the main justifications of the program. He "probed laboriously into assertions that juvenile delinquency had been lessened by the religious education classes...,"[19] a theme introduced by Franklin.

Chapman: "What religion do you think is best for preventing juvenile delinquency?"

Franklin: "Objection."

Court: "Sustained."

Chapman: "Have you ever looked into the question of whether one religion is better than another in dealing with juvenile delinquency?"

Cartlidge: "No."

Chapman: "Has that question come to your mind before?"

Cartlidge: "No. I would think, however, that all are about equally good, speaking only of the ones within our council."

Chapman: "Have you had any contact with those outside of your council?

Cartlidge: "No, but I would say they are as good as those that are in."

Chapman: "Let us take the Holiness Faith Healers. We have seen their pictures in the papers with snakes around their necks. Do you accept them as being just as good as Presbyterians?"

Franklin: "Objection."

Court: "Sustained. It has not been shown that they are involved in this particular controversy."

Chapman: "I offer to prove by this witness that if he were allowed to testify he would testify that he regards Presbyterians as better and more worthy than the Holiness Faith Healers."

Peterson: "Objection, on the grounds that there is no showing that counsel has any [grounds] for the offer."

Chapman: "In making your estimation and evaluation of religion, one being as good as another, do you accept the creed of the Holiness Faith Healers with their snake demonstrations on equality or par with the Presbyterians?"

Cartlidge: "I would like to ask what the creed and the practices of the Holiness Church are?"

Court (to Cartlidge): "A witness doesn't have a right to question a lawyer."

Cartlidge: "I do not know, so I cannot say whether I accept them as equal to my own. There [are] other denominations whose creeds I do not know well enough to compare with my own." (A correspondent later reported: "the courtroom crowd was disappointed when Mr. Cartlidge said he knew nothing about the creeds of the three groups—atheists, free-thinkers and Holiness Faith healers—mentioned.")

Franklin: "I object to the interrogation of the witness regarding any creeds or beliefs of which there is no evidence of their existence in this school district."

Chapman: "The question of whether the teaching was secular or not does not depend on whether anybody in the school district agreed with it, but depends on whether there is a creed anywhere to the contrary. The *New Webster Dictionary* defines sectarian and includes not only believers but dissenters, any organized group."

The court sustained the objection; the examination continued and even produced a small measure of levity.

Chapman: "Can you name one child who has improved during the course?"

Franklin: "Objection."

Court: "Overruled."

Cartlidge: "I have a boy of my own who takes the course. I have found that when it comes to understanding relationships with these young people, many of the things he has learned in these courses make it easier for me to understand and to give him what I consider the ethical relationship between men."

Chapman: "What was the condition of his ethics before he started taking the course?"

Peterson: "Objection."

Court: "Sustained."

Chapman: "What changes have you noticed in his behavior?"

Cartlidge: "I think that I have seen a decided improvement in his attitude toward his sister."

Chapman: "What was his attitude toward his sister before?"

Franklin: "I believe this has gone far enough."

Chapman found it difficult to abandon his inquiry into the alleged notion that behavior was beneficially influenced by the religious classes. He asked: "With reference to improving juvenile delinquency, do not the churches already have religious classes?"

Cartlidge: "Yes."

Chapman: "What keeps them from being able to deal adequately with the problem?"

Cartlidge: "Lack of time."

The minister, upon continued questioning, admitted that, "The reason for continuing these religious education classes in the schools instead of the churches is because of the availability of the children of all denominations and religions; the children of all denominations attend schools better than they attend church."

Chapman then asked: "Do you not go there (the schools) to reach children that do not ordinarily attend church?" This brought a denial from the minister.

The examination ended soon thereafter following intense wrangling among the lawyers over the question of whether or not the witness had "observed an improvement in … ethics and morality [and] juvenile delinquency among children who attend parochial schools and those who attend public schools."

Of much greater interest to both the reporters and spectators was the next witness, Arthur Cromwell. His presence in the courtroom had already been noted by a Chicago reporter in a brief reference to courtroom events of the previous day.[20]

Cromwell's participation in the *McCollum* trial was directly related to the pamphlet that Chapman had discovered on his first visit to Champaign. From that time until the trial, a little more than three months later, the two had exchanged no fewer than 16 letters.[21] Several factors emerge as possible reasons why Chapman was interested in having Cromwell at the trial. Most important, it would seem, was the fact that Cromwell's pamphlet had been included in the pleadings to help illustrate the plaintiff's "views and understanding concerning religion," and that those views differed markedly with what was being taught in the religious classes. Because of its use in the pleading, Chapman may also have thought the pamphlet should be defended. Without question, an appearance by Cromwell was a guarantee that the godless extreme would be placed in evidence to further support Chapman's contention that the classes were sectarian. Finally, there was Chapman's penchant for the sensational. Based upon the dramatic reaction to Cromwell's pamphlet at the outset, Chapman must certainly have anticipated the headline potential of putting the elderly rationalist on the stand.

Barely a week before the beginning of the trial, Chapman, in a brief letter, had asked Cromwell to come: "Our trial begins next Monday. I'm going to Urbana Sunday. I think it might be nice if you could be present. I might even find it helpful to call you as a witness with reference to doctrines of Freethinkers. Could you make this for a visit to Champaign?"[22]

Vashti knew her father well and from the beginning had been against his participation at the trial.

> When Chapman told me he was calling my father as a witness, I protested vehemently, for many reasons. My father's health wasn't good and it was an expensive trip for him to make. And then I didn't want to keep house for a guest during the trial. And in the third place, I knew we were in the doghouse as far as many people were concerned, anyway, and I was sure my father's testimony wouldn't improve our public relations.[23]

Cromwell himself was reluctant to come and his return letter to Chapman cited a number of reasons why a trip to Champaign would be difficult. But he did say that, "If you feel that my being there is absolutely essential to the success of the case, I shall leave all things and come."[24]

Cromwell's response to the invitation was followed a day later by a second letter from Chapman; the missives almost certainly crossed in the mails. In the second letter, Chapman altered his initial request somewhat.

> Yesterday I returned from Champaign where we issued subpoenas for more than a dozen witnesses. Therefore, we shall have sufficient evidence, without your testimony, to show the sectarian character of the teaching. While your presence will not be essential, I would enjoy your company on this occasion.[25]

It is possible that Chapman, reacting to Vashti's objections, had attempted to politely withdraw his invitation. In the interim, Cromwell had warmed to the notion of coming to Champaign; the feisty freethinker had changed his mind. It was with his daughter's extreme, and as it turned out, justified trepidation that he was called to the stand.

Cromwell was described variously as, "short, stooped, hard of hearing,"[26] "small, grey-haired ... elderly,"[27] "a bespectacled man in his 50s, with incisive features and a slight stoop,"[28] and as "a Bible-toting atheist."[29] "Gasps came ... when [Cromwell] failed to take the usual oath of 'I swear by the everlasting God ...' in going to the witness chair. Instead, [he] gave the vow of 'I affirm'."[30] In Cromwell's pocket, he carried to the stand "a thumb-marked Bible, which he said he studied for some 35 years."[31]

Reporters outdid themselves in describing the reaction of the courtroom crowd: "The assembled audience of missionary society ladies, Sunday school teachers, and ministers were suddenly face to face with a man who didn't believe in God and was proud to say so."[32] Another noted: "An audible gasp went up Tuesday afternoon as a courtroom crowd, composed largely of churchgoers, received an introduction to atheism as it figures in the McCollum religion trial."[33]

Chapman wasted no time placing Cromwell's views before the court; "What is the teaching of that sect (the Rationalists) with reference to Adam and Eve being the first man and woman?" After strenuous objections by opposing counsel, Cromwell was allowed to answer.

Cromwell: "We believe the Adam and Eve story is entirely fictitious and founded upon superstition. Adam had nothing to do with our ancestry, and especially the beginning of the earth."

Franklin objected but Chapman was allowed to continue his examination.

Chapman: "With reference to the flood upon the earth by God as told in the Bible?"

Cromwell: "Science had proven that to be a scientific impossibility."

Franklin: "I move to strike."

Court: "The answer will be stricken. The question was whether they believed it."

Cromwell: "We disbelieve it."

Chapman: "Is that what you teach?"

Cromwell: "Yes."

Chapman: "What do you believe and teach concerning the miracles performed by Jesus?"

Cromwell: "They are impossibilities; a miracle is a violation of natural law."

Chapman: "And resurrection after death?"

Cromwell: "It is a physical impossibility."

Chapman: "Do you believe in such things as prophets?"

Cromwell: "No."

Chapman: "With reference to the Bible being the word of God?"

Cromwell: "Inasmuch as we find no evidence that God ever wrote it and we find no authority for accepting that writ, we deny it being God."

Chapman: "Freethinkers teach that?"

Cromwell: "Yes."

Chapman: "Do you deny the existence of God?"

Cromwell: "Yes."

One such denial—there were several—caused "a stir of whisperings (and) prompted bailiff Pat Finnegan to rap for quiet."[34] Another report noted "sharply drawn breaths which were heard throughout the courtroom."[35]

Then came the defense's turn. It had apparently been decided to subject the plaintiff (Vashti) to a detailed examination, especially with respect to "her atheistic or 'rationalist' beliefs as fully as Chapman has required the church and school representatives to do."[36] Cromwell, however, became available first. Peterson in a "sharp cross-examination" which "drew sparks,"[37] probed many of the more pejorative statements Cromwell had written in his pamphlet.

Peterson: "You also hold that (reading from Cromwell's pamphlet), 'Religious worship is a chronic disease of the imagination contracted in childhood?'"

Cromwell: "I do."

Peterson: (again reading) "From the first day that the first crook realized he could hoodwink a few credulous beings into believing he had some personal tie up with an unknown deity, religion and its unscrupulous preachers have fought to perpetuate the racket that permitted them to prey upon the innocence and credulity of the masses.' You believe that?"

Cromwell: "I do."

Peterson (continuing to read from the pamphlet): "'The Bible contains so much that is bad, so little that is good, and little or nothing that is true that it seems impossible that anyone who has read and studied it would recommend it as fit for our youth to read, much less as a moral inspiration.' You believe that?"

Cromwell: "I certainly do."

After continuing in this vein for a period of time, Peterson then inquired: "You don't believe in God unless He makes His personal appearance to you?"

Cromwell: "Absolutely correct. We take the position that we have no evidence of God."

Peterson: "Then you are an atheist?"

Cromwell: "I am proud to say that I am."

The reply, as reported in the Chicago *Sun* was: "I praise God that I am."[38] When Cromwell learned of the quote, he promptly wrote to the reporter, Fletcher Wilson. Cromwell to Wilson (Sept. 29, 1945): "Of course you know I said nothing of the kind, and you also see what a silly contradiction it makes of my philosophy." No retraction was offered in Wilson's reply: "As for that 'Praise God' quote, that was the way it sounded to me. And I thought it did you credit. It was as nicely turned a piece of irony as I have ever heard. Everyone I talked to got a chuckle out of it, considered it an intelligent bit of whimsy, and saw in it no intimation that you were giving a serious obeisance to God."[39] Apparently some papers carried UP reports which Cromwell assumed were taken from the *Sun* story. In a letter to Cromwell from Joe Morgan of the UP (Oct. 3, 1945), the UP report of Cromwell's response was: "I am very proud to say that I am." None of the other Chicago reporters or those from the *News-Gazette* or *Courier* heard Wilson's version either.

Peterson then probed into a new area. "Did you criticize the Bible in the presence of your children?" Chapman objected to the question and was sustained even though Peterson and Franklin argued strongly in its defense.

Peterson resumed his interrogation of Cromwell's beliefs: "Do you believe that when persons pray they think they are teasing God?"

Cromwell: "I believe the beliefs of my organization—yes."

Peterson: "Do you believe that when the President of the United States makes a proclamation of a day of prayer that that is the equivalent of asking the people to tease God?" After an objection, Peterson changed the question from Cromwell's personal belief to that of his organization.

Cromwell: "We believe [the proclamation] is a violation of Constitutional law as far as using the power or duty is concerned."

Peterson then proceeded to quote at length, presumably from the President's proclamation: "At a time when stars hang in the windows of the nation's homes to honor the absent warriors; when millions of Americans live in temporary homes and in migrant centers while they work at war jobs, it is important to urge that the religious education of the country's children be fostered and extended. It is likely that there are millions of youngsters who need initial and basic religious instruction. They should receive it and learn of the fatherhood of God and the brother-hood of man." Cromwell's response was that "a statement of that kind is based upon ignorance and superstition and cowardice."

Franklin then took over the questioning. He asked Cromwell if he "believed that religion is an insane desire to appease an impossible deity."

Cromwell: "I believe that as (I) stated in my pamphlet."

Franklin: "Do you believe that all persons who embrace religion are insane?"

Cromwell: "Yes, to that degree."

Chapman objected but the court allowed Franklin to continue.

Franklin: "Do you believe that every minister of the Gospel is insane?"

Cromwell: "I certainly do to that degree. They are following an insane and dishonest occupation."

Franklin: "Does that apply to Philip Schug whom you know and who sits across the table from you?"

Cromwell: "Yes, if he taught the doctrines of which you are talking."

As Franklin neared the end of his questioning, he asked Cromwell: "Is it true that you talked to Mrs. McCollum regarding the instigation of this suit?"

Cromwell: "No."

A few questions later, Franklin queried: "Would you personally be disap-pointed if she (Vashti) did not prevail in the suit?" After an objection, which was overruled, Cromwell responded: "I certainly would."

Thus ended Cromwell's testimony for the day. The old rationalist had had his day in court. He had "barked" and "snapped"[40] his defiance of a belief system which he had, over many years, grown to despise. "Raised eyebrows and shocked murmurs greeted (his) 'atheist' statements."[41] His "vigorous replies (had) stirred interest in the proceedings to a new pitch, and tears (had come) to the eyes of some of the onlookers as his answers (had) raked across their own religious beliefs."[42]

Vashti was dismayed concerning her father's testimony, a matter she later discussed in some detail.

> I knew that my father's testimony would induce a flood of unfavorable publicity, and, as it turned out, my suspicions were practically under-statements. There were many reasons for my father's conduct in the case; he is hard of hearing, and he was excited and confused; and so he an-swered things he wouldn't have had to answer about his beliefs. He went far too much into details ... It was a line of thinking to which undoubtedly many rational people subscribe, and yet in a small town, in which most people offer a semblance of conformity to religious dogma whether they believe it or not, it set off an explosion.[43]

Cromwell, many years later, reflected upon the same event.

> My daughter looked very distressed and apprehensive (during his testi-mony), wondering what her dad was going to say next. I think I had more or less of a reckless attitude, too, because I thought here was an opportu-nity to really broadcast what I thought religion really was.[44]

As the long and memorable day was drawing to a close, Chapman called James Terry McCollum. He had been present at the trial at least since noon and had "had a field day collecting the used flash bulbs of the cameramen who were snapping dozens of pictures just before the court resumed for the afternoon session."[46] Another reporter noted: "Before court convened at 2 p.m., he had 22 and [he] obtained several after that."[47] Described in one report as "a handsome blue-eyed youth with a crew haircut,"[48] "he made a one-handed attempt to tuck his shirt into his trousers [as he] walked forward to be sworn in."[49] Still another reporter wrote: "But understanding smiles bubbled from mothers and fathers in the audience as James, an alert-eyed lad with a haircut and a Tom Sawyer nonchalance, went forward, stuffing unruly shirttails under his trousers belt."[50]

In his other hand "he carried ... a religious education enrollment card he received at the beginning of the year."[51] He "looked solemnly up as Mrs. Hallie Snyder, deputy circuit clerk ... repeated (as she had done for James' grandfather) the words of the court affirmation. . . . He nodded his head and sat down."[52]

On the stand, James reiterated much information that already had been presented to the court. He said that when his classmate, Elwin Miller, did not take the class, their teacher would accompany both of them to the music room or library. Later when he was the only child not enrolled, the situation changed. "Mrs. Taylor," he said, "did not go with me to the music room or to the library ... she was in the classroom listening to the religious education."

Chapman: "Did Mrs. Taylor ever send you to a place other than the music room or the library?"

James Terry: "Once she sent me out in the hall." Several questions later, Chapman inquired: "What happened when you were out there on that occasion?"

James Terry: "The kids that went by teased me."

Chapman, after concluding his probe into James Terry's activities while the religion classes were in progress, asked if Mrs. Taylor had ever spoken to him regarding his participation in the classes. According to James, she had said on a number of occasions, "Why don't you keep the class 100 per cent?" "She (also) said to me I would get along better if I did take it." This directly conflicted with earlier testimony given by Mrs. Taylor.

Chapman then offered for identification and introduction into evidence the parental consent card for the religious classes, which was passed out to all students—the same card James Terry had carried with him to the stand. After it had been identified and delivered over to the court, an incident occurred which offered some needed comical relief.

> The sympathy of the spectators [towards James Terry] suddenly changed to   perceptible irritation against the court. The boy, on the witness stand, had tried to hold a whispered conversation with [Chapman] ... The opposing attorneys objected. The three judges frowned at the thought of such legal misbehavior.[53]

Chapman, addressing James Terry: "You can't talk to me now."

Then … Peterson … withdrew the objection. He too is a parent, he said, he understands certain things. He intimated that maybe James wanted to visit the men's room. So James was allowed to whisper to … Chapman … Laughter rippled throughout the courtroom as Chapman finally announced: "He just wanted to be sure he gets his card back."[54]

It was explained that once the card was placed in evidence among the plaintiffs exhibits, it could not be returned. But James was a sportsman when he comprehended the procedure. Looking at the three judges he said, "Oh that's all right; you guys can use it."[55]

Chapman sought to contradict Bessie Taylor's damaging testimony of the previous day: "Did Mrs. Taylor talk to you about fighting?"

James Terry: "A little, she asked me why I got in fights and stuff like that."

Chapman: "When Mrs. Taylor testified here yesterday she said that some of the other children complained to her that you kicked them and slapped them and spit in their faces. Were those complaints true?"

James Terry: "Yes."

Chapman: "Was it the whole truth?"

James Terry: "Well, now, not exactly. They beat up on me and I didn't have much else to do."

According to a news report, the "lawyers got into a wrangle over the wording of a question about who struck the first blow and finally Judge Leonard took over. The judge leaned over the bench and said, 'What they're trying to ask you, Terry, is who did which first.' The boy squirmed and swung around in the swivel witness chair and said: 'Oh, I guess they did … We both did … Oh, I'll just say I don't know'."[56]

Chapman continued to pursue the fight issue and what Mrs. Taylor said and did about the problem, but after little new information was developed he moved on to another theme.

Chapman: "Did you want to take religious education?"

James Terry: "Yes."

Chapman: "Why didn't you take the class?"

James Terry: "My mother would not sign the slip."

Chapman: "Did she ever sign (the slip)?"

James Terry: "Yes, the year before."

Chapman: "Then you took religious education at the end of the year when you were in the fourth grade?"

James Terry: "Yes."

Chapman "What was there about this religious education that attracted your attention?"

After an objection from Franklin which was overruled, James Terry replied: "I did not like to be out in the hall and in the music room with the door shut—and I wanted to hear Miss Chapin's opinion." The *News-Gazette* reported that James' reply was: "Different people have different ideas and I wanted to know what Miss Chapin's was."[57]

Chapman continued to pursue the question of why James Terry wanted to take the religious class. The attorney may have hoped that his young client would say that he did not like being separated from his fellows. Instead, the youth said that when he left the room he usually did spelling and arithmetic, which he did not like very well.

Chapman: "Did you like religious education better?"

James Terry: "Yeah, lots better."

Alfred Prowitt of the *Daily News* noted: "Everyone in the court seemed puzzled—somehow it wasn't the expected answer."[58] James also said, "Miss Chapin brought different papers and things to class and sometimes she would have little ornaments and stuff like that from China."

At that juncture, Chapman ended his direct examination. The court recessed until the next morning, at which time the defense would have its chance to cross-examine James Terry.

In Prowitt's account, "The boy and his grandfather gave the crowd some of the most throbbing moments ever witnessed in an American courtroom. There were laughs of amusement, ahs of sympathy and plain shudders."[59]

Prowitt provided the only somewhat critical reviews of James Terry's performance under a heading of "Son Gets Mixed Up On Stand," and he described some of his testimony as a "maze of childish contradictions."[60]

James Terry, if one can judge from the other press reviews, had acquitted himself well. Guy Gentry of the *Tribune* described the performance as "childish but prepossessed."[61] Stanley Pieza of the *Herald-American* noted that he "eagerly answered questions and was at ease as a witness."[62] The headline in the *Daily News* read: "Atheist's Son Wins Trial Fans: Relieves Grimness of Urbana Hearing." The lead paragraph went on to say: "The 10-year-old son of a woman atheist sat on the witness stand in circuit court ... and provoked friendly laughter and 'ahs' of admiration from an overflow crowd of spectators".[63]

The *Courier* report represented a similar view: "His testimony brought freshness and spontaneity to a session that had dragged with wrangling among attorneys and wordy duels between witnesses and their interrogators."[64]

Fletcher Wilson of the Chicago *Sun* was quoted in a New York newspaper: "Under questioning, the 10-year-old swung the witness chair restlessly from side to side but was calm and confident in his answers."[65]

Bruce Taylor of the Chicago *Times* wrote: "With a small boy's disarming frankness, 10-year-old Terry McCollum made Champaign's religious education trial seem a little ponderous and silly today." And, "Cross-examined by two solemn, fatherly lawyers, the youngster, focal point of his mother's fight to halt teaching of religion in Champaign schools, answered them with delightful freshness."[66]

Vashti and her backers, while they could draw some solace from James Terry's performance, had serious misgivings about the way the trial was going. The plaintiff later wrote: "That day [September 11] the publicity was so bad that three of the members of the CAC came down to Champaign. They had not intended to come to the trial, although they were backing me, but they were all businessmen and this talk of atheism was bad for them."[67]

Dissention had been noted in the McCollum camp by the Chicago *Sun* when it had reported: "Support originally given Mrs. McCollum by the Chicago Action Council, a group headed by Robert S. Greenfield, has been withdrawn."[68]

According to Vashti, the delegation's purpose was to communicate the fact that "the conservative" members of the council "wanted to withdraw their backing." She rejoined: "But you can't get out; we've made mistakes, yes, but they're your mistakes as well as mine. You just can't get out of it now."[69]

The fact was that Vashti had not selected the trial attorney; instead she had relied upon the choice of the CAC, and it was Chapman who had been in charge of the legal conduct of the case. The sensational headlines were a direct outcome of his approach, beginning with the pleadings and continuing through the trial to that point. Vashti described the resolution of the matter: "They [the delegation] had the others [members of the CAC in Chicago] on the phone, and after talking to me they went back to the phone and said, 'Sorry fellows, Vashti says we're not quitting'."[70]

Clearly the lack of unity in her own ranks as well as the stress of the trial was taking its toll on the plaintiff. There was also a personal side which Vashti later related:

> Although it seemed as if the law was incontrovertibly on our side, I still wasn't pleased at the way the trial was going. I've never liked to antagonize people, and I hated the position I was in, being on the outs with everyone, disliked and despised all around. I not only wanted the ruling to be in our favor, but I wanted people to understand and sympathize with the principle at stake, and we had definitely lost ground in the way of public sympathy. It isn't pleasant to go into a courtroom and know that everyone is hostile, to know that the friends who are on your side feel that they can't afford to be seen supporting you.[71]

The following day, the *Sun* offered a correction: "The Chicago Action Council, which was reported to have withdrawn its support from Mrs. McCollum's suit, announced today that this statement was incorrect. Backing given her, financially and otherwise, will be continued, according to Esther Alexandre."[72]

Chapter 7

The Trial, Day Three

The dissension in Vashti's ranks was sufficiently substantive to make news in Chicago. At the council of war, held at the McCollum house Tuesday evening, a fundamental change in strategy was determined; it involved "a movement away from stress on religion vs. atheism."[1] Vashti, like Philip Schug, had stressed the narrow legal issue from the outset; this was in contrast with Chapman's more flamboyant and confrontational approach, which had encouraged the press and public to focus upon what was perceived to be an attack on religion. The CAC delegation insisted on driving back to Chicago late that evening, but returned the following morning. Accompanying them were two Chicago ministers, Rev. Erwin A. Gaede and Rev. Karl Baehr, who were to appear for the plaintiff.[2]

At 9 a.m. Wednesday morning, before the trial resumed, the spokesman of the CAC delegation, Chicago attorney Milton T. "Ted" Raynor, held a news conference.[3] He said that he and his associates, the ten members of the CAC, "were dissatisfied with the 'atheistic trend' and wanted to get the case back 'on the beam'."[4] Raynor, speaking for Vashti, went on to say:

> Mrs. McCollum has no objection to religious training or to the type of faith anyone has ... But she is a believer in absolute religious freedom. She believes religious education should be given in the homes and churches and not made a part of compulsory public education. The only issue is whether or not it is proper to bring religious education into the public schools. It is unfortunate that this has come to be regarded as a contest between atheism and religion.[5]

When the trial resumed at 9:30 a.m., James Terry again took the stand, where he was to remain for nearly an hour and a half in what reporter Ted Duffield termed, "the most grueling experience of any of the morning's witnesses."[6] Jean Hurt of the *Daily Illini* said the young witness "battled attorney's questions...and came through with answers that make him a candidate for the famed Quiz Kids."[7]

Peterson began the cross-examination by further probing the issue of James Terry's problems in school, in particular the fights.[8] When that failed to produce anything new, the attorney questioned the youthful witness on his Sunday school attendance (he attended "Mr. Schug's ... when it was open"), the incident when he was sent to the hallway, and Mrs. Taylor's efforts to get 100 per cent participation in the religion classes. Again, no new information was developed.

Then Peterson introduced an entirely new issue: "Did you sign up in the Cub Scouts?"

James Terry: "Yes, in the fourth grade."

A few questions later Peterson inquired: "Do you know that a Boy Scout and a Cub Scout have to take an oath?"

James Terry: "Yes."

Peterson: "Do you care if you have to take the oath?"

James Terry: "No. It is O.K. with me."

Peterson: "When you came into this court room here did anyone ever ask you not to take the oath or did you ask not to take the oath?"

Chapman: "I object, he took the oath."

Court: "Sustained."

At this point, the attorneys gathered at the bench. Franklin then argued:

It is our position that under the law unless the witness asks to be excused, the accepted procedure is to swear on oath by the ever living God; it is only upon conscientious scruples that a witness may avoid taking the oath. We are entitled in this case to have the conscience of the witness pledged to veracity, and I would like to ask the privilege to ascertain by this witness whether his veracity is being guaranteed by any conscientious scruples.

While the three judges and the counsel argued the point privately, James leaned around and tried to hear the conversation. He was sent to another part of the courtroom.[9]

The court recalled Hallie B. Snyder, deputy Circuit Court clerk who administered all the oaths during the trial. She testified that on Tuesday morning, before the convening of court:

Mrs. McCollum came to me and asked if we had another oath that could be administered to her, to her father and to her son. I replied that the only oath was the one we give to witnesses, and that if she did not want to be sworn by that oath we could give the affirmation. She requested that she, her father and son be given the affirmation in place of the regular oath to the witness.

Franklin (on cross-examination): "Did Mr. Cromwell or the witness on the stand, James Terry McCollum, make any such request of you?"

Snyder: "Yesterday noon Mr. Cromwell asked me whether or not I would give him the affirmation in preference to the oath; James Terry did not."

Cromwell was recalled and he affirmed that he had made such a request. Presumably on the basis that James Terry had made no such request, Franklin moved to strike all the evidence the youth had presented.

Court: "This is a boy of tender years. I doubt very much that the boy understands what the nature of an oath is. His testimony will be received for what it is worth in the mind of the court. The proper procedure in the case of one of tender years is to ask that he understands that he is required to tell the truth, and if so, why. That was not asked by either side."

Upon returning to the stand, James Terry was asked by his lawyer, "What does it mean to promise to tell the truth?" "Why, to tell a thing that's true," James answered, looking puzzled over the asking of such an easy question."[10]

Judge Leonard, seeking to shorten interrogation of the boy regarding his oath as a witness, asked, "If you don't tell the truth do you know what might happen?"

James Terry: "As far as I am concerned, I would be thrown in the jug."

One of the defense attorneys inquired of James: "Did your mother ever tell you what to say in court?" The youth "startled the court by answering 'Yes'."

Attorney: "And what did she tell you?"

James Terry: "She told me to tell the truth."

For the time being, those interchanges resolved the question of whether or not James understood the oath and was telling the truth, so the matter was dropped.

Peterson then questioned James Terry concerning his participation In a summer demonstration school at the University of Illinois where he recited the Lord's Prayer and read aloud a Bible story to the class.

Chapman on re-direct-examination: "Did your mother give you permission to study the Bible at the university?"

James Terry: "I do not remember. She does not care if I do or not."

Several questions later, Chapman inquired, "What was the reason (on cross-examination) you said you wanted to go to Sunday school in some ways and some ways you did not?"

James Terry: "I wanted to learn more about religion; I did not want to go because I think I would feel kind of funny there, being an atheist, not believing in God."

(A major effort was made by the defense to show that Vashti was hypocritical in her attitude and actions regarding Jim's participation in religious activities. It is unclear why Chapman pursued the subject.)

On re-cross-examination, Peterson questioned James concerning his religious views. "When you called yourself an atheist, what did you mean?"

James Terry: "I said to myself, I did not believe in God."

Peterson: "When did you say to yourself you did not believe in God?"

James Terry: "Before I went to kindergarten."

Earlier, when Peterson had asked him when he first considered himself an atheist, James had answered: "When I was a little fellow in the fourth grade I called myself an atheist but didn't know its meaning."

Peterson continued: "Who talked to you about not believing in God?"

James Terry: "The only one was my granddaddy (Cromwell) who said it was just bunk."

James acknowledged that in kindergarten, during the brief period he had lived with his maternal grandparents (the Cromwells), he repeated prayers with his classmates before they "drank milk." He said his grandfather had disapproved. When asked what a prayer was, James responded: "As far as I am concerned, it is just a bunch of words."

(The author does not recall religion being a common topic of family conversation prior to the commencement of the religious education controversy. James, however, had spent time with the Cromwells and there, as one might expect, religion was a regular subject of conversation).

Franklin took over, returning to the oath question responses. James Terry indicated he had made no objection to the oath when he was in Cub Scouts and that he personally had made no request to be excused from taking an oath to God in the present case.

Franklin: "What would God do if you didn't tell the truth?"

James Terry: "I wouldn't be punished by God if I didn't tell the truth as there is no evidence of God." James added: "My grandfather has never found any evidence of God nor have I."

Franklin, pursuing the topic: "What have you looked for in the way of evidence of God?"

Chapman: "Objection."

Court: "Sustained."

Franklin: "Have you made any effort to find out whether or not there was a God?"

Chapman: "Objection."

Court: "Sustained."

Franklin: "Aren't you a little in doubt as to whether there is or is not a God?"

Chapman: "Objection."

Court: "Sustained."

As his long stint on the stand was drawing to a close, James "drew" one of several "hearty laughs from the audience and even a smile from the judges."[11] It "came as Franklin quizzed him about testimony that other children 'teased' him about atheism."

Franklin: "Have you spoken to any of your friends about your religious beliefs?"

James Terry: "One Cub Scout."

Franklin: "When did you do that?"

James Terry: "That was when I heard about the Cub Scout oath."

Franklin: "What grade were you in?"

James Terry: "Fourth, maybe fifth."

Franklin: "Do you make it a secret among your playmates and acquaintances that you are an atheist?"

James Terry: "No."

Franklin: "From anyone".

James Terry: "From some of the kids in school I tried to keep it a secret, but I suppose everyone in the City of Champaign knows it now."

Several questions later Franklin asked: "Isn't it fun to be an atheist?"

James Terry: "Well, in some ways it is, and some ways it isn't." In the *News-Gazette*, James was reported as responding: "Well in a way it is and in a way it ain't."[12]

Vashti took exception to the quote:

> I don't know where they got the "ain't," as Jim didn't say it and it isn't
> included in the court record. But it was reprinted someplace and then, as
> those things go, reprinted and re-copied a dozen times.[13]

All of the other reporters in attendance who recorded the interchange agreed
with Vashti.[14] She just credited it to the biased reporting of the *News-Gazette*
reporter, Ed Borman.

Chapman then resumed his questioning in the attempt to support his contention that James was "embarrassed."

Chapman: "Did children tease you about being an atheist?"

James Terry: "Yes."

Chapman: "When would that be?"

James Terry: "When the teacher was not around."

Several questions thereafter Chapman asked: "Which of them teased you?"

James Terry: "All of them that knew I was an atheist teased me."

As one of his last questions, Chapman asked James what an atheist was.

James Terry: "An atheist is a guy who doesn't believe in God, in the Bible and
in stuff like that."

Commenting on this and other responses, one reporter wrote that, "Jimmy …
gave his atheistic views with the sureness of a young Voltaire." The same observer also reported: "Mothers and fathers who filled the courtroom sighed and
shook their heads."[15]

After asking James several questions on re-cross-examination, Franklin
moved "to strike all of the testimony of James Terry McCollum because it appears from his testimony that "he did not have conscientious scruples against the
taking of the oath provided by law." Peterson joined in the motion but it was
denied.

As part of the "new trend in the conduct of the case," the two Chicago ministers opposed to the released time religion classes were called in succession,
following James Terry. Although little of their evidence was allowed, both testified as to their opposition to the Champaign program. Vashti recalled Franklin's
argument.

> The ministers were not from our district, they weren't familiar with
> Champaign, they didn't have children in the schools there. Franklin ar-
> gued that if we were going to start bringing in people and asking them
> what they thought, we could ask everyone in the United States and when
> we ran out here we could start on Europe.[16]

For the record, Chapman asked them both if they were atheists to which both
answered, "No." While their contribution to the court record was slight, Vashti felt
that "the fact that a couple of ministers had disapproved of having religion taught
in the public schools was good for public consumption."[17]

Following the ministers' testimony, Chapman said: "I want to make it clear
that we are not opposing religion, that the purpose of this suit is not to oppose
religion, that it is not an issue at this time, nor do we oppose it because some of

our people are atheists." Franklin moved to strike. The court, however, ruled: "He has the right to state the purpose for which he offers testimony. It may stand."

Chapman called Vashti as his next witness. "This was the moment," in the words of the *Daily News*, "the courtroom crowd had been waiting for."[18] Guy Gentry described her as "looking more like a co-ed than the 32-year-old wife of a university professor..." He continued:

> The youthful Champaign matron proved the star attraction of her trial; for the first time since the opening of the case … the Circuit courtroom on the third floor of the courthouse was packed to overflowing and a waiting crowd filled the hall outside.[19]

The fascination of the Chicago reporters concerning Vashti was extraordinary. From the time her case first made news she received the treatment normally accorded a femme fatale. On the day she took her turn on the stand, even her clothes were described in detail by two of the Chicagoans.

> She was wearing a beige jacket-and-skirt ensemble with a white scarf at her throat.[20]

> [She was dressed] in a trim sand-colored wool gabardine suit, which she made herself; red and white blouse and matching pumps [completed the outfit].[21]

Though characterized by the Chicago press on the first day of the trial as "in the role of a crusading liberal, "[22] and "small, dark and vivid,"[23] Vashti was hardly at full strength as she approached the witness stand. The cumulative effect of Bessie Taylor's testimony concerning James Terry, her attorney's "nervous fatigue," Arthur Cromwell's pejorative testimony, and the threatened withdrawal of her Chicago backers had all taken a severe toll on the plaintiff. Later, in her book, she candidly described her condition:

> [B]y the time they got to me I found it hard to keep my mind on what was going on. I had to concentrate hard just to be lucid. At times I'd get vague and hazy and start thinking, "Now who is this I'm talking to and what am I doing here?" It didn't help me to know that the courthouse was packed and that curiosity seekers were being turned away at the doors. Under such circumstances, anyone wants to appear intelligent, but there were times when I felt my mind was a complete blank.[24]

The plaintiff, like the other members of her family, was administered an affirmation in lieu of being sworn.

Chapman began by leading his client through the background events which resulted in her decision to file the lawsuit. Vashti told of her several conversations with Bessie Taylor, which focused on Jim's problems in school. She testified that at their first meeting, Mrs. Taylor suggested that James might be more readily accepted by his fellow students if he participated in the religion class and changed from the South Side to the Dr. Howard Cub Scout troop.

McCollum: "I told her I was anxious to help him (James Terry) in every way possible (but) had not considered allowing him to take religious education."

Chapman: "Why were you opposed to Jim's participation?"

McCollum: "It was not that I feared that anything taught in those classes would be harmful to Terry, but that I was bitterly opposed to the whole system as being undemocratic. To my way of thinking it defeated the constitutional principle of the separation of church and state. I thought I was being a hypocrite if I allowed him to join in when I opposed it bitterly, merely for the purpose of having him conform to the rest of the children." Shortly thereafter, she admitted: "I realized in taking this stand against religious education classes participation it was doing Terry harm, making it hard for him. I felt in the long run it was the only action that I myself could take."

The second conversation with Mrs. Taylor, according to Vashti, occurred the same afternoon James had been consigned to the hall. "I asked her if Terry had to wait in the hall that day and she said he did during the religious education class; that he was provided with a desk and there was sufficient light, and he had books and material to work with. She said that she was not aware that there had been any [hurt] feelings on Terry's part."

Mrs. Taylor, according to the plaintiff, "said she was sorry, that ordinarily Terry had been allowed. to sit in the music room." Vashti indicated there were problems with that approach also, "that he did not like to be in a room by himself." The plaintiff went on to state, "no boy of mine within the regular school period was going to be made to sit in the hall, to be subjected to ridicule, condemnation or questioning, or in a music room where any teacher would know why he was there or would question why he was there [just] because he was not taking a course in religious education."

Vashti testified that she went to see Superintendent Mellon that afternoon. In great detail, she outlined her arguments to him against the religious classes; he "made no comment" in response to the charge that the "program was unconstitutional and contrary to the basic principle of separation of church and state.

The plaintiff testified that she "admitted" to Mellon "that the teaching itself did not hurt Terry as long as at home we presented an open viewpoint for him … I was going to keep him out of the class because I would not be one of those people that swell the ranks … and sign up for religious education in the school." She went on to charge that some parents who presumably did not approve of the classes, ultimately gave their consent after having been "teased" by their children.

Later, during a recess, the plaintiff told of the experience of a "woman friend with views similar to her own." The friend "finally allowed a daughter to attend the classes. The girl came home with a New Testament prize for being the best student. The mother swallowed her chagrin, Vashti said."[25]

The superintendent, she testified, did tell her "that there had been wide-spread interest in the subject of released time for religious education in connection with the schools; that the Champaign plan had been satisfactory and [there had been] numerous inquiries from other communities regarding the set-up in Champaign; that as a result a letter was being prepared to be sent out to these people who requested information." She further testified that at a later meeting with the superintendent she "asked Mr. Mellon for a copy of the form letter which they were sending out in answer to the inquiries from other localities but was told it had just been made up and was sent to Rev. McDonald for approval before it was printed to be sent out." The plaintiff said she never saw a copy of the letter.

(Rev. Robert McDonald was pastor of the First Baptist Church in Champaign. His association with the CCRE is assumed by the fact that Mellon felt it necessary to clear the letter with him. This added indication of close cooperation between religious and secular officials was pursued by Chapman later on when the Superintendent was called as a witness for the defense.)

After dealing at some length with Vashti's conversations with Mellon, Chapman then attempted to have her contradict some of Mrs. Taylor's testimony.

Chapman: "Did Mrs. Taylor ever say anything to you about children complaining that Terry had kicked and slapped them and spit in their faces?"

Franklin: "Objection."

Court: "She may answer."

McCollum: "Mrs. Taylor told me that Terry was not adjusting well, was not accepted too well in the classroom.

Franklin: "Objection. This conversation has been gone over step by step. Mrs. Taylor was his witness, and he cannot cross-examine as to whether to impeach Mrs. Taylor."

Court: "Objection is sustained. The answer will be stricken."

Chapman: "When Mrs. Taylor testified as to the children complaining that Terry had kicked and slapped them and spit in their faces, had the matter ever come to your attention before?"

Franklin: "Same objection."

Court: "Sustained. You are not permitted to ask an impeaching question."

In keeping with the new approach, Chapman developed Vashti's religious background (which she had already outlined to a reporter); this had included baptism and Sunday school attendance. She further testified that her children currently attended the Unitarian Sunday school. She admitted that aside from her early contacts with religion, she had "not taken any course in any theological seminary or in any colleges or universities." She added: "I have never been particularly interested in religion.

(The latter statement was consistent with her earlier statements on the subject and certainly in agreement with the memories of the author.)

Chapman: "Have you ever joined any organization in opposition to religion?"

Franklin: "Objection. It is not direct examination."

Court: "She may answer."

McCollum: "I have not."

Chapman: "Have you ever engaged in any activity in opposition to religion in the church?"

Franklin: "Objection."

Court: "Sustained."

Chapman: "Have you ever engaged in any activity in opposition to teaching religion in the homes of the people?"

Franklin: "Objection."

Court: "Sustained."

While the effort was frustrated, Chapman did make an attempt to separate Vashti from the "Bible-toting" and "dogmatic atheism" espoused by her father. Chapman then proceeded to enter into the record Vashti's objections to the specific teachings in the Protestant classes, but not without repeated objections from the defense.

Chapman: "Do you accept Miss Chapin's statement that Adam and Eve were the first man and woman as true teaching?"

Franklin: "Objection."

Court: "She may answer."

Franklin: "I object for the reason that there is no foundation laid here to show that the relator is a member of any recognized sect, society, organization, cult, creed or belief, that she embraces the belief of any such organization, doctrine or belief. I do not believe that there could be any question of relevancy unless in some way it is to be contended that her form of religion is interfered with. She cannot have a religion all by herself alone."

Court: "The evidence will be received subject to the objection."

McCollum: "I do not."

Chapman: "Do you desire (for) that doctrine or belief (to be) taught to your child while he is at the age of nine or ten?"

Franklin: "Objection on the ground that the parent's desires with reference to the matter are not the controlling factor with reference to what the child should himself be permitted to learn."

(This seems to be an extraordinary line of objection for the defense to make. Vashti observed in her book: "While many of my critics cried 'Communist' at me for fighting religion in the schools, to me the idea that the parent has no control over what his child is to learn sounds strangely totalitarian."[26]

Peterson: "Otherwise there would be no choice of form of religion for the child."

Chapman countered with the declaration that the constitution provides for freedom from federal or state law, but not from guidance from individuals."

Court: "Objection overruled."

McCollum: "I object to that doctrine or belief being taught to Terry as a creed or dogma. As a story he is permitted to read anything."

Franklin: "We object to all this line of testimony."

Court: "It will be so understood."

Chapman then proceeded, in spite of further objections from Franklin, along the same line until the end of direct examination, which occurred soon thereafter. During Chapman's questioning, one reporter noted that Vashti "answered the questions decisively."[27]

The plaintiff's direct testimony had been interrupted earlier by the noon recess. In her book she relates that Judge Leonard "had given orders that no pictures were to be taken … while [she] was testifying on the witness stand. "

I took this to mean while the trial was going on, so proceedings wouldn't be interrupted, and when one of the photographers asked me to pose in the witness chair between sessions, I went in with him and had my picture taken. Judge Leonard came back and scolded me, explaining he had meant no pictures on the witness stand at any time.[28]

It was just another disagreeable incident in what was to prove a long and unpleasant day for Vashti.

Franklin's cross-examination began simply: "When did you first become acquainted with the doctrine of church and state [separation]."

McCollum: "In high school where it was discussed in the social science class. I have had between thirty or forty hours of political science study since then at Cornell University."

Franklin's questioning further brought out the plaintiff's legal training and a restatement of her commitment to the "doctrine of the separation of church and state."(Franklin was fully aware of Vashti's educational background; it had been a subject of discussion in previous press reports. Ordinarily, it would not have been a productive tactic to pursue the strengths of an unfriendly witness, but considering Franklin's subsequent efforts to portray the plaintiff as hypocritical and inconsistent, the strategy made sense.)

Shortly thereafter, Franklin asked the plaintiff what her reaction would be if her cause did not prevail in the courts. McCollum: "If the court [one would suppose she meant the United States Supreme Court] decides that this is definitely within the boundaries of the constitutional limitations, definitely constitutional, I [would] have no further objections."

Franklin then began to press the plaintiff: "Do you know that many children in the fourth, fifth, sixth, seventh, eighth and ninth grades in School District No. 71 do not take religious education classes?"

McCollum: "Yes."

Franklin: "Do you know that 80 per cent of the students in the junior high and at least 20 per cent of those in the fourth, fifth and sixth throughout the system do not take the courses?"

McCollum: "That may be so; I do not know the percentage."

Franklin: Do not those people have various reasons for non-participation?"

McCollum: "That may be true."

Franklin: "Is it not true that not all of them fail to take the courses because of any religious disbelief?"

McCollum: "That may be true."

Franklin: "Do you admit that a child's non-participation in these classes discloses nothing whatever in regard to his religious belief or lack of it?"

McCollum: "I do not."

To support her opinion, the plaintiff mentioned the instance of Jewish children who did not take the class "because of non-belief in the New Testament." This almost certainly was in reference to the incident concerning the Jewish child who was assaulted after being asked by his teacher in front of the class why he did not participate in religious education. Vashti's point would have been much stronger had she been able to cite the event specifically, but after consultation with the child's foster parents, their anonymity was preserved.[29]

Franklin then interrogated the plaintiff concerning her religious background. After an exhaustive review of her exposure to religion during childhood, a topic already developed on direct-examination, the defense attorney then sought to bring matters up to date. "Were you still toying then [when the plaintiff went to Cornell University] with the idea of believing in God?"

Chapman: "Objection."

Court: "Sustained."

Franklin: "Did you go there (to chapel at Cornell) to worship God?"

Chapman: "Objection."

Court: "She may answer."

McCollum: "'I had no convictions whatsoever."

Franklin: "How old were you at that time?"

McCollum: "I was 19."

The plaintiff, in response to the attorney's questions, went on to testify that at home during her childhood she did not hear doctrines concerning belief in God; neither did she know at that time if her father espoused the same beliefs with reference to God and religion as he had at the trial. "If he told me about it," she said, "it made no impression."

(Cromwell told the author that his anti-religious views were well-formed by the time he was a young man. A check of his letters, of which he wrote and saved many, many hundreds, would indicate, however, that his overt and militant avowal of atheism did not occur until after his two daughters had entered college.)

Franklin, apparently intent upon establishing some positive connection between the plaintiff and established religious belief, asked: "When you were married in February, 1934, were you married by a minister in a religious service or by a civil officer?"

Chapman: "Objection."

Court: "She may answer."

McCollum: "We were married by a judge in Chicago. As far as I can recall no form of religion or recognition of God was included in that service."

In her book, Vashti observed: "I am sure he thought we probably were [married in a religious service], and he was paving the way to ask me why we hadn't objected to a religious ceremony at that date. The answer, of course, was that I had objected and so had Pappy ... I think my reply took Franklin aback a bit."[30]

The attorney, unshaken, then pursued the matter from the opposite direction: "You did not go before a judge in order to escape a religious form of marriage service?"

Chapman: "Objection."

Court: "Objection overruled."

McCollum: "I felt that the civil ceremony was as legal and binding and not subject to conflict with anything that I might believe."

Franklin, with an apparent intent to show that the plaintiff possessed a predetermined hostility towards religion, asked: "Are you a member of the Free Thinkers Society of Rochester or of any Free Thinkers Society anywhere?"

McCollum: "No."

Franklin: "Do you at this time believe that there is no Supreme Being in the world?"

Chapman: "Objection."

Court: "Overruled."

McCollum: "I would have to ask you to tell me what you mean by 'Supreme Being.'"

Franklin: "Do you embrace the opinions of your father, Mr. Cromwell, as expressed in 'Rationalism v. Religious Education in the Public Schools'?"

Chapman: "Objection."

Court: "Overruled."

McCollum: "I cannot answer yes or no."

This response was certainly in keeping with the new strategy—that of downplaying the confrontational tenor of Cromwell's pamphlet. It was also consistent with the plaintiff's own approach to life, one in which religion played a part of little consequence. But the plaintiff's vacillation at this juncture was definitely inconsistent with the tone of the petition for mandamus of which Cromwell's pamphlet had been made a part, and Franklin proceeded to drive the point home.

Franklin: "Do you remember signing a petition for mandamus?"

McCollum: "Yes."

Franklin: "Did you acquaint yourself with the material in the petition?"

McCollum: "Yes."

Franklin: "Was what was in there with your knowledge and approval?"

McCollum: "Yes."

Franklin: "Did you know that it contained a statement that you adhered to the school of thought known as Rationalism, including atheism?"

McCollum: "Yes."

Franklin: "You are not a believer in any religious creed or doctrine and do not accept that part of the Bible as true where it is not in accord with reason?"

McCollum: "Yes."

Franklin: "Did you know that it contained a statement that your views and understanding concerning religion are set forth in 'Rationalism v. Religious Education in the Public Schools,' written by your father, Arthur G. Cromwell?"

McCollum: "Yes."

Franklin: "Is it still true today that those views are your views?"

McCollum: "Yes."

Franklin: "Have you changed your mind since this proceeding was started?"

McCollum: "No."

Franklin, referring to the statement that Cromwell's pamphlet reflected her views, continued, "Was that a correct statement when you signed the petition?"

McCollum: "Yes. I believed it the way I interpreted it."

Franklin: "At that time did you take an oath that the facts set forth in the petition were true?"

McCollum: "Yes."

Franklin: "Do you remember in what form the oath was administered?"

McCollum: "No."

Franklin: "Are you sure that an oath was administered?"

McCollum: "No, I do not know."

Franklin: "Did you at the time have conscientious scruples against taking oaths?"

Chapman: "Objection."

Court: "Overruled."

McCollum: "I would prefer to take an affirmation. If the oath had been 'by the ever-living God' I am sure I would have said something about it."

Franklin: "Do you remember if you affirmed on that occasion?"

McCollum: "No."

Franklin: "I move to strike the verification from the petition for mandamus in this case."

Court: "The motion will be denied."

The defense attorney continued to pursue the oath question at some length over the repeated but unsuccessful objections of Chapman. Finally, when the plaintiff indicated that she had scruples against swearing to the "everlasting God" when she had no proof one existed, Franklin returned to her religious beliefs.

Franklin: "When was it that you first made up your mind that you did not believe in God?"

Chapman: "Objection."

Court: "Overruled."

McCollum: "I could never set a time. I always had the form of belief as I reasoned it out in my own mind."

Returning to Cromwell's tract, Franklin inquired: "Do you subscribe to the references in this document ... [and] to your father's belief as that of an atheist?"

Chapman: "Objection, as not covered by direct examination."

Court: "Objection overruled."

According to the *News-Gazette*, "she became somewhat shaky as Franklin pressed her for further explanation of her religious beliefs." It was at this point "when Franklin was hammering 'Are you or are you not an atheist,'" the plaintiff responded, "I'm not sure." The account went on to report that Vashti then said: "Wait a minute." She "sat quietly on the witness stand for a couple of minutes apparently collecting her thoughts. After the pause she answered: 'I am a Rationalist.'"[31]

Franklin: "Do you subscribe to the expressions in the second paragraph of this petition that 'The relator adheres to the school of thought known as Rationalism including atheism'?"

McCollum: "Yes."

Franklin: "You do believe as atheists believe, do you not?"

McCollum: "I believe as a Rationalist."

Chapman: "I object to the question and move that the answer be stricken."

Court: "Objection overruled and motion denied."

Franklin: "Do you adhere to the school of thought known as Rationalism including atheism?"

McCollum: "Yes, but I believe as a Rationalist."

Franklin: "Is an atheist a Rationalist?"

McCollum: "Yes, but it has never been in my mind that Rationalism and atheism are equal terms.

Franklin: "Are they not synonymous?"

McCollum: "No they are different."

Franklin: "Are you not an atheist?"

McCollum: "I am a Rationalist."

Franklin: "When you made that statement in the petition that you adhered to the school of thought known as Rationalism including atheism, was that true?"

McCollum: "Yes."

Franklin: "Then you are an atheist."

McCollum: "I am a Rationalist. I am an atheist as far as believing in my own mind that there is no God; as a Rationalist I have not proved there is a God in my mind."

Franklin: "Do you deny that there is a God in the mind of any person that believes in God?"

McCollum: "No, but in my mind, I have not accepted a belief in God—I have no proof."

The most intense moments of Franklin's cross-examination were over and the plaintiff had not yielded on her contention that she was a Rationalist. While that term was less pejorative and thus more in conformance with her attitude, she probably would have taken much of the impact out of Franklin's interrogation by accepting the label of "atheist," especially since it had been an assertion contained in the petition which she had approved.

Franklin went on to probe other matters including the fact plaintiff had allowed James to attend the university demonstration class where he learned Bible stories with her knowledge. She steadfastly held to her view that it was all right for her children to learn of religion: it was indoctrination of any sort to which she was opposed.

During a brief re-direct-examination by Chapman, Vashti explained her decision to allow James to take the religious class at South Side for one semester:

In permitting Terry to take religion during the last half of the fourth year, I took into consideration that he had come home and had asked me to be allowed to take it. I did not approve of it or I would have done it in the first semester.

Franklin asked only one question on re-cross-examination and Vashti stepped down from the witness stand. Ed Borman of the *News-Gazette* commented:

The witness [Vashti] was described by metropolitan reporters as 'petite, comely and pert' [as she took the stand to testify]. When she stepped down she was a tired and wilted little woman.[32]

No other reporter commented upon the plaintiff's condition after Franklin's cross-examination, but the "grueling two and a half hour inquisition" must have been an ordeal—certainly when added to all the other trials she had undergone since the evening meeting at the Unitarian Church on Sunday evening barely three days earlier.

Chapman's next witness was Mrs. Kelley of the Board of Education. She had apparently been requested to bring records which would have recorded any payments from CCRE to the Board for mimeographing the permission cards used in connection with the religion classes. It was quickly ascertained that the records she brought to court were not those needed. She was excused though there was an indication she was to be recalled the next day.

Also briefly on the stand was Mr. M.H. Adams. An insurance salesman and resident of Champaign, he testified concerning his opposition to the religious classes and of his refusal several years earlier to allow his son to participate. The defense declined to cross-examine either of the witnesses, setting the stage for the appearance of Vashti's closest ally, Rev. Philip Schug.

Schug, as had Cromwell and the two McCollums before him, chose to affirm in preference to swearing to the "ever-living God." That, along with his testimony, prompted Ed Borman to offer as his lead paragraph on the event: "A new brand of religious thinking was tossed into the McCollum trial Wednesday afternoon by a minister who said he prefers not to be called a 'Christian' because he considers both Jesus Christ and Santa Claus 'folk tales.'"[33]

Several paragraphs later, Borman wrote: "Before he finished (testifying) he startled the packed courtroom with beliefs most spectators had never heard propounded by a man who calls himself 'Reverend'."[34]

Schug "picked words carefully"[35] on direct-examination. Among other things, he testified that "every Unitarian has the right to think as he pleases." He said that circumstance would make it difficult to say whether the truthfulness of the Adam and Eve story was "in conformity with the teachings and doctrines of the Unitarian Church." The minister went on to deny that any teachings of his denomination included "any connection between Heaven and the sky." When asked by Chapman if members of his denomination regarded the belief that Jesus was the son of God with a woman as his mother, Schug responded: "I do not know of any Unitarians who accept that story." Similarly, he denied knowing any Unitarians who accepted the Resurrection.

"The prevailing view among Unitarians," he testified, "is that God is some spirit, a force or thing or agency that lies behind the universe." Shortly thereafter he added, "A large minority of the church take the view that the entire question is outside the scope of human experience, and they hold no opinion as to what he is or where he is or who he is or if there is a god." When asked how Unitarians regard the King James Version of the Bible, he responded: "The majority view in my church does not speak of [it] as the word of God."

Peterson conducted the cross-examination, beginning with an inquiry into the minister's theological training. Schug indicated that he attended both the Evangelical Theological Seminary in Naperville, Illinois, and the Chicago Theological Seminary. He indicated that he had received additional psychiatric training at the Elgin State Hospital.

Peterson: "Isn't that an institution for the insane?"

Schug apparently chose instead to describe the hospital as a place for "the mentally deficient."

With the preliminaries completed, the attorney sought to develop the religious beliefs of the young minister.

Peterson: "Do you believe in God?"

Schug: "I am not sure I can answer that question unless you tell me what you mean by God."

Peterson: "As a minister do you have any God in mind—any God at all?"

Schug: "I recognize that in the thinking of other people there is a relationship called God."

Peterson: "I'm not asking about other people. Tell us about yourself."

Schug: "I do not give any credence to the idea that there is a personal God or anything that seems to be a person behind the universe. When I use the term, I use it much as I might use the word conscience, but I have a working definition of the word as it is used by many other folk."

Peterson: "Do you believe God created the world?"

Schug: "Oh, no. I have no evidence on which to believe that. That's why I do not."

Peterson: "What kind of evidence would you require before you believed it?"

Schug: "I would only believe in it to the extent that it can be demonstrated in keeping with the best scientific procedure of the day."

Peterson then probed at some length the Sunday school program at the Unitarian Church. Schug's approach was ecumenical to say the least: "For the most part [the class] is not based on Biblical stories; the literature in [the class for the youngest group] for the most part is based upon Biblical stories and stories from the scriptures of various cultures." Later, when asked concerning the use of prayers in his church, Schug responded: "If any prayers are said in my church they are said by members or attendants without my knowledge; I do not bring or have any said in my church."

On re-direct-examination by Chapman, Schug testified, among other things: "I teach about the birth of Jesus and I teach about Santa Claus; the story comes on quite naturally as another folk tale that people repeat."

Franklin, on re-cross-examination, was inclined to inquire further into Schug's analogy between Jesus and Santa Claus. The minister qualified his original statement by saying: "The Santa Claus story is not as deeply implanted in the culture as is the story concerning the birth of Jesus." He added soon thereafter: "Otherwise I consider them as just both stories that are quite meaningful to people."

Franklin: "Is there equal evidence of the existence of Jesus Christ as there is Santa Claus?"

Schug: "I cannot give a yes or no answer to that."

When, on re-direct examination, Chapman continued to probe the Santa Claus question, Schug was prompted to say, "I see considerable evidence of the existence of a man named Jesus as we find it in the scriptures, the Bible, and do not deny such a person existed. I find no evidence of the personal or impersonal existence of a Santa Claus except in the imaginations of certain people."

"'Oh come now,' Franklin broke in, 'I thought we had all decided that there is no Santa Claus.' The Court tittered, the bailiff pounded for order, and … Judge Leonard adjourned the court."[36]

The *Courier* version of the ending noted that Peterson "offered to stipulate Santa Claus does not exist ... as the most hippodromic session of the religious education hearing in Champaign County circuit court adjourned."[37]

Chapter 8

The Trial, Day Four

Before the start of the court session on Thursday morning, Chapman distributed a printed statement to reporters. The gesture represented a continuation of the public relations effort initiated 24 hours earlier by Ted Raynor of the CAC. This time, however, the statement was made in behalf of the Chicago Civil Liberties Committee, which may have felt left out the day before. It read as follows:

> There is no issue in this case as to the existence of Santa Claus; nor as to the existence of God. There is no issue of atheism or religion. The question is this: Are some of the churches in Champaign teaching their own religion in the public schools during regular school hours? If so, they are sponging off the public school and taking unfair advantage of the compulsory school law; and that is illegal. The Chicago Civil Liberties Committee, supporting this prosecution, is an organization of people of many creeds as well as of many races, colors and national origins. Religious liberty [is] their only interest in this case.[1]

The first witness was Mae Chapin, who was recalled by Chapman.[2] During her brief appearance, she admitted that some of the parental consent cards, allowing elementary school students to participate in the religious classes, were printed by the school district. She insisted, however, that "the school board was paid for the work done in the office." Miss Chapin testified that parents of junior high students consented to participation merely by accepting the class schedules. On these forms, supplied by the school district, religious education was simply listed as another class. Further questioning revealed that daily attendance at the junior high was handled by the religious education teachers in the same manner as it was by secular teachers, on forms supplied by the district.

Rev. Herbert L. Miller of the Episcopal Church of Champaign, and recently elected CCRE president, was next on the stand. Several years previously, he had been a member of the curriculum committee of the CCRE.

Chapman: "How did you decide what to teach?"

Miller: "The materials for teaching would be displayed on the table at committee meetings and we selected the materials to be used."

Chapman: "What materials did you select?"

Miller: "That was five years ago, and I do not remember."

Chapman: "On what basis did you decide?"

Miller: "We took into consideration all the material that was there, accumulated from several sources by several people."

Chapman: "What was the nature of the material?"

Miller: "It was general religious matter accepted by the great Christian church throughout the world, that is, the general run of Christian churches which are in agreement on fundamentals."

Chapman: "Can you name them?"

Miller: "No, but there are over 200."

Chapman: "Does that include the Catholic church?"

Miller: "Yes."

Chapman: "Did you see their material?"

Miller: "No, it was for them to select their own material; we selected for our group as Protestants."

Chapman: "Was any of the material there furnished by the Freethinkers ?"

Miller: "I doubt it."

Chapman: "Was any furnished by Christian Science?"

Miller: "I do not know."

Chapman: "Did you have some [material] from all the great churches?"

Miller: "No."

Chapman: "Was any [material] furnished by Jehovah's Witnesses or the Mormons?"

Miller: "I do not know."

Chapman: "Would you include the Mormons among the great religious denominations ?"

Miller: "I am not sure, possibly."

When pressed further on the Mormon question, Miller was quoted as saying: "In the light of my statement that all Christian churches are great, I'd say yes ..."

On cross-examination, Miller testified that: "The curriculum committee has had the policy of having churches bring in any material being used, and to prevent any material being used that would bring up controversies or difficulties; the things that are selected for our courses are what is acceptable to the great mass of Christians." Under Franklin's questioning, Miller denied "select[ing] for teaching any doctrinal material or teach[ing] particular beliefs of any church."

Franklin: "Have you ever heard of any Protestant denomination or their representatives protesting to the curriculum committee about the material selected or to the manner in which they were selected?"

Miller: "No."

On redirect-examination by Chapman, Miller stated: "We cannot accept everything [curriculum materials] that is offered; there is too much offered."

Chapman: "When you were on the curriculum committee, was material submitted that was in conflict with the teaching of your own church?"

Miller: "Yes. It was probably not acceptable to a good many churches."

Rabbi Judah Goldin was then called as one of the relator's final witnesses. He had lived in Champaign-Urbana from 1939-1943 and had been the Jewish representative when the religious education program had been formulated. After an

absence of two years, Goldin had returned to the twin cities just in time to participate in the trial.

Chapman established that Goldin had attended an early organizational meeting at Wesley Foundation. The lawyer then asked: "If you remember, do you recall
whether you approved or disapproved at that time?" This and subsequent questions brought repeated objections from the defense. Finally, after Chapman had
prepared an acceptable foundation, Golden was allowed to respond.

Goldin: "At the time it was discussed, I said I wanted to know first whether it
was legal and if it was determined to be legal, the Jewish group which I represented would cooperate. If it was decided that it was not, the Jewish group would
continue as we were with its own supplementary religious education."

According to the *Daily News*, "Questioning of the young rabbi revealed that
he doubted the legality of the school religious program when it began in 1940."[3]
Goldin testified that, in fact, Jews did participate in the released time program for
the first two years. "Since then there has apparently been nobody there to teach
[the class]." As a consequence, the Jewish classes were no longer offered.

Chapman: "When you were here [in 1939-1943] was the teaching in the Jewish religion under your supervision?"

Goldin: "Yes."

Chapman: "Did you teach any of the Christian religion in connection with (the
classes)?"

Goldin: "What I teach is in accordance with the Jewish belief." '

Chapman attempted to illustrate through Goldin's testimony that conflicts
existed between Judaism and Christianity.

Chapman: "Within the doctrines and teachings of Judaism, is it accepted as
true that there was a man called Jesus?"

Goldin: "The records show it."

Chapman: "According to those doctrines, was God his parent?"

Goldin: "Not in the physical sense."

Chapman: "According to its doctrine [Judaism] was Jesus divine?"

Goldin: "No more than any other man."

Chapman: "Do you accept the story as true that Jesus was killed and after he
had been dead two or three days he came back to life again?"

Goldin: "So far as Judaism is concerned, that is a doctrine which history has
given us; that is what the story tells us."

The rabbi went on to testify: "Judaism is a way of life which has a system of its
own. Christianity is a way of life which has a system of its own. Judaism has
nothing to do with Christianity; Christianity has nothing to say about Judaism."

When Chapman again tried to obtain from Goldin a statement of Jewish disbelief in the crucifixion and resurrection, the rabbi continued to be evasive: "My
only honest answer can be: that is what the New Testament teaches us. Acceptance is decidedly mental." Further questioning produced: "Obviously, Judaism
cannot react one way or the other," and "The New Testament is not incorporated
as a part of Judaism."

Chapman's intent had been to show how the teachings in the Protestant class
were in conflict with other beliefs. In this respect, Goldin's testimony would have

been most helpful, especially since the Jews were no longer offering their own classes. His cautiousness was a great disappointment, both to Vashti and to at least one very supportive Jewish family:

> There were at that time some disagreements within the Jewish group about which we knew nothing until later. I was later told that a prominent Jewish citizen had approached his rabbi and said, "Rabbi, this case is being fought for us Jews as well as for Mrs. McCollum. I want you to tell the court that we as Jews are opposed to these classes, we don't condone them; they only serve to call attention to differences and are harmful to us." The rabbi seemed to agree with him, so you can imagine his surprise when, on attending the trial, he heard the rabbi carefully steer clear of any controversial subjects and state his position tactfully and colorlessly.[4]

Elmer Bash was the relator's last witness. It is not clear why Chapman called Bash, and his testimony was supportive of the religious classes.

Chapman: "What is your interest in this case?"

Bash: "I have filed an intervening petition in this proceeding. "

Chapman: "Why?"

Bash: "Because I desire that my daughter, Wanda I. Bash, continue her work in the ninth grade on released time. In my opinion her well being, education and character will be benefited by such education."

The roofing contractor went on to testify that while he did not "claim to base [his] opinion on any particular facts," he believed "that [the class] has taught her tolerance, taught her to get along with fellow classmates much better, and has taught her something about the Bible that she did not have before ... " Franklin declined to cross-examine Bash.

Before beginning its case, the defense recalled Vashti. The purpose was to have her identify the "Defendant's exhibit 300," the note allowing James Terry to take religious education during the second semester of the fourth grade. It read as follows: "Dear Miss Hollingshead: Terry says he wants to join the Religious Ed. class so I'm sending you this note to say it is O.K. Sincerely, Vashti McCollum"

After Vashti stepped down, John Franklin immediately presented, in writing, a motion to dismiss the plaintiff's case. He was joined by Rall. The motion was "overruled ... without prejudice [to the right of the defense] to renew it at the conclusion of all the evidence."

Elmer Bash was recalled as the first witness for the defense. He testified that he had discussed the classes with his daughters when they brought the consent cards home for approval.

Rall: "At that time or at any other time did either of the girls ever state to you that they wished to take the work because if they did not do so they would be unlike other children?"

Chapman: "Objection to the form as leading, and also as calling for testimony out of the presence of the adverse parties and the relator."

Court: "Overruled."

Bash: "No question was ever raised."

Rall: "Did they at the time or at any time in your presence or to your knowledge, criticize any of the pupils who did not take work in religious education?"

Chapman: "Objection; criticize is a conclusion."

Court: "Sustained."

Rall: "Did they ever make any comment in your presence about students who did not take the work in religious education?"

Bash: "No."

Alice Bash was next on the stand. She was described by Fletcher Wilson as "... a comely woman in a severe black dress with her graying hair dressed in a pompadour above pearl earrings ... "[5] Alfred Prowitt termed her as a "religious mother" who was: "... 35, smartly attractive, her graying hair coiffed into a becoming up-do, and quiet in a matronly way."[6]

In the same report, Prowitt described Vashti as "comely" and "restless." To heighten the drama, he wrote: "A religious mother who wants biblical teaching for her child in public schools took the witness stand here today to combat an atheistic mother who wants to save her child from such teaching." The report went on to say:

> "They [Alice Bash and Vashti McCollum] were a contrast as they confronted each other in Circuit Court, whose roominess was again taxed with drama-hungry spectators. The two women eyed each other curiously."[7]

Alice Bash confirmed testimony by her husband that their children participated in the classes with their consent and that, in her opinion, they benefited from them. Like her husband, she denied that the girls were motivated to take the classes through a desire not to be "set apart" or "unlike" other children. Many of their friends did not take it," she testified. "It has not made any difference in their friendship."

On cross-examination, Chapman asked: "In your opinion, is this 30 minutes of religious education in school beneficial to them?"

Bash: "Yes."

Chapman: "Would it be more beneficial if they had an hour of it?"

Bash: "Yes."

Chapman: "How about a day?"

Bash: "That might be overdoing a good thing; there is an extreme in everything."

Eugene Mellon was then recalled, this time as a witness for the defense. Franklin questioned him in some detail concerning school district practices relating to utility use and employment of custodial services. Mellon testified that there were no increased costs in these areas as a result of the religious education classes. He went on to deny that he had told Vashti, "If the American Legion objected I would not allow the Jehovah's Witnesses sect to use the public school buildings for religious education and instruction." This directly conflicted with Vashti's earlier testimony. The American Legion's possible objection was raised in relation to the fact that Jehovah's Witnesses teach that it is wrong to salute the flag.

Chapman, on cross-examination, delved into the matter of response letters mailed to school districts making inquiries concerning the Champaign System. According to the *Tribune*, the lawyer "scored a point" when the superintendent admitted he prepared a form letter, had it mimeographed by district personnel, and mailed it at public expense.[8] As to the matter of the 500 permission cards prepared by his office, he confirmed Mae Chapin's testimony that the school district was reimbursed for its costs, $1.05, which covered "all the expense of the cards and labor."

Chapman was also able, with some success, to lead Mellon into the admission that, in at least one instance, a school area was used for religious classes which was not ordinarily used for secular classroom purposes. It was a "little ante room [at South Side School] with one end of it fixed up as a library" where the Catholic class was held. It had been a defense contention that everything used in the religious classes was also used for secular purposes, so that there were no additional costs to the district.

During redirect-examination, Franklin raised the alternative of holding the religious classes in the churches, but on school time—the dismissed time option.

Mellon: "As a school administrator, I believe it would be very inconvenient and impractical to release children from the school in Champaign for the purpose of their going for religious education to church buildings." He then cited the same reasons used by the board in 1940 when it allowed the CCRE to use school space— danger to children from vehicular traffic and the long distances between schools and churches. Chapman took the opportunity on recross-examination to explore with the superintendent some of the implications of dismissed time.

Mellon: "If they were sent to the churches, there might have to be somebody in charge. I imagine somebody would have to see that they went to the churches and did not go home or play along the way."

It rained most of Thursday afternoon, but the weather "thinned only slightly the courtroom crowd which gathered to hear the last of the trial witnesses ... "For the most part they were, in the words of the *Tribune*, "a parade of youthful Champaign students who marched in and out of the witness chair as defense witnesses to repeat almost without variation testimony tending to prove there was no religious ... dissension resulting from the course and no compulsion in enrollment."[9]

The first was a former classmate of James at Dr. Howard. She denied ever hearing Bessie Taylor either "urge any of the children in the class to take religious education" or "say she would like to have the class 100% in the religious education class." The youngster also denied ever hearing "any of the children ... tease or make fun of [James Terry] about his failure to take part in the religious classes." During cross-examination she admitted she neither knew James very well nor did she sit close to him in class. She "drew a laugh when Franklin asked if she'd ever heard anyone call James Terry an atheist. She said, 'No, I just saw it in the paper.'"[10]

Elwin Miller, James' fellow non-participant at Dr. Howard, offered similar testimony. Elwin did admit that he had been questioned by another student as to why he did not take the religion class. His response to the other youngster was that he would be participating at the "end of the semester."

Twelve other young witnesses, described as "bobby soxers" by a banner headline in the Sun, denied ever being "embarrassed" as a consequence of not taking the classes[11]. Franklin also led them through a common series of questions which were designed to refute allegations in Vashti's pleading.

Franklin: "Did anyone ever expose you to shame, hatred or contempt as a result (of your non-participation in the religious classes)?"

Witness: "No."

Franklin: "Did anyone ever mention it to you or quiz you or ask you why you did not take part in these classes?"

Witness: "No."

Franklin: "Did your public school teacher ever urge you or try to get you to take the work?"

Witness: "No."

Franklin: "Did you ever feel that your religious difference if any was being pointed out by your not taking part in these classes?"

Witness: "No."

The consistency of the testimony and the common background of the youngsters would indicate that they were carefully screened before being produced by the defense at the trial. Vashti afterterwards dismissed their collective evidence:

> ... the children they brought in were children in junior high, who hadn't taken religious education for other than reasons of principle, because they had band practice or other activities. Also they were all children of parents who were influential in the Methodist or the Presbyterian Church, never the children of Christian Scientists or Jehovah's Witnesses. None had stayed out of the classes because of religious scruples.[12]

Vashti was only partly correct. The youngsters who were put on the stand by the defense fit into two categories; six, contrary to Vashti's recollection, were elementary students and appear to have been selected because they were classmates of James Terry either at Dr. Howard or South Side. The remaining eight were junior high students who had previously attended the two elementary schools in question. Most in each group had never participated in the religious education classes, though at least three did at one time or another.

Chapman, during cross-examination, did question most of the youngsters concerning their own religious beliefs. They were, as the plaintiff suggested, children from conventional families and did not remain out of the classes for religious reasons.

An interesting insight was provided by two of the older junior high witnesses. One testified that, "Not many in the [secular] class at Dr. Howard school [when she was there] took the [religious] course." The other, also from Dr. Howard, testified, "When I was in the sixth grade that was the first year the course was given and just a few were taking it." She went on to say: "Those that took it left the room and went to the library."

This seems to indicate that, at least at Dr. Howard, participation in religious education increased steadily after its introduction into the elementary schools. In the fifth grade classes when James was a member just three years later, the situation had reversed itself: in his class all but two participated, while in the other fifth grade only "five or six" out "about 25 or 26" did not take the religious classes. Instead of those who took the religious instruction leaving the classroom, as had occurred earlier, those who did not were forced to leave. Chapman failed to pursue the reasons behind the dramatic change.

Franklin called two additional witnesses; both Bessie Taylor and Rev. Herbert Miller already had been called earlier by the plaintiff. Mrs. Taylor testified that for the last two months of the previous school year, she had sent James Terry to the other fifth grade class when the religion class was in session. She said she had not taken that action earlier because James "caused confusion in our room" and "it was very hard for him to keep his mind on his work." She had not wanted to create "difficulties" for the other teacher. Mrs. Taylor further testified that James Terry "never mentioned that it bothered him when the door [to the music room] was closed."

Franklin then turned to the incident when James was placed in the hall. "What were the circumstances on the occasion when James was placed in the hall?"

Taylor: "The music supervisor was in the building at the time and using the music room. There was a vacant desk in the corridor. I asked James if it was all right if he sat out there. He did not seem to have any fault with it so I turned on the light and allowed him to take his things there."

Franklin: "Did you realize that he was feeling not taking the religious education so seriously that any little movement from the children would be construed as making fun of him?"

Taylor: "No, or I would never have put him there."

Franklin: "Did you ever do it again?"

Taylor: "No."

Mrs. Taylor went on to deny that "from [her] observation [of the] children" James suffered "any embarrassment whatever." She also denied either urging the class as a whole or James Terry privately "to sign up to take religious education in order to make the class 100 per cent." On cross-examination, Bessie Taylor acknowledged that the reason she sent the youngster to the other fifth grade class was because "his mother requested it."

Rev. Miller's brief appearance produced little new information other than the participation figures for the released time program in Champaign schools. At the elementary level, the overwhelming majority of students took part in the classes while in the junior high the situation was just the reverse. (Rev. Miller revealed that only 134 out of more than 800 in junior high took religious education during the 1944-1945 school year. This was just the reverse in the elementary schools during the same period: in sixth grade, 249 out of 295 participated; in fifth, 206 out of 286; in fourth, 196 out of 298.) Chapman's main probe on cross-examination was directed at whether or not the minister was aware that "some schools in Champaign have only colored children." The matter of segregation in Champaign had been mentioned by Ira Latimer at the Sunday evening meeting at the Unitarian church, and it may well have been Chapman's objective to embarrass the local authorities. It certainly bore questionable relevancy to the case at hand.

After Elwin Miller's testimony, the defense offered in evidence a receipt showing that $1.05 had been received by the school district from Miss Chapin, presumably a reimbursement for the cost of producing the consent cards; the defendant and the intervenors then rested.

Mellon was recalled briefly by Chapman as a rebuttal witness to address a number of technical questions, the importance of which has been obscured by time. Chapman then also rested his case. The last event of the day was John Franklin's renewal of his motion to dismiss the complaint. The court agreed only "to take the motion with the case" and the stage was set for final arguments, scheduled to begin the following morning.

Contending counsel had agreed upon a three and a half hour limit per side for final arguments. When court re-convened on Friday at 10 a.m. attendance had "thinned ... as many of the rain-soaked on-lookers grew bored with the legal testimony."[13] Chapman opened arguments for the plaintiff. (Since no verbatim transcript of final arguments exists, what is provided here represents the author's best effort to reconstruct what was said from the extant first-hand accounts, most of which are cited in other notes in this chapter.)

"I think," he began, "there is very little for me to say. All points of the mandamus petition [have] either been admitted or proved by undisputed evidence."[14] Speaking in a "cagey and soft-spoken"[15] manner, Chapman continued: "The reason for bringing [religious] education into the public schools is to get more children into religion; not for the welfare of the children, but for the benefit of the churches. But if the government is going to finance religion, then the government is going to regulate religion; and people are not going to be free to teach and worship as they please, or openly pray for anything they want."[16]

"When we begin to let churches use school funds, we are letting them feed at the public trough. And when we do that, it means the beginning of the end for most churches." ... "I can see only one church, the Catholic, which could benefit. Like pigs at a trough, the larger ones crowd the littler ones out." ... "Then we will be back to the Dark Ages with a union of church and state."[17] "Religion should be taught [at] the expense of those whose creed is taught; it shouldn't be in the public schools."[18] Chapman concluded his presentation after only ten minutes. According to the *Gazette*, he said that "he expected to offer much more argument after he heard 'what, if anything' the defense had to offer."[19]

Owen Rall opened the argument for the defense. He said he would present the "issues," Franklin would carry the "main burden" of citing law, and Peterson would summarize the defense's case.[20] According to Rall, there were three main issues involved. The first was "whether the program as it exists ... is within the power of the board of education; the second was "whether or not [the religious education program] infringes on the national.and state constitutional guarantees of the freedom of religion." The final issue, in Rall's view, was "whether or not the program [was] in violation of Illinois statutes and laws pursuant to the appropriation of public funds to sectarian purpose[s]."[21] Rall promptly launched into a discussion of the first issue:

The board of education has power to release students for any purpose it considers proper. Under the law and our established tradition, school boards are practically autonomous. The legislature has wisely left control of schools to local boards because no subject is closer to the people than their schools. This court is not called upon to pass on the policy of the board. If the court finds the board has the power, it does not become the concern of the court whether the plan is wise or unwise. Once the question of power is resolved in favor of the board, this lawsuit is ended.[22]

Rall then moved on to the question of constitutionality, the main question raised by the plaintiff.

The phrase "separation of church and state" about which we have heard so much from the relator is a shibboleth which does not furnish a rule for deciding this case. It is only a philosophy or doctrine. The only way to decide this case is to turn to the Constitution. As I apprehend the relator's position, she contends her son's right of freedom of religion [is] being violated because there is social pressure to coerce him to take these courses. We want to make a sharp distinction between a compulsory system that is subject to [abuse], and a system that is in fact purely voluntary. The evidence in this case has shown that in the Champaign system of religious education there is no urging to participate, no penalty if they do not participate, no social pressure, not even an inquiry why when they do not participate. The Champaign system is voluntary in fact as well as in name. [23]

"Freedom of religion as guaranteed by the Constitution," Rall continued, "means freedom of religious worship. The Constitution is not designed to protect atheists from the consequences of their own decision to be atheists. The United States Supreme Court has said this is a religious nation. The Illinois Supreme Court has said Illinois is a religious state."[24] "When it is disclosed that Mrs. McCollum and her son have no religion, they are not entitled to rely on constitutional provisions for freedom of religion, except in that they may not be forced to adopt a religion."[25] "The Constitution does not protect atheists against the results of their being atheists."[26] The attorney went on to warn: "If this suit is sustained, the liberties of the parents who desire this religious education for their children will be infringed upon."[27]

Rall also returned to the oath question, specifically the reason Vashti, her son, father and minister (Schug) all gave for refusing to take the traditional oath and swearing to the "everliving God." It "embarrassed" them, according to the defense attorney. He said this could be carried to absurd extremes. "Under their position ... no one in the courtroom could be required to take an oath to God if it 'embarrassed' Mrs. McCollum to refuse it." He added: "These propositions are preposterous, but the woman is driven to them if she says she is deprived of religious liberty by the school education program."[28]

Franklin then took over the argument from his colleague. He chose first to respond briefly to Chapman's comparison of pigs feeding at the trough with churches competing with one another to obtain public benefits. The analogy, said Franklin, was "particularly inappropriate as to taste."[29] "But," the attorney went on to say, "this is a cornbelt county where we know little about atheists and much about hogs. We know that when pigs are fed at a trough one alone does not get fat; they all do. So, if we must use this analogy, I say let them all grow fat at the trough together."[30]

Franklin then became serious and proceeded to make one of the most widely quoted declarations of the trial: "Just as we are concluding a costly and bloody war which ended in victory over unchristian and infidel nations, the struggle of these unchristian and infidel forces against religion is being transferred to this little courtroom in central Illinois."[31] And, "This is an aspect of this case which we may not forget as men and which we must not forget as judges and lawyers. I am not trying to be emotional, but Christianity is a part of us and our government and our law is interwoven with it."[32]

Chapman later countered: "But I thought Communist Russia was our ally in this war; I thought atheism was on our side in this case."[33] "They [the Soviets] showed more sympathy with democracy than 'religious' Italy, Spain or Japan."[34]

Franklin had "lined the long counsel table with twenty law books borrowed from the University of Illinois Law Library [from which he then began to cite] court rulings which have allowed the church to come into the schools in some manner."[35]

The chief defense counsel then questioned whether the exemption of church property from taxes violated the principle of separation of church and state. "School District Number 71 exempts tens of thousands of dollars worth of church property from taxes each year—are they then to deny them the use of the public school buildings?"[36]

Continuing in the same vein, Franklin drew laughter from the courtroom audience with another analogy. "The City of Champaign," he said, "recently appropriated a great sum of money for a fire truck. Does Chapman contend," he inquired, "that if the Methodist church should catch on fire some night, the appropriation of this expensive piece of equipment has been made to sectarian purposes?"[37]

Referring to the First Amendment to the United States Constitution which prohibits Congress from passing "any laws respecting an establishment of religion," Franklin insisted: "This does not divorce the state from Christianity or religion generally or exclude any benefit to religion generally." He went on to declare: "This is a Christian nation; we have oaths in our courts. Congress opens with a prayer and so do our legislatures; the Christian religion is incorporated into the warp and woof of our government." Using similar reasoning, Franklin directed the court's attention to the fact that the state purchases Bibles for inmates of the criminal institutions, "but these people here want to stop little children from reading the Bible."[38]

Returning to an argument previously made by Rall, Franklin maintained: "Mrs. McCollum has no religion, and so there can be no violation of her religious freedom."[39]

Addressing the "embarrassment" issue, Franklin argued that James Terry was "no more subjected to embarrassment than a Catholic boy is when he passes up meat on Friday in the school cafeteria or a Jewish boy when he passes up pork."[40]

The noon recess intervened during Franklin's presentation. When he resumed, Franklin delved into what he termed "parents' rights" in determining what should be included in their children's education. "According to our relators," he said, "if you want your children educated in religion during the week, the only way to avail yourself of it is to send them to private or parochial schools, and a majority of parents cannot afford such schools. If the Supreme Court [says] they have a right to control the education of their children, they have the right to determine if children are to take 30 minutes of religious education each week."[41] Franklin went on to suggest that "if atheists could stop religious education classes they could prevent [the] reading of the Declaration of Independence or the singing of America since both contain references to God."[42]

It was then Abe Peterson's turn to wrap up the case for the defense. The Chicagoan charged, "There is no evidence that children have had their secular education impaired because a half hour each week is devoted to religious education."[43] He went on to attack the plaintiffs assertion that mimeographing and distributing parental consent cards constituted giving aid to religious denominations. "Can anyone say that this school board should be prevented from doing little incidental things without cost to the board to help provide religious instruction for children under its jurisdiction?"[44]

On a related theme, Peterson said: "I wonder if there is any court in the land that would sustain a petition against the government for paying chaplains of various faiths to accompany our men into battle."[45] Then, in an apparent reference to Chapman's repeated mention of the Holiness Faith Healers and their snake-handling practices, Peterson added: "That they [the military] do not have snake charmers does not in any way impair the constitutionality of this."[46]

Judge Watson interrupted Peterson's presentation with the inquiry: "What do you say about the rights of atheists to teach in the schools?" Another version indicated that the judge's question referred to the "situation in regard to Jehovah Witnesses' classes in the schools."[47] Peterson replied: "I could not commit the school board, but I would say that if atheism is a religion the board would give them the same privileges as any other group; whether anyone would come to listen to them is another matter."[48] Franklin later referred to the Jehovah's Witnesses, noting that "they had not taken advantage of the school religion program, but, I think the evidence is clear that they may if they wish."[49] He also pointed to the board's answer to the suit which expressed "willingness to allow atheists to teach on the same basis others are allowed to conduct their classes."[50]

Two very interested spectators, Superintendent Mellon and board president Huxtable, "said that apparently they would be required to allow the sects to hold classes in the schools if a request were made; they wondered, however, if Jehovah's Witnesses could offer a curriculum which would not be in conflict with other denominations."[51]

Before concluding, Peterson argued specifically in behalf of his clients, Elmer and Alice Bash, the intervenors. "If Mrs. McCollum won her suit, the Bashes and other parents who desire that their children receive religious education would be denied their fundamental right to have a voice in the education of their children."[52]

The remainder of the time belonged to Landon Chapman. He vigorously defended his contention that the teaching of religion in the schools represented a union of church and state. "We shouldn't have a compulsory law to send people to school and then send someone around to try to convert them; religious teachers have no more right in the school building than a peanut vendor. If the school superintendent allows them to go in he is misappropriating public funds."[53] This made good copy and was widely reported.

Chapman "hammered away" at the contention that the classes were sectarian. "The fact that all sects are invited to participate does not make the courses non-sectarian; [it just] makes them a conglomeration of all sects. There isn't one thing they teach that isn't sectarian. The Freethinkers are a sect and we've shown they don't believe in anything that's being taught."[54] Chapman added: "There is no such thing as nonsectarian religion."[55] "You can't teach religion without practicing a certain amount of religion, and that is what happened in these classes."[56] As a further indication of the sectarian nature of the instruction, Chapman pointed to "evidence [which] showed the financial responsibility for the religious education program was divided ... that the Protestants paid for Protestant teachers, Catholics for the Catholic program and Jewish support paid for the Jewish program."[57]

Arguing to sustain another important point in his case, Chapman "insisted that the testimony of James Terry specifically proved that he had been subjected to embarrassment and pressure." He dismissed the testimony of the children produced by the defense. "They brought in some children from the Methodist and Presbyterian and Christian churches, the biggest and the most popular in town; of course they suffered no embarrassment. Why didn't they bring in Jehovah's Witnesses pupils or Seventh Day Adventists?"[58]

In apparent reference to testimony from James Terry and his mother that he desired to participate in the religious instruction, Chapman charged that the youngster was "sold on the idea of joining the class by social pressure." Chapman continued: "Most children would take it anyway, even if they didn't want to, so that they wouldn't be called to attention; little children should not have to be subjected to disclosing their religious views. Freedom of religion includes freedom from religion."[59]

Chapman "belittled" defense conclusions that if the court ruled against the religion classes, school children would be precluded from contact with historical documents and traditional songs which mentioned God. "Of course [school children] could read the Declaration of Independence. They could sing hymns like 'Swing Low Sweet Chariot,' if they sang them for music—not worship. They could even read the Bible, so long as they read it as history or literature or even science and not as religious or a subterfuge for religion."[60]

Responding to Franklin's insistence that "this is a Christian nation," Chapman argued, "it is also the nation where we have atheists and agnostics and where there is practiced Shintoism and Mohammedanism. The government protects religion after it has been established but it is not the duty of government either to start or foster any religion."[61] Chapman went on to point out that there is no mention of God in the Federal Constitution and he quoted George Washington from a treaty with Tripoli, "The United States Government is in no sense founded upon the Christian religion."[62]

On the same theme, Chapman distinguished between the situation of chaplains in the army and religion in the public schools. "The government is not trying to make religionists out of soldiers who are not. It merely provides religious privileges for those who were taken away from the privileges they had at home. But the school board is taking those with no religion and trying to give them some."[63]

As to Franklin's assertion that atheists could participate in the religious classes on an equal basis with the other groups, a concession contained in the board's answer, Chapman said that the wording allowed only that "atheists may apply and have their application acted upon just like any other group. They would [still] have to obtain school board permission; the board would decide if there was enough interest to justify a course. If there is freedom of religion, there is no censorship of religious practices; if they have a right to go into schools, they have a right to go in without permission."[64] In another report, Chapman went on to charge that the situation in Champaign schools made Mellon a "potential religious dictator."[65]

Chapman also referred to University of Illinois president-elect George Stoddard's earlier ruling as New York state commissioner of education, that religious instruction must be discontinued in the public schools.[66] Considering the publicity the ruling had received in the local press three months earlier, in June, it was by no means new news.

In contrast to the defense, which cited "more than a dozen higher court decisions which they said [would] sustain the school board's position," Chapman offered less than six. He argued that "they were so in point that they entitle Mrs. McCollum to the order she asks against the religious classes."[67]

Vashti was absent for most of the afternoon's arguments. She rejoined Schug at the counsel table just before Chapman finished.[68] Beset with a severe migraine headache, she had been driven to the hospital in an effort to obtain relief.[69] It had indeed been a trying week for the plaintiff.

In closing, Judge Leonard set October 8 for Chapman to file his brief, October 22 for the defense to reply and October 29 for Chapman to reply to the reply. Leonard said that he and his colleagues would render a decision within 30 days.[70] The delay was occasioned by a defense request for the written briefs because, in its view, the case was "too important to be decided off the cuff."[71]

With some literary license, one of the Chicago reporters summed up the charged, occasionally dramatic trial as follows: "If God had been on trial in Circuit" here this week, the decision would be simple. On the evidence—and emotions—presented during the hearing ... the answer could be given today: God would win. He went on, with considerable accuracy, to outline the tasks that lay ahead for the attorneys and judges:

Within a month, however, attorneys for both sides will file briefs outlining their arguments. These arguments will be presented in the cold terms of constitutional law and judicial precedent. And that is the issue—not God. It is on these points that three Circuit judges from the Corn Belt—sometimes referred to as the Bible Belt—will decide whether the Champaign school board is right.[72]

Chapter 9

In the Interim

While the trial was still in progress, Ruth Cromwell was prompted to write her daughter in Champaign:

I'm like Will Rogers; "All I know is what I read in the papers!" I might still be wondering if Art found his way through the Illinois Central depot [in Chicago] if I hadn't seen his picture in the paper. Well, I can imagine you all have your hands full.[1]

There was no dearth of information on the *McCollum* case in Rochester. The two major daily newspapers were especially attuned to events in Champaign-Urbana due to Cromwell's earlier, highly publicized activities in New York with respect to church-state separation and the father-daughter connection. Upon his return, the newspapers filed additional reports. The unrepentant rationalist declared himself to be the "proudest father and grandfather in seven states."[2] According to Cromwell: "Terry was anxious to be on his toes to answer questions in a straightforward manner. He gave the questioners a definite idea of his disbelief in God, but he didn't show off and didn't act like a big shot."[3]

He went on to say that James Terry "did not once contradict his philosophy despite the attempts of the lawyers to confuse him and prove that he had been subject to indoctrination to his mother's and grandfather's beliefs."[4]

Many religious leaders, as well as the groups they represented, were quick to express their views concerning the celebrated hearing. Opinion was divided, even among religious liberals. The legal position of both Cromwell and his daughter was supported by David R. Williams, minister of the Unitarian Church in Rochester.

I do not agree with Mr. Cromwell's view about the existence of God. To me all life is a living witness of the fact of God. In the United States [however] it is Mr. Cromwell's inalienable right to believe as he sees fit. With regard to the unconstitutional attempts now being made to foist the teaching of sectarian religion into the public schools, Mr. Cromwell is 100 per cent right in his opposition. The most vicious system in the world is a combination of church and state. This country was founded to get away from this evil and the results I believe speak for themselves. Let those who criticize Mr. Cromwell take the beam out of their own eye."[5]

Rev. Ellis Pierce of the First Universalist Church in Urbana disagreed:

The position of all liberal churches in such a situation is not easy. [At] a former parish, because of the extreme sectarianism of certain teachers, I felt it necessary to recommend that my church withdraw from membership in the Council for Religious Education and that families in my parish should withdraw their children from religious instruction in all classes in one school and certain classes in others. This is not a unique situation and liberal churches are divided as to the proper solution. However, to my mind, the cure suggested by Mrs. McCollum seems worse than the disease.[6]

In Argo, Illinois, Rev. Erwin Gaede, who had testified at the McCollum trial, commented on the event in his Sunday sermon: "A recognized minority of clergymen are strongly opposed to the program of religious education known as 'released time' because it opens the way toward many abuses in our democratic tradition."[7]

Among more conservative denominations there was generally favorable support for the released time program, although it was by no means unanimous. Dr. John A. Leimer of Hope Lutheran Church in Chicago was quoted as saying: "The church and state should be strictly separated and this separation can exist only when the church has its own religious education program completely independent from the state."[8]

Siding with the Champaign Board of Education was Rev. Dr. Torrey Johnson, head of the Youth for Christ movement. Speaking in Chicago, he said: "The people of Champaign made their decision; they voted to give [the] opportunity for religious instruction to their own children. This does not interfere with the school program. This is not paid for out of school funds. This does not violate the separation of church and state."[9] (Johnson apparently was unaware that neither a public discussion nor a vote had preceded the installation of the classes in Champaign schools.)

During the week of the trial, in the *New World*, official journal of the Roman Catholic diocese of Chicago, the Rev. Edward V. Dailey wrote: "If the state will, by court order, become an absolutely independent entity in society, freed from all accounting to God, we have fascism and totalitarianism which apparently the freethinking opponents of religious training unwittingly invite."[10]

In another offering from the *New World*, as reported in the *Tribune*, Rev. John Evans asked Vashti if her will should "be legally imposed upon many stalwart Americans who believe that God and the things of God should be kept close to the hearts of our people?" He went on to add:

When it comes to imposition we might think of the straight thinkers who will be severely penalized by court action against religious teaching during released time in a program which has been carefully worked out by civic and religious leaders. They had decided on the program as a constructive plank in the shaky moral structure of American life, feeling, no doubt, that they were definitely laboring for a better democratic life.

They must have been duly shocked to learn that some of their opponents had practically sloganized them into the class of Benedict Arnold.[11]

Meanwhile, much closer to home, the 95th annual convention of the Illinois Disciples of Christ met at the University Place Christian Church in Champaign the week following the trial. Among the resolutions adopted at the conclave was:

> We recommend approval of the efforts of those interested in weekday religious education to further the work through the support of the defense of the McCollum Case. We approve the formation of a non-profit corporation to receive and disburse funds to this end. All interested churches may send money to the Illinois Church Council for this purpose.[12]

The secular press was also quick to express its views on the *McCollum* case. The *Courier* carried a short editorial on Friday, September 14, the last day of the trial. "Various questions by counsel," observed the writer, "occasionally facetious or calculated to provoke humorous replies, have dealt with some of the issues handled so entertainingly in the Scopes Trial." The editorial went on to say:

> But questions of doctrine and of personal religious belief have been permitted to overshadow, or even eclipse the constitutional issues at stake. The judges are sitting to determine a point of law, not as a church council to decide whether there was a flood or whether the whale actually swallowed Jonah.[13]

The *News-Gazette* carried no editorial concerning the case, relying instead upon the regular reports of Ed Borman and the comments of nationally syndicated columnist George E. Sokolsky to enlighten their readership. Sokolsky, in three columns which appeared in the *News-Gazette* two weeks after the trial, differed strongly with the position taken by Vashti. In the first he raised two issues: "The right of the parents to control the education and culture of a child," and "The place of religious education in American life." In the discussion of the former, he proceeded to equate "Mrs. McCollum's position" with the situation "in Soviet Russia, in Nazi Germany, in Fascist Italy and in all other totalitarian countries where man has been a thing of the state ... " With respect to the latter issue, the columnist raised a rhetorical question:

> The question then arises whether the child's mind should be exposed to the mythology of current sociology but not to the 5,000 years of relationship to God's world; whether Karl Marx is legitimate as an historical figure, but not Moses and Jesus Christ; whether the nonsense of Henry Wallace is more serviceable to human culture than the wisdom of Isaiah and Paul.[14]

Two days later Sokolsky began with an even stronger indictment of the plaintiffs case:

> I was reminded of the Book of Esther, in which Queen Vashti is portrayed as an angry and vengeful woman, when I read of Mrs. Vashti McCollum's suit to stop all children of Champaign, Ill., from having religious educa-

tion on released time because she objects to her son hearing the Word of God since she is a rationalist, a freethinker, an atheist.[15]

Sokolsky argued that the "social pressures" to which James Terry was subjected resulted from the fact that Vashti herself "made an exception of him." This, the writer said, "of course is true in adult life of all who choose to mark themselves off from the normal type of any community." Concluding, he wrote in part: "What our modern Vashti asks, however, is that because she does not want her child to know of God, all children should be deprived of that knowledge."[16]

For the last column in the series, Sokolsky took on Philip Schug and "his own views of God." Relying on "the reports written by Ed Borman, who covered the case most thoroughly for the *News-Gazette*... ," Sokolsky proceeded to repeat selected excerpts of Schug's testimony, which the columnist termed "astonishing, not for its contents but because of his vocation." The minister's beliefs were not those of Unitarians who, asserted Sokolsky, "do not reject God." He then proceeded to summarize the issue Schug and the "so-called free-thinkers" were really pursuing: "The case tried in Champaign County only technically involves the use of school funds for religious education. Basically, it is an attack on God, on the concept of God; on the moral basis of our society."[17]

It is unclear whether or not Schug had read Sokolsky's last column before taking pen and paper to offer a reply. In a letter dated Sept. 28, the same date as the last column appeared, but omitting mention of the personal reference, Schug took issue with Sokolsky's interpretation of the Vashti story in the Bible. The minister wrote:

> According to the story in the Book of Esther the king, Ahasuerus, had spent six months impressing his subordinate princes and their army leaders with his wealth and power. Determined that the impression shall last he concludes these diplomatic maneuvers with a seven-day feast and drinking bout in the gardens of the palace.
>
> Merry with wine, the king calls for (Queen) Vashti to display her charms before his guests, and in all modesty she refuses to come at the king's command. The king's anger burns within him. He calls the wise men, and they advise him to quickly depose the queen, for if he does not "this deed of the queen will come abroad to all the women" and they will follow her example.
>
> ...Vashti is deposed, and a decree goes out "that every man should bear rule in his own house" and that women must not deny their husbands any wish, however great or small it may be.
>
> ...Vashti, deposed and despised ... is never allowed to see the king again, [and] becomes the first great champion of women's rights that we know in the Bible. Her modesty and her good sense, as well as her courage, are ignored by Mr. Sokolsky, who labels her an "angry and vengeful woman."[18]

Another well-known columnist, Elsie Robinson, agreed with Sokolsky and made known her non-support of Vashti:

As you [the reader] probably know, she [Vashti] complained that her small boy had been "embarrassed" and "ostracized" by his school mates because she refused to let him attend the school's religious classes. Well, that's one way of being a smarty and commanding the spotlight. Or influencing dimwits. And personally I have no objection to smart alecks, being frequently one myself. But when it comes to throwing spitballs at God, even I have not enough courage—nor stupidity.[19]

Elsa Maxwell, still another national syndicated columnist, disagreed with her colleagues. She called Vashti a "fighting mom" who "is undoubtedly right when she says this religious training in public schools makes for discord rather than harmony." She went on to quote an "atheist friend": "I was brought up on the principle of being concerned with man's relation to man rather than man's relation to God—and if there is a God, it seems to me, He'd be more concerned about that too." Her final thought was: "I only regret that Clarence Darrow, himself an agnostic, isn't here to plead the case with his waving arms and convincing oratory. But it will be interesting to see how the rights of the minority—in this case a minority of one—come out."[20]

Even the *Saturday Evening Post* entered the editorial fray with a piece entitled, "What Would Robert G. Ingersoll Say About This?" "Sometimes," the unidentified writer began, "it looks as if the freethinkers were trying to earn the reputation for intolerant solemnity formerly enjoyed by the more puritanical practitioners of religion." The editorial went on to state that, "The resort to the civil arm (the courts) it appears, is as tempting to antireligious people in a pinch as it used to be to authoritarian theologians." The ending was particularly offensive to James Terry's grandparents, the Cromwells, who promptly wrote to the magazine:.

If "freethinking" is to get anywhere as a movement, its followers will have to be made of sterner stuff than this. The saying that "the blood of the martyrs is the seed of the church" has a wider application. It suggests at least that an unbeliever who can't take a little embarrassment, who has no disposition to "dare to be a Daniel, dare to stand alone," and whose mother has to go to law to protect him from the sight of other children taking religious instruction, is likely to end up a choir boy.[21]

Arthur and Ruth Cromwell, in a six-page, single-spaced, margin-to-margin response, sharply took the *Post* to task.[22] Frederic Nelson, of the *Post*, quickly responded.

Of course we had no knowledge of the facts as you state them as to the experience of your grandson in attempting to stand up for his principles in the Champaign Schools. I assure you that if we had known about the outrageous treatment of the boy as reported by you, we should not have used the episode as the occasion for what we thought would be a piece of innocent merriment.[23]

Nelson asked for "newspaper clippings or other material" which substantiated their statements. Cromwell responded with another long communication with the supporting materials requested. Months later, Nelson returned the "several pictures and documents" which Cromwell had provided.

> No concise way [Nelson wrote] of going into this again seemed to suggest itself and, inasmuch as the boy's name was not used in the original piece, I still think that bringing it up again would have done more harm than good. I still agree with you that the facts as presented in your letter indicate an excess of zeal by the Champaign School authorities, and I wish to express my regret that we printed that little piece based on inadequate newspaper reporting.[24]

An unidentified clip from Rockford, Illinois, like much of provincial America, sided with the Champaign Board of Education:

> With all deference to the Bill of Rights, has Mrs. McCollum, an atheist, any more constitutional authority for challenging the teaching of religion than somebody else, an anarchist would have for challenging the teaching of civil government? Or than a confirmed fundamentalist would have for challenging the teaching of geology or biology?

The writer chose to end with a more personal observation, one which no doubt also weighed heavily on Vashti's mind:

> Still, the big issue does not really seem to matter as much as the little boy. Possibly the writer of this editorial, being himself the father of a ten-year boy, is unduly sensitive on the subject. But it really does seem that, if Mrs. McCollum had had a due regard for her son's comfort and peace of mind, which is the reason she gives for bringing the court action, she would never have brought such an action at all.[25]

Two Chicago newspapers saw the matter much differently. The *Daily News* committed itself while the trial was still in progress. As part of its editorial it reprinted a statement of the Chicago Schools Committee:

> The principles of separation of church and state and of complete freedom of worship are basic to American democracy. It is clear that the only advantage to the church in released-time religious education is the help of compulsory attendance laws. For the church to ask the state thus to sponsor its teaching is to confess its own weakness and to imperil its ultimate freedom from control by the state.

Referring specifically to the situation in Champaign: "The feeling stirred up by the lawsuit should make us glad that we do not have the Champaign system in Chicago." But the writer saved for the final paragraph the strongest statement:

> We should remember that the worst moral breakdown took place not where religion was free but where it was not free. In Germany and Japan, the rulers strove to make it a tool of the state. One of our first responsibilities in the new world is to spread religious freedom. While we are en-

gaged in that task, we shall be well advised not to mix denominationalism with our own public school system.[26]

The Chicago *Sun* was also supportive of Vashti's legal effort:

The issue in the religious-education trial now concluded at Urbana was
not the religious or nonreligious belief of any party or witness. It was not
whether religious education is essential. The issue to be decided is simply whether such education has [a] proper place in schools supported by
all taxpayers, whatever their views on religion. This newspaper believes
that religious education is out of place in the public schools. We believe
it has a vital place in the churches and Sunday schools and in religious
homes. To inject it into the public schools means a harmful division of
schoolmates into Protestant, Catholic and Jewish groups. However "voluntary" attendance in the classes, heavy social pressure and consequent
frustration are felt by children whose parents' conviction forbids their
conforming to the pattern.[27]

Written comment and opinion in the press was one thing, direct mob action
was quite another. It occurred on the Halloween night following the court hearing.
John McCollum had left to attend a lecture. "Ironically enough," noted the plaintiff
later, he went to hear "Ely Culbertson on 'World Peace' ... ," leaving Vashti home
alone with the three children.[28]

During the evenings of the week preceding Halloween itself a "teenage" crowd
of nightly "serenaders" had visited the McCollum home. Their "theme song," according to Vashti, seemed to be "Onward Christian Soldiers." The serenaders
returned that All Saints Eve and rang the door bell. Vashti McCollum recalled
rushing to the door to pass out treats before the impatient visitors resorted to
tricks.

As I opened it [the door] I was met by a shower of everything the victory
gardens had to offer that year. Rotten tomatoes smashed against the walls,
splattered in my hair and over my clothes. Huge cabbage plants, roots,
mud and all, came careening through the open door and into the living
room.[29]

Vashti called the police, who arrived too late to apprehend the culprits. After the
police had departed, the mob returned and charged the heavy front door "with
such violence," she recalled, "that our whole house, a stone one, seemed to shake."

All family members retain vivid memories of that Halloween night. It was a
terrifying experience for the McCollums, and fortunately was not repeated.[30] While
the *News-Gazette* of the next day mentioned specifically numerous calls for police assistance, that from Vashti was not included.[31] The *Courier*, covering the
evening's happenings similarly, did note the attack.[32] Either the *Courier* reporter
had done a more thorough job of reading the police blotter or, as Vashti believed,
the omission represented just another instance of the biased reporting of the
News-Gazette.[33] Philip Schug informed his congregation of the attack in the church
newsletter. His heading: "Christian Halloween."[34]

There was, however, a much more constant reminder of the battle. It was the "fan mail," as she termed it, that arrived day in and day out.

During and after the trial we were swamped with letters, sometimes as many as two hundred a day. We opened them and sorted them in piles of "pros" and "cons," and in the beginning I tried to answer them all. Finally it got so hectic I could answer only the "pros," and then it got still worse, so with the help of a girl, who had asked if there was anything she could do to help, I sent out a form letter to the "pros," thanking them for their interest, explaining the issue and the complications and leaving enough margin at the bottom of the letter to write in answers to specific questions.[35]

In the form letter, Vashti noted that "of the 200 or so signed letters not supporting my stand, none attacked my legal grounds—only the religious angles." She went on to say: "The question of my own personal beliefs is entirely beside the point. I have never meant this to be a question of religion versus atheism; but rather, a definition of the separation of church and state. I am firmly convinced that both the church and the state have benefited by this separation."[36]

Vashti vowed in the letter, to "carry this question all the way to the United States Supreme Court to get a favorable decision ... " She acknowledged that "there has been some question as to whether [a higher court] will review the case." Even if it did not, she felt there was still value to the effort "If the experience I have had in this suit can be of any help to [others] in their local situations." With each form letter, the plaintiff enclosed a copy of a pamphlet prepared by the Chicago Action Council.[37] It was the statement prepared earlier by Philip Schug and published by the *Courier* and excerpts were quoted in Chapter 4. Vashti noted on one of the copies of this letter which she saved: "First form letter to 'pros,' 750-1,000 sent."

Vashti saved all of the letters, boxes and boxes of them, for a number of years following the U.S. Supreme Court decision in 1948. In her book, she included a chapter-long discussion of her mail.[38] Afterwards, the collection was consigned to the McCollums' coal-fired furnace, converting to physical warmth the moral warmth and the fire and brimstone of the "pros" and "cons" respectively.

Many of the letters also contained religious tracts which were saved until 1971. At that time, they were given to the University of Illinois Library in Urbana. An inquiry a number of years afterward failed to locate them. While the entire collection of letters, had it survived, might have formed the basis of an interesting sociological study, the chapter covering the mail in *One Woman's Fight* makes fascinating reading.[39] In that chapter, Vashti noted that "there were more letters in my favor than opposed to me: in fact, three-fifths pro to two-fifths con." Commenting on the latter she said later: "Some of them were not only unprintable, but unspeakable, unwhisperable, unimaginable. Filth, bitterness, sadism, hatred—and all of it in the name of Christianity."[40]

Meanwhile, on October 19, a second effort was made to develop local support for Vashti's stand, the first being the Sunday evening meeting immediately preceding the trial sponsored by the CCLC. This time the impetus came from the CAC and the meeting was not public, although there was a reporter present. Eight members of the CAC were in attendance including its president, Robert Greenfield, Boris Steinberg (who led the discussion) and Ted Raynor. Also present in the "group of about 30" were Vashti, Philip Schug, and hosts Dr. and Mrs. David Bourgin.[41]

Raynor, reflecting upon the events at the trial, asserted that it was the defendants who were responsible for obscuring the real issue at the trial. He went on to offer an explanation for the tactic.

> The efforts of the defendants to make it appear that God and religion were on trial is an old legal trick that every lawyer knows will sometimes work when you don't have much of a case. You try to clutter up the [court] records and make the judges decide on points that are not even at issue. Besides it often gets favorable publicity when a discussion of the issues would not.[42]

Raynor accurately outlined the CAC attitude from the outset, that the issue be narrowly focused upon the legality of the religious classes. But, it must be remembered, it was Landon Chapman, the plaintiff's attorney, who determined the direction of the trial, not the defense. Greenfield, however, agreed with Raynor and went on to express optimism that a clarification of the issues would be favorable to Vashti's cause.

> Now that the smoke screen of atheism versus religion that some religious groups succeeded in throwing around the McCollum case has cleared, and people are discussing the real issue of the legality of sectarian religious teaching in our public schools, things are really beginning to happen. Over the entire country this practice is now getting publicity that its promoters never desired, and when the American people learn the facts you can trust them to do the right thing.[43]

Greenfield's optimism was debatable and the objective of the meeting was not realized; no organized local support group developed.

While she awaited the work of lawyers and judges, Vashti had other matters more directly related to the lawsuit with which to deal. Of these, the most important were the difficulties which developed in the relationship between the CAC and the Chicago Civil Liberties Committee (CCLC). Though initially caught in the middle, she found the approach of Ted Raynor and the CAC much more compatible with her own inclinations than that taken by the CCLC. Reflecting upon the situation in her book, she wrote:

> From the time things first got under way I felt that my conception of the case was entirely different from Landon Chapman's and Ira Latimer's. Under them it became a civil liberties fight in the form of the *McCollum* case, while I wanted to keep it a simple legal case of using public-school buildings for sectarian purposes. I felt that the law was clearly on my side. We didn't have to have all the trimmings of a Scopes trial. My reli-

gious convictions, it seemed to me, were of less importance than the legal rights involved. I could have filed the same suit had I been a member of almost any church.[44]

In this respect, it should be remembered that Chapman had been recommended by Latimer and the CCLC. Further, Vashti had differed with Chapman and Latimer on the proper approach almost from the beginning. She felt from the outset that the use of Cromwell's pamphlet had been a mistake. Some members of the CAC agreed. As the trial approached, the plaintiff had been clearly against Chapman's idea of calling Cromwell as a witness. Vashti even appears to have been less than enthusiastic about the public meeting held at the Unitarian Church just before the trial, which was Latimer's idea; she certainly was dismayed by the statements made by Chapman and Latimer that evening.

More conservative in nature, the CAC was far less antagonistic in the manner in which it supported Vashti. After the first day of the trial a number of its members were so displeased with the direction in which Chapman was headed that they were in open revolt (see Chapter 6). The result was the CAC delegation, headed by Ted Raynor, which arrived in Champaign on the second day of the trial to demand a change in tactics or, failing in this, to withdraw their support.

(Cromwell's attitude was, as one might expect, far more confrontational than that of the CAC. In a letter to the McCollums dated October 17, 1945, the freethinker noted several cases similar to the *McCollum* case which were not going well. He contended that "their cases are being smothered under because of the lack of ballyhoo that Chapman knew you would have to have in order to get a fair trial. If your case had been conducted in the quiet, under-the-table manner with a very sedate writ of mandamus, there would have been only one judge hearing the trial and you would never have gotten it [the lawsuit] to the U.S. Supreme Court." Cromwell certainly had prescience here; the U.S. Supreme Court hearing of the *McCollum* case was some two years in the future.)

Differences continued after the trial. One of the points of friction was with respect to fund raising for, and financing of, the lawsuit. Both the CAC and CCLC actively, though separately, solicited funds to support the case. The former sent out a one-page "Dear Friend" letter. Though undated, it is clear that it was composed before the trial began. It was an amateurish effort, mimeographed and contained numerous typographical errors. Even the plaintiff's name was misspelled in both places it appeared. The actual appeal read: "Financially, we are dependent upon our contributors. This case IS going to take a great deal of money. We are asking you to participate by sending in your contribution to help us carry on the fight until we win."[45]

In contrast, the CCLC appeal was a printed brochure, much more professional in appearance. It is not clear when the material was prepared and distributed. Like the CAC, the CCLC used the *McCollum* case to solicit funds.

All persons interested in religious liberty should join now in support of the *McCollum* case. Funds are absolutely necessary. The CCLC has set out to raise $10,000 to maintain religious liberty, with separation of church and state, and to prosecute this case to a complete, fair and final decision.[46]

Chapman wrote Cromwell in late September. "I think," he said, "our Chicago forces are working together very well."[47] No mention was made of money or strategy problems. In less than a month, both were at the forefront of the friction between the CAC and the CCLC.

The first public symptom that all was not well in the plaintiff's camp appeared on October 8, just before the filing deadline. At that time, Chapman requested a delay in presenting his first brief, with October 25 as the new date. Leonard agreed, setting October 25 as the new date.[48]

Vashti wrote to her father on October 15, alerting him to the serious attorney-client problems which had developed since the trial:

> I'm very sore at Chapman. He didn't get the briefs in on time, indeed hadn't even started them. And all the time, he was busy trying to arrange speeches, radio talks etc., for himself. He is still hollering for more money, and I have taken the trouble to check up, and find that it is the consensus of opinion that the $1,100 he has been paid to date, is plenty to cover the writing of the briefs... I talked to Phil Schug, and then called Ted Raynor in Chicago, and told him to lay the law down to Chapman, and if he wouldn't get the briefs in pronto, we'd get another lawyer.[49]

Then, in a release of her frustrations, she wrote, "This case has me nuts. Everyone working at cross purposes, and it has to be my name plastered to every mistake that is made."[50]

In a second letter to her father, undated though written about the same time, Vashti again dealt with the problems she was having with Chapman:

> Chapman is concerned only with his own publicity and publicity for atheism. He wants to form a national, or at least a Chicago, freethinking group and you'd please me if you'd avoid tactfully any connection with his operations. I'd like to win this case and see similar victories all over the country. If we can get Christians to help us, I'm all for it. Why antagonize everyone and make it appear that this is an atheist movement when, in reality, it is purely a legal matter.[51]

Chapman, in a letter dated October 18,[52] wrote Cromwell and, among other things, complained of financial disagreements between the CAC and the CCLC. In his response, Cromwell had the benefit of the information contained in his daughter's letters. Denying what he knew, he tried to be a peacemaker.

> I note your reference to financial difficulties with the two organizations that [are] interested in this case of Vashti's. Please, I do not know anything about it all, and I should much rather not become involved in any of it. I do not know what it is all about, and I most deeply regret that there is or has been any misunderstanding among you all out there. This case of Vashti's is far too important to endanger by any trouble or quarrels among any of you. I wish you would do all in your power to make peace in the family and concentrate on *winning* this case.

Then in reference to Chapman's apparent interest in becoming involved in freethought activities, Cromwell cautioned:

Of course I am made happy in knowing that you are interested in organizing a Freethought Society, *But*, and it is a big *But*, I do not believe that you should be in any way involved in any such thing at this particular moment. You have pleaded your case before the court of law and before the court of public opinion that you are fighting Vashti's case on purely legalistic grounds, and that there was in no sense any contest between Atheism and Christianity. *Let it remain just that way* ... until after this case is won.

The veteran freethinker continued:

My lawyer here has just as many Atheistic desires as you, yet he has kept [them] out of the picture entirely and it has been much better for us. The public is all too quick to charge us with bigotry and intolerance—be it true or false—and we have so little opportunity to fight back and win public opinion.

Cromwell then returned to finances:

... if you feel that you have not received full payment, you should have had a better understanding at the time you took the case. And, I also feel that if you are as concerned in this case as you profess, and I believe [you], no such questions as finances should enter this case. Our lawyer won our case here for us for only $125.00 and would accept nothing more as he felt it was up to him to do his bit to assist the cause of keeping religion out of our New York state schools.

He concluded by adding his own altruistic but probably unrealistic view of the fight for freethought.

I work here in my office 8, 10 and even 16 hours a day on the cause of freethought and I have never received a dime in pay and [have] put hundreds of dollars into it. My interest in freethought is not measured by what I can get out of it financially but what I can put into it to make the mind and body of all men truly free.[53]

In the meantime, Chapman met the deadline of October 25 by filing a 59-page brief with the circuit court. He was accompanied by Ted Raynor.[54]

Chapman responded to Cromwell's letter of October 24 with one dated October 27. It has not survived although some indication of its contents can be gleaned from Cromwell's follow-up letter of November 5.[55]

In my remarks regarding compensation for legal services, I did not intend to imply that you should work for nothing or just for the love of the cause, but I did mean to convey that in movements of this kind, money is darned scarce and thus much work has to be done at a minus-profit basis.

Cromwell went on to duly register concern over Vashti's predicament:

I do keenly feel that it has been a mighty unfair and unkind thing that all this trouble has come up and Vashti had to be the go-between ... It does seem to me that you all, ... the CCLC and the CAC and Vashti and Phil Schug [should] get together and put your cards on the table and clear up your differences and then go ahead with your fight against religion in the schools.

Then Cromwell questioned Chapman about a major new development:

Our local paper had a short notice of the CCLC filing a suit with you as attorney ... What is the idea behind this suit? Is not the suit you have already started covering this whole thing? Are you planning to start a new suit and drop work on the present one?[56]

The new case Cromwell referred to was one filed in Chicago on October 26 by Ira Latimer and the CCLC, challenging the practice in that city of releasing public school children for one hour each week for religious instruction off school property.[57] Little did Cromwell suspect that the new case was being heard on the same day he dated his letter.

Also caught by surprise were Vashti and Philip Schug; she later described the new action as a "small bombshell."[58] As late as October 19, in a statement contained in its newsletter, the CCLC still appeared to be solidly behind the prosecution of the *McCollum* case. The statement read in part: "If separation of church and state is to be maintained (the fundraising efforts of the religious groups) must be countered and the case of Mrs. Vashti McCollum against the Champaign School Board must be fought through to a successful conclusion."[59]

In its newsletter of November 2, the organization's position appears to have changed. The big announcement related to the filing of the *Latimer* case; the *McCollum* case considered so important just two weeks earlier was mentioned only once and then only incidentally.[60]

Had the two Chicago groups been cooperating, the Latimer case most likely would never have been filed. Conventional wisdom would have dictated that the stronger action would be the one to be pursued. In this respect, the Chicago case lacked the issue of actual use of public school property on school time as well as the fact that no specific discrimination was alleged, merely the potential for abuse. Vashti noted later, perhaps wistfully, the difference in progress between her own case and that of *Latimer*:

It (the *Latimer* case) was not a three-ring circus. It had a brief hearing and a short record. It was heard on November 5, and on November 17 the Superior Court in Chicago ruled against them (Latimer and Chapman). They had filed five months after I had, but got their decision first.[61]

Chapman, according to Vashti, acknowledged that he and Latimer had ulterior motives for filing the Chicago case:

... he admitted (over the telephone) that they rushed through the Chicago case, so that "the Latimer Case will reach the Supreme Court first, and be for all time, the classic case which determined the separation of church and state." So it seems quite apparent that he and Latimer are much more concerned about the publicity than winning their cases, for a victory in my case would greatly have helped them to a victory in theirs.[62]

The defense had also been at work. On November 20, Franklin filed the defense brief.[63] It was delayed first by Chapman's extension, then by a printing strike in Chicago.[64] "They're (the Illinois Association for Religious Education) talking of printing 10,000 copies," Franklin said of the brief. "Maybe," he continued, "I'm the author of a best seller."[65] Four days later, Peterson and Rall, quick to exploit Chapman's defeat in Chicago, filed copies of the *Latimer* decision with Judge Leonard in Urbana.[66]

When Cromwell learned of the defeat, he wrote Chapman, expressing sorrow over the decision.[67] Eight days later, on December 2, Cromwell again wrote Chapman. In this communication, he was openly disillusioned with, and critical of, the attorney. "I am sorry you ever started the Chicago action until *after* you had cleared the case in Champaign, and I am more disturbed that you lost the case." Later in his letter, Cromwell continued:

If you [had gotten] your briefs in when you promised and the defendant's attorneys [had done] likewise, [the Champaign] decision [would have been] due ... Why did you not devote all your time and attention to the Champaign case [that] you had started and [gotten] that clear and on time and a decision received *before* you attempted another?"

And there was more to Cromwell's castigation.

Then you say [in the letter] that if you lose your Chicago case, Vashti has little or no chance to win hers. You add that your opponents produced a 95-page printed brief which is the product of some thousands of dollars. I may be dumb, but I just cannot see where any great cost in legal assistance or research is required or necessary to prepare the brief in defense of your case, and regardless of how many pages the opponents deemed necessary to put across their arguments, it still remains of no consequence to you, just so long as *you* fully and properly prepare your brief in substantiation of your claims and charges. *You* had all the law on your side; they had only the usage of illegal methods and infractions over a period of time infringing upon state and educational laws. They *had* to make their brief look important and impressive for they had little or no legal grounds to substantiate their defense.[68]

Chapman's reply was quick. In a letter dated December 4, he defended himself:

You can be absolutely sure that I am doing everything in my power mentally and financially to win Vashti's case. Not only that, but I have been crying for help so that more can be done. You can also be sure that no lawyer in the world ever took more interest in a client's case than I have in this one, or was ever more diligent or loyal.

Concerning the briefs, Chapman explained:

I never promised to write any brief at all, and suggested to the three judges that we be not asked to write [them]. Our opponents insisted upon [the] opportunity to present briefs. The three judges, desiring to make the proper decision, and wanting the same advantages that the Supreme Court will have later in-so-far as possible, did direct us to furnish briefs. Then I asked for an extension of time in which to present them, and have since asked for further extensions of time.

He then addressed the financial wrangling, clearly taking the side of the CCLC:

During the trial the CAC promised to pay for the trial, preparation, briefs and everything else. They haven't yet paid for the trial, and have paid nothing whatever for briefs. With Vashti's help, I am sure we could have had the CCLC take over the case and have financed it. We would be better off if that had been done last summer. We would have had more financial backing.

The attorney then pleaded his own financial difficulties.

You ask why I did not devote all my time and attention to the Champaign case. I have to do something else as a means of earning a living and paying overhead. I was being paid for the work I did on the Chicago (Latimer) Case, and on other cases, at least enough to meet expenses. I think if Vashti had abandoned the CAC and had almost any other organization sponsor her case, we could have obtained financial expenses for her case, too.

In closing, Chapman fired off a final shot at the CAC:

... I do suggest that you relieve your mind of worry about me, and get after the CAC. Either make them pay the bill, or take it [the case] away from them, and let someone else have it that will finance it.[69]

Thus ended this most revealing interchange of letters. (The two corresponded again two years later, but only briefly and then only to exchange copies of various briefs filed in the *McCollum* case.) It is clear that by early December, 1945, Vashti had totally lost confidence in Chapman and was determined to see him replaced. In a letter to her father, she wrote:

After the lacing out that I gave him [Chapman], he may realize that he is to be thrown off the case as soon as we get a decision in this court and so refuse to write the final brief which is due ... So last night, I called Raynor, and warned him, and he said they'd be prepared with other lawyers.[70]

Vashti was destined to make the final comment on the financial settlement: "And it ended up with the CAC assuming the bulk of the financial responsibility, some $20,000, while the other organization's (CCLC) contributions totaled $94."[71]

The problem of finances was certainly not being neglected by the proponents of the Champaign system. On October 11, the *Courier* reported that the Illinois Association for Religious Education (IARE) had obtained $3,421.68 in payments on pledges. The unpaid remainder of the pledges totaled $6,831. David Lindstrom, chairman of the finance committee, reported that a check for $2,000, the first installment of attorney's fees, had already been mailed, presumably to John Franklin. Eckert and Peterson had yet to submit a bill, but in a letter to the IARE, Peterson indicated that their fees and expenses would "probably amount to about $5,000." He went on to warn that there would be additional costs related to preparing the brief and other documents as well as the appeal to a higher court.[72]

In her book, Vashti indicates that she met in Chicago "with Chapman and Latimer and the men from the CAC ... [and] the differences were ironed out..." This occurred even before the Latimer Case was filed.[73] While relations remained strained between lawyer and client, the effort continued. During the preparation of the final brief the plaintiff wrote: "Phil Schug and I worked on the two briefs yesterday, making notes, corrections and suggestions, and today Phil is up there passing our suggestions on to Chapman and Raynor sitting in joint session."[74]

The arrangement worked sufficiently well that Chapman and Raynor managed, on December 7, to file the second and final brief on behalf of Vashti in the circuit court at Urbana.[75]

In spite of Vashti's opposition, Chapman did make speeches and even engage in a debate relating to the issues involved in the Champaign case. The latter event was staged on January 17 in Danville, just 30 miles east of Urbana. Chapman faced Danville minister Rev. J.T. Myers; the question was, "Resolved: That Religious Education Should Be Banned From Public Schools."[76] Chapman announced in advance that he believed that "Freedom of religion includes freedom from religion." He went on to preview his argument.

> Our public schools should be conducted for the welfare of the pupils rather than the churches. They should teach knowledge, not mere beliefs; and science not superstition. They should prepare children for life in this world which is a certainty, but leave them to the homes and churches to be prepared for heaven and hell or wherever they are going, if anywhere, after they die.[77]

Chapman, apparently unable to resist a dramatic gesture, added: "Rev. Myers, who does profess faith, will be asked to perform for the audience, one of the Bible miracles, one of his own choosing."[78] For some reason, Chapman did not call upon the cleric "to perform" during the debate.[79]

Later that same month, but before the circuit court decision, Chapman challenged Rev. Hollis of Champaign to a debate; the latter accepted, the date to be set for some time after the January 26 court date.[80] But the debate was never held.[81] Chapman's extracurricular activities, especially so close to home, could hardly have been welcomed by his client.

Chapter 10

More Fire and Brimstone: The Stoddard Controversy

Into the heavily charged, post trial atmosphere erupted another controversy with religion and Champaign-Urbana at its epicenter. The explosion occurred on September 30 at a Catholic mass in Joliet. Before an overflow congregation which included Archbishop Stritch of Chicago, Bishop James A. Griffin launched an attack against the president-elect of the University of Illinois, George D. Stoddard. This was the same Stoddard who, as New York State Commissioner of Education, had ruled that released time religious classes were unlawful in the public schools of that state the previous June on a petition from Arthur Cromwell.

The bishop's 45-minute sermon,[1] insofar as possible, has been reconstructed from newspaper reports. The bishop began:

> Out of the holocaust of Hiroshima ... the paralyzed world heard the voice of a strong man, sounding the warning I reecho today, and giving to mankind the prescription for a lasting peace.[2]

The "strong man" was General Douglas MacArthur. The cleric went on to quote a small portion of the general's remarks made that past summer at the Japanese surrender ceremony:

> Military alliances, balances of power, League of Nations all in turn failed ... we have had our last chance. If we do not now devise some greater and more equitable system, Armageddon will be at our door. The problem basically is theological and involves a spiritual recrudescence and improvement of human character that will synchronize with our almost matchless advance in science, art, literature, and all material and cultural developments of the past 2,000 years. It must be of the spirit if we are to save the flesh.[3]

Building upon the general's words, the bishop went on to say:

> I have tried for the past few minutes to bring into focus the crisis of civilization as it exists today. The swing back to Christ, prescribed by thinking men all over the world, will be a task worthy of Hercules. For in our very midst, we have materialistic die-hards who still cling to the

futile promises of their "brave new world" which has collapsed. Over and against the stirring words of MacArthur we hear such feeble rumings as these:

(Quoting) "Feeble in mind are the persons whose intact brains, giving the highest promise up through childhood, (as shown by insight into school subjects and other relationships) have been so systematically drugged with the vapors of dogma, superstition, and pseudo-logic as to fail at the lowest attribute levels."

(Quoting) "Manmade concepts such as devils, witches, (totems,) original sin, (divine right predestination, reincarnation, salvation-through-death-in-battle,) and divine revelation, (related to no genetic patterns, but) kept alive in an unending chain of emotionally tinged spoken and printed words, have distorted the intellectual processes of millions of persons over the centuries."[4]

The bishop then asked:

Were these words penned by a Thomas Paine or by an Ingersoll? Or were they, perhaps, issued from the Kremlin or from Berchtesgaden? No, quite to the contrary. These words appear in a book entitled, *The Meaning of Intelligence*. And the author of that book, and those words, is the man who happens to be at the present time, the president-elect of the University of Illinois, George Dinsmore Stoddard.

It would be interesting to see what would happen if Dr. Stoddard stood face-to-face with General MacArthur and told him his "intellectual processes" were distorted. As long as men like George Dinsmore Stoddard sound the keynote of modern education, our "last chance"—a return to spiritual values—will never be realized. What are you, citizens of Illinois, going to do about it?[5]

Griffin went on to voice support for the "unimpeachable plan for world peace" offered by Pope Pius XII and to warn that it would never be realized in America "until our people, particularly the youth, have become God-fearing Christians."[6] He then continued his attack:

And that means, among other things, cleaning the Augean stables of our non-sectarian universities of those godless and conscienceless educators who, for the past two decades, have been robbing the youth of this land of its rightful heritage—a belief in, and a love and service of God.

America, the America of the future, will never be able to "measure and weigh human statutes," as the Holy Father admonishes, according to the holy, unshakable rules of Divine law, until it first recognizes that there is a Divine law. Today, countless young men and girls are going down from our great universities, carrying away in their minds nothing that can compensate them for what they have lost in godless classrooms, and in the silence and emptiness of their young hearts, they must often hear a distinct echo of that bitterest of all human cries: "They have taken away our Lord ... and we know not where they have laid Him."[7]

Concluding his remarks, the bishop said:

And until the spirit of Godliness begins to permeate, not only the American scene, but the world as well, the threat of war will always be with us. Even now, the words of the Latin poet sound their timeless challenge: "The sins of thy forefathers thou shall expiate, till thou restorest the crumbling temples of the gods."[8]

(It is surprising that such lengthy and detailed reports were carried in the two Champaign-Urbana newspapers of a happening in Joliet, especially the long quotes attributed to the bishop. Either the local papers had been "tipped off" or copies of the text of the sermon had been supplied them in advance.)

Stoddard was reached by reporters the next day while he was on an inspection trip with state legislators.[9] The educator, according to the *Courier*, "expressed the opinion that perhaps the bishop had seen only isolated quotations lifted from context."[10] Stoddard was quoted as saying:

That can be done even with the Bible. Take some things out of context, and you won't like what you read. I can't believe the bishop would have made those comments if he had read the book. Actually, the book urges a return to religion and is at all times sympathetic to religion. All of the references to religion are favorable. There are definite passages that can be quoted in support of this statement.[11]

Stoddard went on to note:

While anyone may obtain the book, it is not on sale generally and may be difficult to find; it is a technical book. The book is religious; it also is scientific; it is democratic and it is liberal. It has been praised by clergymen who liked the liberal outlook and the liberal religious spirit. There are references in the book to the feudal days when men were not supposed to develop scientifically, and to medieval thinkers who opposed the development of science and that is the setting in which such references are placed. The day has long since passed when man received his knowledge of astronomy or biology from his religious dogma.[12]

In a related Associated Press report, Stoddard added:

We in the modern world should not place as much emphasis on creeds and doctrines as we do but (rather) on a living Christianity. I think we should have a return to the basic moral and ethical ideas contained in early Christianity.[13]

On October 2, two days after the bishop's sermon, Champaign-Urbana newspapers carried an amplification by Griffin of his initial attack. The *News-Gazette* appears to have printed the new pronouncement in its entirety:

The people of Illinois want to know what they're paying for. The people of Illinois have a right, and under the present circumstances a grave duty, to demand a profession of faith from George D. Stoddard, to whom they propose to pay a high salary for educating their sons and daughters at the University of Illinois.

We want to know what we're paying for; and while we're at it, we might as well find out something along the same lines about those employees of ours who hired Dr. Stoddard.

Already the president-elect of the State University has gone on record as saying that those who believe in divine revelation, original sin and hell are "feeble in mind" and that such "manmade concepts" have distorted the intellectual processes of millions of persons over the centuries. Thousands of future students who will attend the University of Illinois under Stoddard's regime [will] believe in the objective validity of these concepts.

But, according to the commissioner of education from New York, these sons and daughters of good Illinois people are feebleminded and distorted in the intellect. If he is a sincere educator he will evidently try to dispossess his charges of their "feeblemindedness and intellectual distortion;" that's what we want to find out now.

I purposely had photostatic copies made of several pages of Stoddard's *Meaning Of Intelligence* in anticipation of the haphazard charge that I had taken his words out of their context. These photostatic prints will appear in the next issue of the *Western Catholic*, diocesan news organ.

Dr. Stoddard's doubt concerning whether I had read his book is groundless, but even though I had not read *Meaning Of Intelligence* in its entirety, I would be as well qualified to condemn the author's views as he is to lampoon sacred doctrines without having read the whole Bible and Biblical commentaries.[14]

In a supporting article, "Bishop's Attack Centers On These Words By Stoddard," the *News-Gazette* quoted much of pages 33 and 34 of the president-elect's suddenly controversial book.[15] While the article included much material omitted by the bishop, it still failed to convey the basic thrust of Stoddard's book which was, as the author had described it, "a technical book."

The controversy had grown sufficiently even in just two days to prompt a statement by the president of the board of trustees, Park Livingston. He said tersely: "The whole board, faculty, alumni and general advisory committee, is satisfied that Dr. Stoddard is an outstanding Christian. That was the one point with which we were much concerned."[16]

Although Stoddard and Livingston chose to say nothing more publicly, Philip Schug was quite vocal on the matter. He announced plans to "open the fall season of the church" with a sermon entitled "The Catholic Hierarchy and Dr. Stoddard."[17] While Schug appears to have made no connection publicly between the *McCollum* case and the Stoddard controversy, his primary concerns were the same, individual religious freedom and the integrity of the public school system.

Schug also devoted the first page of his church newsletter to the Stoddard affair. Under the heading, "Copernicus, Galileo and Stoddard," the minister sought to draw parallels between the manner in which the Catholic Church had treated scientists and thinkers in the past and its attitude towards these people now. After a brief recounting of history, Schug concluded:

> Three hundred years later the Catholic hierarchy selected Dr. George Dinsmore Stoddard, president-elect of the University of Illinois, as its victim of a modernized inquisition. Dr. Stoddard is a bold man, an educator of vision, and his scientific pronouncements do not please Bishop Griffin of Springfield and Archbishop Stritch of Chicago. "A profession of faith" is demanded as the price of his job!!!
>
> Is the Inquisition to be brought to twentieth-century America? Have the freedoms of speech, press, and religion no meaning to the hierarchy? Is Dr. Stoddard to be crucified at the altar of Catholic orthodoxy?
>
> We must answer these questions. The skill of the hierarchy in operating the inquisition is not to be denied: the question is, "Is it to be allowed; are we, or are we not, free people?[18]

Schug delivered his sermon on October 7. Both the *Courier* and *News-Gazette* carried extensive reports of the crusading minister's vigorous counterattack. The sermon has been reconstructed as follows:

> The attack upon the American public school system was carried forward this past week by Bishop James A. Griffin, Roman Catholic bishop of Springfield, when he publicly censured Dr. George D. Stoddard for holding views of religion not in accord with Catholic orthodoxy.[19]

Schug indicated that he was not surprised:

> Our public schools as they now exist have been constantly under fire from the Catholic hierarchy for the past 100 years, that is, ever since the various states took an active interest in the education of [their] people. So heated has been the attack that in the fall of 1884 the Third Plenary Council of Baltimore commanded Catholic parents to send their children to parochial schools unless the proper official gave certain of them permission to do otherwise.

Schug then read the decree from *Essays On Catholic Education In The United States* by Roy J. Deferrari, published by the Catholic University of America Press.

> In 1929, after the attack on our present school system had become of sufficient importance to call for action by Pope Pius XI, we find this pope categorically declaring in his encyclical on education (of) December 31, 1929, "Education belongs preeminently to the church ... as for the scope of the church's education mission, it extends over all peoples without any limitation, according to Christ's command: 'Teach ye all nations.' Nor is there any civil power that can oppose or prevent it..." Pius XI made it exceedingly clear that no system of education that is not under the direction of the [Catholic] church is "a fit place for Catholic students."[20]

Schug then quoted Pius XI, reading from the Deferrari book.

"In order that a school may accord with the rights of the church and the Christian family and be a fit place for Catholic students, it is necessary that all of the teaching and whole organization of the school and its teachers, syllabus and textbooks in every branch be regulated by the Christian spirit under the direction and material supervision of the church, so that religion may be in very truth the foundation and crown of the youth's entire training; and this in every grade of school, not only the elementary but the intermediate and then higher institutions of learning as well."

[Thus] our University of Illinois as it is now conducted under President Willard, according to the pope, is not a fit place.[21]

After citing other Catholic authorities, Schug continued:

These instances could be multiplied over and over again. [They] show that the attack upon Dr. Stoddard is not an isolated or petty personal attack. It is a part of a picture, a part of a fabric of which this is just a thread. If it were not Dr. Stoddard, it would be some other person of importance in the educational world ... No, this is not an isolated attack upon our president-elect. It is a part of the opposition of the Catholic hierarchy to public education as now conducted. I want this to be clear, I am not saying opposition to education, but to public education as now conducted.[22]

If the hierarchy were allowed to run our public schools, censor the textbooks, supply or choose the teachers, and make them places of Catholic religious education—or, at the least, free of anything that might call into question the validity of Catholic doctrine and dogma—[their]—opposition would cease.[23]

We the people of Illinois, the people of the entire United States, must constantly make the choice between the basic freedoms ... and the comparative slavery of controlled thought and expression.[24]

[Our basic freedom] will not cease as long as our schools hold high the banner of unrestricted inquiry, the banner of scientific methods, the banner of creative thought.[25]

Schug said that it was difficult to determine from the bishop's statements whether or not the cleric actually claimed he had read Stoddard's book in its entirety. "I know I haven't," said Schug. "To really read it," he continued, "would take several weeks. It is 500 pages long and is certainly no novel." The minister then went on to address specifically the material contained in the two pages of Stoddard's book of concern to the bishop.

They come in a book that is exceedingly technical in the field of education ... It is a dissertation of a scientific nature within the field of psychology and it is no picnic to read unless you happen to be a Ph.D. in this field. They come as a part of the efforts of the author [Stoddard] to clarify his field of study. He has completed a seven-section discussion of the word "intelligence." He says, in effect ... that really intelligent behavior resists emotional blocking.[26]

Dr. Stoddard pleads, and I quote from page 33, "What is needed is science and logic, together with a forthright truth-seeking honesty." On the same page he pleads that we recognize these things for what they are and "retain them if they serve a generally recognized social purpose." The crux of the entire matter is that Bishop Griffin and the hierarchy disagree with Dr. Stoddard and millions of other Americans on the identification and proper use of these emotional blocks.[27]

Schug contended that the bishop's statement attacking "men like George Dinsmore Stoddard" represented "an attempt to arouse the masses and thus endanger the rights of one of our citizens." Referring to the demand for a "profession of faith," Schug said:

The Catholic hierarchy has always demanded professions of faith from people under their control. Galileo was forced on his knees to profess his faith ... But in our country and in the state of Illinois, we must place these demands and pressure of Bishop Griffin against the article of our state constitution on religious freedom. [Schug then read Article II, Section 3 of the Illinois Constitution of 1870 which was then in effect.] If we once allow ourselves to indulge in the sport of witch-hunting nobody is safe.[28]

Fundamentally this is a clash of two opposed philosophies of education, and we must recognize this point. The official position of the Catholic hierarchy is that the state recognize and support religion, and by religion it means the Christian religion, and of the 258 different brands of the Christian religion, it means the Catholic religion, and among the several "Catholic" religions, it means the Roman Catholic religion ... You will find this clearly stated in *Catholic Principles of Politics* by Ryan and Boland. This book is copyrighted by the hierarchy's main agency, the National Catholic Welfare Conference.[29]

All education which in any way affects the people over whom the hierarchy has charge should be either innocuous or carefully controlled. Contrasted to that is the American public school where academic freedom, critical inquiry and constructive thought is the ideal. However imperfectly realized, that is the ideal. There lies the clash. It is not a matter of personalities, but of basic philosophies.[30]

I am not here to defend Dr. Stoddard personally. I am here to bare the basic difficulty and challenge us to see clearly and act wisely in order to protect not only Dr. Stoddard's rights, but our own.[31]

The next day, the diocesan office in Springfield responded to Schug's sermon. It took the form of a statement released to the Associated Press.

In the direct issue involving Dr. Stoddard, his Urbana coreligionist has not only missed the ball, but he's wound up in the wrong ball park. The point at issue is Dr. Stoddard's disrespect for the beliefs of millions of

Protestants, Catholics and Jews as contained in his treatise, *Meaning of Intelligence.*

The red herring spawned today by the Unitarian minister in Urbana doesn't merit an answer from Bishop Griffin, who is concerned at present with an entirely different matter, namely Dr. George D. Stoddard's public admission that he considers people who believe in some of Christianity's fundamental doctrines "feeble in mind" and intellectually distorted. The allegation (by Schug) that the American hierarchy is opposed to the existing public school system is news to this office.[32]

While others were reluctant to relate the Stoddard affair with the *McCollum* case, the Bloomington *Pantagraph* was not. On October 3 it published the following editorial which identified the attacks by Bishop Griffin as an outgrowth of the religious education suit.

The stage is being set for some witch burning at the University of Illinois. What could and should have been a friendly suit to test the legality of teaching religion to pupils who have been released from public school classes for the purpose has developed into a fight as to what constitutes religion. Those who brought the suit did their full share of beclouding the issue.

[The] latest outgrowth is the criticism of George D. Stoddard, President-elect of the U of I, by Bishop James A. Griffin of Springfield. The question now seems to be not religion but the degree and brand of religion a man has.

It is exactly that issue that has kept religion out of the schools for so many years in this country. So many who profess to favor the teaching of religion in schools, when pinned down, want their own creeds and dogmas taught to the exclusion of others. Such a view makes those who are keenly aware of the need of basic morals and conscience still reluctant to permit the teaching of religion in schools. They fear it won't be religion in its broadest sense.[33]

Less than two weeks later, the *Pantagraph* carried a response from the bishop. "You made," he began, "an excellent point in [your] editorial in stating that one of the stumbling blocks to the teaching of religion in the schools is the possibility that some overzealous advocates of this program 'want their own creeds and dogmas taught to the exclusion of others'." He said he did not know "whether or not this was the trouble in the so-called 'Urbana Case,' ... since I haven't really been following it too closely." His response continued:

The reason for my lack of concentration on (the *McCollum*) case is that this is a controversy carried on, as I understand it, by the Protestant ministers of the community. If any Catholic clergymen are prominent in the case, they are merely assisting the ministerial group. It is chiefly a Protestant affair. It's not my point in this letter to argue the relative merits of the case, but merely to call to your attention that my attitude toward Stoddard has been formed for almost a year now, and that I was surprised to read that you considered it to be the "latest outgrowth of the 'Urbana Case'."

I liked your editorial. I was, however, honestly unable to see any connection between the teaching of religion in the public schools of Urbana and the agnosticism of the president-elect of Illinois University. I certainly intended no connection, since I have actually nothing to do with the former, and the latter is a matter of grave concern to me, as it should be to every citizen of the state.

It is, I realize now, unfortunate that these separate controversies happen to be centered in Urbana. Perhaps that's what suggested to you that they were correlated. I assure you, very honestly and sincerely, that I had been preparing this attack on Stoddard many months before the Urbana case ever broke.[34]

Bishop Griffin continued his offensive by devoting much of the October issue of the diocesan newspaper, the *Western Catholic* edition of *Our Sunday Visitor*, to the Stoddard matter. The lead article began with an analogy between an ancient Greek myth and the bishop's view of the situation at the University of Illinois.

Once upon a time, according to the story, there was a beautiful casket, a gorgeous chest, a gift of the Gods, that no one was supposed to open. One day, however, a little girl named Pandora pried the lid off this box. Within it was revealed a horde of evil things.

And once upon a time, there was a beautiful state university, its ivy-bound towers and million dollar buildings, its landscaped quadrangles and gabled rooftops, making it the envy of other state universities. One day, however, on September 30, 1945, to be exact, someone pried the lid off this modern Pandora's box. What was found therein started a nationwide flare-up. It was discovered that this beautiful state university contained some reprehensible business behind its classic facades. The people of the state, all of a sudden, began wondering how long this sort of business had been going on.[35]

There followed, in chronological order, the chain of events leading to the bishop's demand for a "profession of faith," which was then reprinted. Also reprinted were photostatic copies of the now familiar pages 33 and 34 of Stoddard's book, with the offending sentences marked with black rings and the Japanese surrender proclamation delivered by General MacArthur.[36] The unsigned article continued:

Unfortunately, for the great and hitherto respected university at Urbana, shrewd and public-minded citizens of the state began to do a little investigating. How was it possible that the trustees had selected a candidate like Stoddard to head the state university? The whole matter of his selection had been done with a minimum—if not an entire lack—of publicity. But the play was too involved. Someone fumbled.[37]

George D. Stoddard, as president of the University of Illinois, will be the foremost educator in the State of Illinois. Therefore, if he is sincere and if he adheres to his conscientious beliefs, he will be expected to do all in his power to "correct" what he considers to be intellectual distortions in those placed under his charge.[38]

In other words, if consistency prevails, he is faced with the unwholesome prospect of dispossessing thousands of Illinois boys and girls of their deep faith and intellectual conviction in the fundamental religious doctrines handed down to them, as a rich heritage, by their good parents. For those are the things which have drugged their minds, according to Dr. Stoddard.[39]

The citizens of Illinois, now that the tocsin has been sounded, are gravely concerned over the future of their state university. It's not entirely due to the fact that they face the prospect of paying an educator of Stoddard's mentality to teach their sons and daughters, but it's also the disturbing realization that they have elected a board of trustees for their university that condones this sort of mentality.[40]

[The "profession of faith" called for] is not of such a nature that either Stoddard or the trustees are expected to announce their particular creedal affiliations, but merely that the president-elect will give to the parents of Illinois the solemn assurance that he will, in every way, respect the religious beliefs of their children.[41] (In order to do this, Dr. Stoddard) will be constrained to repudiate the statements referred to by the bishop ... The board of trustees must likewise guarantee that this pledge, if forthcoming from Stoddard, will be carried out.[42]

In other words, no one cares whether Stoddard is a Protestant or a Jew or a Catholic. That's his personal concern and anyone who attempts to investigate his particular religious denomination is violating the standards of religious freedom, so sacred in the laws of this country.[43]

Apparently, the board of trustees at the University of Illinois slipped up a bit on this in making Stoddard's Christianity a point of much concern in the selection. What if Stoddard wasn't a Christian? Is that any reason why he shouldn't be president of the University of Illinois? That's one for Park Livingston to mull over in his spare time.[44]

Elsewhere in the edition, there was a response to Stoddard and Schug that possibly the bishop had not read the book in question. The statement was clear and unequivocal.

... not only had he [Griffin] read the book, but that he had seen to it several of his friends in the education field had read it as well. To Dr. Stoddard's doubt we might comment, "one need not eat the whole egg to know it is rotten."[45]

Resolving the Stoddard affair appears to have been the major concern of the University Board of Trustees at its regular meeting on October 18. Board president Livingston read the following telegram from the president-elect.

On the occasion of your October Board Meeting I feel that you should
have a statement from me concerning the recent controversy as President of the University of Illinois. My fixed policy will be to uphold our
democratic institutions in which is embedded the right to religious freedom. The University of Illinois belongs to the people of Illinois who erected
it and who support it. It must be administered in the light of their social
ideals and principles. Freedom of religion involves respect for the religious beliefs of the citizens of Illinois. While adhering firmly to my own
personal convictions I shall administer the University within the limits of
academic freedom, and I shall respect and endeavor to make respected
the religious beliefs of all students. In these critical times educators
recognize the responsibility of stressing the moral values which religion
inculcates and supports. In twenty years of professional life I have had no
interest in the private beliefs of any person, and I have not known, save
incidentally, the church affiliation of any student, colleague, or associate. I will follow the same policy at the University of Illinois.[46]

Trustee Chester R. Davis then announced that the Board's Committee on General Policy (which had met privately earlier in the day) had drafted a statement of
policy with respect to the Stoddard situation and recommended it to the full board.[47]
The statement, which was unanimously adopted by the board, read as follows.

The Board of Trustees is committed to the principle, which it now reiter-
ates and clarifies, that every student of the University of Illinois and each
member of its faculty and administrative staff is entitled to freedom of
religious belief. Included in that principle must be the practice that no
member of the faculty, or any administrator of the University, may do
anything by word or act to influence, change, or criticize the faith or
religious conviction of any student.

Freedom of opinion and religious faith are fundamental to American
life. The employment of any member of the faculty or any administrator
has attached to it the condition that untrammeled freedom of faith and
opinion will be respected and observed. Any member of the faculty of the
institution is entitled to entertain such beliefs, disbeliefs, or opinions as
his conscience may dictate.

Dr. George D. Stoddard was employed on the basis of a distinguished
record as an educator. He is now the President of the University of the
State of New York, and Commissioner of Education of that State, and, as
such, the head of the educational system of that State. His educational
qualifications are of the highest.

On thorough inquiry, the Board of Trustees of the University of Illinois ascertained that Dr. George D. Stoddard is in complete harmony
with and fully committed to our firmly established basic principle ever to
maintain this great University and its affiliates free from any and every
religious controversy and prejudice. We are assured by Dr. Stoddard that
in his twenty years of professional life as an educator he has never made
inquiry into the church affiliation or beliefs of any student, colleague, or

associate, and that he will demand strict adherence to this policy as President of the University of Illinois.[40]

Griffin was quick to accept both the sentiments expressed by Stoddard in his telegram and the policy declaration of the Board of Trustees. The bishop's statement was short and conciliatory:

Dr. Stoddard has graciously promised without qualification to respect and to make respected the religious beliefs of all students at the University of Illinois. In this statement released by the University's Board of Trustees, Dr. Stoddard has cleared the atmosphere. The sincere fulfillment of this pledge will automatically involve an unequivocal reversal on Doctor Stoddard's part from some of the views expressed in *Meaning of Intelligence* and the people now have every reason to expect that their religious beliefs will be accorded fitting respect during Doctor Stoddard's tenure of office as president of their state university.

The Board of Trustees of the University of Illinois has also clarified its policy. Its statement was a wholesome guarantee of the fundamental democratic principle of religious freedom. On the strength of today's statement from the board, the citizens of Illinois are forewarned that any professor who so much as dares 'to do anything by word or act to influence, change or criticize the faith or religious conviction of any student' violates the principles of the University.

This particular commitment will come as a definite reassurance to the students of the various branches of philosophy, history, sociology, and kindred subjects. My request for a profession of faith from Doctor Stoddard and the Board of Trustees has been convincingly granted [49]

The bishop failed in his demand that Stoddard repudiate those statements in the *Meaning Of Intelligence* to which he had taken exception, if indeed that was all he had sought to achieve. Griffin was able to obtain from the president-elect and the board only an affirmation that they accepted and would adhere to the principle of religious freedom. That, in itself, seems hardly to have been worth the bishop's effort.

On the other hand, there is the possibility that the attack was designed to attain a much larger objective—that of Stoddard's voluntary resignation or a withdrawal of his appointment by the board. Then there is the question of whether the bishop was acting under the direction or with the approval of higher authority. The presence of Archbishop Stritch would strongly support this speculation. It is also speculative as to whether or not the attack was prompted by the connection Stoddard had with the *McCollum* case—his ruling in favor of Arthur Cromwell's petition against released time religious education in the public schools of New York some four months earlier. Whatever the real motivations were, the bishop was either personally content or instructed by higher authority to declare victory and let the matter drop.

Griffin's earlier statement to the *Pantagraph* did contain an important and correct observation—that the leadership in support of the religious classes in

Champaign came primarily from the Protestant clergy, not the Catholic. Of equal importance was the fact that no Protestant support developed for his crusade against Stoddard, in spite of the fact that Stoddard's controversial statements could have been easily construed as critical of Protestant theology. Even his Catholic coreligionists publicly stayed away from the fray, although this could have been due to a desire not be embroiled unless success seemed probable.

Shortly after the war with Japan had ended, General MacArthur requested that the War Department send a commission of educators to study and recommend reforms in the Japanese educational system. As irony would have it, Stoddard was not only named to the commission, he was appointed to head it. He met the general on three occasions, all official. It is virtually certain that the two never exchanged views on religion or discussed Bishop Griffin's attack.[50]

In his autobiography, Stoddard failed to mention the Griffin controversy although he mentioned others that occurred during his tenure at the University of Illinois. He did note that certain portions of his book the *Meaning Of Intelligence*—and those which gave offense to Bishop Griffin are mentioned specifically—were the subject of criticism. Stoddard blamed "a journalist of shady reputation" for taking the material "out of context, thus initiating a denunciation of the author as godless, atheistic, communistic."[51]

Chapter 11

The First Decision

On decision day, January 26, 1946, "less than 100 were in the courtroom throughout the approximately two hours required for the reading of the decision."[1] Vashti McCollum and Philip Schug sat in the audience along with local ministers, members of the CCRE, the school superintendents of both Champaign and Urbana and David Lindstrom.[2] The plaintiff recalled: "... before the reading began, Phil was far more confident than I. The length of time it had taken to prepare the decision had only added to my doubts."[3]

Many years later, Schug spoke for himself:

My most vivid memory of the *McCollum* suit is ... the shock that I felt when the decision of the three circuit court judges was read. I was so certain of the legal and logical necessity to rule that the released time program was unconstitutional that I saw no way that three judges could reach a different decision. Yet they did—as smoothly and as easily as if the issue had never been raised. With all of the majesty that they could muster they denied the relief we sought...[4]

Early on in the reading of the decision it was clear that the "findings of fact" were predominantly in favor of the board of education and the intervenors. The decision stated:

What it all amounts to is that the pupils who take religious education use a thirty-minute study period which otherwise would have been devoted to study for recitation in their regular lessons; that on this released time they study religious education; while those who do not take religious education simply have a thirty-minute study period while waiting for the pupils in religious education classes to rejoin them for the regular secular studies.[5]

The evidence does not sustain relator's charge that the interest and attention of such pupils is wrongly diverted from their regular secular and lawful studies in the schools, but on the contrary, the evidence shows that the courses in religious education are similar to the extracurricular activities, such as music and art, which are taken with the parents' permission in so many of our public schools today.[6]

In her book, Vashti took exception:

They weren't similar at all. The students didn't have to get permission from home to study music and art. They weren't divided into labeled groups. They weren't required to move and change around. They were all in the room and the music or art teacher arrived and taught the class intact.[7]

Access to the schools was not discriminatory according to the court:

The defendant school district has been willing to grant its permission for the similar, free and equal use of rooms school buildings when not in use for school purposes, to any faith or group which desires to make use of the school belonging to the defendant, for instruction in the tenets or belief or unbelief of such other faith or group.[8]

Vasti again took exception: "If the school buildings are not in use for school purposes at nine thirty and ten o'clock in the morning, when are they in use?"[9]

The court reviewed the procedures by which other groups would be allowed access to the schools and concluded that: "An honest attempt" had been made "to permit religious instruction to be given by qualified outside teachers of any sect to people of their own faith."[10]

Concerning sectarian differences, the court did conclude that the evidence proved their existence in the Champaign program.

The Jewish classes of course would deny the divinity of Jesus Christ. The teaching in the Catholic classes of course explains to Catholic pupils the teaching of the Catholic religion and are not shared by other students who are Protestants or Jews. The teachings in the Protestant classes would undoubtedly, from the evidence, teach some doctrines which would not be accepted by the other two religions. Likewise it is true that the teaching of Protestant, Catholic and Jewish teachers in these courses would all be in conflict with the teachings of Atheists as those beliefs were testified about by the relator and her father, Mr. Cromwell. They would probably be in conflict with that branch of the Unitarian Church represented by Rev. Philip Schug.[11]

Chapman should have taken some comfort in this finding; he had made it a fundamental element of his case to prove that the classes were sectarian.

As to the plaintiff's contention that James Terry had been ostracized because of his non-participation in the religious classes, the court found: "The evidence is undisputed that James Terry McCollum had difficulties with the other students in his school, but there is no evidence except his own, that his want of religion had anything to do with these difficulties."[12]

The court went on to say: "... his difficulties were due to his own personality problems, entirely disconnected from any question of religion. On the witness stand he was plainly nervous and excitable."[13]

Vashti rejoined:

Perhaps Jim did seem "nervous and excitable" on the witness stand. If so, I didn't notice it. He was on the stand for four hours, and in that time he swiveled around in his chair frequently, but I don't know what ten-year-old wouldn't have. He answered the questions promptly and unhesitatingly, which to my mind would be sign of intelligence and quick thinking rather than nervousness and an inability to adjust.[14]

The court concluded its findings of fact by holding "that no public funds have been directly appropriated by the defendant for private use." The judges did acknowledge that "... to some slight extent the defendant has indirectly appropriated public funds for the use of these [religious] classes, by the furnishing of rooms in public service, light, heat, janitor service, and so forth ..."[15]

As to the law of the case, two-thirds of the opinion dealt with a discussion of the constitutional questions raised. With respect to the federal constitution, the case most heavily relied upon by Chapman was *West Virginia vs Barnette*.[16]

There, a state statute required public school students to salute the American Flag. The circuit court held that, not-withstanding the fact that the case was brought by a religious sect, the Jehovah's Witnesses, it "was not concerned at all with the question of whether the State or Nation was establishing religion." The conclusion of the court was:

It may therefore be said that so far as Federal constitutional provisions are concerned, and conceding that they are binding upon the State of Illinois, and on the defendant school board, there is nothing in any expression of the Federal Supreme Court that remotely indicates there is any constitutional objection to the Champaign system of religious education.[17]

The circuit court panel, in considering the federal and state constitutional language on the church-state question, believed "that one covers the same ground as the other; that if anything our own State Constitution is more specifically stringent than the Federal."[18] It was also the panel's opinion that, as to the state constitution, the relator rests her entire case for all practical purposes on the case of *People ex rel. Ring vs Board of Education*.[19] (Chapman was convinced that all he had to do was illustrate that the classes were sectarian and the *Ring* case would dictate a decision in favor of his client.)

In the beginning of its discussion of the *Ring* case, the court paraphrased an observation made by John Franklin in his advisory opinion to the board of education the previous June. The panel wrote: "However, as authority for a decision on the facts in the case at bar, it is peculiar that the *Ring* case is not mentioned in any of the later decisions by the Supreme Court of Illinois construing religious freedom clauses of our Constitution."[20]

The opinion went on to state:

Then, too, the language in the later opinions (of the Illinois Supreme Court) would tend to narrow and circumscribe what was said in the *Ring* Case. The authority of the *Ring* Case is weakened by the fact that it goes farther than any other case in the United States in its language.[21]

It was acknowledged by the three judges that:

Were the *Ring* Case presented to us as a matter of first impression we would have arrived at the same conclusion as did our Supreme Court, for under the compulsion executed by the public school teachers in that case on Catholic pupils, we would agree that their constitutional rights were violated.[22]

But the court ruled:

The fact remains, however, that James Terry McCollum was not required to take the religious education courses and he was sent away from the room where the exercises were going on, so there could be no claim that any actual compulsion was used against him.[23]

The opinion went on to read:

In the *Ring* Case there was a combination of prayer, Bible reading, and the singing of hymns. In the cases from other states which we have examined there is almost always a similar combination, plus the fact that an earnest sincere minority of religious people, usually Catholics or Jews, were compelled to join in religious services that were abhorrent to them. In the case at bar no prayers were offered in any of the religious classes, and no hymns were sung. The Bible was used as a textbook and outlines and other reading material founded on the Bible were taught.[24]

Thus, the court held: "Believing as we do that no constitutional or statutory rights of the relator and her son ... have been violated by the Champaign system of religious education as it is conducted, according to the testimony in this record, the petition for mandamus will be denied."[25]

Before going to court, both her husband and Schug had urged Vashti to prepare two statements, one in case she won, the other if she lost. She wrote: "I tried to do so but couldn't get down to it, so while the judges were reading, I wrote my statement and had it all ready. I wrote just one; I knew which way it [the decision] was going."[26]

She handed what the *News-Gazette* described as "a hurriedly written statement" to a reporter on the way out, presumably for all members of the press to share.[27] The most complete report of that statement was carried in the *Courier* report of the following day. The plaintiff wrote:

It certainly is a blow to the guarantee of personal freedom of which we all have been proud. [The decision] tends to limit the freedom of religion to the mere choice between several of the denominations and aggressive sects and it makes the separation of church and state little more than an empty phrase. Fortunately for the freedom of all the people, this decision need not be final. We shall certainly take an appeal.[28]

To a reporter who asked her if she was disappointed, she responded: "Disappointed? I wouldn't have brought this case if I hadn't wanted to win."[29] She and

Schug paused briefly for a photographer; both even managed to smile in spite of the defeat.[30]

Chapman did not appear to be as disappointed as was his client. He said that he was prepared for such a decision but went on to say:

> I don't feel this is just my case. It is for the people of Illinois. As far as I am concerned, however, the trial went very well, except for the final decision, which is upside down. But the trial court did permit us to make what I think is a good record for appeal, so that the Supreme Court may have an opportunity to reverse the decision. And for this, the three trial judges honestly deserve our gratitude.[31]

Franklin apparently had less to say. Concerning the religious education program, which he described as being "to some extent experimental," it "has now received the stamp of approval of the law and has established a standard by which other fair-minded people may be guided in setting up similar programs."[32] He was also quoted as saying: "The cause of religious tolerance and freedom has been greatly advanced by the decision."[33]

While Chapman was reported as saying he would "appeal to the Illinois Supreme Court as quickly as possible," his association with the case was terminal. It was left to Ted Raynor to speak officially for the plaintiff as well as the Chicago Action Council.

> We feel that the court's decision was indecisive and indefinite as to the fundamental issue which was involved in the case, namely the maintenance of the tradition of separation of church and state. The court based its opinion on the voluntary procedure of the religious program and thereby did not decide the issue to the constitutional aspects of separation of church and state. Consequently, we are taking a direct appeal to the Illinois Supreme Court to decide the issue.[34]

As might be expected, the decision stimulated additional editorial comment. The *Chicago Tribune*, previously silent on the *McCollum* case, took the occasion to express its opinion on the issues involved:

> A three judge panel at Urbana has dismissed a suit seeking to stop the operation of a voluntary plan of religious education by the public schools of Champaign. It is possible that the verdict of the court can be explained in some part by the disreputable character of some of the people connected with the attack on the program. At any rate the program itself is not sound public policy.
>
> The plaintiff made her petition for mandamus a vehicle for speeches on atheism which had about the same intellectual and logical content as the thunderings of an Arkansas Bible slapper.
>
> The action was promoted by the CCLC, which some time ago lost such respectable members at it had and became an outright and shameless servant of the Communist party. The temptation to rebuke such an aggregation must have been considerable.

One very sound objection to such a program is that it is unlikely to accomplish, to any large extent, the good things expected of it. Religious education is peculiarly a private thing, the function of the home and the church. If parents and ministers, priests and rabbis can't carry out that function successfully, it is hardly likely that better results will be accomplished by shifting the burden to the public school system. The schools already are being asked to do too many things that ought to be done in the home.

The doctrine of the separation of church and state, like the guarantee of religious freedom, was incorporated in our constitution partly to protect the church against the encroachment by the state. Time has demonstrated the wisdom of the constitution's precautions. In a time when government is seeking more and more to encroach on every aspect of the citizen's life, religious congregations of whatever denomination should take warning.

If they start yielding to governmental institutions—even local institutions over which they have the most effective control—the functions which traditionally have been performed by the churches and by their members in their homes, they are yielding to just that extent a part of their religious freedom. And religious freedom is not easily divisible. Religion is either free or not free, and if government has a finger in it, it's not free.[35]

The *Sun* continued in its support of the plaintiff. Its editorial read:

The provocative issue raised by the suit to halt the teaching of religion in the Champaign public schools is still unsettled. The basis of the suit was a test of the constitutional guarantees of the separation of church and state. The ruling of the three-judge court, upholding religious teaching in public schools on a voluntary basis, has failed to come to grips with this issue.

Although the classes are not "compulsory," social pressures can exert compulsion similar to law. In addition, the court skimmed over the fact that the injection of such instruction inevitably results in an undemocratic division of schoolmates as Protestants, Catholics, Jews and "non-believers."

"The doctrine of separation of church and state," [the court held] "does not mean that there is any conflict between religion and the state." This was not the question. No one has stated there was such a conflict. Religion has a vital place in churches, Sunday schools and religious homes; religious freedom is guaranteed by the Constitution. The question is—does it have a place in the public schools? It is good that the issue is to be carried to the Illinois Supreme Court.[36]

The Toledo, Ohio, *Blade* saw the matter differently:

The decision of a Circuit Court refusing to ban non-sectarian classes in religious education from the public schools of Champaign, Ill., is a reminder that the majority has some rights which need not always be set aside for the benefit of the individual.

Apparently the only one bothered by the religious instruction was the wife of a University of Illinois professor who takes her "rationalism or atheism" very seriously. She complained that time was lost from regular school subjects because of these other [religion] classes; she complained that her young son was embarrassed by being the only child in the fifth grade who didn't attend them. Thus, without exactly putting it that way, she petitioned the court to require all the other boys and girls to get in step with her son.

In turning down that rather large order, the court held that none of the constitutional or statutory rights of the mother have been violated. We are not sure the same thing holds true for her son. It's pretty tough on a 10-year old to be sent into the world to battle society all alone in behalf of his mother's fanaticism. We thought that form of religious persecution had gone out with the Puritans.[37]

Feelings concerning the decision were strong. Basic questions remained unanswered. For example, were the classes, as Chapman maintained, sectarian? Was there a usurpation of public school facilities for religious purposes? Was there compulsion for students to participate? Did the program favor some denominations over others? Did the religious classes sort students out according to religion? Were the classes unconstitutional?

Vashti thought the answer to all was "yes," and was determined upon an appeal though she as well as the CAC were convinced that there had to be a fundamental change in strategy. Likewise, the Champaign Board of Education and the intervenors were committed to defend the decision to the Illinois Supreme Court— and beyond.

Chapter 12

Round Two: The First Appeal

Before, during and after the trial, strategy was a source of continuing discussion in the McCollum camp. The plaintiff later reflected:

> During the trial we received many comments and much unsolicited advice, most of it criticism from well-meaning friends. The friendly criticism did much to undermine my shaky morale. "You should never have had all that atheism in the case," they would tell me. "You never should have brought your father's pamphlet into it..."[1]

Schug had been sensitive to the latter criticism and offered a justification to the readers of the church newsletter, a justification even before the trial had begun:

> It is ...interesting to note that almost all the press releases take only a few words from the 22-page petition and concentrate almost entirely on a pamphlet written by Mrs. McCollum's father, a pamphlet that was filed with the petition to avoid any possibility that the defense might successfully argue that the views expressed in the pages of the petition were not held by others and to make unnecessary any greater elaboration of Mrs. McCollum's own position on religious ideas. The petition, after all, is long enough.[2]

The liberal minister felt called upon to again deal with the issue after the trial in his October newsletter:

> Many people have asked about the way the recent religious education trial was handled. Why was it brought by an atheist? Why all this bother about Santa Claus? Why the scrutinizing of personal beliefs? And many other questions of similar nature.
>
> The answers are very simple. Illinois state law and the Illinois Constitution, to begin with, say nothing about teaching or not teaching religion in public schools or any other place. They do, however, have much to say about sectarian religion. It is sectarian religion that can not be aided or supported by state agencies, including school boards. It was necessary, therefore, to prove conclusively that we were dealing with a

matter of teaching sectarian religion in the public schools during school hours. This was done, and it was this part of the trial that made the headlines day after day. If the attorneys for the school board had admitted that sectarian religion was being taught, most of the trial would have been unnecessary.

Concerning the introduction of atheism, Schug wrote:

He (Chapman) became convinced that the case would get a better hearing if the petitioner were not an adherent of any recognized faith. Several similar actions had been compromised by judges because it was a matter of some Baptist not liking what some Methodist teacher taught, for example. Wanting a thorough constitutional test he asked Mrs. McCollum if her rationalistic position could be called "atheism." She did not think it could, but she did agree that it might be said to include atheism ... That was the way the petition was written, and to expand this term "Rationalism including atheism"—as it is used in the petition—a pamphlet written by Mrs. McCollum's father was appended as an exhibit.[3]

Nevertheless, Vashti needed no convincing that serous mistakes had been made in both the pleadings and at the trial. All this was aggravated to the breaking point by the disagreements over money and the filing of the *Chicago* case by Chapman in behalf of Ira Latimer and the CCLC. Thus, even before the circuit court decision in her own case, the decision had been made to replace Chapman. The main reason a change was not made earlier was that a change during the critical time immediately following the trial would have broadcast the dissension which, in all probability, would have done more harm than good.[4]

Soon after the circuit court decision, Vashti and Schug met with George Washington Goble of the University of Illinois College of Law, seeking advice with respect to Chapman's replacement.[5] Goble asked for a few days to consider the situation and discuss the matter with a colleague. Shortly thereafter, he provided her with a list of possibilities. As Vashti recalled, all the lawyers recommended were "capable and highly respected." All but one, however, was associated with large Chicago law firms and that meant expensive.[6]

The exception was Walter F. Dodd. Though he practiced in Chicago, Dodd was elderly and worked by himself. He was semi-retired, and concentrated on cases that appealed to him for their legal and scholarly interest rather than for remuneration.[7] He was Vashti's first choice, but as she recalled, "If we couldn't have persuaded Dodd to take the case, I suppose we would have agreed to take a lesser man at a higher fee, because we were determined to continue the case."[8]

Dodd was a man of distinguished background. His vita included authorship of *Modern Constitutions*, a two-volume work published in 1909, along with other works on constitutional law and state government. During the years 1908-1915 he was a professor of political science at the University of Illinois, leaving there for the University of Chicago; he served later at Yale from 1927 to 1930.[9]

When Vashti suggested his name to Ted Raynor the latter responded "Why, that name sounds like a prof I had at college, but he doesn't practice law."[10] Raynor was both correct and incorrect. By chance, Dodd's office was right across the street from Raynor's. Vashti recalled:

> It was a small, unpretentious office, and Dodd was a small, unpreten-tious-looking man. White-haired and somewhat shriveled, Dodd (had) a brilliant mind. He (had) a tendency to stutter and stammer in a somewhat crackly voice ... Dodd was interested in the case and said he'd been following it in the papers and hadn't approved of the way it had been fought. It was difficult to decide to enter a case that had been so involved, he said frankly, and he'd "have to do some thinking about it."[11]

Dodd's answer was in the affirmative. Afterwards, Vashti reflected upon the importance of that decision. "His acceptance marked more or less of a turning point in the case, and from then on our legal associations were comparatively free from friction."[12]

Vashti and Schug traveled to Chicago to inform Chapman of his replacement. "We parted amicably," she recalled.[13] It would be difficult to believe that Chapman was surprised. In a terse statement, he said: "Mrs. McCollum has hired another lawyer, Walter F. Dodd, to direct her appeal; Dodd is a fine lawyer. I am more interested right now in the *Latimer* case—if we win that one it will knock the bottom out of the Champaign case."[14]

Since the *Latimer* case was ahead of the *McCollum* case in the judicial process, coupled with the similarity of the issues, Chapman probably had good reason for feeling that the former had become the more important of the two actions.

News of Chapman's replacement broke in Champaign-Urbana on March 19, 1946. Vashti declined comment on the report, but the *Courier* article did note: "... she had indicated in off-the-record discussion immediately after the decision in Champaign County Circuit Court...that the handling of the case by ... Chapman ... was contrary to her desires."[15]

The *News-Gazette*, on the following day, did carry a brief statement from Vashti that left little public doubt why the change was made: "[Chapman] didn't present the case the way I would liked to have had it tried. The trial got off into side tracks that were beside the point."[16]

She indicated further to the reporter that the connection with Ira Latimer and the CCLC had been severed. Attorney Dodd was also contacted for comment and he left no doubt that a fundamental change in approach was in the offing: "The case will be presented to the (Illinois) Supreme Court on legal issues alone, purely independent of what individuals might believe or not believe. There will be no issue of atheism or anything of that sort."[17]

Raynor, also quoted in the report, agreed with Dodd. He termed the "atheism versus religion" issue as "surplusage which had no bearing on case." He contin-ued: "So far as the legal issues are concerned, the plaintiff could have been a devout Catholic." Raynor indicated that he would remain connected with the case.[18]

John Franklin was quick to respond to the effort by the plaintiff's new attor-ney, as well as by Raynor, to disassociate the case from its anti-religious overtones. "We do not intend," he said, "to let Mr. Dodd whitewash the facts just because he is a new face in the case; we will insist that the case be tried in the Supreme Court on the evidence heard in the Circuit Court and on the law as it applies to that evidence."[19]

One day preceding the announcement of Dodd's association with the *McCollum* case, Judge Leonard suffered a heart attack while attending church; it was reported to be his second that spring. The first attack was reported to have occurred while Leonard was in Chicago "attending conferences on the McCollum religious suit..."[20]

Chapman had argued the *Latimer* case before the Illinois Supreme Court on March 21.[21] Dodd was particularly anxious to get the *McCollum* case before the court during the May term.[22] By so doing, the McCollum forces hoped that the Supreme Court would hold its decision in the *Latimer* case and consider it together with the Champaign case.[23] Franklin, according to a newspaper account, "said he and his Chicago associates ... have assured Dodd they also are eager to get a Supreme Court decision as soon as possible and that there will be no delaying tactics on their part."[24]

It was an ambitious undertaking. The record in the Champaign case was long and involved. To hurry the effort along, Champaign attorney John A. Appleman was engaged to make necessary appearances in the local court and to do whatever else related to the case that required legal attention in Champaign County. Announcing his association with the case, Appleman issued a statement that raised several new facets:

> I was asked originally to associate with Landon Chapman in the handling of the *McCollum* Case prior to the filing of the suit. Upon reading the complaint, I disagreed violently with his attacks on Christianity and his propounding of atheism and I asked him to delete four pages from his complaint and to communicate my requests to his principals. Upon his refusal to change his pleadings I declined to handle the case.
>
> Thereafter, during the progress of the trial, Mr. Chapman's principals requested me to enter the case, stating that he [Chapman] had failed to communicate my demands to them and expressing a wish to discharge him at that state of the proceedings.
>
> I refused to take the matter on at that time, feeling that the case had degenerated into a contest of religion versus atheism, instead of the legal issue of the validity of using public schools for the teaching of religious subjects.
>
> I was again contacted with reference to handling of the appeal, which I declined. Thereafter, Professor Dodd, whom I have known for many years and for whom I have the greatest respect and liking, asked that I handle the mechanical details of court procedure in this county to save him from making trips to this area.
>
> As an accommodation to my old friend, I have consented to act as water boy for these purposes, but the appeal will be handled by Professor Dodd.[25]

Appleman's statement was neither authorized nor cleared with Vashti. In her view, the statement was "cowardly" and she was "furious" with Appleman. As to the substance of the statement, Vashti had a vague recollection of Chapman talking with Appleman before the suit was filed, but she insists the latter was not asked by her to step in during the trial and was never considered as Chapman's replacement for the appeal.[26] Like so many other happenings in her long struggle, it was easier to let the matter pass than attempt a rectification.

The restructuring of her forces did not put an end to Vashti's problems. There had been a three-week delay in court reporter Louis Temple's preparation of the trial transcript from his notes.[27] Concerned about the deadline for the May term of the Supreme Court, Vashti called Judge Leonard concerning the transcript; this prompted action and the record began to arrive right away. She recalled:

> ... as soon as the parts of the record were finished, I would take it volume
> by volume to Chicago ... we dared not trust our only [copies] to the mails.
> At the time I was under the impression that the work was being done by a
> professional abstracter. Only [afterwards] did I learn that Ted Raynor had
> been the "abstracter." Slowly and painstakingly, sandwiching the job in
> between his other numerous professional tasks, he had ground out our
> abstract—another mammoth undertaking for which our cause is ever-
> lastingly in his debt.[28]

In spite of the help, Dodd was unable to meet the deadline for filing for the May term. The *McCollum* appeal was delayed as a consequence until the fall term. Vashti's reaction to the setback was carried in the *Courier*.

> We naturally are disappointed that the brief and abstract were not ready
> for filing in time for the May term, but because of the delay at first when
> the transcript was held up, we knew it would have been a tight squeeze.
> The entire time schedule was thrown off when the transcript was not
> ready for the attorney at the time he had set aside for working on it. After
> that, he had other commitments for his time, and we just never were able
> to catch up.[29]

Shortly after learning that the American Educational Fellowship, following the lead of its New York branch,[30] and the American Ethical Union favored her cause,[31] Vashti McCollum made plans to journey to the east coast for further backing. On her itinerary were speeches to a Rationalist convention in Philadelphia and afterwards to the newly formed National Liberal League (NLL) in New York City.[32]

Arthur Cromwell was one of the founders of the NLL[33] and was anxious that it encompass all activist, secularist factions in a united effort to promote church-state separation. In a letter discussing her speech to the NLL, Cromwell offered advice which tended to indicate that even he was beginning to see the wisdom of moderation, especially with respect to rhetoric.

> The nature of your speech is entirely up to you, but it is my suggestion
> that it be along the lines of giving a case history of this whole battle ... in

its legalistic terms, you yourself are anxious to keep shy of atheism and religious differences. Your frank, friendly way of telling how this has all come about will appeal to the listeners and at the same time in no [way] be called or considered "rabble-rousing."[34]

It seems likely that Cromwell wished to exploit his daughter's newly-acquired status in the promotion of the NLL; in this, her moderation would most surely be an asset. But, as this additional excerpt from his letter reveals, the old freethinker continued to believe that a defensive stance was not solely the answer in the promotion of church-state separation.

Also in your talk, I would suggest that you bring forth the necessity of [a] nation-wide organization [presumably the NLL] to "hold the line" as you put it. The battle of attrition—for lack of a better phrase—is of questionable value, but I am not in the mood to argue this with you. To hold the line means that at least one of the two lines must eventually recede or break up, and I am not so sure that we are in a position either financially or in organized numbers to just hold the line. Flank attacks such as you and I have thus far waged are of far more value in winning any battle than just "holing in" and waiting for the other side to retreat.[35]

On her way home from the meetings, Vashti stopped in Rochester for a short visit with her parents. At her father's invitation she delivered a talk to the Rochester Society of Freethinkers. She was quoted as saying:

I agree that a little religion never hurt anybody, but it seems to me that when religious education is given in the public schools the problems arising are greater than the benefits received. The argument that religious education in the schools is necessary for the prevention of juvenile delinquency is based on the assumption that people are naturally bad, and that training in Christian culture is needed to correct that condition.[36]

Schug also had been on the road looking for "moral support,"[37] meeting with the Board of Directors of the American Unitarian Association, as well in New York City with representatives of other religious and educational groups.[38] While these trips helped publicize the cause and perhaps even helped raise funds, the bulk of that responsibility fell to the CAC. By late January, 1946, the CAC was able to announce that $9,600 in cash and $3,500 in pledges had been raised.[39]

By May 21, Vashti was back in Illinois. On the advice of her allies in the CAC, she journeyed to Chicago to attend a board meeting of the CCLC. Chapman was on the agenda to explain his status with respect to the Champaign case. Though the CCLC was no longer connected with the *McCollum* case, its membership remained interested in the issue. Her CAC supporters felt that the plaintiff should be present "to answer any questions or misstatements that were made."[40] The clear indication was that the distrust of several months earlier had not abated.

Vashti sat inconspicuously in the rear of the room. Before the meeting began, she was notified that she had a long-distance telephone call from Champaign. It was from a *News-Gazette* reporter seeking her reaction to the defeat of the *Latimer* case which had been announced that morning. After offering a brief statement, she returned to the CCLC meeting only to learn that Chapman would not make his presentation. Disappointed, she nevertheless remained and when the opportunity presented itself, she introduced herself and explained the reason for her attendance. In her book, she related what happened next:

> Then I dropped my bombshell. "First of all," I said, "I want to tell you how sorry I was to hear the *Latimer* case lost in Springfield." They were sitting there, very calm, very composed, and suddenly it hit them between the eyes. They hadn't known it! To this day they're probably wondering how I found out before they did. "We've lost one battle in the fight," I continued, "and it's an important fight. In the second place, it goes without saying, this [the Latimer decision] will hurt my case." Apparently my few words made an impression, for many people came over to shake my hand and express good wishes. I left the meeting happy.[41]

In an interview that occurred while this manuscript was in preparation, Vashti said she told those in attendance at the CCLC meeting that her case was the stronger of the two cases and that an appeal of the Latimer decision would jeopardize the cause.[42]

The *Gazette* reported Vashti as saying she was "very sorry" about the Supreme Court's decision in the *Chicago* case, but left no doubt as to her resolve to pursue her own suit. She said that she and her supporters "always regarded the Champaign case as much stronger ..." Commenting on Franklin's statement that the *Latimer* decision represented a "final disposition" of her action, she distinguished the two cases, "The infringement is much greater in the Champaign case."[43]

Ira Latimer announced that he intended to appeal the decision in his case to the United States Supreme Court.[44] This prompted renewed concerns among the supporters of the *McCollum* case. Again, the weaker case, in their view, was compromising the stronger. Latimer, in fact, petitioned the Illinois Supreme Court for a rehearing of his case, which was denied on September 13, shortly before the *McCollum* case was formally submitted to the same court.[45] In the end, Latimer declined to follow through with an appeal to the United States Supreme Court. According to Vashti, representatives of the CAC credited her impromptu appearance before the CCLC board as the decisive factor in the decision not to appeal the *Latimer* case.[46] Whatever the reason, it came as a great relief to Vashti and her supporters.

The *Courier* commented editorially on the *Latimer* decision and its relationship to the *McCollum* case. As the following excerpts indicate, the writer felt that the *Chicago* case did not settle the issue:

> Few Illinois residents were aware of the Chicago case in litigation. But the *McCollum* Case was tried in a hippodrome atmosphere and the statutory issues were obscured by attorneys' questions dealing with the Old Testament stories of Jonah and the whale, and with the nature of the Deity. Finally, the case of the plaintiff was prejudiced by her free admis-

sion that she is a free thinker, an atheist. The Champaign case, stripped of its Dayton "monkey trial" aspects, should afford the State Supreme Court an opportunity to rule finally on an issue which is regarded with serious interest throughout Illinois. More than the Chicago case, it deals with the basic question of the separation of church and state.[47]

The first brief filed for the plaintiff-turned-appellant was submitted in mid-September. Raynor was listed as "Attorney for the Appellant," while Dodd's status was that of "Of Counsel."[48] (Such identification would imply that Raynor, not Dodd, was the principal author of the brief.)

The appellant's brief sought to deemphasize the not-so-subtle antireligious overtones introduced by Chapman's pleadings at the outset of the suit and sustained by him during the first two days of the trial itself. In the section dealing with the factual background, Raynor and Dodd briefly referred to the matter:

Many other matters of fact appear in the pleadings and evidence which are only incidentally relevant or material to the issues of the case, and for them neither party can entirely blame the other.[49]

First in the short list that followed was: "The religious views of appellant are developed both in pleading and in evidence."[50] Later, in the arguments, the subject was briefly discussed:

The portions of the record in this case with respect to appellant's religious views are immaterial as to her right to bring proceedings to prohibit religious instruction in the public schools ... There is no doubt of her right to bring this suit as a taxpayer, and the issue as to her religion is merely incidental to the reason for her action in this case and to its effect upon embarrassment which her son may have suffered.[51]

The brief went on to assert that the appellant "has the same constitutional rights as those belonging to [Protestant, Catholic or Jewish religions] or other religions, or no religions." It then quoted the *Ring* case: "The free enjoyment of religious worship includes freedom not to worship."[52]

For its remainder, the brief adhered to constitutional and statutory arguments that Vashti and her CAC backers had favored from the outset. They were organized under the following seven points:

1. The issue of this case is not limited to a school district of Champaign County nor to the embarrassment of plaintiff's son.[53]

2. That all persons are entitled to freedom of religion and religious independence is guaranteed by both Federal and State Constitutions.[54]

3. Publicly segregating students in public schools into sectarian groups for religious education in the schools and in school hours is violative of constitutional guarantees of freedom of religion, and is not validated by providing that students may be excused from religious education.[55]

4. The use of public funds for sectarian education violates the Constitution of Illinois.[56]

5. Sectarian teaching of public school students in public school build-ings during school hours is violative of the Illinois School Code.[57]

6. The discretion vested in this case [to the school superintendent] constitutes a delegation of legislative power in violation of the Constitu-tion of Illinois and the Constitution of the United States.[58]

7. The appellant's position in this case does not conflict with the court's opinion in *People ex re I. Latimer v. Board of Education of the City of Chicago*; nor does it seek to defeat religious education of children who may go to public schools and who may also desire such education.[59]

Vashti objected to the inclusion of the last point: "I didn't feel we had to polish any apples and say they [the Supreme Court justices] were perfect. We didn't have to antagonize them, but I didn't like our saying the Latimer decision was all right."[60]

Rall and Franklin, in their response, were not going to allow the issue of the plaintiff's religion drop:

At the outset of our consideration of this argument, the question naturally arises how can one who espouses no religious belief, who denies the existence of a Supreme Being, and who places her reliance upon a politi-cal principle, namely, separation of church and state, rather than upon religious scruples, invoke a guaranty of religious freedom?[61]

In answering the question, their brief stated in part:

It is our contention that persons who have no religion have no right of religious freedom because they have no religion; they are entitled only to be protected from being compelled to embrace a religion, but this certainly does not give them any right to prevent religious education for those desiring it simply because of the fact—if it is a fact—that their own failure to participate in the program exposes their own lack of reli-gion.[62]

Later:

If one denies the existence of such a relationship (as defined under "reli-gion" by *Webster's New International Dictionary*—1927) between God and man, as does the relator, he has no religion and obviously cannot be impaired in the free exercise thereof. As well might a person without property complain that he has had it taken without due process.[63]

The main response of the brief relied upon four arguments, the first three of which cited the Latimer decision as their prime authority:

1. The defendant Board of Education has the statutory power to ex-cuse pupils from public school attendance for a period of from thirty to forty-five minutes each week to attend religious education classes.[64]

2. The voluntary religious education classes do not violate any right of religious freedom guaranteed by (the Constitutions of either the United States or the State of Illinois).[65]

3. The defendant Board of Education has not made "any appropriation" or paid "anything in aid of any church or sectarian purpose," nor has
it granted or donated any "land, money, or other personal property" "to
any church or for any sectarian purposes."[66]

The final point, for which the *Latimer* case was of no help, was the actual use
of the public school property, the classrooms:

4. The use of public school classrooms by religious education classes
during school hours, in the sound discretion of the Board of Education is
authorized by the School Code and no illegal discretion has been vested
in the Superintendent of Schools.[67]

During the course of the second argument, the brief went to some considerable length to distinguish the *Ring* case, which the appellant's attorneys had
relied upon so heavily. Given the fact situation in the *Ring* case, the appellees'
brief conceded the correctness of the decision. However, the brief argued that the
language of the decision—the obiter dicta—went beyond the actual holding.

The brief then identified what its authors' felt were six material differences
between the current suit and the 1910 case. First, the *Ring* case involved members of an organized church; in the *McCollum* case the plaintiff was an atheist.
Second, in the *Ring* situation, the exercises were a part of the school program; in
Champaign, pupils in religious classes were excused. Third, the teachers involved in the religious classes/exercises were not public school employees in
Champaign as they had been in the *Ring* situation. Fourth, the *Ring* case involved
actual religious exercises, "repetition of the Lord's Prayer and singing of hymns,"
while in Champaign "the religious education courses [were] on an educational
level..." Fifth, in Champaign, the religious classes were voluntary; in the *Ring*
situation the religious exercises were not. And sixth, embarrassment and social
pressure on non-participants "was assumed to exist" in the *Ring* case, while in
Champaign such was "affirmatively shown not to exist..."[68]

The appellant, through her attorneys, submitted a short reply brief; as in the
earlier brief, Raynor was listed as Vashti's attorney and Dodd as "Of Counsel." In
a continuing effort to blunt the religion issue, the brief charged: "On the matter of
legal issues, Appellees' brief seeks to prejudice this Court against the Appellant
on the ground that this case is one of attack upon the Christian religion and an
effort to prevent any form of religious education."[69]

Elsewhere in the brief it was stated, "The appellant's views are not at issue in
this case ..."[70] and, "The appellee fails to recognize that all religious views, including atheism, are subject to constitutional protection."[71]

The brief went on to accept the proposition that school boards had the authority to release students from public school to attend religious education classes
..."[72] Not content with merely accepting the *Latimer* decision, Raynor and Dodd
made an effort to argue that "the opinion in the Latimer Case strengthens [the]
appellant's position."[73] Much of the remaining argument concerned amplifica-
tions and clarifications of propositions already advanced in the earlier brief.

In the meantime, Judge Leonard had recovered sufficiently from his March heart attack to return to his duties on the Circuit Court bench. As it developed, he was far from a healthy man. In early September, he suffered a cerebral hemorrhage and died after a few days.[74] At age 55, he was the first important figure involved in the *McCollum* case to pass from the scene.

Later that same month, it was announced that the religious education program not only was being continued, but had been expanded. Enrollment for the fall semester was put at 962, an increase of 173 over the previous year. Most of the growth was accounted for in the extension of the program to the third grade.[75]

Oral arguments before the Illinois Supreme Court occurred on November 20, 1946. From the Associated Press report carried by the *News-Gazette*, it would appear both sides strayed little, if at all, from previously announced strategies. Dodd presented the case for the appellant. Staying close to the legal and social aspects of the case, he said he thought it was "obvious that the teaching is to some extent sectarian." He went on to charge that "segregation into religious groups violates [constitutional law], which forbids participation by schools in religious teaching and which forbids the use of public money for that purpose." According to Dodd, the social consequences were serious. "This system of religious education," he said, "advertises and develops to a greater extent a type of friction which unfortunately exists in this country."[76]

Franklin argued: "This suit was started as an instrument and vehicle for expounding her [Vashti's] atheistic and political views."... "One thing the relator alleged and proved at great length," he pointed out, "was that she was an atheist."

Pursuing a familiar theme he asserted, "Constitutional guarantees are for religious people and for people who prefer religion; this is a religious nation and state" and religion should receive "incidental benefit from the government." Concerning the difficulties or problems experienced in school by James Terry—which he did not admit—he said, "We can't, as judges and courts, protect people from social consequences resulting from their choice of religion."[77]

Both Vashti and Philip Schug were disappointed in the hearing before the Illinois Supreme Court. The former remembered that, "The courtroom was terribly hot the day we were there, and now and then one of the judges would start to nod and fall asleep."[78] Schug was expansive in his criticism of the High Court:

> I was ... convinced that the law was so simple and clear that the outcome was inevitable, but the session before the Illinois Supreme Court only added to my consternation. I sat there and watched at least one third of the judges doze off and sleep soundly, then jerk to attention and doze off again. It was a significant performance but I did not grasp its meaning. I was concerned that they were in no condition to consider the issue that we were presenting. What I did not realize was that my concern was not their concern. Their concern was to see that the lower courts in Illinois shielded the people and the officials of Illinois from the power of a superior law. The lower court had done its job well. They [the justices] could sleep soundly. All was well.[79]

As might be expected, neither Franklin nor Rall offered any criticism of the Illinois Supreme Court. Both, in interviews conducted many years after the event, indicated that they expected to win the appeal at that stage.[80] Armed as they were with the *Latimer* decision, they had reason to be pleased and confident.

Just over two months after oral arguments, on January 22, 1947, the State Supreme Court denied Vashti's appeal. The opinion was short and accepted the appellees' view of the case. Perhaps the biggest obstacle for the court was the language contained in the *Ring* case; the problem was overcome when the justices concluded that that case and the *McCollum* case were "plainly dissimilar."[81] In doing so, the court relied upon the appellees' arguments that the exercises in the *Ring* case, in contrast with the *McCollum* case, were "actually worship services," "compulsory," and a "part of the public school program" conducted by public school teachers.[82]

The justices refused to accept the effort of Raynor and Dodd to distinguish their case from the Latimer decision. Instead, the court ruled that the two cases were "to all intents and purposes exactly the same ... excepting only that the classes [in the Latimer situation] were held outside the schoolrooms."[83] Thus, since no illegal segregation was found in the one case, none existed in the other.

As to allowing the religious teaching in the school rooms, the court held such use of school property was "incidental," and no legal problem was found to exist with respect to sectarian religious teaching in the public school.[84] Further, according to the court, there was "little if any" disruption of the regular class schedule.[85] Finally, as to the use of illegal discretion, none existed since no sect had been denied use of the school facilities.[86]

On the last page of the decision, the court offered a philosophical statement to help define the relationship between the state and religion: "The government does not recognize a particular faith but this does not mean that it is indifferent to religious faith. To deny the existence of religious motivation is to deny the inspiration and authority of the constitution itself."[87]

Vashti had no great expectations after oral arguments. Her response to a *News-Gazette* reporter was low key and seemed to indicate that she regarded the state court ruling as only another lost battle in a long legal war. "We have no overall campaign," she said. "We are just taking this lap by lap and have made no definite plans pending the state court decision."[88] As usual, when the opportunity presented itself, she reiterated her objections to the "Champaign System":

> We are convinced the method is undemocratic and unconstitutional. It weakens both the public school and the church. The church shows its weakness in relying on compulsory school attendance to present its teachings. When the churches thus attempt to avail themselves of public funds they are curtailing religious freedom as well as establishing a definite hindrance to [the] efficiency of the public school system.[89]

In some contrast to earlier descriptions of the appellant, the *Gazette* reporter described her as "mild mannered"[90]—he must have been new on the job.

The *Courier* report noted that Vashti was "admittedly disappointed over early reports of the ruling," but her statements to the reporter were hardly those of a vanquished person:

> Similar cases involving either use of schools for non-school purposes or for so-called released time for religious instruction, are pending in several states; quite obviously a final decision as to the proper use of school property, teachers' time and educational programs must eventually be handled by the Supreme Court of the land. I hope that our case, with its clean-cut issues, is the first such case to reach the highest court.[91]

In an article printed four days after the court decision, a reporter for the Chicago *Times* described the appellant as "vivacious" and carried quotes which also must have come from a personal interview.

> Many religious groups and educational organizations have come forth with encouragement and aid since the Illinois Supreme Court held against me. [Among those she reportedly mentioned were: the American Unitarian Association, the American Educational Fellowship, the Christian Adventists, a number of Lutheran churches, the Chicago Citizens' Schools Committee and the Scottish Rite Supreme Council.] The court overlooked the fact that such practice [the religious classes] is really the attempt of certain churches to propagate their objectives by taking advantage of compulsory school [attendance] laws—"If children don't come to us," they say, "we will get to them."[92]

The reporter could not resist bringing up the question of religion. Vashti indicated her children went to the Unitarian Sunday school. "I don't tell them to go, they just get up on Sunday morning, dress and go off to Sunday school of their own accord." When asked if she were an atheist, her answer was somewhat evasive though consistent with her other public utterances on the subject:

> That (the word atheist) was an unfortunate term during the Circuit Court trial. I don't know enough about theology to describe myself as an atheist, who is a person who says there is no God. To me, any concept of God is mental, and I have no such concept in my mind, but I know that God does exist in this form in the minds of many other people, so I do not go so far as to deny that He exists.[93]

Raynor and Dodd left no doubt as to Vashti's intention to appeal the decision. The two indicated that they would immediately seek a writ of certiorari from the United States Supreme Court, and Raynor expressed optimism that a hearing might be held by early fall.[94] Dodd, in obvious disagreement with the Illinois Court said, "The point at issue is whether even voluntary segregation of pupils in public schools for religious instruction is a restriction on the freedom of religion. We believe it does constitute a restriction."[95]

Much less space was devoted to what the proponents of the religious classes had to say. Franklin, described as "confident," declared: "We're over the biggest hill now; she will have even less chance [in the federal court]."[96] That surmise was based upon the legal reality that the United States Supreme Court would be limited only to questions involving the federal Constitution; the Champaign System had obviously passed the state test. Also in his favor was the fact that the federal high court hears only a small fraction of the cases presented to it for review; in Vashti's action, review had yet to be granted.

Thomas West, the Chicago patent attorney and perennial supporter of released time religious education classes in the schools, declared that with the Illinois court decision, his organization "can now set out to strengthen the weekday religious education system throughout the state." Concerning the appeal, West reported that under the direction of David Lindstrom, $15,000 had been raised for legal costs.[97]

Comment was almost immediate in the Chicago press. Referring to Vashti's motives and state of mind, the *Daily News* stated:

> It probably would be futile to suggest to one of Mrs. McCollum's militancy that her son would lead a more contented life if he learned the appearance of conformity with prevailing customs. She has eminent clerical backing for her argument that ideas implanted in the young are not readily lost. Furthermore, history has given a high place to some who have suffered martyrdom for their convictions.
>
> It doubtless would be equally vain to point out that if a child IS to be reared an atheist it would do him no harm to learn what it is he doesn't believe in. Mrs. McCollum is fighting for a principle. She holds that since school attendance is compulsory the churches should not take advantage of that fact to instill religious faith. She maintains further that it is an invasion of liberty to have their differences in belief pointed out to the pupils.[98]

The editorial, in noting that, "The law now seems well established ... ," accepted the fact that, as far as Illinois was concerned, the final arbiter had spoken. It concluded: "The court's decision simply means that this is a question that every community must settle for itself and express through its school board rules. The law will say only that no child shall be forced to receive instruction in a belief alien to the family convictions."[99]

The *Tribune* recognized that:

> The Champaign program ... must now be considered lawful, but it cannot be considered sound public policy in spite of the high motives of the people who organized it and their effort to avoid the interdenominational strife that followed experiments with Bible reading in the schools years ago.

The latter is probably a reference to the *Ring* case. Reference was then made by the editorial writer to the more sweeping language of the State Supreme Court decision quoted earlier:

> Of this program [the Champaign System] the court said: "Our government very wisely refuses to recognize a specific religion but this cannot mean

that the government does not recognize nor subscribe to religious ideals. To deny the existence of religious motivation is to deny the inspiration and authority of the Constitution itself."

The *Tribune* was not impressed:

It is a far stretch of logic to conclude from the fact that our government recognizes and subscribes to religious ideals that it is the function of government to inculcate those ideals. There are few people in this or any other American state who will side with the plaintiff in the Champaign case in doubting the value of a religious education. It is not the American plan of government, however, to make the state a participant in all desirable activities, much as the extreme New Dealers would like to do that. We have seen what that system produces in other countries; the thing that it is least capable of producing is the fear of God and the love of one's fellow men.

If the foregoing had not been enough, the writer left little doubt what the newspaper's views were on the subject: "Religious training in this country has always been the function of the family and the church, working together. The fact that these agencies may not be doing as good a job as might be hoped for is no excuse for turning over any part of the task to the public schools."[100]

Neither the *Courier* nor the *News-Gaztte* carried editorials concerning the state court decision. The former did, however, carry an interesting commentary from the Collinsville *Herald* under the heading, "By the Judge's Cousin:"

Two weeks ago the Illinois Supreme Court, ignoring the constitution, the anti-Bible reading decision [*Ring* case] and the legislature's refusal to "legalize" the "religious teachings" practice, held, in an evasive opinion, that the Champaign program did not violate the constitution, and since it did not violate any specific statute it could not be forbidden by the court. The opinion was written by Justice Charles H. Thompson of Harrisburg, who is a third cousin of mine, not a particularly able lawyer, a nice fellow who is inclined to go with the wind and not to step on anybody's toes. The gist of his opinion was that since the dismissals of students from class were on consent of the parents, and the receiving of the religious instruction was "voluntary," there was no state interference with or aid to religious inculcation.

I know nothing of the type of religious programs which were given in the Champaign schools nor anywhere else in the state. That is immaterial so far as the constitutional question is concerned, but is interesting as relating to the mental attitude of the ministers and others who introduced them and the parents who consented to them.

The programs may have been a mere homily on morals and manners, or an ethical credo, or an inculcation of out-and-out denominationalism, or a scrambling of all three. Morals and manners and ethics may properly be taught in the schools as a phase of secular training in personal conduct, taught well enough by either laymen or clerics. But anything smacking of denominationalism, or even recognizing it, promotes division and emphasizes divergence and is alien to our system of free schools, and violative of the constitution, no matter how "voluntary" it may be.[101]

Whether or not the writer's sentiments reflected those of the editorial staff of the *Courier*, it is certainly clear that they conformed to Vashti's.

The legal issues raised by Vashti continued to be overshadowed by her religious beliefs, both actual as well as perceived. *Time* Magazine, in a report where the dividing lines between news and commentary, fact and fantasy were somewhat blurred, hardly improved matters.

Children may now legally study the Bible in Illinois public schools. After due consideration, the State Supreme Court has said it is all right. But Mrs. Vashti McCollum, 33, an angry atheist of Champaign, who brought the subject up, planned to appeal to the U.S. Supreme Court. Her eleven-year-old son James had been "embarrassed" she said, because he was the only pupil in his class who had declined the voluntary Bible lesson. Religion, fumed Mrs. McCollum, is "a racket based on fear and prejudice and a chronic disease of the imagination contracted in childhood."[102]

There seemed to be no escaping Cromwell's pamphlet and the other anti-religious elements interjected by Landon Chapman. That strategy, in Vashti's view, had proved to be a positive detriment in the court of public opinion as well as in the two lower courts of law. The big question, she believed, should the nation's highest court agree to hear her case, was the relative importance it would assign to the religious versus legal questions raised.

James Terry McCollum, Vashti
Cromwell McCollum, Arthur G.
Cromwell. (Photo courtesy the
Champaign-Urbana *News-Gazette*)

James Terry McCollum
and Vashti Cromwell
McCollum, Champaign
County Courthouse,
Urbana, IL, September
1945. (Photo courtesy the
Champaign-Urbana *Courier*)

Organizers of the released-time program: A. Ray Cartlidge (center), flanked by religious education teachers Mae Chapin and Sarah Grace Jorgensen. (Photo courtesy the Champaign-Urbana *News-Gazette*)

Attorneys for the defense: Owen Rall, John Franklin, Abe R. Peterson, Champaign County Courthouse, Urbana, IL, September 1945. (Photo courtesy the Champaign-Urbana *News-Gazette*)

Attorney Walter Dodd
(Photo McCollum archive)

Vashti McCollum the day following her
victory. (Photo courtesy the Champaign-Urbana
News-Gazette)

Left: Knolton Theodore "Ted" Raynor;
Right: Rev. Philip Schug. (Photos
McCollum archive)

Chapter 13

The Final Assault

On February 10, 1947, less than a month after judgment was rendered by the Illinois Supreme Court, the United States Supreme Court rendered a decision which was of considerable importance to the contending parties in the *McCollum* case. The issue, raised by Arch R. Everson of New Jersey, was that of a local school board's right to provide bus transportation for parochial school students. In a close decision (5-4), the court ruled that the practice did not violate the First and Fourteenth Amendments to the United States Constitution; any aid to religion, the court ruled, was incidental and the primary purpose was to promote the public welfare, not religion.[1]

John Franklin, who said he had anticipated "no difficulty"[2] prior to the New Jersey decision, commented afterwards that it "bears very much on the local case." He expressed his disappointment that the decision was not unanimous."[3] Many months later, he admitted that the complexion of the *McCollum* case was "utterly and completely changed" by *Everson*. He acknowledged that he faced a "tough fight" before the Supreme Court. He concluded: "We may have to convince the court it was wrong in [the *Everson*] case."[4] Years afterward, he was even more candid:

> From [the *Everson* decision] on, we thought we would lose the case. The issue of letting parochial children ride a public school bus was so narrowly approved, and the formulation of [religious] doctrine in young students' minds was so blatant in comparison with the *Everson* facts that we thought we would lose it.[5]

When called for her comments on the *Everson* decision, Vashti steadfastly adhered to points she had made all along in the protracted struggle.

> My objection is not to the teaching of religion, but to the use of the public schools for that function. There are about 70 churches in Champaign-Urbana. I realize that many people who advocate religious education in the schools feel that the few hours of religious classes in the churches are insufficient, attendance inadequate, and the quality of the teaching not always entirely satisfactory.

She then asked rhetorically:

> If a weekly class in a church or church school given by a clergyman trained in the teaching of religion is not sufficient, then what potency can there be in one hour per week of religious education in the public schools, taught by non-professional teachers?

In answering her own question, she claimed: "That potency is presumed to lie in the overwhelming prestige of the state in compulsory school attendance laws, acting through public school boards and their staffs."[6]

The McCollum forces, while disapproving of the result, were encouraged by the *Everson* decision. On the basis of what he read, Walter Dodd had advised his client that she had "a good chance of winning. "[7] In her book she wrote:

> Like John Franklin, I, too, felt this decision had great bearing on the McCollum case. I, too, regretted the split decision and especially the fact that one vote caused such a decision at all. But I felt that at least we had four men on our side. Our job was to convince the other five.[8]

Offering particular encouragement to the twice-defeated appellant was the language—the obiter dicta—in the majority opinion by Justice Hugo L. Black. While having no direct value as precedent, the language seemed to give some indication as to the direction the court was going with respect to church-state issues.

Especially disconcerting to Franklin and those he represented was the following wording from Black's majority opinion—wording later included in the majority opinion in the *McCollum* case.

> Neither a state nor the Federal Government can set up a church. Neither can pass laws which aid one religion, aid all religions, or prefer one religion over another. Neither can force nor influence a person to go to or to remain away from church against his will or force him to profess a belief or disbelief in any religion. No person can be punished for entertaining or for professing religious beliefs or disbeliefs, for church attendance or nonattendance. No tax in any amount, large or small, can be levied to support any religious activities or institutions, whatever they may be called, or whatever form they may adopt to teach or practice religion. Neither a state nor the Federal Government can, openly or secretly, participate in the affairs of any religious organizations or groups and vice versa. In the words of Jefferson, the clause against establishment of religion by law was intended to erect "a wall of separation between church and State."[9]

Some of the *Everson* language found its way into print much closer to home. The *Tribune*, in a long editorial, quoted at length from Justice Jackson's dissenting opinion, which discussed the background of the "establishment of religion" clause of the First Amendment. Jackson wrote:

It was intended not only to keep the states' hands out of religion, but to keep religion's hands off the state, and, above all, to keep bitter religious controversy out of public life by denying to every denomination any advantage from getting control of public policy or the public purse.

This policy of our federal Constitution has never been wholly pleasing to most religious groups. They are all quick to invoke its protections; they are all irked when they feel its restraint. This court has gone a long way, if not an unreasonable way, to hold that public business of such paramount importance as maintenance of public order, protection of the privacy of the home, and taxation may not be pursued by a state in a way that even indirectly will interfere with religious proselytizing.

But we cannot have it both ways. Religious teaching cannot be a private affair when the state seeks to impose regulations which infringe on it indirectly, and a public affair when it comes to taxing citizens of one faith to aid another, or those of no faith to aid all.[10]

The editorial concluded by relating the *Everson* decision to the situation much closer to home than either Washington D.C. or New Jersey:

As we said recently, in connection with the controversy over religious instruction in the schools of Champaign, Ill., the teaching of religion should be encouraged in every way so long as it is carried out by the citizen himself in his home or thru his church. It is not a matter with which any public body can safely concern itself, however indirectly.[11]

In Toledo, Ohio, there seemed to have been a shift in the editorial position of the *Blade*. In agreeing with the *Tribune*, its editorial writer concluded:

Though last week's decision is applicable to only one church and draws the line at which a church can receive support from the state, it lets down a historic barrier. From now on, all churches, creeds, and sects can scramble for public funds and set up schools to justify them. In which case, the American public school system could be sadly disrupted. And the consequences to American democracy might be disastrous.[12]

While *Everson* offered strategic encouragement to the McCollum forces, the situation on the home front had deteriorated. Without question, her prosecution of the suit had multiple negative impacts on her entire family, but they were most severe and direct on her oldest son. (In her book, she detailed some of the precipitating events which culminated in her decision to send James Terry away to school.[13]) Less than a week after the New Jersey decision, the McCollums attempted to quietly withdraw their son from school. Later the *News-Gazette* carried a short notice of the event: "Terry McCollum, 12, central figure in Champaign's religious education suit, withdrew Monday from classes at Champaign Junior High School and will be enrolled in a private school at Rochester, N. Y., according to his parents ... "[14]

"Of course it was expecting too much to think that Jim could leave town quietly," wrote Vashti, but she was angered by the newspaper's falsely attributing the story to her and her husband. In an angry telephone call to the editor she recalled saying: "I've never tried to crash your society columns and I'm not picking this time to try. You know I didn't send you that information and it wasn't given "according to his parents."[15]

Though a *Courier* reporter had seen Vashti at the school officially withdrawing her son the day before the Gazette story ran, at her request he had refrained from reporting it.[16]

While other press reports failed to offer a reason for the transfer, the Rochester *Times-Union* was direct and to the point. The lead paragraph read:

> Hounded by his schoolmates in the swanky South Side Junior High School in Champaign, Ill., because of his religious disbeliefs, a 12-year-old lad sought refuge in an unidentified private school here this week.[17]

James, as he then preferred to be called, was actually in Rochester and enrolled in Harley School at the time of his official withdrawal from the Champaign school. He was to remain in Rochester, living with his grandparents, the Cromwells, for over a year until the Supreme Court ruling on his mother's appeal. There were difficult adjustments for both boy and grandparents as well as a substantially increased financial burden on the McCollums, but such was a "cost of doing business" when challenging the system.

Vashti had another though less immediate concern relating to Dodd's effectiveness in presenting oral arguments. On May 5, 1947, Cromwell received a hurriedly-written card from his daughter expressing optimism over the chances of a Supreme Court review as well as a request for his help and advice in seeking legal assistance for Dodd. She wrote:

> Chances are that we'll have a U. S. Supreme Court decision in our case by this fall. I'm looking now for another lawyer to supplement Dodd. I want someone absolutely sold on the case, but not rabid, a fine convincing speaker [for the oral argument in Washington] who will check over Dodd's briefs before they are filed and perhaps collaborate with him in their writing. ... Can you suggest anything... Let me know immediately.[18]

Cromwell wrote immediately to a man prominent in Freemasonry, seeking his advice and help. He also checked to see if there was anyone suitable among the Rochester legal fraternity. The person he found he described to his daughter as follows:

> He is a fine young man, about 34 years old, and has had considerable experience before the U.S.S.C [the United States Supreme Court] and worked for Fred Vinson, the chief justice. He worked four years in Washington during the war and knows a lot about the setup there.[19]

The young attorney was none other than Sol M. Linowitz, a man who in subsequent years was to make an impressive name for himself.

But before matters went any further, Cromwell received a second postcard from his daughter.

Forget about the last card I wrote you. Have seen Bear [Theodore Bear, a prominent attorney in Peoria, Illinois, and a quiet supporter in the *McCollum* cause] and made arrangements for all the legal help I need without any expense to me or the Chicago Action Council. This new firm will work with Dodd, I hope. I'll be in Chicago this Friday to see Dodd and Raynor and advise them of this new help and the arrangement for division etc. of the work. I'm sitting on top of the world right now.[20]

In a follow up letter sent the same day as the card, she indicated that the entire matter needed to be kept in confidence. "I'm not telling the Action fellows (the CAC) who the fairy godfather is because they might let him shoulder their obligations. Also, I suspect Bear to be anti-semitic and I don't want them to meet head on."

She went on to write:

Now all of this must be kept absolutely quiet. The opposition feels they are sitting pretty and have us licked easy, but they haven't. If they get wind of our new forces, it'll give them impetus for a new drive for funds and legal aid. And I'm just hoping to get a lawyer that'll make John Franklin look like a damn fool in Washington without the latter having any idea of his opposition ...

Concerning Dodd's sensitivities, she wrote: "With Raynor, I'll go to see Dodd and tell him that at long last we have secured help for him etc. I expect all to go smoothly. Dodd will still be in the driver's seat, but must understand that he has to confer with and take suggestions ..."[21]

Cromwell responded immediately expressing pleasure over the news. He also shared parts of his daughter's letter with Linowitz. The latter took the news graciously.

[Linowitz] is also happy with the news and says that if in any way he may be able to assist he will be most happy to do so... Both your mother and I thought very highly of him ... and we believe he would have been a real scrapper for you in this case.[22]

The Masonic official to whom Cromwell had initially written did respond both to Cromwell himself as well as to Vashti, but his help was no longer needed.[23] Five days after his letter to his daughter, Cromwell wrote Bear. While expressing appreciation for his help, the old Freethinker warned: "Every effort will be made to arouse the maudlin passions and prejudices of the mob. Every effort will be made to blacken the life and character of every person that has any part in assisting Vashti in this fight."[24]

On June 2, 1947, local newspapers reported that the United States Supreme Court had agreed to review the *McCollum* case. When reached by a reporter from the *Courier*, Vashti was jubilant: "I'm so thrilled, I don't think any comment is necessary."[25] In her book she wrote: "I was too excited to comment."[26] Franklin, who had asked the high court to reject the case, called the action "more or less routine." He went on to say: "The court's action means merely that it has agreed a federal constitutional question has been raised. We will go on now to an exchange of briefs and oral arguments before the court in Washington."[27]

Vashti noted in her book that another factor began to emerge which was favorable to her cause:

> One of the arguments we had used was that the schoolrooms were needed for secular work; the other side maintained that classes in religion were held on "released" time, when the rooms weren't needed. Yet early in the Fall of 1947, more and more local headlines attested to the crowded conditions of the schools.[28] Indeed, by early June, 1947, voters in Champaign had approved overwhelmingly bond issues to construct additions to two elementary schools, one of which was South Side.[29]

The mere fact that the United States Supreme Court had agreed to hear the case also appears to have worked for Vashti; " ... all of a sudden," she wrote, "we began to acquire friends." She continued:

> From the day our case was accepted by the Supreme Court a number of groups approached us requesting permission to file in our behalf. In the beginning, we turned all these groups down. Dodd said that while these amici curiae briefs might have helped in the state court, in the Supreme Court, right not strength, was the important thing.[30]

"Why," Dodd argued to his client, "give the Court a lot of extra briefs to go through?"[31]

The first religious groups wishing to participate in the case as amici curiae and that received public attention in Champaign-Urbana were Jewish. The Synagogue Council of America and the National Community Relations Advisory Council, which reportedly represented "more than 80 per cent of Americans affiliated with Jewish organizations," filed a brief before the Supreme Court. Both the *Courier* and *Gazette* carried the story. The brief included the following qualification:

> We wish not only to disassociate ourselves completely from the antireligious views of the appellant, but wish also to deplore the fact that the sponsors of the original petition chose this case as a means of inscribing such anti-religious matter on the public record and for confusing the basic issue in this case by dragging into it the unrelated issues of atheism versus religion.[32]

An outraged Vashti wrote to her parents and enclosed the news clip containing the disclaimer. Cromwell responded:

> After reading your letter and then the news clipping I am not so sure that you are right in your anger or that the news item or the Jews' attitude is in any manner harmful to your case or cause. On the other hand, I believe it is one of the smartest things that could have happened for you; and let me tell you why.

After explaining his thoughts several different ways, Cromwell wrote succinctly:

> I say again, I was truly thrilled to see the clever and smart way these Jews came into the picture to give you a helping hand. Their open denouncement of your opinions and, as they charge, attempt to bring antireligion in the case, forestalls any and all criticism against them and their purpose and at the same time gives all others, favorable to the thing you are fighting for, a clue and excuse to get in and help put it over.[33]

Though the offer of the brief by the Synagogue Council was declined by Vashti on advice from her attorney, the group "successfully petitioned the Supreme Court for permission to file in [her] behalf."[34] There was a lamentable side locally to the Jewish involvement nationally as Vashti explained later in her book.

> Champaign has an anti-Semitic element, and as soon as the news got around that Jewish groups were supporting us, phone calls and letters began pouring in: "You dirty Jew ... we knew the Jews were in back of this all along," et cetera, et cetera.[35]

Other religious groups, as Cromwell had predicted, expressed an interest in submitting their own briefs. Vashti decided that more than just the feelings of nine justices of the United States Supreme Court were at stake in her fight: "I knew that if we were to win our case in the court of public opinion as well as in the court of law, we had to let people know that this was neither an anti-religious nor an antiChristian case."[36]

After discussing the matter with Dodd, the latter agreed, saying, "Since we can't keep everyone out, we might as well let everyone in." A letter was sent to the Supreme Court removing any objections to the amici curiae briefs.[37] Vashti shared the contents of Dodd's letter with the local press:

> In the case, I contemplated the plan of joining all arguments for the appellant in a single brief; such a plan has failed. The National Community Relations Advisory Council has, I understand, filed a brief and motion. The American Civil Liberties Union, the General Conference of Seventhday Adventists, and the committee representing the several large organizations of the Baptist church, also desire to file separate briefs as amici curiae.
>
> Under the circumstances, I consent to the filing of these or any other briefs as amici curiae presented in this case. I do not wish to insist upon motions or to defeat additional briefs under Rule 27 of the Supreme Court... This letter is written to you because others may file briefs before service has been had on these [briefs from the groups already mentioned].[38]

Franklin was quick to protest, saying that additional briefs "will only confuse the issue." Ironically, that position was not all that dissimilar to Dodd's original stand. The Board's attorney went on to challenge the right of a Washington, D. C., attorney to speak for all Baptists. "Baptists," he said, "are organized on a congregational basis in which each church makes its own decision on policy."[39]

Local Baptists were quick to join Franklin in the dispute. Rev. McDonald called together other area Baptist ministers and after the meeting offered a statement:

> The pastors of the local Baptist churches repudiate the statement that Baptists are united in their support of Mrs. McCollum's case before the Supreme Court which would prohibit the teaching of religion in the public schools. The claim of Mr. Jackson [E. Hilton Jackson, the attorney representing the national Baptist group] that he represents the four great Baptist groups of the United States—14 million strong—is false. Baptists are congregationally organized as local church bodies and no one person is authorized to speak for Baptists as a whole.[40]

The local Baptist ministers did not leave matters there; they requested "a statement from headquarters" concerning the denomination's position nationally.[41] "We want replies from two or three authorities," said McDonald. He went on to add:

> I don't know who would authorize such a statement that the Baptists would unite on this question. It isn't very good publicity for the Baptist churches. When we get additional word on it, we will probably have another meeting here and decide what further steps we should take.[42]

Jackson, a trustee of the First Baptist Church in Washington, D. C., as well as a lawyer, was contacted by the Associated Press for comment. The attorney attempted to clarify matters: "The action of the Committee [the Joint Conference Committee on Public Relations on which the four Baptist conventions have representatives] does not commit the entire membership; Baptists frequently have differences of opinion on public questions."

He added: "The Committee felt that the teaching of religion in the public schools of Champaign was a violation of the First Amendment separation of church and state."[43]

The "trail of headlines" kicked up over the dispute between the local Baptists and their national representatives caused Vashti some concern for, as she pointed out, "they hadn't yet filed a brief." She added: "I could only hope that the national Baptists would maintain their original interest and not be scared off. Later on, when I met E. Hilton Jackson ... I realized that he wasn't the type to be easily scared."[44]

Nationally, the Baptists were determined to enter the case. Less than a week after McDonald and his colleagues met to repudiate such an action, the *Gazette* reported that Baptist attorney Jackson had notified John Franklin of the filing of the amicus curiae brief.[45] Several days later, the *Gazette* carried another story on the matter. Rev. McDonald had received a response from Dr. Joseph Hazen, corresponding secretary of the Northern Baptist Convention. Hazen indicated that he had received McDonald's request to the chairman of the Joint Committee on Public Relations. Leaving it up to that group to speak for the national organization, Hazen undertook to venture an ambiguous statement of his own concerning the matter: "We must get together on this thing, and it seems to me that we should have a clear understanding so that we should all be trying to do the same thing."[46]

Meanwhile, Methodist Bishop G. Bromley Oxnam of Boston and several other prominent Protestant theologians announced they would meet in Chicago on November 20 to form a national organization stressing the separation of church and state. "We are by no means," said Oxnam, "limiting our activity to Protestants, but including educational, fraternal and secular organizations and all others who stand with us in respect to this matter."

Schug was named to attend the conference representing the American Humanist Association by the organization's executive secretary, Edwin H. Wilson. In commenting on the meeting, Wilson pointed out that he saw the goal of the group as one which would be difficult to achieve: "The one point at which we may prove out of step is in my very earnest conviction that Protestants themselves have compromised the principle of separation of church and state by entering into the released time religious education program."

He added:

> May I raise my voice once more for the position that in order consistently to stand for complete separation, the Protestants should renounce and begin to withdraw from the released time projects and improve their own methods of quality ... religious education, pursuing [such education] on their own premises and with their own time, money and leadership in complete divorcement from public authority of the public schools over their children.[47]

Oxnam's group at their meeting was unable to develop a consensus with respect to the released time issue; many supported the religious classes if they were conducted on church property. A statement was issued, however, which reflected some general agreement: "The organization has been called into existence because this principle [church-state separation] has been and is being violated and threatened with further violations in certain areas and by certain acts of both government and church."[48]

The group, which came to be known as Protestants and Other Americans United for Separation of Church and State (POAU), later shortened to Americans United for Separation of Church and State, resolved to meet again in less than two months, on January 12, 1948.[49]

While POAU failed to specifically come to Vashti McCollum's aid, the concern the group expressed along with the direct action of the Jews and Baptists seemed to indicate that there had been some rethinking of the church-state issue by many religious people. It was reflective of the developing opposition which had defeated the Clabaugh Bill in the Illinois legislature just over two years earlier.

For over two years, the Board of Education, local religious leaders and their allies had enjoyed a virtual monopoly of support by organized religionists. The news of religious support on the national level for Vashti must have been most disconcerting. Announcements of more such support continued to come in. On November 25, the American Unitarian Association submitted a brief in her behalf.[50] Also filing support briefs were the American Ethical Union and Hazel Franklin Lewis, a private citizen from nearby Danville, Illinois.[51] John Franklin, years later, reflected upon the amici curiae briefs and offered his perception as to how they were regarded by the High Court:

> I was amazed to find that the practice before the Court is to liberally permit amici curiae briefs, and then to treat their representations as factual... When the Jewish council, or whatever they were called, filed their amicus curiae brief and said there are thirteen million practicing orthodox Jews in the United States, or whatever the figure is, they just accept that—they accept the fact that this council represents the whole thirteen million adherents. That was a new experience for me, as a country lawyer where we fight over the record endlessly as to whether this or that should be heard by the court and is fully authenticated.[52]

Originally, oral arguments before the Supreme Court had been set for mid-November, but as news of growing support for the *McCollum* case by religious groups continued to make local news, the Court announced a postponement until December 8.[53] This was good news for John Franklin. He had indicated just days before the announcement that if he could not obtain a delay in a case in neighboring Piatt County, his colleague, Owen Rall would be presenting oral arguments in Washington by himself.[54]

While outside support was accumulating on Vashti's behalf, a report was circulated that George F. Barrett, Illinois state attorney general, was "thinking" about intervening on behalf of the Board of Education. Barrett had earlier submitted an amicus curiae brief in the *Everson* case in support of public bus transportation for parochial school students; his counterparts in five other states did the same thing. Initially, when contacted by reporters, Barrett was evasive: "Now where would something like that [his rumored support of the Board of Education] come from," he queried, although he was not reluctant about expressing his interest in the case.

> All I've been doing is thinking about the case and I haven't told anyone about that. Possibly in four or five days I will be able to say what I will do. Right now I have the flu and you know how it is when you got the flu.

When asked directly if he planned to intervene he responded: "I can't answer that question."[55]

Barrett, on December 4, did announce his participation. Franklin, as might be expected, lauded the decision:

> I think that the State of Illinois has a very legitimate interest in this case. It will determine to what extent the state can control its public buildings and that is distinctly a matter of states' rights. It is also contended by the opposition that this case involves educational policy and that, likewise, has always been a field of exclusive local control rather than national control. The State of Illinois is naturally interested in preserving state control in the field of education.[56]

In mid-October, during this period, there was a short but revealing news item in the *Courier*. It was reported that Superintendent Mellon, in the weekly news bulletin to school staff, wrote: "This time the [Supreme Court] justices are to decide the question, may a public school system provide its classrooms to church groups for sectarian education."[57] This represented a substantial admission on the part of the school authorities; it had previously been the board's contention that the classes were nonsectarian.

At the end of October, Philip Schug was again in the news. He had accepted a new position as minister of the All Souls Unitarian Church in Lincoln, Nebraska. It represented a significant advancement for the young minister; Lincoln was nearly twice the size of Champaign-Urbana, as was the new congregation.[58] The city contained the University of Nebraska and was also the state capital. The diminutive pastor could look back upon an eventful four years in the twin cities. In addition to his support of Vashti's cause, he had defended president-elect George Stoddard and had been one of the founders of the Student Community Interracial Committee.[59] The latter group represented the beginning of the postwar effort to promote racial equality in Champaign-Urbana.

In spite of his causes, which were regarded by many as radical, Schug had seen his small congregation double in size.[60] He left in December,[61] before oral arguments were made before the Supreme Court. But psychologically, the case seemed to have turned; from having only a few friends, Vashti by then had many. Phil Schug's support was no longer essential—even though he must have left with regrets over not being able to see Vashti's case through to the finish. To be sure, he had made a difference when it counted.

As headlines announced each new milestone in the case, there followed a flurry of editorial comment. The approach of oral arguments before the Supreme Court stimulated its share.

The *Daily Oregonian*, after briefly outlining the legal controversy, came to a non-committal conclusion:

> Just recently in Oregon City a Baptist minister, speaking publicly, pointed out with "regret, but with a fear it is true" that the campuses of our large universities were "great barren places spiritually." The Champaign plan no doubt was a community effort to touch a spiritual response in young people of school age but the old church and state controversy apparently is not so easily worded.[62]

The Catholic diocesan paper from Boston was much more committal. Its editorial treatment began with: "Two million children in 46 states enjoy the benefit of the 'released time' method of religious instruction in the public schools." Apart from this statement favorable to the concept of religious education in the public schools, the editorial did acknowledge that Vashti did have one legitimate concern: "Of this woman's objections, the only valid one is her concern for Terry. Children dread being 'left out.' It must be painful for this small boy to find himself alone and peculiar."

But then the writer queried: "But is it fair that two million children should be deprived of a benefit because of one parent's atheistic bigotry?"

The editorialist then offered his or her interpretation of what the "establishment of religion" clause really means:

The First Amendment of the Constitution was aimed squarely at the "church-state" idea. It was intended to prohibit favoring one church over another. It did not commit the government of this nation to unfriendliness or even neutrality. Historically, recognizing that there can be no morality without religion, America has always encouraged religion and eased its burdens.

The editorial concluded:

Terry McCollum ... is a child whose plight would touch any heart. But religion is an anti-toxin against an evil worse than diphtheria. And if Terry were the only child in the schoolroom whose mother would not permit him to be immunized against the diphtheria virus, no court would rule that every other child in the class must be deprived because of one parent's perverse obstinacy.[63]

In Charlotte, North Carolina, where there was a similar released time program, the *Observer* commented:

Since she (Vashti McCollum) is fighting so relentlessly against a program supported jointly by representatives of the Jewish, Catholic and Protestant faiths, there is ground for the suspicion that she may be inspired by other motives than the fear that the principle of separation of church and state is in jeopardy. Being an atheist, she probably objects to the teaching of the Bible and religion in churches or anywhere else just as much as in public school buildings.[64]

In Champaign-Urbana, the *Courier* offered two non-committal editorials on the subject. In one, the writer attempted to at least make clear the question involved: "The basic issue in the *McCollum* case, one forgotten in the 'monkey trial' atmosphere of the original court hearing, is the use of public schools built and maintained by public tax money for teaching classes in religion."[65]

The other editorial, while not advocating a particular outcome, supported the challenge:

Americans glory in the guarantee of religious freedom in this country and in the separation of church and state. They point to the fact that the very first article in the Bill of Rights, the first ten amendments to the Constitution, provides that Congress shall make no law respecting an establishment of religion, or prohibiting the free exercise thereof."

That stern provision may have forestalled necessary interpretation by the courts. The *McCollum* Case currently before the U. S. Supreme Court, may compel clarification of issues which have been only whispered heretofore. Thus it serves a useful purpose.[66]

Fifi Nella of *The Churchman* was supportive of Vashti, and thus consistent with the second thoughts many Protestants were having concerning the released-time programs. Of interest in the commentary was the expression of a growing feeling that strict church-state separation would help reduce what was perceived to be the growing influence of the Roman Catholic Church in public affairs. Nella wrote:

> Many parsons keep telling their hearers that education doesn't educate unless religion is included in the curriculum. The religion-in-the-classroom bug is gaining momentum. No doubt these good parsons are sincere, and no doubt they believe public school religion will promote peace. *But:* How are they going to teach religion in public schools without making the kids sectarian conscious? How are they going to get around the teachings of the Roman Catholic "one true church" concept? Don't they know from experience that constant pressure, constant agitating, on the part of the Roman Church—with the sympathy of the press, the radio, the government, big business—will eventually win over the "tolerant" Protestants?

The rhetorical questions continued:

> What's the matter with the Sunday schools? Aren't they teaching the principles of Jesus effectively? Would it please God more to have denominational controversy in the public schools, than to have the children taught to use the Golden Rule which all religions—even our much denounced "secularism"—have? Would God be just as pleased if His law of love were taught in the home, in the church, in the school—instead of an emphasis on being "different," which denominationalism fosters?[67]

Close to home, the St. Louis *Post Dispatch* also stepped forward to support Vashti. After outlining the facts in detail, it reprinted the basic arguments used by Henry Epstein in his amicus curiae brief on Vashti's behalf. The editorialist concluded:

> The public school is no place to teach sectarian beliefs. Denominational teaching is the responsibility of pastors and parents. The places for it are the church, the Sunday school and the home.
>
> One of the greatest blessings of the American people is that they have not been blighted with strife and hatred in the name of religion to the degree which has caused so much suffering over the world. We hope Mrs. McCollum will be upheld, not because· of her disbelief, but because of her right to it. If she is not free to bring up her son according to her convictions then other parents are not secure in their freedom to train their children in their beliefs.[68]

In the nation's capital itself, Vashti garnered even more editorial support. While lamenting the controversy brewing at the time in the New York City public schools concerning the singing of Christmas carols—raised by Jews—the editorial laid the blame squarely upon "the Protestant and Catholic churches" that had built up the nation's largest released-time program of religious instruction in that city. "For wherever this program has been forced upon our public schools, the tensions," wrote the author, "created among the children, their parents and the local communities have almost invariably resulted in unfortunate manifestations of one kind or another." After a lengthy discussion of the New York City released time program and its problems, the editorial continued:

> Fortunately our church and school authorities in Washington have had the good sense to maintain the independence of both these institutions, a practice which has been the custom in our country for over a century. Have the Christian churches elsewhere-especially the Protestants, who initiated the released-time program—ever really studied its devastating effects and asked themselves whether it is, in fact, a moral act consistent with their religious principles when they inject among little children the regrettable dissensions of their adult intolerances and rivalries?

The conclusion somewhat anticipated the decision of the United States Supreme Court in the *McCollum* case: "We hope the religious groups who still advocate the release program will withdraw from the public schools before court decisions or popular indignation subject them to the damaging effects of an enforced retreat."[69]

Thus went the public debate, though the debate that counted was that waged by contending attorneys and subsequently among the Supreme Court justices themselves. With the submission of briefs and the presentation of oral arguments before the court, the stage was set for the final resolution of Vashti's long battle. Clearly she had made some progress; from having very few friends, she had progressed to a point where she had many—not freethinking fellow travelers, but concerned, thinking people who represented a wide variety of religious persuasions.

Chapter 14

Briefs and Oral Argument

Dodd's brief, at 34 pages, was short, succinctly reiterating points made in earlier written arguments. It concluded:

> The appellant asks this court to determine whether sectarian groups may be permitted to teach in public school buildings during school hours, and substantially a part of the public school system. If such teaching is permitted, Appellant asks if school authorities may be permitted to determine who shall teach and what may be taught.[1]

In contrast, the appellee's brief was 168 pages, continuing the pattern already established by the relative lengths of earlier briefs submitted by the parties. "This brief is longer than we would ordinarily think proper,"[2] acknowledged Rall, the principal author. He then proceeded to justify the length on two grounds.

The first, Rall wrote, was "to anticipate and answer whatever contentions may be raised in the briefs of the numerous attorneys ... acting as amici curiae ... only one of which ... we have had the opportunity to examine .... "[3] The second justification was related to Rall's concerns over the language contained in both the majority and dissenting opinions in the *Everson* case. Almost certainly on the defensive, he felt it necessary to "direct the attention of the Court to highly pertinent interpretative data with which it had apparently not been furnished at the time of [that earlier decision] ... " Specifically, he mentioned "expressions in the majority opinion and language in the dissents which lend encouragement to what we believe to be an erroneous argument as to the establishment of religion clause of the First Amendment."[4] Rall continued:

> These expressions the appellant now seeks to have this Court enforce as the law of the land. It is our respectful suggestion that this is a field heretofore reserved entirely to State power; that subjection of it to Federal control or review will constitute an unnecessary and unwise substitution of national control for state control...
>
> And: "... a decision denying to the State the power to confer upon religion even the incidental aid of government will operate to restrict the high right of parents to control the education of their children..."

And: "... such a decision (against the Board of Education) will necessarily terminate efforts on the state level to provide balancing influences against the increasing emphasis upon materialism and secularism that many sincere persons believe is endangering the very foundations of American life.[5]

George F. Barrett, the Illinois attorney general, submitted a very short brief—six pages—on behalf of the Champaign Board of Education. Devoid of substantive legal argument, the brief maintained:

If appellant's constitutional thesis is correct, although children may be compelled to study the history of the Western World, a history that has been dominated in many of its respects by the writings in question (the Bible), nevertheless they may not be even permitted, much less compelled, to read those writings themselves on school property. And this is true, according to appellant, nothwithstanding the fact that the parents—whose responsibility for their children's tutelage must remain primary amoung a free people—desire that their children be tutored in *this* great literary work.[6]

The brief went on to direct the High Court's attention to "a wide consensus on the part of the state authorities ... " tolerating Bible reading and Bible study in the public schools." Barrett's brief then asserted: "Had the State Legislatures been told that their ratification of the Fourteenth Amendment would proscribe the voluntary reading of the Bible on school property, it is very doubtful that the amendment would have been adopted at all."[7]

Afterwards, the lawyer who had prepared Barrett's brief saw Dodd and asked rhetorically: "Well, our brief didn't hurt you any, did it?"[8]

In its brief, the Protestant Council of the City of New York sought to acquaint the Court with the New York released time statute. It argued strongly on its behalf and in an outline of the program as conducted in that state listed the following provisions, among others, in an apparent effort to distinguish it from the Champaign System.

- The religious instruction is given outside the school buildings and grounds;
- The religious organizations, in cooperation with the parents, must assume full responsibility for attendance at the religious center and for the program of religious instruction thereat; and
- The school authorities have no responsibility beyond that assumed in regular dismissals.[9]

It would seem that the Protestant Council, in light of the *Everson* decision, was motivated at least to some extent by a feeling that the Champaign System was vulnerable.

The amicus curiae brief submitted on the appellant's behalf by the American Civil Liberties Union represented its only active involvement in the *McCollum* case while it was in progress. In responding to Vashti's request for extra copies of the ACLU brief, attorney Kenneth W. Greenawalt wrote: " ... I am very glad to send one ... to you, except for whom the case would not have been brought—It takes a great deal of courage, sincerity and stamina to bring and carry on a case like this."[10]

In a 31-page appendix, the ACLU brief provided the constitutional and statutory provisions of all of the states—then 48—and the District of Columbia, which either affirmed or mandated support for the principle of church-state separation.[11]

The brief submitted by the Joint Committee on Public Relations of the four Baptist Conventions was short, containing, in nearly equal amounts, legal and public policy arguments. Lacking is any indication of why the Baptists, alone among the major Protestant denominations, felt the issue important enough to enter the case on Vashti's behalf.[12]

Henry Epstein, in his brief for the two Jewish organizations, left little doubt as to their concerns:

> The divisiveness which inevitably results whenever sectarianism enters the public school affects all American children, but is particularly harmful to children of minority faiths. Jewish groups base their opposition to the released time program on many grounds, but no consideration bulks larger in that opposition than the divisive effects of the program.[13]

Epstein's brief was endorsed in its entirety in a two-page statement filed by the American Ethical Union.[14]

The remaining religious minority groups submitting briefs were influenced quite likely by the same concerns expressed openly and obviously by Epstein. Attorneys Homer Cummings and William Donnelly, filing for the Seventh-day Adventists, did address the issue, though somewhat indirectly:

> The Council of Religious Education [in Champaign] was conscious of the dangers of religious distinctions and differentiation among children of tender years; so conscious that it chose to invoke censorship in religion rather than run the risks inherent in teaching the controversial subjects of religious belief, the tenets which are the distinction between the sects. Thus the very proponents of religious school training in effect admit that exercise of the constitutional right to propagate religious beliefs can not, as a practical [matter], in its full scope be permitted to all the sects in the public schools without engendering disruptive differences among the children and consequent religious controversy among the parents. The result is to destroy the privilege of non-conformity which is the very essence of the constitutional right and necessarily to create among the school children the impression that our vaunted Bill of Rights is in some respects at least a mere set of platitudes.[15]

Edward C. Park, in behalf of the American Unitarian Association, offered a somewhat unusual version of the compulsion argument:

> We believe that for many ten-year-old boys, and perhaps for James, a choice between pursuing regular studies in public school and attending classes in religious education may be regarded as one between two evils.

In any event, he was in substance, offered a release from compulsory attendance in public school only upon condition that he elect to pursue a course in religious education. He was in effect told that he must take such a course or else continue his regular studies. We think he was thereby constrained by public authority to attend the class in religious education. Moreover, as the record discloses, the constraint, though not absolute, became under the circumstances severe in that by not volunteering he was isolated from other pupils and singled out as a non-conformist.[16]

Unquestionably the most unusual brief was that submitted by Hazel Franklin Lewis, a private citizen of Danville, Illinois, on her own behalf. Mrs. Lewis took issue with both Dodd and Franklin for their opposition to the Court's acceptance of her brief. With respect to the former:

Attorney ... Dodd refused his consent on the grounds that an amicus curiae brief must carry the signature of an attorney qualified to appear before the Supreme Court of the United States. I am not an attorney, nor do I have funds to hire an attorney ... Furthermore, there is nothing in the Constitution of the United States vaguely hinting at an exclusive right of attorneys to operate in our tax-supported courts.[17]

Concerning Franklin's objections:

(He) refused his consent ... on grounds that parties wishing to discuss the national aspects involved rather than the facts of the initial controversy are merely confusing the issue.

She countered:

Any aspect of provincialism attached to the controversy vanished into nothingness when appeal was made to the Highest Court in this land. What the Court says binds every citizen in these United States.[18]

Most of her brief was devoted to arguments against the Champaign system on grounds of public policy. She concluded, however, with a personal note:

Some five or six years back feelers were being put out locally on sentiment with regard to religious teaching in public schools. I protested to the School Board, [and] to the Danville Ministerial Association with a copy to the Principal of Danville Public Schools. The plan was not put in operation, but certain parents belonging to a particular sect withdrew their offspring from the public schools and sent them to parochial schools of their faith. A bus was chartered for the purpose, and a group of these children congregated one block from my home. It was necessary for me to pass that corner as I took my two daughters to high school. These children waiting for their bus to come to take them to the parochial school they attended would shout "communist" as I passed, spit at the car, and stick out their tongues as they made ugly faces. That did not bother me in the least, but how would children under compulsion to attend school feel if such manifestations of hate were directed at them?

... I have often wondered what deep-seated planning [presumably for the proposed program of religious education] was frustrated to bring on such actions on the part of these children. No good purpose will be served by any plan that establishes the conditions that make some children subject to the insults of other children who shout only that which they hear at home. If religionists have failed to draw children to their churches they must not bring added failure into our public school system that is the bulwark of everything that is our way of life.[19]

With the submission of all but two briefs, it was then time for the argument of the pen to give way to the force of the spoken word—the showdown before the Supreme Court itself.

As it turned out, the additional legal help offered by Theodore Bear earlier in the appeal process was not required. Bear, in its stead, undertook to underwrite all further personal expenses for Vashti related to the prosecution of the lawsuit. These included the trip to Washington D. C. for the oral arguments before the Supreme Court. "So," the appellant wrote afterwards, "for the first time in my life, I traveled first class [to Washington D. C.] on the Capitol Limited." It was the same train John Franklin was to take.[20]

In a desire "to achieve a happy balance between chic and respectability," Vashti, after much deliberation, decided to purchase a stylish coat of black cloth with ermine trimmings. It was rather expensive, and in spite of her husband's urgings she had had misgivings concerning its purchase. The proprietor of the store, a friend, finally settled the matter. On Saturday, December 6, the day before she was to leave for the nation's capital, he most persuasively argued: "A girl who can make up her mind to file a lawsuit and take it all the way to the Supreme Court ought to be able to make up her mind about a coat."[21]

For most of the remainder of that Saturday, a severe headache kept Vashti in bed.[22] She was well enough, however, to respond to a *Gazette* reporter who asked her if she had a "last-minute battle statement."[23] After a very brief review of her basic arguments concerning both the efficacy and propriety of religious education in the public schools, she declared:

This country's greatness was built on the principle of separation of church and state. If that wall is broken down, with the public treasury on the other side, there will be an attempt by all religious groups to get control. Smaller denominations will be crowded out and the process will be continued until one is predominant.

She continued:

The wall between church and state has been weakened by several attacks. A decision against me would be a very severe blow to [the] church. No matter how much value is attributed to religious education, I still say the price is too high.[24]

"Is there any chance that [the headaches] will keep you from going to Washington?" The reporter asked. "Not a chance in the world," responded the obviously determined appellant.[25]

The same reporter contacted John Franklin, who was in Chicago for "last-minute conferences" with Owen Rall. Franklin referred to the recent order in the public schools of Brooklyn, New York, banning the singing of Christmas carols. He said the occurrence represented a "small indication of what may happen if the Supreme Court rules in favor of Mrs. McCollum." He went on to state:

> This decision will either give great impetus to secularism and material-
> ism not only in public education but in all phases of American life, or it
> will fortify the promotion of spiritual values in the education of America.
> Complete secularism of all phases of education would flow from a deci-
> sion against the school board. A great deal more depends on this case
> than is generally realized. If its full significance were understood by the
> public, it would be one of the greatest issues before America today.[26]

Vashti was at the Supreme Court early on the morning of December 8, 1947. She found the hearing room already crowded though she did find a place in a section in the rear reserved for spectators. At the request of photographers, who wanted her picture, she went outside. On the steps of the Supreme Court building, with the dome of the Capitol in the background, she posed in her ermine trimmed coat. The result was probably the most widely published photograph of the lawsuit. Upon her return, she was accorded a seat in the front in the section reserved for attorneys admitted to practice before the High Court.[27]

All of the morning was devoted to the reading of decisions in cases heard earlier by the Court. Finally, at 12:30, Walter Dodd rose to present the argument for the appellant. The aging attorney was described as "tall, slender, gray." He stood behind a tall lectern and began reading from a typewritten manuscript "in a low voice, slowly and so quietly that his words could not be heard in the back of the courtroom."[28]

It became clear almost immediately when Justice Reed interrupted Dodd's presentation with a question, that the court was not going to be satisfied with a dull recitation of arguments. "Did the parents," Reed inquired, "ask the school to permit their children to attend the religious classes?"

Dodd: "The schools distributed cards prepared by the Religious Education Council on which parents might indicate their approval."

Justice Frankfurter, not satisfied with the response, wanted a more direct answer: "What you are saying is that the school asks the parent—I assume the contrary, the parent asks the school."[29]

The questioning continued with Frankfurter pursuing the interrogation "most sharply of all."[30] Frankfurter: "Will the decision in this case affect other States?"

Dodd: "Probably, yes."[31]

In a follow-up question Justice Burton asked: "Would your objections apply if the religion were taught away from the schools on released time as is done in New York and elsewhere?"[32]

Dodd: "The two systems need not necessarily be linked together."[33]

Chief Justice Vinson: "I understand certain sects are not in and never have been in on this plan—are there certain children who receive no instruction of their sect?" Dodd: "They may join in [the program]."[34]

Frankfurter: "Nine Protestant denominations have gotten together on a common denominator, is that correct?" Dodd: "That is practically true."[35]

Frankfurter: "What did I understand you to say about the attitude of Jehovah's Witnesses?" Dodd: "The Witnesses have not chosen to be represented."[36]

At this point the *Courier* reporter present noted: "There was some whispered exchange along the bench and all broke into smiles without explaining their own little joke."[37]

Reed: "Can anyone teach religion in the schools who wants to? Who decides what persons may teach?"

Dodd: "The Superintendent of Schools."

Frankfurter: "Is there any evidence that school authorities exercise any judgment about the qualifications of those religious teachers?" Dodd: "The record does not show that the school authorities have questioned appointments by the sects."[38]

Reed: "Do all other activities—reading, writing and arithmetic—cease during the religious classes?" Dodd: "The religious teachers come in and take over."

Reed: "Assume that in a room of 30, there is one who does not take religious education, what happens to him?" Dodd: "That is very important in this case. Appellant's son did not participate, and he was put out in the corridor and later in a music room."[39]

With some difficulty, Dodd worked his prepared presentation in among the numerous questions. Summarized by Ed Borman, the attorney emphasized four main points:

1. Teachers support the classes by distributing cards on which parents give permission for children to enroll;
2. The teaching is sectarian;
3. Use of school buildings constitutes expenditure of public funds for religious purposes;
4. Division of students by faiths creates "friction" and religious stigmas.[40]

In emphasizing the latter point, Dodd said: "There is a sharpening of differences between Jewish and non-Jewish children that often leads to trouble."[41] He continued: "Anti-Semitism and anti-Catholic views at an early age will be accomplished by segregating for religious teaching."[42]

Justice Jackson interrupted: "It is the legal and constitutional question we must consider here; can a state commandeer students' time then give back some of that time if they will study religion? Whether there are good or bad effects from this practice we can't consider."[43]

Rutledge then asked: "I take it that the School Board does not permit use of its facilities to teach atheism", to which Dodd responded: "On the basis of the testimony in the record by the Superintendent of Schools, the classrooms are open to all groups—in fact, there have been no classes on atheism."[44]

As Dodd's time was nearly over, Frankfurter asked: "What do you say *is* the crucial element of infringement of the Constitution by this plan?"

Dodd: "It is the establishment of a religious organization in the public schools which will be dominated by the predominant group. This action is not intended as a means of preventing children from taking religious lessons; the point is, if they take them in the schools friction and trouble is sure to develop."[45] He went on to dispute the Board's argument that equal treatment of all sects made the program legal: "It is sectarian teaching and will be done in relation to sectarian numbers; control will go to denominations with the greatest numbers."[46]

Frankfurter: "A child can attend a parochial school altogether. Why can't he divide time between school and church?"

Dodd, noting that his time was running short, promised to respond to the question after presentation of the Board's argument[47]—during the 15 minutes of additional time awarded him by Chief Justice Vinson.[48] In later years, Rall offered the following explanation as to how the award of additional time came about:

> Felix Frankfurter prided himself in not reading anything about a case before oral arguments—he wanted a fresh view. Because he had not read anything about the case, he asked Mr. Dodd a lot of silly questions which disrupted his argument. At one point Dodd paused to re-gather his thoughts, prompting Frankfurter to say: "Mr. Dodd, Mr. Dodd, you should get on with your argument." A voice came from the left side of the court, Justice Jackson, which said: "I submit that Mr. Dodd has been making extraordinary efforts in that direction."[49]

While Franklin had taken the lead role at both the trial and in the arguments before the Illinois Supreme Court, he had suggested to Rall, whose specialty was appellate work, that they switch roles. As Franklin remembered it:

> When we went to Washington, I urged Mr. Rall to take the lead argument, but he, through perhaps modesty, insisted on my making the principal and opening argument before the Supreme Court. He said that he "would pick up the pieces," as we say, and make the closing argument and would only ask for five or ten minutes at the close of the argument.[50]

Thus it was that Franklin stepped forward, at 2 p.m.,[51] first to formally be admitted to practice before the Supreme Court,[52] then to make the lead presentation. The attorney had barely begun when he was halted by a 30-minute lunch break.[53] When he resumed, as Rall remembered it, "The justices were standing in line to ask him questions."[54] Indeed, Franklin's argument was punctuated by sharp questioning, perhaps to an even greater extent than was Dodd's. In contrast to Dodd, whose responses were described as so unargumentative "that one might have had trouble deciding which side he represented,"[55] Franklin, to the "amazement" of "veteran court observers ... 'talked back' to the black-robed justices."[56] Chief Justice Vinson pursued the question of membership in CCRE: "Is it fair to infer that groups (sects) that did not come in did not want to come in?" Franklin: "Yes. Any religious group that wishes to make use of the school buildings may do so."[57]

The attorney was "questioned closely" by Frankfurter and Reed "as to whether all creeds and faiths were equal under the plan." Franklin: "The school authorities had abided by the Constitution by barring instruction from no one who wanted it. It was not found possible, however, to set up classes for a sect unless a sufficient number of pupils of a sect applied."[58] "The plan is open to any religious, irreligious or unreligious group which desires to participate."[59]

Frankfurter: "Suppose all you say about the place of religion is true, is the public school the place to introduce it, when it may be a source of conflict? Is that good or bad?"[60]

Franklin: "We are not here as legislative censors; this is a court trying a constitutional question."

Frankfurter: "But the Constitution is not something up in the blue."

Franklin: "No. It's something in the Constitution. A question as to whether the classes are good as a practical matter is not a proper one. I can only ask your honor to go on the record which shows that such classes are being taught in at least 1,000 communities in 46 states, and there is nothing in the record to show that they are bad."[61]

Justice Rutledge asked Franklin to discuss the relationship between the *Everson* and *McCollum* cases. Franklin: "In the New Jersey Case, the court held a tax could not be levied for religious purposes, but, thank God, it didn't say that once facilities are established, they can't be used for the benefit of religion. The constitutional provision that 'Congress shall make no law respecting an establishment of religion' does not prohibit all aid to religion—all it means is that government shall treat all religious groups equally."[62]

Jackson: "Are you saying it means that, 'Congress shall make no law respecting an establishment of religion' but may establish religious instruction?"

Franklin: "No. The 'establishment of religion' clause has had a well defined meaning for 160 years, and it means that one particular church cannot be given preference over another."[63]

Reed: "Would it be all right if religious instruction went so far as to receive children into the church?"

Franklin: "No. It would not be proper to hold a revival in a school building. Education in religion is taught rather than the doctrine of any church; it is kept on an educational level and an interdenominational basis."[64]

Reed: "If they taught children to join the Methodist Church ..."

Franklin: "That is not taught."

Frankfurter: "Why don't you answer that it's none of the School Board's business—that for a half hour children are turned over to religious teachers to teach what they want to?" Franklin: "That is not the answer. I am trying to answer Justice Reed's question. The content of the Bible is taught, not the doctrine of any church."[65]

Justice Black: "If the Illinois practice of setting aside an hour or less a week for religious instruction in public schools were constitutional, would four hours a day, six hours a day, seven and a half hours a day be constitutional also?"

Franklin: "It might be unwise, but I do not think it would violate the Federal Constitution."[66]

Black: "Would you go so far as to say that the State of Illinois can contribute $5,000,000 a year to religion so long as all religions are treated equally?"[67]

Franklin: "I certainly do; the State of Illinois spent more than that last year."[68] When Black asked how, Franklin responded "Through tax exemptions on properties held for religious purposes."[69] It was an argument Franklin and Rall had thought to include in their brief.[70]

The *Courier* reported that Franklin "and Mr. Justice Black literally stood toe to toe slugging it out" during the exchange.[71]

At one point Franklin pointed to the tablet depicting the Ten Commandments on the frieze above the High Court bench. "If," he said, "you want to legislate religion out of our civilization, you must take that down."[72] The "oratorical outburst" continued as Franklin "waved a quarter" in front of the justices and declared: "If you declare this program of religious education unconstitutional, you must strike out 'In God We Trust' from millions of coins minted by the government. Your honors cannot strike out of the American people an interest in religion."[73]

This prompted a retort from Justice Jackson: "I think it is going a bit far to say that because people do not agree with this system they are irreligious; there are many devout people who do not believe public money ought to pay religious costs, and so do not believe the state ought to compel people to be religious."[74]

Frankfurter was also "nettled" by Franklin's burst of eloquence. After alluding to the number of briefs filed by dissenting religious bodies in support of Vashti's suit, he said: "The very fact that we have these briefs proves that religious controversy has been introduced into the public schools."[75]

Franklin's argument, interrupted as it was by repeated questioning from the justices, ran one hour and ten minutes. By Franklin's reckoning, 30 minutes of that time was taken up in responding to questions from the justices.[76] The attorney "apologized to the Court for taking more time than he anticipated and leaving only five minutes for his colleague (Rall)." One of the justices responded: "That is a matter for you and your colleague."[77]

Rall later recalled: "I did have the longest undisrupted argument of the day ... even Justice Frankfurter didn't get any questions in."[78] The attorney contended, in the brief five minutes of defense time which remained, that the right of religious freedom was a relative right. "Eight hundred fifty pupils," he said, accepted the religious courses and only one objected; there must be a balancing of rights."[79] Rall also argued: "Objections raised to this plan run to its wisdom, not its constitutionality, and they should be left to the school board."[80] There was a check against abuse: "There is no public body more closely watched than the local school board," Rall said, "and it may be depended upon for discretion in the public welfare."[81]

Franklin reflected years later: "The justices peppered me with so many questions ... that I never really made the connected argument that I had come to Washington to make, though, upon a review of it afterwards, we had touched upon all the major points in a disconnected fashion."[82] Rall agreed: "The night before the hearing, John and I worked up a wonderful oral argument. The night after, we compared notes and found we had covered everything we had planned the previous evening."[83]

In the time he had reserved for a rebuttal, Dodd unexpectedly allowed former U.S. Senator Edward Burke of Nebraska to argue in behalf of the numerous groups that had filed amicus curiae briefs in support of Mrs. McCollum. Since his appearance came late in the day, the only references to his participation came in follow-up reports carried the following day in the *Courier* and *News-Gazette*. According to the former, Burke said:

> "The wall separating State and Church must not be breached."[84] The latter reported: "Burke asserted the Champaign School Board had made an unlawful contract which allowed churches to 'impart their creeds to children assembled under the school board's authority'."[85]

On the day oral arguments were presented, Superintendent Mellon was quoted extensively concerning possible consequences of a court decision upholding Vashti. "Of course," he said, "it depends on what the court decides to do." Mellon continued:

> But if they [the justices] decide to ban religious education, just how far will they go? Will it mean that we have to give up our Christmas plays? They're about religion you know. Will it mean that anything about religion that is taught in the grade schools will be taboo? Religion is connected with history. In the grades, these courses aren't electives; all the pupils have to take them. Just what this will mean, I don't know.

Mellon did point out, even in the event of an adverse ruling, "We can still release our pupils to attend these classes if they are not held in the school buildings." The Superintendent concluded: "If they decide our way of conducting religious education classes is proper, all the other schools will want to know how we do it; I guess we'll just get up a mimeographed form."[86]

In an interview back in Champaign, Franklin admitted to being somewhat nervous as he began his argument before the Supreme Court. The account continued:

> But after he started speaking everything straightened out for the school board attorney and he forgot about the crowded courtroom and the fact that most of the crowd was against him as he launched into a vigorous and aggressive defense of the teaching of religious education in the Champaign schools.[87]

Vashti was also contacted by the press on her return. Described as "a peppery, attractive woman," she responded that she "certainly wasn't impressed" with Franklin's arguments. "But," she added, "I was very proud of my attorney." Concerning James Terry, she said: "I'm awfully sorry now that I didn't take him with me. He wanted to go, but I decided against it. I should have taken him because I know it would have made him feel good to see how people there were on his side.[88]

In hopes that James Terry would be home for the following school year, Vashti indicated she had applied for his admission to University High School, an experimental school run by the University of Illinois College of Education. She had given up, as far as James Terry was concerned, on the schools run by the Champaign Board of Education.

While she refused to speculate as to the outcome, she did acknowledge that her base of support was stronger outside of Champaign-Urbana. When asked if she had lost friends locally over her long fight she said that she did not think so. "There are," she said, "some people who don't know whether they should speak to me or not." The reporter asked if she thought there would be any change in local attitudes should the Supreme Court should declare her position to be correct. "Do you think," she answered, "that anyone who's thrown garbage in my front room will change his mind just because the Supreme Court says I am right?"[89]

All that remained was for the two attorneys to file supplemental briefs. This resulted from the fact that several of the amicus curiae briefs had been submitted after Franklin had filed his. The *Courier* reported that most of the defense's final, 19-page brief was prepared by Franklin and his colleague Rall as they returned to Chicago from Washington. It was in Dodd's hands within four days following oral arguments.[90] Dodd's response followed in less than a week of that event. The final paragraph read:

> Even if it were possible to establish state religion supported by taxation and with an effort in good faith to apply equal treatment to all sects, an equality cannot be maintained in any area in which a religious group has stronger organization and larger membership than others. Our Constitution has forbidden both state and national religion for this reason. From the beginning of our civilization religion has been the primary basis for war and other human friction, and public schools should not be employed to continue religious friction.[91]

Franklin took public issue with these sentiments and issued a statement in which he said: "She [Vashti] has closed her case as she started it, in an angry and unfounded attack upon religion." He continued:

> This is typical of her attitude toward religion as expressed throughout this litigation. The United States has engaged in seven major wars and we are not acquainted with any authoritative suggestion that any one of them was caused by religious friction. Certainly no one has given any such interpretation of the causes of World War I and World War II. The charge of religious friction in the public schools is equally without basis. Actually, religious tolerance has reached a new high in Champaign and other communities where cooperative programs of religious education have been instituted.[92]

As to the prosecution of the lawsuit, the work of the parties was over; all that remained was to await the Court's decision.

Chapter 15

A Landmark Decision

Vashti was sound asleep on Monday, March 8, 1948, when she was awakened by a call from a *Courier* reporter. The latter had caught a Washington, D.C. dateline on the teletype and had dialed the McCollum number assuming that the forthcoming story concerned the Supreme Court decision in the *McCollum* case. By the time she answered, he was able to read: "The Supreme Court ruled today that public school systems may not be used to assist religious groups in giving religious instruction; the decision was eight to one.[1] The subsequent story recorded her reaction.

Vashti was silent for a moment. Then she spoke: "Honestly? Oh ... (pause) ... Oh ... (brokenly) ... Oh." Then, recovering, she said: "I'm going right upstairs and tell my husband."[2] John McCollum was in bed, home sick that particular day. Vashti related what happened next:

> I opened the door and stood there, trying to look nonchalant. "Pappy," I said, "guess what happened?" Sick as he was, Pappy grinned broadly. "You needn't tell me," he said. "I know."[3]

After the rush of excitement passed, she drafted a statement for the newspapers.

> The preeminence of this nation is in large measure due to the complete separation of church and state and the resulting secular public school system. The Supreme Court has by this decision safeguarded our school system from sectarian domination.
>
> There are and will be still more attacks made upon the secular nature of our schools and eternal vigilance is. necessary to see that we maintain the school system which is our heritage. Still more, the principle separating church and state has been fortified. It is the obligation of all who cherish democracy to fight any attack on this principle. I am deeply indebted to the Chicago Action Council who, seeing the threat, liberally gave of their energies to carry on the fight and to Mr. Walter Dodd, who, realizing the great responsibility in this case, handled it with the utmost care and integrity, which impressed me as it must have the justices in Washington.

My main concern all along was to get this case before the U. S. Supreme Court. I have always had the greatest admiration for this bench and felt confident that there I would have a fair, complete and non-political hearing.[4]

In Rochester, New York, Arthur Cromwell and James Terry, his temporary ward, were contacted for their reaction. The latter was brief and to the point: "I knew Mom was right. Everybody thought Mom and I were wrong, but now they can't think that unless they think the justices are wrong, too."[5]

Cromwell was quoted by a Rochester newspaper: "Americans who would keep America truly free can well be thankful for this decision by the Supreme Court."[6] The *News-Gazette* carried, in its words, a "blast" from the old freethinker. "The concerted and insidious attempts of religious leaders and zealots to parochialize our public schools has met with defeat. The ruling has served to hold back the religious tide that is trying to sweep America back into another medieval dark age."[7]

Attorney Dodd was also contacted for his perspective on the decision. He was inclined to be cautious: "The judgment in this case applies only to Champaign, but the determination by the court will be controlling throughout the nation. Other suits may have to be brought if there are violations of the principles enunciated by the court."[8]

Dodd was asked if he thought revisions could be made, consistent with the Court's decision, which would allow the religious education classes to continue. "I don't know just now where you would draw the line," he responded. The report continued:

"Thinking out loud," Dodd indicated that he thought it would be permissible to dismiss all students an hour early one day a week to allow those so choosing to attend religious classes. He emphasized "all students" for if the schools exercised any selection of the students to be dismissed or attempted to determine which students attended "there would still be the use of the schools for religious education purposes."[9]

When asked to comment on Cromwell's "blast," Dodd declined, saying only: "I'm interested in the legal aspects and would like to confine the case to that."[10]

Support for Vashti from local clergy, in the absence of Philip Schug, came in the form of a mild statement from only one, Rev. Ellis E. Pierce, pastor of the Universalist Church in Urbana. "[The Supreme Court's decision] would be in accord with the official position of both the state and national associations of our church. We have felt that week-day released time for religious instruction is not in the best interest of either the church or school."[11]

John Franklin, reached early by the *Courier*, was initially guarded in his response: "[I have] no comment until I know more about what the Supreme Court said. Of course, it goes without saying that I disagree with them. The importance of the decision and its full effect here will depend upon exactly what the Court said in its opinion."[12] When asked if further appeal were possible, the attorney quipped: "Not unless it's to the United Nations."[13]

By noon on that momentous Monday, Franklin was prepared to speak at greater length regarding the decision, this time to the Champaign Rotary Club. Excerpts were reported the following day in the *Daily Illini*.

The U. S. Supreme Court is too concerned about rights of minorities... I would rather argue a case for any minority group, right or wrong, in the Supreme Court, than for any majority group, no matter how right. Those in the Supreme Court are not representative of the people. Practically all were appointed by the same president.[14]

Franklin acknowledged that he had not "thought well" of the justices before he appeared before them in Washington, though he admitted that he came away with respect for them. Nevertheless, in Franklin's view, the justices were "left" in their thinking on Constitutional matters.[15]

The following day, after studying the text of the decision, the Board's attorney issued a lengthy statement that was printed in a follow-up news article:

The decision is a severe blow to religion, which is not softened by Justice Black's assurance that it is delivered without hostility. Religion like everything else may be killed with kindness and good intentions as well as by design. Only Justice Reed, who dissented, and Justice Jackson who concurred with expressed misgivings, seem to have appreciated the dangers in the decision and the force of our arguments to the Court. It is perhaps a cause for gratification that four of the judges in the majority have specifically limited their decision to the facts of this case and have left open to later decision other forms of cooperation between government and religion. But the decision leaves the constitutionality of every form of released time religious education open to serious question.

One of the most regretted aspects of the opinion is that the Court found itself unable to agree upon or express any rule of decision to control other cases and leaves open to attack every form of cooperation between religion and government.

By this decision the Court has enacted into law its philosophy that religion should be quarantined to the home and the church. As I do not believe that the Court's fellow Americans are willing to commit religion to such a subordinate role, I do not believe that this decision will live in our law.

In the meantime, it is the duty of every religious citizen to work for its constitutional change and to strive to build an appreciation of spiritual values in our youth through agencies outside of the school.[16]

On March 10, perhaps after even more study, Franklin said: "The majority opinion is much more sweeping than I supposed possible, but we at least changed one man's mind [Reed]. We didn't make any progress with the others with the possible exception of Justice Jackson."[17] In other reports that day, the Board's attorney declared less charitably:

There is no end to what crackpots can and will do under the decision. It places in jeopardy every phase of religious practice with which government has any association. Literal compliance with the majority opinion would make the United States the most secularized and materialistic nation in the history of the world.[18]

And: "They'll [the Supreme Court] be flooded with litigation from crackpots who may want church buildings taxed or chaplains removed from the army, or the (in) 'God We Trust' taken off coins. I give them several months to start this."[19]

While minds might differ over what causes one would have to espouse to be labeled a "crackpot," there was logic to Franklin's interpretation of where the *McCollum* decision might lead.

Ministerial opposition to the court decision was quick. Rev. Cartlidge, by then the most familiar religious figure associated with the released time program locally, was quoted at length in the local papers. The *Courier* version read:

The decision looks as though it is a victory for a definite commitment of our nation to an irreligious stand that can now be used by groups antagonistic to religion to prohibit any benefit of government toward religion. It verifies my conviction that the Supreme Court of the United States is not interested in the will of the people but in its own social program which it has in mind. It seems they have set themselves up as a legislative body more than a judicial body.[20]

The *Gazette* version added: "When the CCRE ... has time to study the matter we will make a statement as to our future policy. We hope that some legal way may be found to carry on our work on released time."[21]

Rev. Northcott, another major force behind the program, said that he was "shocked" by the decision. "The task of religious education has received a setback, but it will stimulate an even greater effort among religious forces of the community to meet the religious needs."[22]

Baptist minister Bromley, another early supporter, was also quoted:

I think all of us realize the need of moral and spiritual training in connection with education. There is no sectarianism in the Ten Commandments or the Golden Rule or the Sermon on the Mount. They are a valid part of our culture and it is one of the purposes of our educational system to pass on the finest things in our culture.[23]

In another report, Bromley sounded almost as if he had adopted his church's national position. "If the decision actually separates the churches and state—so that no financial compensations will be given to religious groups for education and schools—the outcome will probably be beneficial."[24]

Rev. Higgins of Holy Cross Church in Champaign stated: "I think the Communists will rejoice over the Court's decision."[25]

Rev. Albert Akley Belyea, pastor of the First Methodist Church in Urbana and Chairman of that city's CRE, said: "It may work out best in the end. We will have to find another way to teach religious education. We as churches will have to do a better job than we are, and there is room for us to do so."[26] In a second statement, he was equally moderate:

> I was not surprised by the decision, and there is certainly nothing we can do to alter it. The churches must work harder. Sunday school is not enough and we do not have adequate teachers. We are not reaching our goal and will have to plan something bigger or try something else.[27]

Lay churchman David Lindstrom was also interviewed. He said his main interest in the case was "to get the law cleared up so that we will know where we stand." He continued: "It was my belief that local school boards should be given the privilege of determining how their buildings should be used when not being used for school purposes."[28] Lindstrom, like Rev. Belyea, appeared to accept the finality of the High Court pronouncement but expressed, as did others, that some way needed to be found to accomplish the same result as that provided by the now banned practice. "[The decision] clears up the matter once and for all. (Religious education in the schools) is now out the window. Religion is a part of our total culture and some way must be found to impart this teaching to young people."[29]

Local school officials were contacted. Donald E. Vance, president of the Champaign Board of Education, said the decision was not a complete surprise; "Franklin had indicated the Court might rule that way."[30] Superintendent Eugene Mellon said he had "no comment" until he knew more of the details. "There might be several angles to the decision," he said. When asked when the schools would end the religious education classes, assuming that a study of the decision shows that to be the only course of action, Mellon, who had avoided talking too much throughout the long legal process, responded tersely: "1 don't know yet."[31]

Superintendent T.H. Cobb of the Urbana schools was far more definite in his response: "We will undoubtedly have to give over in Urbana. We will want to be in compliance with the Supreme Court mandate. I will have to think it over before making any further statement."[32]

In Springfield, the state capital, Vernon Nickell offered his perspective:

> I felt that if any of the various programs used in the state were constitutional, the Champaign plan was. The Board of Education there was careful not to spend any tax money to support the program. Up to now [my office] has maintained a hands off policy on religious education but with the Supreme Court decision we might have to take a definite stand.[33]

Around the state and nation, there was no shortage of persons expressing their views. Beginning close to home, Bishop Griffin of Springfield and George Stoddard critic opined: "The cause of religion suffered a deplorable setback by this decision, not however because of the action of the Supreme Court justices, but because anti-God elements persisted in making of this whole issue a battleground between atheism and religion."

But, he added:

The clear-cut decision of the Supreme Court of the United States with reference to the teaching of religion in the public schools was based on an authoritative interpretation of the First Amendment. In the Roman Catholic Church we have a saying: "Roma locuta, causa finita—Rome has spoken, the case is closed." Similarly, every good American should adopt the same attitude toward this recent judgment of the Supreme Court. The Court has spoken; that ends all dispute.[34]

Bishop Griffin's fellow churchman in Springfield, Episcopalian F. William Orrick: "If this court ruling means that children won't be able to get the training, I think it will be a tragedy."[35]

Frank E. Karelsen Jr., vice president of the Public Education Association in New York City:

All of us who have been opposed to the inroads of religion in the schools are very much heartened by this decision. [It] should be a milestone toward true democratic education. I foresee that this will lead to the elimination of sectarian influences in our schools and particularly I am in hopes that it will end released time in the New York City school system.[36]

A. Ralph Eckberg, president of the Brighton, New York School District: "The ruling is ridiculous; there must be rejoicing in Moscow today.[37]

Gerald Landis, Member of Congress from Indiana: "I'm in favor of religious education in schools. It will not hurt anybody. We may need a constitutional amendment to clarify the situation."[38]

His colleague, Herbert Meyer of Kansas:

This decision shocked, and rightly so, all God-fearing people in America and made them wonder just why and how the Court made its findings at a time when Communism is conducting a vicious attack upon religion and religious institutions everywhere. We can only wonder too, what is coming next if the Supreme Court stands in the way of religious instruction in a public school when it is by no means compulsory.[39]

Dr. Edwin McNeill Poteat, president of Colgate-Rochester Divinity School and president of Protestants and Other Americans United For Separation Of Church and State:

While I have been interested in the so-called "released time" program of making religion available to school children, I have never been quite satisfied that it has been sufficiently protected against violation of the principle of separation of church and state. I wish there were some way religion in a non-sectarian form could be more generally taught. However, I am not surprised at the stand taken by the Supreme Court.[40]

Dr. Joseph R. Sizoo, president of the New Brunswick, New Jersey, Theological Seminary:

[The schools are] now being forbidden by the Court to give spiritual content to education. Education in a democracy is never safe if it is to be lacking the content of spiritual values. It is rather regrettable that in the public mind ecclesiasticism should be confused with spiritual values. The problem which rests before the country now is how it shall educate its children in spiritual values. This is now a very grave and great responsibility.[41]

Charles S. Longacre, secretary of the Religious Liberty Association of the Seventh-day Adventists: "[The decision] is not hostile to religion but friendly toward it—both religion and the state prosper and enjoy friendly relations better under a program of complete separation than under a commingling of functions."[42]

Rev. Terrence A. Seery, principal of St. Philip High School in Chicago:

The decision is a denial of the parents' rights concerning whether their children should receive religious instruction. We don't see where the Constitution was violated. The decision will discourage cooperation among all of America's religious faiths.

According to the Court's decision the public schools will have to stop buying fish to serve Catholic children on Friday in the cafeterias—and Kosher food for Jewish pupils—because that is cooperation between the schools and the churches.

Permitting religious instruction in the schools is merely a favor by school boards and does not establish a church-state union.[43]

Paul Mitchum, principal of Pipkin Junior High School in Springfield, Illinois:

[I don't believe the Supreme Court] could make any other decision in this case. It's a matter of traditional separation of government and church. I don't think the decision means, however, that schools or government cannot recognize religion. That's what Springfield schools try to do, recognize religion and religious values.[But America's traditional] freedom of religion also means freedom from religion, if that's the choice of the individual. Some mistaken people would like to see the schools take over responsibilities belonging to the church; if they're having trouble getting their young people to attend church, they think the schools ought to fill the vacuum and take over.[44]

After several day's reflection, both opponents and proponents of released-time in Champaign-Urbana began to make pronouncements as to what the practical effects of the decision were. On Wednesday, after she had appeared at a press conference in Chicago sponsored by the CAC and attended by her attorney, Vashti "made it plain ... that the [CCRE and presumably the Board of Education] will have another fight on [their] hands ... if the schools have any connection with the new plan." She then offered her view of what would and what would not be permissible in the light of the Supreme Court decision:

If the School Board wants to dismiss all children earlier than usual and let them go to religious classes away from the schools, I think it would be all right. But the schools must have nothing to do with it. School authorities can not distribute cards or assist in the enrollment, check on attendance, or keep in school the children who do not attend the classes. Any lining up or other segregation of the children who attend the various classes must be done off the school grounds.[45]

Board President Vance promised that the Board would decide at an "early meeting" the action it would take. Before making any "statement" [and presumably before taking any action] he said the Board would have to consult with its attorney."[46] Franklin went to Chicago the day after the decision, as did Vashti. There, he met with his associate in the case, Mr. Rall.[47]

In Champaign on Wednesday, Franklin met with the CCRE. He prefaced his interpretation of the court decision with: "This is as unhappy (a) time for me as it is for you." Franklin went on to tell the assemblage: "My professional intuition tells me we'd do better not filing" a petition for rehearing before the Supreme Court. "I see no reason for a rehearing. If I had the opportunity to write another brief, I couldn't for the life of me do anything but tear out pages of our first brief and turn them in."[48]

In another account: "We had ample time to prepare our briefs and I doubt that any new points could be made which could change the justices viewpoint at this time.[49]

Franklin went on to say that, "Justice Reed has done a great service to the nation. This may be a rallying point for public opinion, I hope, that may eventually lead to a change of view by the court."[50]

While one or two of the ministers were in favor of discontinuing the classes until the following year, the majority initially stood behind Lutheran minister Kaiser, who stated: "People are looking to Champaign to see what we're going to do. We're on the spot. Let's go a step farther and ask the School Board for more."[51] The end result, after vowing to "work out some program for continuance of the training outside the schools," was a recommendation to the Board of Education that the present released time program be terminated before Easter in an "orderly, unhurried, unpanicky fashion."[52] On Thursday, the CCRE issued a statement:

> The Supreme Court has ruled that the Champaign plan of religious education in the public schools must be discontinued in its present form. Therefore, as loyal citizens, we will comply. However, if there is some legal way we may continue, we will endeavor to do so.
>
> We believe as a council that the real issue should not be obscured. The threat to democracy is not religion but a lack of it. When religion goes, morals go.
>
> We believe that we as a council must endeavor to educate the young people of our community in religiously-based moral values. Anything that blocks a reaching of our young people with these values, prohibits

religious freedom and opens the way for the disintegration of our democratic state.

Therefore, we challenge the religiously-minded people of our community to rally to their churches and to implement with their cooperation and support the paths still open to us to continue the essential task before us.[53]

In Urbana, Superintendent Cobb, after a conference with Board President F. R. Steggerda, ended the religious classes Wednesday afternoon. The director of the program, Mrs. E. E. Latowsky, spent the last day telling her students why the classes were being ended. "It was difficult," she said, "to explain to the pupils that the court had prohibited the classes which were entirely voluntary and which were popular in the class program."[54]

On Friday, the Champaign Board of Education met at a special meeting, the original purpose of which was to open bids for the sale of school bonds. The Supreme Court decision, however, became the main issue of the meeting. Mellon began by reading a letter from Rev. Cartlidge, representing the CCRE.

The CCRE is prepared to terminate the classes in religious education as soon as the School Board desires. If it would be more orderly and convenient to the school system for us to continue until the Easter season, say March 26, or stop at once, whichever is your desire, we will do so.

We wish to extend to you and the employees of the Board our sincere appreciation for the spirit you have manifested to us in our work in the schools and through the long period of litigation through which you have passed.

Although noxious motives have been imputed by some to the School Board and to the CCRE for instituting this work, both are aware that it was done because it was in the best interests of the youth of our community and with true democratic fairness.[55]

Attorney Franklin, as he had done to the CCRE, recommended to the Board that the classes be ended. In the ensuing discussion, one board member asked if Christmas carols could still be sung. "I wouldn't discontinue any practice," said Franklin, "other than religious education."[56] The Board minutes make only a brief reference to the action taken:

Mrs. McGinty moved, seconded by Mr. Colbert, that the classes in religious education conducted in the Champaign Public Schools terminate with the Easter vacation, March 24. Motion carried unanimously, Ayes 6, Nays 0.[57]

Almost immediately following the decision in the *McCollum* case, the CCRE indicated its interest in an alternative program of religious instruction. The week following the decision, Rev. Cartlidge had a new proposal for consideration by the Council. It asked:

1. That the Council continue to function as a group representing the various church denominations.

2. That it consider a plan requesting that the School Board dismiss all pupils one hour early one afternoon a week, with the Council sponsoring religious classes at the ... YMCA, the churches or at other properties outside the school premises for boys and girls wishing to participate.

3. That the Council sponsor and direct a cooperative summer vacation Bible school, five half days a week for a month's period following the close of the spring school term.[58]

The new program, as proposed by Cartlidge, would seem to have met the guidelines delineated earlier by Vashti. Practically speaking, dismissed time programs, where the public school did not enforce attendance at the off-school site, have not fared well. Children, when offered the choice between religion and play seem to prefer the latter in spite of the desires of their parents and ministers. In view of this, it was not surprising that no dismissed time program was established in the Champaign schools.[59]

The High Court in Illinois declined to interpret the opinion of the United States Supreme Court in the *McCollum* case. It chose instead to remand the case to the Circuit Court for "proceedings not inconsistent with the opinion." With the death of Judge Frank B. Leonard, the unpleasant task of issuing the order reversing the original Circuit Court decision devolved upon his colleague, Judge Grover Watson.

At the first hearing on the matter, Franklin argued that, since District 71 had been reorganized into a larger consolidated district, "the defendant was dead."[60] This collaterally brought up the question of the constitutionality of the Illinois school consolidation law then pending in the Illinois courts. Dodd, apparently taken by surprise by the argument "eventually made an oral motion to make the Community Unit School District No. 4 a defendant in the religious education proceeding."[61]

As a fall-back position, Franklin maintained that should District 4 be recognized as the defendant, that any order should apply only to that portion of the new district that had formerly been included in District 71.[61] Mrs. McCollum "hotly disputed" the point. "If it is illegal in one district or in one state, it is illegal in the rest of the country, and it shouldn't take court action to enforce a Supreme Court ruling."[62]

It seemed clear that the reorganization question was a subterfuge; the real issue was the scope of the final order that Watson would issue. Dodd argued that the scope should be broad, consistent with the Supreme Court's decision. He proposed the following wording.

It is ordered that a writ of mandamus issue out of this Court directed to the Board of Education compelling such Board, (1) to prohibit within its district a use of the State's tax-supported public school buildings for the dissemination of religious doctrines, and (2) to prohibit within its district the use of the States compulsory school machinery to help provide pupils for religious classes of sectarian groups by providing that pupils compelled by law to go to school for secular education be released in part from their legal duty upon the condition that they attend the religious classes.[63]

Franklin, arguing for the narrowest interpretation possible of the Supreme Court ruling, offered his own wording:

It is hereby ordered that the Board of Education immediately adopt and enforce rules and regulations prohibiting all instruction of and teaching of religious education in the manner heretofore conducted by said public school district in all of the public schools and in all public school houses and buildings in said district when the same are occupied by public schools.[64]

On behalf of his point, Franklin contended: "It would be presumptuous for this Court by interpretation to give a wider or more comprehensive interpretation of the opinion of the Supreme Court than necessarily arises from its decision that the petition of the relator [Vashti] should have been granted upon the original hearing."

He continued in his combative style: "We need not be overawed by the fact that this case has gone to the Supreme Court of the United States. All this Court needs to do is give Mrs. McCollum what she asked for originally."[65]

At the conclusion of the hour-long "informal" session, Judge Watson continued the hearing until August 12,[66] but not before Attorney Dodd "dropped a broad hint" that if Watson's final order was unsatisfactory from his and his client's point of view, they might appeal it back to the United States Supreme Court.[67]

Walter Dodd returned to Champaign-Urbana on August 12 for the continued hearing. After a "ten-minute conference" in the judge's chambers,[68] Watson emerged to issue an "oral"[69] order that followed, "almost word for word," Franklin's proposed language. Afterwards, Franklin savored his victory:

We were anxious that no order be entered that would be interpreted as ruling against something that we did not do here. We wanted the court order to adhere to the strict facts of our case and thus avoid unnecessary damage to others—and we succeeded in doing that.[70]

Vashti was worried that the order would permit released time classes which would "present the same abuses." She added: "I definitely am not satisfied with the decision (of Judge Watson) and certainly am going to take action against it."[71]

Judge Watson, questioned afterwards, offered clarifications as to what his order meant:

It [the order] prohibits the teaching of religion and each and every act attendant with the teaching and the use of school property. The order did not discuss released time at all, but as to the use of school records for encouraging children to go to religious education classes outside of the building, I don't think it can be done. I think I have gone as far as I should have under the Supreme Court ruling.[72]

Before a final written order could be issued, Walter Dodd needed to comply with Judge Watson's request that he send down his suggested wording. When reached in Chicago on September 24, Dodd indicated that he still had reservations concerning the Franklin-Watson approach:

> Judge Watson told us in a conference in his chamber [on August 12] that he thought his ruling would [bar the use of school records]. But his construction [of the order] is rather broad and I would rather that the order include a specific reference to this. As the order was given, it says schools may not in public school buildings do any religious teaching. It is a part of teaching to keep records—and perhaps punish [the children] if [they] don't go to religious education classes. If it will prevent that, then the order will have done all we need.[73]

The anti-climatic but official conclusion of the *McCollum* case occurred on September 25, 1948, when Judge Watson held the final hearing on the matter. Vashti recalled the hearing:

> Walter Dodd called from Chicago to tell me that he was coming to Urbana for a hearing on the final court order to be issued to the School Board. He asked that I meet the train and take him to the court house, which I was glad to do.
>
> After some initial hesitation about my going in, [a conference held in the judge's chambers] he decided it was all right but cautioned me not to say anything: "It's just a matter between the lawyers and the judge."
>
> As to the wording of the final order, Dodd spoke first in his halting, retiring manner. Franklin spoke decisively and forcefully. The order, he argued, should be specific—that the court said that what the schools had been doing was wrong and that the order should be limited to the Champaign fact situation.
>
> When they had finished, Judge Watson said: "I am inclined to go along with Mr. Franklin's thinking." I interrupted: "You mean that after three years of fighting this case in the courts, and winning, that now, conceivably, any slight variation in the plan could be permitted under the order? Have you read the Supreme Court decision?"
>
> Judge Watson admitted that he had not. He called a recess to read the decision. When he came back, he included the wording that I wanted. Afterwards, Dodd admitted that I had saved the day.[74]

Watson's decree ordered the Champaign Board of Education to:

> Immediately adopt and enforce rules and regulations prohibiting all instruction in and teaching of religious education in the manner heretofore conducted by said school district...in all public school houses and buildings in said district when occupied by public schools; and to prohibit within said district the use of the state's public school machinery to help enroll pupils in the several religious classes of sectarian groups.[75]

The order, with the inclusion of the second part, represented a compromise. Franklin, who lost ground, still expressed his satisfaction:

> The order is in a form that does not cast reflection upon released time programs generally. It does not condemn anything but a form of religious education which involves holding classes in public school buildings during public school hours or the actual use of public school machinery.

Vashti "expressed pleasant surprise"[76] at the inclusion of the additional wording, but took exception to Franklin's implied suggestion that the use of public school buildings would be acceptable at times other than during school hours: "If the religious classes are held after school in the school buildings, of course, that angle is out."[77]

She reiterated her concerns relating to any religious instruction held during school hours: "It is just when the classes are given during school time (presumably at locations other than in the public school buildings) and when school authorities have anything to do with it that we feel it isn't right. It should be a matter between the churches and the parents absolutely, and the schools should have no part in it."[78]

Dodd expressed his concern over the use of the word "enroll" with respect to the use of the "public school machinery." He would have preferred additional wording which would have included a ban on "requiring attendance." He added: "If the order can be construed to prohibit any pressure, it will cover the opinion of the Supreme Court."[79]

After quoting much of Watson's order, a *Post-Dispatch* editorial concluded afterwards:

> This is precisely the action Mrs. McCollum called for in the beginning when she objected to the treatment of her son, Terry. Because she was not cowed by school board members, courts and prosecutors, she has seen her position proved right in the end. It is a big achievement for one small woman.[80]

Apparently, Vashti thought similarly for, in spite of her remaining reservations concerning the wording, she chose not to appeal the order.

Chapter 16

The Right of Jimmy McCollum to Go to Hell

Reaction of editorial writers and commentators was immediate. The wrath of the losers was probably exacerbated by the fact that, with the exception of those following the case most closely, the result was unexpected. The decision prompted the *News-Gazette* to break its editorial silence on the case:

> The Supreme Court of the United States has spoken, and Terry McCollum can return to the Champaign schools without the "embarrassment" his mother said he suffered because she wouldn't let him take religious education.
>
> Terry's strong-willed mother, Mrs. Vashti McCollum, has the satisfaction of knowing that the nation's highest court found she was right all along, even though Champaign county's three circuit judges and Illinois' Supreme Court said she was wrong.
>
> Terry's militantly atheistic grandfather, Arthur G. Cromwell, trumpets from Rochester, N. Y., that the "religious tide which is trying to sweep American back into another medieval dark age" has been turned back. The family has a hard won victory to celebrate, but the decision gives an entire nation cause for genuine concern.
>
> When the U. S. Supreme Court speaks, its words become the law of the land. The final word in a dispute between Mrs. McCollum and the Champaign School Board touched 2,000,000 children now enrolled in religious education classes and millions more who might have received this training if her suit had not been filed. That was the objective of the organizations which supported and financed her three-year fight.
>
> Destruction of a workable system of religious education is a serious matter, but it can be rebuilt if churches will find a new way to arouse and hold interest of children away from school buildings. The cause for concern goes deeper than loss of the system.
>
> The Supreme Court has committed the United States to a course of hostility to religion. When Circuit Judges Grover Watson, Martin E. Morthland and the late F. B. Leonard first decided the case against Mrs. McCollum, on the law as they then understood it, they declared, "This is

a religious nation." When the Illinois Supreme Court upheld them, it said, "To deny the existence of religious motivation is to deny the inspiration and authority of the constitution itself." But the U. S. Supreme Court has made new law now. And Justice Jackson of that court interprets the decision as granting Mrs. McCollum a writ that "bans every form of teaching which suggests or recognizes that there is a God." Justice Jackson should understand the decision for he concurred in it, even though he said it went too far.

There is nothing in the Constitution to prevent the teaching of atheism, but now there is the decision in McCollum vs. Champaign Board of Education to be cited whenever anyone wants to interpret the Constitution as prohibiting encouragement of religion—any religion.

The potential strife which the decision will encourage also was cited by Justice Jackson—and remember he is a concurring, not a dissenting justice.

He said, "Authorities list 256 separate and substantial religious bodies in the continental United States. Each of them through the suit of some discontented but unpenalized and untaxed representative has as good a right as this plaintiff to demand that the courts compel the schools to sift out of their teaching everything inconsistent with its doctrines.

"If we are to eliminate everything that is objectionable to any of these warring sects or inconsistent with any of their doctrines, we will leave public education in shreds. Nothing but educational confusion and discrediting of the public school system can result from subjecting it to constant law suits ... It is idle to pretend that we can find in the Constitution one word to help us as judges to decide where the secular ends and the sectarian begins in education. Nor can we find guidance in any other legal source. It is a matter on which we can find no law but our own prepossession."

Justice Jackson is at least frank when he concedes that the present high court decides cases on "prepossession" rather than law. Author of the "separation of church and state" phrase on which Mrs. McCollum relied was Thomas Jefferson. His prepossession did not prohibit him as a trustee of the state-supported University of Virginia, from recommending that students be "expected" to attend religious meetings during school time.

So far as government is concerned, the prepossessions of other men now have relegated religion to a forbidden role. The strength of the nation's religion will determine if its people are willing for that role to be a minor one in their daily lives.[1]

From elsewhere, Oklahoma:

Have those persons who oppose the weekday Bible school paused to consider the fate of peoples whose states have opposed teaching about the creator, be they atheists like Mrs. McCollum or rigid sectarians?

People have a right to disbelieve. But have they also a right to attack the faith of others in a Christian way of life?

Multitudes are hungry today, not only for food or other material things but for things that are spiritual. They need a religious faith that will carry them through tribulations that no amount of material wealth can prevent.

Thousands of children, growing up to face what conditions we do not know, would never come into touch with the Bible and its teachings were it not for the weekday Bible schools of the nation. Let those attacking these schools think again.[2]

Buffalo, New York:

Justice Jackson said the court's language was so general that it might make trouble in teaching subjects which touch on church architecture, sacred music, the historical effect of religious movements, the Bible as literature or biology with its theory of evolution. He argued also that the Court majority failed to set up any rules as to how far a school may go on religion.

Until that last point is cleared up, it cannot be assumed that the decision interferes in any way with the "released time" religious instruction provided in our own public schools. But, even if it should interfere, we are sure that people would go right on being religious and having religion taught to their children. No Vashti McCollum can go to court and get an injunction against God.[3]

Mansfield, Ohio:

Now that the Champaign, Ill., woman—an avowed atheist—has won her point in the matter of freeing her 12-year-old "embarrassment" of attending a school in which a brief weekly period was given to religious education, it may be wondered what she will do about handling United States coins in which it is asserted, "In God We Trust."

It would appear that she must be in total disagreement with this recognition of the existence of a Supreme Being, and that it must therefore be "embarrassing" to her to handle coins bearing this inscription.[4]

Salisbury, North Carolina:

Mrs. McCollum successfully contends that the Constitution "protects" her son against religious education. She maintains that he is embarrassed when other children voluntarily go to a class which teaches things his Mummy considers rude fairy tales.

We do not concur in the belief that Bible courses like those being taught in Salisbury break down the "barrier" between the State and Religion. The school scrupulously avoids actual sponsorship. Courses are elective. They do not come near attempting to establish a State Religion, and although entirely Protestant here, they only reflect the background of the pupils they instruct. Were the population less homogeneous, the situation would indeed be different.

The tendency to treat religion as a one-day-a-week proposition is far too widespread already. The teaching of "great truths or affirmations" of the Bible has as much educational value as a course in Egyptian art.

It seems unwise to cast aside the small progress made toward treating religion as a part of secular education simply because the offspring of one over-educated college wife suffers embarrassment among his schoolmates.[5]

Scranton, Pennsylvania:

The big majority of Americans, regardless of religious affiliation, will sincerely regret the United States Supreme Court has ruled religious instruction in public schools ... is unconstitutional. In an especial way there will be regret the Supreme Court's ruling was handed down in connection with a protest entered by an avowed atheist who said her son, attending a Champaign school, has been "embarrassed" by being the only child in his room not attending religious classes.

Regardless of the ruling by the Supreme Court, it can be said there is a growing belief by American parents, teachers and others that some form of daily religious instruction of the youth of the land must be developed; otherwise we are apt to grow into a godless nation. At the same time no one wants a joining of church and state in violation of the federal constitutional mandate.

It is admittedly a bit discouraging that an atheist could sprag a well developed interdenominational plan of religious instruction.[6]

Washington, D.C.:

Thus the Supreme Court can be called on to deny that an American child shall, in a tax-supported school, look on a picture of Raphael's Madonna or study a drawing of the Cathedral of Sts. Peter and Paul that dominates the ridge along Wisconsin Avenue here in Washington, D. C., and which is commonly known to all of us as "The National Cathedral."

Queer, queer thinking. Something is surely loose in the world that was not here before. The Constitution surely was never meant to be read in any such way. The rule forbidding legislation on religious matters, surely was meant to protect people against *enforced* religious attitudes.

Yet here the Supreme Court *enforces* a religious attitude. The attitude it *enforces* is the attitude of atheism and anti-religion.

It not only denies teachers the power to *force* religious information on children, it *forbids* them to give that information. We are into something here that every thinking man and woman had better examine closely, again and again.[7]

Also from Washington, D. C.:

On the face of the Supreme Court's latest interpretation, the doors of the public schools have been closed to any form of religious instruction. It would appear that the ban extends even to such a thing as the recitation of the Lord's Prayer. If this is true, if the court has gone to such an extreme in the enforced separation of church and state, then it is a matter which ought to be of the utmost concern in an age in which the old spiritual guides are crumbling under the impact of materialistic philosophy.

Is it now unconstitutional for children to sing Christmas carols at school plays? What about the chaplains in the military establishment, or the compulsory religious services at Annapolis and West Point? Must these things go too?

It is not the layman's function to challenge the correctness, as a matter of law of what the court has done. But it is proper for the layman to appraise as best he can the practical effect of the decision on the world in which he lives.

The First Amendment was adopted in the light of conditions which do not exist in this country today. It was written by men whose ancestors were familiar with religious persecution. Many of them had come to this country to escape it. If the founding fathers erected a wall between church and state in fear of dominance of the latter by the former, it cannot be said that, in their time, the fear was without basis.

But that was more than a century ago. Today's world is an entirely different one. The influence of religion is much weaker now than it was then. And we are the worse because of it. In our day religious instruction is disappearing from too many American homes. The position of the church is weakening. And one may well believe that these things, in part at least, are responsible for such disturbing trends as the turn away from the old concept of family life, the deplorable picture of one in three marriages ending in divorce, the futile, fevered quest for happiness in material things, the groping by hundreds of thousands of people for some higher standards, some better guides, to live by.

In dealing with economic and political questions, the members of this Supreme Court have never viewed the Constitution as being rigid and inflexible. On the contrary, and rightly so, they have treated this great charter as being a flexible thing, intended by its authors to be susceptible of appropriate adaptation to meet changing conditions and changed times. Why then, in a matter affecting the separation of church and state, should it be applied so narrowly and so rigidly? What has become of that flexibility without which no constitution can serve the continuing needs of a people?

The great challenge to the freedoms which we know and which the Constitution would safeguard does not come from religion or any teaching of religion. It comes from the advance of a Communist philosophy which, as practiced, is the antithesis of religious doctrine—an advance which is facilitated by our own embracement of materialism at the expense of the things of the spirit. In this setting, it is neither necessary nor reasonable to erect an insuperable barrier to the kind of religious instruction that was practiced in Champaign. Would it not be much better for us if, instead of forbidding appropriate religious instruction in the schools, we were to encourage it in every reasonable way? If one's answer to this question is in the affirmative, then it must be most earnestly hoped that the Supreme Court will not let this decision stand as the law of the land.[8]

Yet another commentary entitled, "The Supreme Court Endorses Communism," came from a source unknown:

> The agnosticism which denies the rights of God and the rights of men is not new in America. Its imprint was visible in the abolition of prayers for guidance, in deference to Soviet Russia, at the World Charter meeting in San Francisco. The pattern has been followed in detail in American foreign policy, to the point that the world does not know what we stand for. And it is evident in the continued appeasement of Godless Communism at home and abroad, with Congress refusing on one hand to outlaw this hateful ideology and the administration on the other hand continuing to give material assistance to Russia.
>
> The founders of this nation, in decreeing a separation between church and state, never intended to banish the Bible from the schools. As a matter of fact, their absolute reliance upon Divine guidance sorely needs to be emulated today. The Bible remains the greatest textbook in the world, despite the Pilate-like decision of the highest court in the land. Its message and inspiration were never more sorely needed than in today's struggle against Communism. Public education, long criticized as inadequate for dealing with the Godless forces menacing the world, has been done a rank disservice.[9]

The most unexpected negative commentary on the *McCollum* decision was printed in, of all publications, *The Progressive*. It was preceded by a disclaimer which ended with the following:

> Sometimes we ... let a regular writer get away with murder. Milton Mayer's the perfect example. An incorrigible individualist and one-man band, Mayer pays no attention to instructions, the Editor's pleas, and the magazine's policies. He literally writes as he pleases, and mostly we give him his way. His article in this issue is precisely on the subject we didn't want him to cover, for his views are so totally different from ours, but he chose it, and for reasons we'll never understand ourselves, we succumbed again.[10]

Excerpts from Mayer's remarkable exposition:

> The Supreme Court has just upheld the Constitutional right of Jimmy McCollum, age 12, to go to hell. Americans everywhere will rejoice, and the reason they will rejoice is that the Court has saved Jimmy, not from damnation, but from knowing about it. The Court holds, in effect, that ignorance of beatitude is bliss, and so do Americans everywhere. We are now, under the First Amendment, squarely committed to the free exercise of the pagan materialism we oppose when Hitler and Stalin exercise it. "God Bless America" is now officially a mammy song designed to

persuade our young men to go and get their heads shot off, and "In God We Trust" is frankly a blemish on the American dime.

Jimmy's Ma is the wife of a university professor and a professing atheist in her own right. Like all you good modern American liberals, she denies God, Who is Love. She sued the Champaign, Ill., public schools for exposing the young to Love when their parents permitted it. Jimmy, who was 7 or 8 at the time, was not permitted to be exposed to Love, but his Ma averred that he was "embarrassed" even to be in the same schoolhouse with it. His Ma won.

This country is now safe for Hate. You would think that, with Hate way out in front in this country, the Court would have been willing to give Love a sporting chance. But the Court went to Jefferson; found that the First Amendment, ... was intended by Jefferson to erect "a wall of separation between church and state;" and, after taking due, if tacit, cognizance of the national hypocrisy which proclaims this country religious, felt compelled to give Hate another boost. What this country wants, it gets.

The victory in the McCollum suit was a victory not for the religious against the churches, but for the antireligious against them both. The choice between the churches and their enemies is a dismal choice, but if I have to make it, I have to take the churches; not for what they are but for what their enemies mistake them for.

The Court, in telling Jimmy McCollum, age 12, to go to hell, destroyed the Champaign program on the grounds of "the use of tax supported property for religious instruction." Now Army posts and battleships are tax supported property—supported, indeed, by 79% of all the taxes we pay— and are used for religious instruction by chaplains who, in addition to being given the hall, are paid, and paid by the taxpayers ...

The American document par excellence is The Declaration of Independence, which proclaims, in the words of this same Jefferson, who is now cited as the Protector of the Faithless, that "all men are endowed by their Creator with certain inalienable rights." The school children of this country, including Jimmy McCollum, age 12, have all been taught to sing the hymn whose fourth stanza runs as follows: "Our Fathers God To Thee, Author of Liberty, To Thee may our land be bright with Freedom's holy light, Thy might, Great God, our King."

What happens at suppertime in the happy McCollum home, with its sampler reading "Man Bless Our Home" on the wall, when Jimmy says, "Ma, if we don't get our inalienable rights from our Creator, where in the devil, then, do we get them?"

What does Ma believe in? I'll tell you what she believes in; she believes in God. And the reason I know she believes in God is that she insists she's an atheist. If she didn't believe in God, she would leave Him alone. Ma McCollum will know she believes in God when, like the atheists on the Western Front, she finds herself in a foxhole. I venture that I am not misquoting Ma McCollum if I say she says, "I'm doing all right without God." But how will she do when she isn't doing all right?

The Court says, in the McCollum decision, that "both religion and government can best work to achieve their lofty aims if each is left free from the other within its respective sphere." What the lofty aims of government are, with God, Who is Love, left out, the Court doesn't say. It doesn't say because it can't. Jefferson, when he wrote the Declaration, knew better than to try.[11]

Arthur G. Cromwell was indignant concerning the commentary, and as was his inclination, and as did his President several years later in defense of his own daughter, he did not suffer quietly. In a letter to the editor of *The Progressive* he had, among other things, the following to say:

I have seen some material that should never have soiled [your] pages, but a new low was established ... when you lacked the moral and intellectual courage to take the Milton Mayer editorial entitled "Come All Ye Faithless," and throw it into the trashcan instead of smearing your own magazine and [the character] of a brave American woman.

Mayer has not in any sense attempted to treat the true and real issues of this Constitutional issue, his only purpose appearing to be to smear the name and character of any and all who would fight for religious freedom. His very reflections on the members of the Court should condemn him, and to follow his own remarks: "His Ma doesn't slap his sassy face for him," I declare here and now that in the name of my daughter, my grandson, the members of the United States Supreme Court, and every other fair-minded American, if I ever meet up with this punk, I'll personally slap *his* sassy face.[12]

One of the most vigorous attacks upon Mrs. McCollum's victory also singled out her Protestant allies for criticism:

Bishop Oxnam and friends, are you just a bit worried? Has your movement been too successful?

You oppose secularism, or the complete divorce of God from Government, business and social life. At least you say you do. The decision in favor of the atheist mother from Illinois was a great boost for secularism. Are you sure that is what you wanted?

Oh well, the "Fascist-breeding Romanism" was soundly thrashed into good behavior. Pat yourself on the back, you and all your buddies. Atheism is certainly better than Catholicism, isn't it, Bishop Oxnam?

With frightened glances over their shoulders at the "monsters" of Catholicism, Protestants pushed our country one step further along the path the Soviet Union has worn so smooth.

The furor created by Protestants United [the group of which Bishop Oxnam was a member] undoubtedly influenced the judges of the Supreme Court to arrive at the decision that officially bars God's entrance into public schools. The judges must have felt that the decision was necessary to preserve religious peace. If tax-supported schools may not be used to the advantage of any particular believers or unbelievers, then it

is time we Catholics bring a few cases to court. The Supreme Court declares that the atheistic McCollum woman must not be forced to pay
taxes to support the spread of belief in God. All right then, we who believe
in the existence of God must not be forced to pay taxes to support atheistic professors in our state schools.

Arise, believers in God, oust from our state universities those who
propagate atheism and materialism. It is "sinful and tyrannical" to force
us to pay for the propagation of opinions which we disbelieve.[13]

Vashti, however, was not without her supporters. In contrast with the Catholic
newspaper's view, a Lutheran publication saw the situation much differently:

The all but unanimous Supreme Court decision in favor of Mrs. Vashti
McCollum ... repairs some of the damage that has been inflicted in recent
years to the sturdy wall which the Constitution erected in its First Amendment to keep church and state separate.

It cannot be denied that there has been church-state interference as
well as state-church interference. Catholics, Protestants, and government have been cultivating vines of interference on both sides of that
sturdy wall, and there was real danger that the vines would obliterate the
wall and, eventually, break it down.

There can be no quarreling with the facts in the Champaign ... case
and the Supreme Court ruling that the churches in that community were
wrongfully using the facilities of the public school system to establish
their separate creeds.

The court's decision is being assailed as a vote for an atheistic or, at
best, an irreligious America. This is an assumption. The First Amendment does not require the state to oppose or ignore religion. It does not
call for a separation of state and religion, but for a separation of state and
church. There is nothing in the Constitution to prevent the state from
teaching the Ten Commandments in its own schools.

Whereas the decision in the McCollum case bars further released
time religious instruction, the Court decision in the New Jersey [*Everson*]
school bus case continues to sanction the use of public funds in support
of church-sponsored education. The Court labeled such support "a social
service". If such support is a social service, it is not a state-sponsored
public service but a private service sponsored by an organized religion
for the promotion of its own institutional welfare.

The Supreme Court has placed itself in the awkward position of en-
dorsing governmental interference in behalf of an organized religion
while, in the McCollum decision, it denies to the churches a right it exercises, of interfering benevolently with the functions and prerogatives of
the state.

If church-state interference is wrong, then state-church interference
is equally wrong.

As the situation now stands, government may interfere patronizingly
with the functions of organized religion while holding the churches to a

strict interpretation of the First Amendment.

It should become apparent now whether the latest Supreme Court decision will affect the unconstitutional privileges of the Roman Catholic Church in certain states that permit nuns, priests and brothers, who are pledged to the promotion of their religious beliefs, to teach in state-sponsored schools at public expense.

If the Supreme Court decision handed down in the McCollum case does not now oust the scores of Catholic nuns, priests and brothers from the public schools—in New Mexico, for instance—; if it does not now put a stop to the payment of salaries from public funds to these representatives of the Roman Catholic Church; if it does not now bar the payment from public funds of rent monies for the use of church-owned property, the Protestant accusation that government is discriminating in favor of the Roman Catholic Church will be true.[14]

From Richmond, Virginia:

The decision of the High Court sustained her, but it also raises the question of how that Court can reconcile Monday's far-reaching decision with its decision of last February, when, by a vote of 5 to 4, it upheld the right of the State of New Jersey—and 16 other states by implication—to use public funds to defray the cost of bus transportation for pupils not only of public schools, but of sectarian schools as well.

The inconsistency of the two decisions becomes evident when we apply a test "in reverse." Atheism, the denial of God or a God, is the very negation of religion, but it is nevertheless a form of intellectual conviction subscribed to with quasi-religious fervor by those who spurn the conventional concepts of man's relation to the universe.

Would those who have condoned or advocated religious education in public and transportation to conventional religious schools, approve or tolerate the teaching of atheism under the roof of a tax-supported school, or the transportation of pupils to atheist schools, in tax-supported buses?

Yet, under the Constitution, the atheist has as much right to his beliefs as the Protestant, Catholic or Jew. If those who derive their belief from accepted sacred writings wish to deny state sanction to atheism—as prevails in Russia—they must also deny such sanction to their own beliefs.

To maintain that rigid impartiality toward all beliefs, positive or negative, is the intent of the First Amendment, as interpreted by the Court. Yet in order to be consistent, the Court should have applied the same touchstone to the question of school buses. For the buses, being publicly owned, tend to facilitate the growth of "approved" sects or creeds thereby benefited. An eventual reversal of the school bus decision would seem to be in order.[15]

From St. Louis, Missouri:

This decision is a victory for the separation of church and state in the United States. It is in the high tradition of James Madison, who led the fight for this constitutional principle in the Bill of Rights. Madison and Jefferson knew, as did others of their time, that "there cannot be freedom of religion guaranteed by the state and also intervention by the church in the state's domain or dependence on the state's largess."

Mrs. McCollum's victory is a victory for freedom of conscience without which there can be no freedom of religion. She is not a Catholic, a Protestant or a Jew. She does not belong to any one of the many denominational sects. She is a free-thinker, sometimes called an atheist. It was her argument that the Bill of Rights' separation of church and state protects her in her efforts to train her children in freethinking just as much as it protects those in denominations with memberships running into the millions.

It can only be regretted that Justice Black did not see the issue as clearly in the New Jersey school bus case, whose majority opinion he also wrote.

Either he has changed his views or he thinks that a little mixing of church and state is all right.

We prefer to think that the Supreme Court has learned a lot from the sound criticism of the New Jersey decision in the press, in law reviews and indeed in religious circles. We prefer to think that the McCollum Case is not only the latest word but also a revised judgment. We prefer to think that it will be followed by decisions which will reverse the New Jersey decision and earlier decisions permitting the use of tax funds to pay for school books for church schools and otherwise to support church schools. We prefer to think this notwithstanding Justice Black's pains to harmonize the McCollum and New Jersey decisions.[16]

From the same newspaper a day later:

The Rev. C. Oscar Johnson, president of the St. Louis School Board, is right when he says there is a difference between the St. Louis and Champaign systems for religious instruction through the public schools. St. Louis' procedure is to release students on request of parents for sectarian classes on school time but away from the school premises [similar to the New York system]. The Champaign plan brought religious teachers into the schools and used classrooms and other facilities.

This difference is, in our opinion, the difference between a small encroachment on the separation of church and state and a larger, and therefore more dangerous, encroachment.

The encroachment lies in the fact that any plan which employs the public school system in any way does so because it uses the great body of public school students as already recruited material. If churches can make use of students organized through the public schools and of time otherwise allotted for school classes, the churches are spared a great load of work at the very outset.

There can be no question as to the good intentions of those citizens who have set up these religious training programs in some 2200 American communities. These inter-denominational groups mean well and in most places their differing systems have worked without disturbance. Even so, the mildest form is an invasion, however slight, on the basic principle that church and state be kept separate.

As long as some church groups use the public schools in released time religious training, other church groups will have an argument for tax funds for parochial schools, books, bus fares and other support. Such competition for the favors of the state would inevitably bring sectarian animosities and dissensions which should be scrupulously kept out of our national life.[17]

From the same newspaper on March 14:

The value and the desirability of religious instruction for the young is not here involved. What is involved is the American principle of strict separation of church and state. Religious instruction of course makes its own contribution to public morality. This, however, should not be made on a sectarian basis within the public school framework.[18]

From a Jewish publication from Detroit, Michigan:

Mrs. Vashti McCollum deserves commendation for the courage with which she pursued the fight for separation of church and state in her suit to stop religious education—through the "released time" program—in the ... public schools. Her victory...is a triumph for American traditions and for that group in American life which has consistently opposed the introduction of religion in our schools. It was a victory for the First Article of the Bill of Rights which provides that "Congress shall make no law respecting the establishment of religion;" and for Roger Williams who, in 1636, in Rhode Island, asserted that "civil power should never intermeddle in religious matters ... " In congratulating Mrs. McCollum, we pay honor to the founders of our Republic, to all who are ready to fight for the ideals which are the foundation of our country and to the Supreme Court whose wise judges have acted so decisively in reaffirming a basic principle of Americanism.

The Supreme Court ruling will undoubtedly strengthen the hands of those who are battling against allocation of public funds for parochial schools. It would be natural to contend that it is right to allocate funds for Catholic schools, why not also support Protestant educational projects and *our* Talmud Torahs? And once this is done, what will happen to the Bill of Rights? Let's stick to the old traditions; let's keep the state and the church apart; and we'll have a better chance to remain free.[19]

From Washington, D. C.:

The advocates of released time for religious education in the public schools are fond of asking "why not?" A prior and more pertinent question is "why?" There is ample opportunity for religious instruction outside school hours, on Sundays, or, if this is not sufficient, on weekday afternoons when secular classes have been dismissed. It is hard to escape the conclusion that the released-time program has been pursued ... precisely because it subjected pupils to a kind of compulsion to participate; at least it made nonparticipation awkward and conspicuous.[20]

From Tulsa, Oklahoma:

But millions of other mothers [apart from Mrs. McCollum] believe their children ought to have religious training during their school years. They now face the responsibility which has been slipped upon the over-burdened school teachers. The public has expected them not only to educate boys and girls but to teach them their manners and morals. This is simply too big a job for our school system. Nor can churches who get the kiddies an hour or two on Sunday be expected to turn little barbarians into well-behaved upright youngsters.

The home is the only place where religious training can be done and where it takes. Parents must be the instructors. If we want our children to know anything about the Bible we shall have to read it to them; if we expect them to live according to Christian principles it's up to us to instill such principles into them, during their tender years.

The Christian American parent is on the spot. The courts have said that this nation still stands on the principle of the separation of Church and State.

From now on, there can be no more hedging on the Issue. Teachers have been relieved of an impossible duty—for the schools can only supplement in the classrooms the training which the children get at home. Dad and Mother must buckle down and do the job which has always been theirs—but which they have dodged for a good many years.[21]

From St. Petersburg, Florida:

That's a rather awesome amount of legal procedure [Mrs. McCollum's court fight] to go through to protect one small boy from not wanting to be exposed to religion.

It's even more awesome when one considers that if all the atheists in the United States were lumped together, in the words of a cynical old newspaperman we know, "they couldn't carry their own precinct."

But the Supreme Court upheld her contention, holding that public schools may not teach religion. It protected the rights of a minority so infinitesimal, so seemingly unimportant, that many people don't even know it exists.

We don't know of another country in the world where such a thing could happen. Possibly England, the fountain-head of Anglo-American law, might be equally judicious, but in view of the lingering attachment between the Church of England and the State, we doubt it. Certainly such scruples would not be observed by any other nation on earth.

As a matter fact, we imagine, there are certain quarters in which this decision may be regarded as another symbol of "the decadence of democracy." If 99.44 per cent of the people think one way, then the other fraction of a per cent ought to keep their mouths shut and conform. That's the way the reasoning goes. To be more accurate, if the ruling minority thinks one way, then the subjugated majority had better keep its mouth shut and go along.

We like it better our way. As long as our Supreme Court will hear the plea of an almost friendless minority and extend its broad mantle of protection, we have no fears as to the "American Way of Life. "[22]

From Tampa, Florida:

The fact that the case was brought by an atheist may be newsworthy but it is relatively unimportant. The significance of the decision is found in the phrase that religions and government "can best work to achieve their lofty aims if each is left free from the other within its respective sphere." We hail the ruling. We consider it a fine contribution to the desirable end of keeping education for character apart from indoctrination in moral theology or religious dogma.

The arrangements in hundreds of communities in the country whereby public school children are released for special programs of religious education are, in our opinion, contrary to sound public policy. Much has been said about the voluntary and cooperative nature of these religious classes. But that becomes an illusion in view of the powerful social pressure which children may exert upon a non-conformist.

The moment children are separated for religious instruction they are made conscious of differences that have no place in a public school. Such emphasis tends to promote discord by singling out the churched and the unchurched. Certainly if religious freedom has any meaning at all, it must mean freedom from compulsion to conform.

Long experience has demonstrated that a resolute separation of church and state is an indispensable foundation of both religious and political freedom. For this reason, such a separation was made a cardinal principle of American society. We think it undeniable that the introduction of religious teaching into public school classrooms, however desirable the teaching may be in itself, and however much it may be desired by a majority or even by all of the pupils and their parents, breaches this principle.

Despite the pressure of groups of people, unquestionably sincere, we must preserve the integrity of the public school and keep it as an institution that respects both the religious conviction and the sincere doubts of

those who entrust their children to its care. That integrity will be preserved if the Supreme Court ruling is followed with education and religion free to flourish in their respective spheres.[23]

And, from Rockford, Illinois:

The opinions of the justice[s] left no doubt that further questions of church
and state separation are likely to be raised. There is no use discussing
them in hushed voices. The salvation of our system is that it avoids public feuding over religious questions. The best way to prolong that situation is to discuss these questions without heat and accept the final court
decisions with good grace.[24]

Before the year was over, two large, metropolitan newspapers carried long
feature articles on Vashti and her family. The first appeared in the St. Louis *Post-
Dispatch* and was unabashedly sympathetic. Written by Clarissa Start, it carried
many direct quotations from the embattled housewife on the morrow of her victory:

It's hard to go out against religion. You're just a no-good if you dare say
anything against it. If I'd known just how hard it was I might not have gone
through with it but I've always been one of those dreamers I guess.

I'm not anti-anything. I've always considered myself liberal and tol-
erant...

We've always been kind of free lance people anyway and I'd say we
have more friends now. There are some—like the neighbors who used to
speak and don't speak anymore. And the lady two doors away who claimed
she had trouble selling her house because no one wanted to live close to
"that Mrs. McCollum."

Then there were the anonymous phone calls. I'd tell them, "When I
had a complaint, I went to court and signed my name to it; you can do the
same." But they kept on and there so many nasty ones my husband
wouldn't let me answer the phone.

As for the letters, we've received over 5,000, as many as 199 in one
day. It got so I could tell what the letters would say without opening them.
If the envelope was addressed in pencil with a tattered old stamp, there'd
be a letter inside on note paper that didn't match, unsigned, and damning
me for an atheist. They never attacked the real issue at all. They'd just
send me quotations. "The fool hath said in his heart, there is no God" was
most frequent. But there were also letters from doctors, lawyers and
ministers backing my stand.

Some of the opposing letters were filthy and obscene. There's a Four
Square Gospel woman evangelist who's been trying to convert me. She
used to come out and call me honey and darling and sweetheart me until
she figured she'd softened me up sufficiently and then she'd put on the
pressure. So one day I brought out some of the letters I'd received and
showed them to her. I watched her face getting redder and redder. Finally

she said, "Oh Mrs. McCollum, no Christian ever wrote these letters." I said, "Well, it's a cinch no atheist ever wrote them."

I think a person must be well studied in theology to say that [they were an atheist] and I'm no theologian. I've never read Tom Paine or Ingersoll or Voltaire or any of them. My father meets with a group that calls themselves the Freethinkers, but I don't know if they're atheists or not. They're preponderantly agnostics.

I was tickled to death when they asked me to teach [dancing] again. It's kind of tough feeling that you're in everybody's doghouse.

The article was especially noteworthy because it contained one of the very rare instances where a reporter managed to get a statement from John McCollum. It was not long but it left little doubt what his opinions were concerning the court fight and his religious views:

I'm not one to pick a fight with anybody, ... that's her business. She's an educated, intelligent woman and knows what she's talking about. There's been much favorable response to the suit on the part of the faculty [at the University of Illinois]. Many of my colleagues are philosophers but not for organized religion. Myself, I never could see how you could go to your laboratory and strain at a gnat and then go to church and swallow a camel.[25]

The second article had quite a different tone. Entitled "The Atheists' Child," it appeared in December in the *American Weekly*, a feature supplement to the Chicago *Herald American*. Aside from the reference made to the McCollums living "in one of the best residential neighborhood districts" in Champaign—as did Clarissa Start in her feature story—one would hardly have guessed that the story concerned the same family. Vashti and her husband were characterized as indulgent, profane—"where discipline was no more evident than the Creator and the only credo was the right to self-expression." James Terry was labeled maladjusted:

From the time he started school, Terry had not been able to get along very well with his schoolmates, but no one suspected that his pampered pride, plus his mother's anti-religious views, would bring about a United States Supreme Court decision which threatened to keep 10,000,000 American children from voluntarily devoting any part of their school hours to religious education.

The reporter, who spent several days in Champaign, apparently interviewed numerous persons besides the McCollums. Bessie Taylor, who had been James Terry's fifth grade teacher, was one. She related a somewhat different version concerning the incident in the hallway than she had a little over three years earlier at the trial under oath. (In the first version, she said the reason the boy was placed in the hall was because the usual place he was sent during the religious classes, the music room, was occupied. In the second version she attributed it to his misbehavior—"he kept coming out and finally one day I put him in a chair in the hall.") She candidly repeated in detail her testimony that James Terry was a trouble-maker and not accepted by the other children. She concluded:

> It seemed to me that Terry must have told his mother that he didn't get along with his classmates because he didn't attend religious classes. To save his own face, he may have given that explanation time and time again. It wouldn't be unnormal for a mother to accept such a story readily.

Without question, the most distressing portion of the article, as far as the McCollums were concerned, purported to prove that, in addition to being irreverent, they were also vulgar and crude:

> If there was atheism—the essence of profanity—in the McCollum home, there was also obscenity. While an *American Weekly* reporter was interviewing Terry and his father, the other two sons entered the room. Errol, 8, sat for a few minutes and then departed, remarking: "I'm not going to listen to that __ ." The elder McCollum just smiled at the gutter expression. "Errol can take care of himself," he said, "and so can Dannel. When anybody calls Dan an atheist, Dan just calls him a ___ ___." The reporter, who had heard such epithets in barrooms but never in a respectable home, was taken aback. Dannel, 10, and Terry laughed, and their father guffawed.

In the final paragraph, the story concluded that locally all had worked out well, in spite of Vashti's efforts:

> What she actually succeeded in doing was to encourage a spontaneous religious revival in Champaign and Urbana, where Jewish, Catholic and Protestant parents, planning a new and more intensive training program outside the schools, were determined that their children's rights to religious education would not be abrogated because of tales brought home by one maladjusted boy.[26]

The story failed to carry a by-line—the reporter received anonymity for his efforts. Deeply wounded, the McCollums considered a libel action against the newspaper but were advised by lawyers and friends that it would not be worth the effort. That was the view that prevailed—most people in Vashti's camp had had enough of courtrooms for a while.

Chapter 17

One Woman's Fight

In 1951, three years after her victory, Vashti's personal story of the law suit appeared in book form. She had been aided in the project by Clarissa Start. It is of interest to note that the manuscript for *One Woman's Fight* was prepared within a year after the Supreme Court decision. It was accepted by Doubleday & Co., publishers, shortly thereafter. Vashti then waited for nearly two additional years before the book actually appeared.[1] This seemed strange to her at the time, especially since such a long delay could not possibly be in the best interest of sales. According to Vashti, she never received a satisfactory answer from her publisher concerning the matter. In her view, the delay was deliberate—that Doubleday had second thoughts about having accepted the book due to its controversial nature.[2]

The book was widely reviewed; most of the critiques appear to have been favorable, though by no means all. In those falling in the former category, Vashti McCollum was described variously as "courageous,"[3] "intelligent, perceptive and ... indefatigable,"[4] and a "woman of steel."[5] In a more neutral review, her book was characterized as "a play-by-play account" that was both "personal and argumentative."[6] Another described her as the "ball carrier for 75 million unchurched Americans."[7] It would be safe to conclude that the book was received more or less on the basis of how the reviewer regarded Mrs. McCollum and the issue over which she fought.

In all likelihood, the most widely printed appraisal was that of E.B. Long, whose syndicated reviews appeared in numerous smaller newspapers around the country. "Mrs. McCollum," according to Long, "writes in a straightforward, interesting and very readable style." The positive review ended:

> This book is the frank story of a woman who battled for what she thought was right despite unpopularity, barrages of rotten fruit, and being known as "that awful McCollum woman."[8]

The Chicago *Tribune*, which had been supportive throughout the long battle in the courts, remained consistent:

> Mrs. McCollum has told her story well. The specific detail of episode, letter and conversation is present throughout, but nowhere does the story lose momentum or bog down in personal trivia or legal technicalities.

Enough is told so that the issue is early and clearly defined—not only as the plaintiff saw the issue, but as defendants and different commentators saw it also.

The reviewer alluded to the fact that the attitudes of big city editors, on the whole, tended to be supportive during her long court battle:

The story is told in terms of flesh and blood people, but also with effective attention to the impersonal, institutional aspects of the problem. If in the telling Mrs. McCollum seems clearly to have the better of it—well, most metropolitan editorial writers, many worthy folk in the general public and the Supreme Court thought she did in fact have the better of it.

The review ended:

The subject of finding legally and morally acceptable means of transmitting valid religious instruction is a weighty one. This book tells of one way not to do it. The subject of securing a citizen's access to a fair and dispassionate hearing in the courts both of law and of public opinion is likewise a weighty one. This book tells of ultimate success in law, but of such accompanying insult, intimidation and violence from numerous people as to give occasion for dismay and shame. The subject of the future of nonsectarian public schooling in America is by no means un-contested or to be taken for granted. This book gives a powerful witness for its preservation.[9]

In St. Louis, The *Post-Dispatch*, as the *Tribune*, continued its support of Vashti in its favorable review, though concentrating more on the issue than on the book itself:

If ever a book bore the right title, it is *One Woman's Fight*, the newly-published story of the personal experience of Mrs. Vashti Cromwell McCollum. She is the young mother of three boys who carried the celebrated issue of sectarian education in the public schools all the way to the United States Supreme Court.

It *was* one woman's fight. It was her fight through the School Board at Champaign Ill., where she lost. It was her fight through the Circuit Court where she lost. It was her fight through the Illinois State Supreme Court where she lost. And it was her fight through the long and difficult appeal to the highest court in the land, where she won, 8 to 1.

Yet, from the beginning, although at first it was not recognized, Mrs. McCollum's fight was for others too. She suffered the isolation in her community, where her husband was a member of the University of Illi-nois faculty, she took the insults from letter writers over the country, to bulwark religious freedom for all citizens, regardless of church, creed or belief.

Yes, it was one woman's fight, but in the end it turned out that many religious groups came to see its significance and so joined her as friends of the court in her appeal to Washington. That only made her victory—

and her vision—the greater. It is not often that a story possesses the combination of human interest and social importance of Vashti McCollum's brave story of a free mind in action.[10]

The Louisville *Courier Journal* provided this review:

Awe-inspiring is the courage of Vashti McCollum ... who carried to the Supreme Court of the United States her fight against religious instruction in public schools. Written by Mrs. McCollum, this is the play-by-play account of her determined battle, which ended in a hard-won, expensive victory. In easy-to-read style, she tells about her principles, her family's reactions, legal proceedings, the thousands of sympathetic and otherwise messages received and the over-all shock and heartbreak of her public efforts to uphold separation of Church and State.[11]

There was an even more positive review in the Salt Lake City *Tribune*, an area known for its religious conservatism:

Through it all, possibly because of iron nerves and possibly because all the persecution gave Mrs. McCollum the feeling of a crusader, this amazing suburban housewife kept her eye on the issues and shrugged off the epithets. She won her case and went on to tell about it in a book that is a bit impish in tone at times but is always both entertaining and amusing.[12]

Perhaps the most informative review appeared in the *Courier*, written by Bruce Taylor, who "had a ringside seat as a reporter for the Chicago *Times*" during the trial six years earlier. Of particular interest were Taylor's comments concerning Mrs. McCollum's trial lawyer:

There were a number of mistakes made by the Plaintiffs' side—as Mrs. McCollum freely admits. She is, on the whole, much more generous in her attitude toward her first lawyer, Landon Chapman, than were several of us from Chicago who covered the trial.

As for the book itself, he wrote:

She could not possibly be judged fairly in the public mind without this book. Whether the reader is for or against the principle for which she was fighting and the reasons she was fighting for it, the evidence was not complete until Mrs. McCollum told her personal version of why she decided to challenge religious education in the public schools and what she had to go through because of it.

Her book is a human story of personal courage as well as a disturbing social commentary on the way fundamental questions can get lost in the smokescreens of prejudice, misinformation and misunderstanding. It is a readable, straight-forward, sincere story of a woman who stood up for a particular conviction in the face of an outraged community .... It has a restraint and an appeal that give it the quality of a good novel.

The book did have its limitations, according to Taylor:

It can not be regarded as a telling intellectual argument for the basically
rationalist attitude Mrs. McCollum has toward religion. In fact the three
chapters toward the end ... that she devotes to an exposition of her opinions on religious education in general and parochial education in particular are not very sound. They weaken the character and impact of her
story.[13]

V. T. Thayer of the *Saturday Review* saw these chapters differently: "These
chapters remind us that eternal vigilance is still the price of liberty."[14]

The *News-Gazette* also carried an article concerning the book, although it
was markedly different in tone and substance. Unlike the *Courier*, there was no
discussion of the issues. The unidentified writer was content to use isolated quotes
from the book in which Vashti offered her assessment of the local community and
various persons associated with the case.

The book will afford Champaign-Urbana readers an opportunity to learn
what Mrs. McCollum thinks of them. She describes Champaign-Urbana
as "a small college town in the heart of the Midwest Bible belt," a town
with all its horror of "what will the neighbor's think?" and far more important, "what will my employers think?"

Of Vashti's meeting with Rev. Northcott:

She describes Northcott as "frowning," "hostile," "antagonized," and "defensive" when she talked with him.

Of her views of Rev. Cartlidge:

She says Reverend A. Ray Cartlidge ... once called her a "publicity seeker."
She comments, however, that after that time Cartlidge was "quite nice"
and is "still one of the few Champaign ministers with whom I have a
speaking acquaintance."

Of her husband:

She relates efforts to have her husband, Professor John P. McCollum—
whom she calls "Pappy" throughout the book—fired from the UI horticul-
ture department. She says "Pappy" is a "longsuffering and wonderful man
who would rather have his wife be right than be a college president." She
adds: "Although my case didn't advance his campus career any, he never
failed to be for me all the way."[15]

Of Phillip Schug, who aided her in the fight, Vashti says, "Through all this
commotion and conflict, Phil Schug stood out like a light over a stormy sea, to me
a symbol of hope and serenity."

The writer concluded:

Throughout the book, Mrs. McCollum is critical of the *Gazette* for what
she calls its "sensational" coverage of her case. She concedes, however,

that when she was on her way to Washington for the U. S. Supreme Court hearing, she "filched" a copy of the *News-Gazette* from Reporter Ed Borman while he was sleeping on the train.

There were other reviews of Vashti's book that were equally unsupportive. Some, especially in Roman Catholic publications, were in all probability prompted by the final chapters of the book to which Bruce Taylor had taken exception. The reason would seem to stem from Vashti's criticism of what she considered violations of the principle of separation of church and state by the Catholic Church. Particularly onerous to her were increasing pressures for public support of parochial schools and Catholic influence in public schools.

One of the most direct counterattacks, though it avoided reference to the broader issues raised by Vashti, was a review written by Fr. John S. Kennedy and printed in the Catholic diocesan newspaper in her home town of Rochester, New York.

Responsible persons have gravely said that the decision, in effect, bars God from tax-supported American schools. A momentous step, surely, and one which naturally brought notoriety to its instigator, Mrs. Vashti McCollum.

But not quite enough notoriety, it seems. For the lady has now written a very curious book ... The title is sober enough, in all conscience. It might serve as a label for a study of Harriet Beecher Stowe or Florence Nightengale, in whose class the author seemingly considers herself.

But the contents are, for the most part, at odds with the title. For one thing, they are permeated with frivolity. For another, they keep disclosing that the fight, although purportedly on a constitutional issue, really is an effort against religion and in favor of militant atheism. The latter is repeatedly denied by Mrs. McCollum, but again and again out of her mouth there comes evidence to the contrary.

Fr. Kennedy's conclusion:

In short, this extremely peculiar book will inevitably destroy the author's reputation as a keen, courageous crusader. It is an absurd and often offensive muddle, whatever one's convictions. Its giddiness and confusion will make the judicious wonder about the merits of a cause so advocated. I would say that for every fanatic it confirms in opposition to any link between education and religion, it will induce ten balanced people to look seriously and searchingly into the arguments pro.[16]

In New York, reviewer Marcus Duffield of the *Herald-Tribune* was sympathetic to the book and attempted to offer a different view of its author:

What manner of woman was this, to subject herself and her family to such odium for the sake of a principle? Her book reads much like a letter—friendly, bright, candid. Piecing things together, it appears she is a reasonably young and comely woman. She likes stylish clothes, but is usually too busy to bother about them or too short of money to buy them.

She would seem to be high-strung; is subject to migraine; is full of restless energy. During the years of her court fight she was not only looking after her husband and three children, conferring with lawyers, hunting up witnesses, answering mountains of mail and thousands of telephone calls; but also she was teaching square dancing, canning a prodigious amount of vegetables and fruit from her garden, taking a pre-medical course, and braiding a big rug. She is the stuff of martyrs. Perhaps the chief appeal of her book is that one sees a martyr in action and gets some inkling of what makes a martyr tick.[17]

The book was not a financial success and after repeated efforts, all rights were obtained by Beacon Press, the Unitarian publishing house, which reissued the unsold books of the original edition[18] and then, in 1961, published a second edition in paperback.[19] It dropped the last three chapters, the same chapters which *Courier*-writer Taylor felt had detracted from the book. Substituted was a revised epilogue, an update on church-state issues by Paul Blanshard and the full text of the Supreme Court decision. Finally, in 1993, the book was reissued a final time by the Freedom From Religion Foundation of Madison, Wisconsin. It sold briskly enough to warrant a second printing.[20]

This author's views of *One Woman's Fight* can be found in the references to the book contained in the preface. The most serious criticism is the book's "chatty" approach. This was, no doubt, the work of Clarissa Start and her peculiar feature-writing style, including as many contractions as possible in the quote material. Nevertheless, what emerges is vintage Vashti. Over the several years during which the manuscript for this book was being prepared, there was seldom a need to discuss with her the case and its repercussions. The book just about said it all in a refreshing, candid, unguarded and open manner.

It would not be inappropriate here for the author to offer his own insight into what made a person like Vashti "tick." She was not a martyr. She never saw her cause as a losing proposition; she was always optimistic as to the outcome. She was driven by the view that she was right and she expected to win and be vindicated in this life—for her there was no next. Vashti was not a person in search of a cause. As her book reveals, she was simply a person who circumstances trapped in the most uncomfortable position of either going along with the crowd and accepting sectarian religious training in the public schools or taking a stand. History trifled with the wrong person. She was of that exceptional breed that not only would refuse to suffer quietly but also would wage a vigorous fight for her principles.

When her fight was over, she wrote her story and remained involved in civil liberties issues for a number of years. And she enjoyed her status as a minor celebrity. She did not, however, make the court fight the centerpiece of her life. To her, the event was episodic; she won and then proceeded to go on and do new and different things.

Chapter 18

Parting Shots

Owen Rall, reflecting on the *McCollum* decision 36 years afterwards, still felt the position of the Champaign Board of Education, as put forward by himself and John Franklin, should have been sustained by the United States Supreme Court. In commenting on the Court's interpretation of the "establishment of religion" clause, he said: "The Constitution does not prevent the recognition of religion. In holding that the Champaign program established religion, it enlarged the Constitutional prohibition."[1]

In an interview 30 years after the decision, John Franklin offered his perspectives:

> I was disappointed when the Supreme Court struck down my argument, but was not surprised. We realized it was a very serious constitutional question and it could have gone either way.

He also observed that there had been some retreat by the Court from its position in the *McCollum* case:

> I think the line is not drawn as sharply as it appeared to be by that decision. Change is jerky; it is not smooth. The public and the court have realized that there has to be some necessary cooperation between the church and state. The pendulum has begun to swing back to the middle.[2]

In what was probably his last interview on the subject, Franklin seemed somewhat philosophical about the matter:

> I have come to think that the [*McCollum*] case, on both sides, was much ado about nothing, and that it isn't true that religion, organized religion, has been hurt by exclusion from the [public] school. And it isn't true, conversely, that there would have been harm to non-believers if it had been permitted. In my present frame of mind, I would probably, regardless of the adjudications that have been made, tell the Board of Education that this is a controversial subject and that they ought to concentrate on the field of education that is devoid of religious emphasis. I admit that my feeling may be influenced by a kind of protective device of saying this was a hopeless cause and, therefore, I ought not blame myself for not

having convinced the Supreme Court of the United States otherwise. But, I can't believe that either non-believers or religionists would be much harmed by a decision of this issue one way or another.[3]

Superintendent of Schools Eugene Mellon, who had said little during the long journey of the case through the courts, apparently had misgivings about the practice of religious education in the public schools even at the time.

I was just doing what the School Board had set up as our school plan. I probably never would have instigated [such] a plan. Even then, I was ... much [interested in the] separation of school and church. But this released time for religious education, you must remember, was rather prevalent then—quite a number of schools did it. It just seemed kind of a thing to do. Now when you get up before a judge ... about all you can testify to is what you are doing and why you are doing it. I don't think they asked me what I really felt about it.[4]

Mellon continued to be interested in the church-state issue afterwards:

I think [the *McCollum* case] made me more of a student of the First Amendment and all its ramifications. [After the decision] I was president of the Horace Mann League, an organization made up most of school people, whose main purpose is to uphold separation of church and state. We have to fight [the issue] over and over, because if you are a student of it you know every year the state legislatures [consider] bills to appropriate ... money for private or parochial schools, for bus transportation, grants for textbooks etc. Those things all have to be fought year after year.[5]

During the long ordeal, and especially on days one and three of the trial, Vashti probably regretted having anything to do with the court case. By the time she offered the following statement, possibly a script for a radio address she delivered on November 25, 1945, she had had time to modestly recover her composure.

If I had realized that raising an objection to a religious project involved nation-wide publicity, inadequate and often false representation of my position, 1,100 pieces of correspondence, malicious gossip and false accusations, I'm afraid I wouldn't have had the courage. But I'm not sorry; it has all served to give the whole movement of religious instruction in relation to our public schools a long overdue airing.[6]

McCollum, *Post-Dispatch*, March 14, 1948:

It's hard to go out against religion. You're just a no-good if you dare say anything against it. If I'd known just how hard it was I might not have gone through with it, but I've always been one of those dreamers, I guess. It's kind of tough feeling that you're in everybody's doghouse.[7]

McCollum, *The Churchman*, Jan 1, 1949: "My religious feeling is not a controlling factor in this case, it is purely a matter of separation of church and state, a secular action."[8]

McCollum, Louisville *Courier-Journal*, Feb 11, 1961:

There is recognition that the law is there, but they [the supporters of religious education], go on. The strange thing is that they bring something into the schools that is supposed to build good character although it is unlawful. It's easy to take the idea that "we have a little delinquency, so a little more religion would help," but there's no correlation between church membership and moral living.

In the same article, when asked if she would do it again knowing in advance what she would face: "That's a hard question, I think I would, but I had no idea what a fight it would be."[9]

McCollum, Houston *Post*, 1962: "No, I did not have such great courage, I got into this thing and I knew I had to keep going."[10]

Courier headline, Sept. 1965: "She'd File Famed Suit Again, Vashti Says, 20 Years After."[11]

McCollum, Chicago *Tribune*, Midwest Edition, Sept. 19, 1976:

It appears to me that religion is again getting its foot in the public school door. There are all kinds of churches with all kinds of time, such as summer vacations, weekends, and after school hours, to have Bible lessons with youngsters. I don't see why they have to bootleg it into the schools.[12]

McCollum, *Courier*, Mar. 8, 1978:

It's not that we were anti-religious. We weren't really, and we never have been. I was baptized Lutheran, and there was no anti-religious doctrine in our home, but we didn't practice it, and we weren't going to have them give it to [our children] in school.

Basic to all other arguments is that it's illegal—and for a very good reason. The founding fathers had seen how divisive religion could be. They decided to free their conscience and their pocketbook as well. When you're supporting a public school system and part of that time it is used to indoctrinate children with religion, then you're being forced to support religion.[13]

When she realized that James was taking physical abuse, "at that point, I regretted having done it." Several paragraphs later, she concluded by saying, "I think I have to admit I'm proud of (the case)."[14]

McCollum, *News-Gazette*, Mar. 8, 1978:

I didn't like [the religious instruction in the public schools.] I felt it was wrong and that it was unconstitutional. It was a practical means of breaking down the wall between church and state. It was a very important issue and I was very, very happy when the court sustained my argument.

Franklin, in the same article:

Religion is so woven into our society that a wall cannot be built between the two. We still grant subsidies to churches through tax relief. It is obviously impossible to segregate religion from education in an extreme manner, just as it is to separate sexuality from human life.[15]

McCollum, *News-Gazette*, Mar. 23, 1986:

I didn't stop to think how far I would have to go. When I saw it not only got into the local papers but front pages from all over the country then I realized I was in for something. I enjoyed being a celebrity, but at the time I was deadly serious and I worried a lot about it. I began to see that it was hard on the boys and I worried about my husband's job. It was hard financially—we had to cough up a lot of money. I was really convinced that I was right; I had no doubt that I was right.[16]

William Sholem, letter, Dec. 3, 1994 (excerpts):

At Dr. Howard primary school, only half a block from our home in Champaign in the 1940s, I watched my classmate James McCollum being victimized repeatedly. His mother was an outspoken atheist amidst the "town versus gown" unease which pervaded the farmer-academician social core of the Twin Cities. Notions labeled "liberal" encountered vigorous hostility in those years when our nation was just coming out of a war with foreigners and when "right" action and beliefs were easily defined without too much concern about civil liberties of minorities.

James paid the price. I saw him verbally abused and badly beaten in a school environment where bullying was otherwise absent. I cannot recall the exact epithets used against James, but memory of the place (the window wells on the then-south wall), the hate in my classmates eyes and actions, and the tears are etched in my memory as if I was there today. There is no question in my mind that the on-site religion classes at Dr. Howard School were the catalyst for that hate ...

Vashti McCollum spoke out. Why did not I speak out as an eleven year old boy? As you know, I was "different" too. Not only was I Jewish, but I was very self-conscious because I was terribly overweight. I could not keep up with my peers on the then-all-important school playground, and I tried to compensate by being a scholarly "good boy" both at home and at school. That meant keeping one's head down by not inviting controversy by inviting attention to oneself. In the atmosphere which prevailed, I got off relatively lightly with the usual "Jew Boy", "Shoe Jew" and "Christ Killer" insults and an infrequent (but telling) thrashing, usually by a child of fundamentalist, evangelical Christian upbringing.

I do remember in Bertha Malzahn's sixth year classroom repelling the tears while trying to sing Christmas Carols in the best possible voice in order to "fit in". There indeed was an exquisitely-taught lesson in self-hate and Jewish identity erosion administered in the open classroom in concentrated daily doses by a well-meaning lady of whom I thought the world.[17]

McCollum, *News-Gazette*, June 18, 1995:

I asked my lawyer if there would be anything in the newspaper about it. Of course, there was a great deal. It was traumatic and expensive. But we had a happy home life and [we] were sufficient unto ourselves and not too dependent on others. And I knew I was right.[18]

McCollum, *News-Gazette*, Mar. 8, 1998:

After we lost in circuit court in Champaign County, I remember saying it would be nice if we would lose in the Illinois Supreme Court as well so when the U.S. Supreme Court make its decision it'll be the law of the land and not just of the State of Illinois.[19]

She knew that she was right. Would that have been enough had she known the costs of challenging the system to have deterred her action? We shall never know because it is impossible to re-script history. We do know that the faint of heart stall and retreat when the going gets tough and pay about the same price as those stalwart few who march on quixotically to the end. Without doubt, Vashti Cromwell McCollum was of the latter category.

Endnotes

Chapter 1

1. Cromwell, letter to Vivian Corbly (National Adjutant of the Disabled American Veterans), Jan. 6, 1934, copy in possession of the author.

2. Cromwell, *Memoirs of a Freethinker* (Rationalist Press, 1964), p. 14.

3. Cromwell, *Rationalism vs. Religious Education in the Public Schools* (Rochester, NY: A.G. Cromwell, 1940).

4. Ibid., 12.

5. Ibid.

6. Ibid. 4.

7. Ibid., 3. This statement bears the imprint of Jean Meslier (1678-1733), a French cleric who stated: "Devotion is a disease of the imagination contracted in infancy." *See* Meslier, *Superstition in All Ages* (New York: Peter Eckler, 1890), 154.

8. John and Vashti McCollum to Cromwell, undated letters c. 1940 in the possession of the author.

9. Cromwell, "Religious Education in the Public Schools," (radio script), 1940, in the position of the author.

10. Vashti Cromwell McCollum, *One Woman's Fight* rev. ed. (1951; Boston: Beacon, 1961), 16.

11. Malcom Nygren, "Released-Time Religious Education in Champaign, Illinois, 1940-1948: Its Implications for Co-operation Between Parish Churches and other Religious and/or Secular Agencies in Mission" (Doctor of Science of Theology diss., San Francisco Theological Seminary, 1980), 19. Rev. Cartlidge was quoted extensively in this work.

12. Cromwell, Personal Papers. This source indicated that he also sent copies of the pamphlet to Urbana school officials, in the possession of the author.

13. Cromwell, interview with the author, Feb. 21, 1980.

14. Ibid., 10; McCollum, *One Woman's Fight*, 34.

15. "Gideons Plan School Bibles In Meet Here," *Democrat and Chronicle*, Oct. 16, 1940, p. 21.

16. "Free Thinkers Oppose Bible Gift To Schools, "*Democrat and Chronicle*, Oct. 20, 1940, p. 1C.

17. "Gideons Win Fight To Place Bibles In Public Schools," *Democrat and Chronicle*, Oct. 31, 1940, p. 21.

18. *Times-Union*, Feb. 1, 1944, p. 3A. When this article was originally written for publication ("Arthur Cromwell and the McCollum Case," *American Rationalist* magazine, September-October, 1981, pp.36-39), the author failed to record the caption of the article, which has since been lost.

19. Cromwell, Personal correspondence to the editor of the *Saturday Evening Post*, Oct. 5, 1945; *see also* Cromwell to Religious News Service, June 27, 1945, copies in possession of author.

20. Ibid. The potential for bias in these letters exists, but they represent the only account available of Cromwell's investigation, and they were written only a year after the fact, when the events were fresh in his mind.

21. G.D. Stoddard, Opinion in the matter of the petition of Arthur G. Cromwell in respect to the actions of the Board of Education of Central School District No. 1, June 7, 1945, in the possession of the author.

22. "Freethinkers To Meet," *Democrat and Chronicle*, Nov. 4, 1944, p. 19.

23. "Religious Classes In Schools Halted," *New York Times*, June 14, 1945, p. 21C.

24. P. Fallon, Copies of Broadcast Bulletins and Wire Reports, WHAM Radio, Rochester, NY, June 14, 1945 (in the possession of the author); *see also* "Mrs. M'Collum's Father's Petition Stops New York Religious Classes," *News-Gazette*, June 14, 1945, p. 3.

25. Ibid., 19; *see also* Ibid., 10, McCollum, *One Woman's Fight*, 38.

26. Ibid., 21, Stoddard, Opinion, June 7, 1945.

27. Stoddard's caution was well-advised. The president-elect was to be severely criticized by Bishop James A. Griffith of the Catholic diocese of Springfield, Illinois, for his religious views; *News-Gazette*, Oct. 1, 1945, p. 3. While the New York decision was not mentioned in the bishop's attack, it could have been the igniting factor.

28. Ibid., 23.

29. Group Fights Pupil Credits For Religion, "*Democrat and Chronicle*, June 14, 1945, p. 21.

30. Cromwell to Arthur E. Sutherland, April 29, 1949, in possession of the author. The same story with only slight variations was related by Cromwell in *Memoirs of a Freethinker*, 17-18.

31. Cromwell to Landon L. Chapman, May 28, 1945, in possession of the author.

32. Ted Duffield, "Mrs. McCollum Tells Why," *Evening Courier*, June 14, 1945, p. 3.

33. Cromwell, letter to the editor, *Democrat and Chronicle*, July 8, 1945, p. 15A.

34. Ibid., 33.

35. Ibid., 33.

36. Ruth C. Cromwell, letter to the editor, *Democrat and Chronicle*, Nov. 15, 1945, p. 16.

Chapter 2

1. McCollum, *One Woman's Fight*, rev. ed. (1951; Boston: Beacon, 1961), 16.

2. Eugene H. Mellon, interview with the author, May 20, 1980.

3. "Religion Plan Sponsor Tilts With Opponents," *Evening Courier*, September 10, 1945, p. 3, MA II, p. 2.

4. Ibid., 1, McCollum, *One Woman's Fight*, 56

5. Ibid., 1 55-58; and Ibid., 3.

6. The stories were carried in both the *Courier* and the *News-Gazette* from March through August, 1940.

7. "Student Church Proposal Told By Nickell," *News-Gazette*, March 8, 1940, p. 2.

8. "Religion May Be Taught In School System," *Evening Courier*, March 8, 1940, p. 3. The relevant provision of the compulsory attendance law, which exempted from school attendance "any child over twelve and under fourteen years of age during the hours while in attendance at confirmation classes." See Laws of Illinois, 56 G.A. (1929), p. 726.

9. Ibid., 7.

10. Ibid., 8.

11. Ibid., 7.

12. Minutes of the Champaign Board of Education, March 7, 1940.

13. Transcript Of Record, Supreme Court of the United States, October Term, 1947, No. 90, *McCollum v. Board of Education*, transcript, p. 128,

14. "Religious Study Is Considered," *Evening Courier*, April 14, 1940, p. 3.

15. Ibid., 14.

16. "Study Of Religion Planned: Ministers To Sponsor Public Meeting April 28," *Evening Courier*, April 16, 1940, p. 3.

17. "Champaign-Urbana Clergymen Took The First Step In An Effort To Initiate Weekday Religious Training In The Public Schools," and "School Religion Plan Is Studied by Ministers," *News-Gazette*, April 15, 1940, p. 5.

18. On Cromwell's remarks, see Cromwell to Chapman, June 25, 1945, in the possession of the author. In accounting for his detailed recollections, Cromwell explained that they were taken from a letter he had written on May 6, 1940.

19. Ibid., 18.

20. Malcolm Nygren, "Released-Time Religious Education in Champaign, Illinois, 1940-48: Its Implications for Co-operation Between Parish Churches and Other Religious and/or Secular Agencies in Mission," (Doctor of Science of Theology dissertation, San Francisco Theological Seminary, 1980), p. 23.

21. Cromwell had published the tract in February, 1940.

22. "Plan To Study Classes In Religion: Clergy To Appoint Committee May 6 To Investigate Possibilities," *News-Gazette*, April 28, 1940, p. 7.

23. Ibid., 22, and "Urbana Schools End Religious Survey," *News-Gazette*, April 26, p. 12; "Study Church Education Program," *News-Gazette*, May 5, p. 3, 1940.

24. Ibid., 23, *News-Gazette*, April 26, 1940, p. 12.

25. Ibid., 23, and "Study Church Education Plan," *News-Gazette*, May 5, 1940, p. 3.

26. Ibid., 20, Nygren, "Released-Time Religious Education in Champaign, Illinois," 23.

27. Ibid., 20.

28. A. Ray Cartlidge to author, Dec. 5, 1980; original in author's possession.

29. "Rev. Cartlidge Chairman Of Education: Presbyterian Minister Named Committee Head For Religious Instruction," *News-Gazette*, May 6, 1940, p. 12.

30. Cartlidge said that he was asked to be chairman because he "had knowledge of what was being done in Cincinnati, Ohio; Cartlidge to author, September 11, 1980; original in the possession of the author.

31. Ibid., 30, p. 29.

32. Ibid., 30.

33. Minutes of the Champaign Board of Education, June 6, 1940.

34. Ibid., 33.

35. "Board Approves Religious Plan For Schools," *News-Gazette*, June 8, 1940, p. 3.

36. "School Rooms To Be Used In Religion Study," *Evening Courier*, June 7, 1940, p. 3.

37. Ibid., 36.

38. Ibid., 36.

39. Ibid., 33, Minutes of the Champaign Board of Education, June 6, 1940,

40. John Franklin, interview with author, May 27, 1980.

41. "Form Council Of Religious Ed" *News-Gazette*, July 25, 1940, p. 3; "Churches Form New Council," *Evening Courier*, July 26, 1940, p. 7.

42. Ibid., 41, *Evening Courier*, July 26, 1940, p. 7.

43. "Religion Study Budget Is $800," *Evening Courier*, Aug. 13, 1940, p. 3.

44. "Religion Study Jobs Offered," *Evening Courier*, Aug. 14, 1940, p. 3; "Name Religious Teachers At Aug. 22 Meet; Personnel Committee Sets Standards For Applicants, To Pick Two, "*News-Gazette*, Aug. 14, 1940, p. 2.

45. "Explain Religious Courses To Jr H Students," *News-Gazette*, Sept 4, 1940, p. 15.

Chapter 3

1. McCollum, *One Woman's Fight*, rev. ed. (1951; Boston: Beacon, 1951), 17.

2. McCollum, Ibid., 1, p. 18.

3. Ibid. 1, p. 18.

4. Author's recollections.

5. "Never Argue over Religion," Chicago *Sunday News*, September 16, 1945, p. 17C, MA II, p 84a, and "It's Not The Religion, But The Principle Of The Thing," *Sunday News*, July 29, 1945, MA I, p. 64, respectively.

6. McCollum, Ibid. 1, *One Woman's Fight*, 18.

7. Ibid. 1, p. 19.

8. Ibid. 1, p. 19

9. Ibid. 1, p. 20.

10. Ibid, 1, p. 20.

11. Ibid. 1, p. 20.

12. Ibid. 1, p. 21.

13. Philip Schug, interview with author ca. 1985. The author had a number of visits and long discussions with Schug at his retirement home in San Antonio, Texas.

14. Author's recollections.

15. Schug, Ibid. 13.

16. Schug, "The Religious Modern," January, 1945, in possession of the author, *see also* McCollum, Ibid. 1, *One Woman's Fight*, p. 22.

17. Clabaugh to McCollum, Jan. 14, 1945, copy in possession of the author; *see also* McCollum, Ibid. 1, *One Woman's Fight*, p. 22.

18. Peters to McCollum, Feb. 27, 1945, copy in possession of the author; *see also* McCollum, Ibid. 1, *One Woman's Fight*, p. 22.

19. Dillavou to McCollum, Jan. 17, 1945, copy in possession of the author; *see also* McCollum, Ibid. 1, *One Woman's Fight*, p. 22.

20. McCollum, Ibid. 1, *One Woman's Fight*, p. 23.

21. Ibid. 1, p. 23.

22. Ibid. 1, pp. 24-25.

23. Eugene H. Mellon, interview with author, May 20, 1980.

24. McCollum, Ibid. 1, *One Woman's Fight*, p. 27.

25. Ibid. 1, p. 28.

26. Ibid. 1, p. 28.

27. Author's recollections.

28. McCollum, Ibid. 1, *One Woman's Fight*, p. 29.

29. "Action Council Will Publicize Religion Issue," *Courier*, June 24, 1945, p. 15.

30. McCollum, Ibid. 1, *One Woman's Fight*, p. 30.

31. Howard Landon Chapman, telephone interview with author, Dec. 21, 1985. See also obituaries: *Chicago Tribune*, July 11, 1979, p. 15; *Chicago Sun Times*, July 11, 1979, p. 90; *New York Times*, July 12, 1979. No page number was noted on the clip.

32. McCollum, Ibid. 1, *One Woman's Fight*, pp. 30-31.

33. Ibid. 1, p. 33.

34. Ibid. 1, p. 33.

35. Ibid. 1, p. 34.

36. Ibid. 1, p. 35.

37. Ibid. 1, p. 35.

38. Ibid. 1, p. 36.

39. Ibid. 1, p. 36.

40. Author's recollections.

41. John Franklin, interview with author, May 27, 1980.

42. McCollum, Ibid. 1, *One Woman's Fight*, p. 38.

43. Ibid. 1, p. 34.

44. Cromwell to Chapman, May 28, 1945, and June 20, 1945, in possession of the author.

45. Chapman to Cromwell, June 3, 1945, in possession of the author.

46. Ibid. 45.

47. Ibid. 45.

48. McCollum, Ibid. 1, *One Woman's Fight*, p. 28.

49. John Franklin, interview, May 27, 1980.

50. "Religious Education Test Suit Filed Against School Board," *News-Gazette*, June 12, 1945, p. 3; McCollum, Ibid. 1, *One Woman's Fight*, pp. 37-8.

51. McCollum, Ibid. 1, *One Woman's Fight*, p. 37.

52. Ibid. 1, p. 38.

53. Ibid. 1, p. 84.

Chapter 4

1. Transcript of Record (prepared for the appeal to the U.S. Supreme Court), p. 17, in the possession of the author.

2. Ibid. 1, p. 17.

3. Ibid. 1, p. 17.

4. Ibid. 1, p. 10.

5. Ibid. 1, p. 5.

6. Ibid. 1, p. 9.

7. Ibid. 1, p. 14

8. John Franklin, legal opinion shared with the author.

9. *Nichols vs. School Directors*, 93 Ill. 61.

10. Ibid., 8.

11. *People ex rel. Ring vs. Board of Education*, 245 Ill. 334.

12. Ibid. 11.

13. John Franklin, Ibid. 8.

14. Hazel MacDonald, "Press Fight to Bar Religion in Schools," *Chicago Times*, June 14, 1945, MA I, p. 5.

15. "School Board Pledges Fight in Writ Suit," *News-Gazette*, June 13, 1945, p. 3, MA I, p. 3.

16. Minutes, Champaign Board of Education, June 12, 1945. Champaign Unit 4 Schools, Champaign, Illinois.

17. *News-Gazette*, Ibid., 15.

18. Fletcher Wilson, "Mother of 3 Leads Fight on Religion in Schools," *Chicago Sun*, June 18, 1945, pp. 1 & 5.

19. "Religious Education Test Suit Filed Against School Board," *News-Gazette*, June 12, 1945, p. 3; "Religion Class Ban Requested for Champaign," *Evening Courier*, June 12, 1945, p. 3 MA I, pp. 1 & 3 respectively.

20. "Religious Education Test Suit Filed," *News-Gazette*, June 12, 1945, p. 3, MA I, p. 1.

21. "Religion Class Ban Requested," *Evening Courier*, June 12, 1945, p. 3, MA I, p. 2.

22. *News-Gazette*, Ibid. 15.

23. "Mrs. McCollum's Father's Petition Stops New York Religious Classes," *News-Gazette*, June 14, 1945, p. 3; "Religion Classes Stopped On N.Y. School Property," *Evening Courier*, June 14, 1945, p. 3, MA I, p 6.

24. McCollum, *One Woman's Fight* (1951; Boston: Beacon, 1961), p. 38.

25. "785 Public School Students Studied Religion in '44-'45," *News-Gazette*, June 14, 1945, p. 3, MA I, p. 7.

26. Ibid., 25.

27. Ted Duffield, "Mrs. McCollum Tells Why," *Evening Courier*, June 14, 1945, p. 3, MA I, p. 9.

28. "Vashti McCollum Wants Separation of Church, State," *Daily Illini*, June 19, 1945, p. 1, MA I, p. 26.

29. Ibid., 28.

30. Wilson, "Mother of 3 Leads Fight," *Chicago Sun*, June 18, 1945, p. 3 & 5, MA I, p. 23.

31. Chapman to Cromwell, June 14, 1945, in possession of the author.

32. Ibid., 31.

33. MacDonald, Ibid, 14, *Chicago Times*, June 14, 1945, MA I, p. 5.

34. Rev. Philip Schug, "Free Schools Lauded," *Sunday Courier*, June 17, 1945, p. 6, MA I, p. 21.

35. Ibid., 34.

36. Ibid., 34.

37. "Ministers Outline Position On Religious Education," *News-Gazette*, June 17, 1945, p. 3, MA I, p. 16.

38. Ibid., 37.

39. Ibid., 37.

40. Schug, "The Religious Modern," July or August, 1945.

41. "Urbana Ministers To Back Schools In Religion Suit," *News-Gazette*, June 19, 1945, p. 3, MA I, p. 28.

42. Schug, Ibid. 40.

43. "Board Will Reply to Religion Suit," *Courier*, June 17, 1945, p. 3, MA I, p. 20.

44. Ibid. 43.

45. Cromwell to James Terry McCollum, (date ?) in possession of the author.

46. Ed Borman, "Clabaugh Asks Legalization of Religious Study," *News-Gazette*, June 19, 1945, p. 3, MA I, p. 27.

47. "Clabaugh Bill Advaces; Bare Earlier Stand," *Courier*, June 20, 1945, p. 3, MA I, p. 29.

48. McCollum, *One Woman's Fight*, Ibid. 24, p. 39.

49. "Mrs McCollum Says Clabaugh 'Changed Mind,'" *News-Gazette*, June 20, 1945, p. 3, MA I, p. 30.

50. "House Rejects Plan to Forbid Atheists At UI.," *Courier*, June 19, 1945, p. 3, MA I, p. 27.

51. Ibid., 50.

52. McCollum, *One Woman's Fight*, Ibid. 24, p. 42.

53. Ibid. 24, p. 46.

54. Ibid., 24, p. 46.

55. "Religious Freedom," *Daily Illini*, June 26, 1945, p. 2, MA I, p. 49.

56. Ibid., 55.

57. "Action Council Will Publicize Religion Issue," *Courier*, June 24, 1945, p. 15, MA I, p. 34.

58. Ibid. 57.

59. "House Approves Religious Classes," *Courier*, June 26, 1945, p. 3, MA I, p. 38.

60. Peters To Rush Legislation To Senate OKEH," *News-Gazette*, June 26, 1945, p. 3, MA I, p. 40.

61. "Religion Bill Given Senate After Hearing," *Courier*, June 28, 1945, p. 3, MA I, p. 42.

62. Ibid., 61.

63. "Schug Heads Objectors In Senate Fight," *News-Gazette*, June 28, 1945, p. 3., MA I, p. 41.

64. Letter, Chapman to Cromwell, 6-?-45, in possession of the author.

65. Schug, Hot Potato Letter, MA I, pp. 43-45.

66. Ibid., 65.

67. Ibid., 65.

68. McCollum, *One Woman's Fight*, Ibid., 24, p. 40, and interview with author.

69. Schug, letter to author.

70. "Senate Kills Religion Bill By 20-14 Vote," *Courier*, June 29, 1945, p. 3, MA I, p. 47.

71. Ibid., 70.

72. Ibid., 70

73. Franklin, interview with author, May 26,. 1980.

74. "Vashti McCollum Wants Separation Of Church And State," *Daily Illini*, June 19, 1945, pp. 1 & 3, MA I, p. 26.

75. Dismissal Denied In Religion Case," *Courier*, July 6, 1945, p. 3, MA I, P. 52.

76. McCollum, *One Woman's Fight*, Ibid., 24, p. 44.

77. "Three On Bench For Religion Suit," *Courier*, June 31, 1945, p. 3., MA I, p. 65.

78. "Board's Answer In Religious Suit Highlights Issues," *News-Gazette*, August 10, 1945, p. 3, MA I, p. 74.

79. "McCollum And Scopes' Cases Compared," *Courier*, August 2, 1945, p. 14, MA I, p. 69.

80. Jack Prowell, "Champaign's Religion Suit Evokes Memories of Evolution Trial," *News-Gazette*, September 9, 1945, p. 4, MA I, P. 86.

81. *Courier*, Ibid., 79.

82. "Churches Hire Attorney For School Fight," *News-Gazette*, July 21, 1945, p. 3, MA I, p. 62.

83. "School Budget Slightly Higher For Champaign," *Courier*, July 11, 1945, p. 3, MA I, p. 58.

84. "Chicago Group May Aid Suit," *Courier*, July 11, 1945, p. 3, MA I, p. 32.

85. *Courier*, Ibid., 83.

86. "Churches Hire Attorney For School Fight," *News-Gazette*, July 21, 1945, p. 3, MA I, p. 62.

87. Ibid., 86.

88. "West Chairman Of State Group In Religious Suit," *Courier*, August 3, 1945, p. 3, MA I, p. 71.

89. Franklin, Ibid. 73.

90. "Religious Suit Poll Approved," *Courier*, July 20, 1945, p. 3, MA I, p. 61. and "School Religion Meet Tonight," *Courier*, August 2, 1945, p. 2, MA I, p. 69.

91. "State Churches Back Board In Religious Case," *News-Gazette*, August 3, 1945, MA I, p. 70.

92. "Association To Back Religion In Schools," *News-Gazette*, August, 24, 1945, p. 5, MA I, p. 75.

93. Ibid., 92.

94. McCollum, *One Woman's Fight*, Ibid. 24, p. 94.

95. Ibid., 24, p. 47.

96. Ibid., 24, p. 48.

97. Ibid., 24, The woman's name was not revealed in the book to protect the family, but is offered here with their permission.

98. Ibid., 24, pp. 50, 51.

99. Ibid., 24, pp. 51, 52.

100. Ibid., 24, p. 55.

101. "Civil Liberties Group To Hold Meeting Sunday," *Courier*, September 6, 1945, p. 3, MA I, p. 79.

102. Advertisements in *Courier*, September 9, 1945, p. ?, and *News-Gazette*, September 9, 1945, p. 22.

103. "Grill Champaign Teacher On Religion In Schools," Chicago *Daily News*, September 11, 1945, p. 3, MA II, p. 6.

104. Annabel Scott, "School Board 'Bootlegged' Classes In Religion," *News-Gazette*, September 10, 1945, p. 3, MA II, p. 1.

105. "Religion Plan Sponsor Tilts With Opponents," *Courier*, September 10, 1945, p. 3, MA II, p. 2.

106. *Daily News*, Ibid., 103.

107. *Courier*, Ibid. 105.

108. Ibid. 105.

109. *Daily News*, Ibid. 103.

110. *News-Gazette*, Ibid. 104.

111. Ibid, 104.

112. *Daily News*, Ibid. 103.

113. *Courier*, Ibid. 105.

114. *Daily News*, Ibid., 103.,

115. "Large Religious Training Impairs Secular In Hearing In McCollum vs. School Board," *Daily Illini*, September 11, 1945, p. 1, MA II, p. 18.

116. Ibid. 115.

117. *News-Gazette*, Ibid. 104.

118. Ibid. 104.

119. McCollum, *One Woman's Fight*, Ibid. 24, p. 56.

120. *Daily News*, Ibid. 103.

121. Ibid. 103.

122. *Courier*, Ibid. 105.

123. Vashti McCollum, interview with the author.

124. *Daily News*, Ibid. 103.

125. *News-Gazette*, Ibid. 104.

126. Ibid. 104.

127. Ibid. 104.

128. *Daily News*, Ibid. 103.

129. *Courier*, Ibid. 105.

130. *News-Gazette*, Ibid. 104.

131. McCollum, *One Woman's Fight*, Ibid. 24, p. 56.

132. Ibid. 24.

133. Ibid., 24, *Courier*, Ibid., 105.

134. *News-Gazette*, Ibid. 104.

135. *Daily News*, Ibid. 103.

136 *News-Gazette*, Ibid. 104.

137. Franklin, Ibid. 73.

Chapter 5

1. Guy Gentry, "Suit to Bar Religion from School Opens," Chicago *Tribune*, September 11, 1945, p. 1, MA II, p. 11.

2. Present were Guy Gentry of the Chicago *Tribune*; Stanley Pieza, Chicago *Herald American*; Fletcher Wilson, Chicago *Sun*; Alfred Prowitt, Chicago *Daily News*; and Bruce Taylor, Chicago *Times*.

3. Fletcher Wilson, "Religious Education Issue Faces Court Test Today," Chicago *Sun*, September 10, 1945, pp. 1, MA II, p 4b.

4. Eugene Mellon, interviews with author, May 20, 1980 and April 18, 1984.

5. Alfred Prowitt, "Teacher Heard on Religion," Chicago *Daily News*, September 11, 1945, p. 1, MA II, p. 5.

6. Ibid., 5.

7. "Frank B. Leonard, Circuit Judge, Dies," *Courier*, September 5, 1946, p. 3.

8. Franklin, interview with author, May 26, 1980.

9. Constitution of Illinois, 1870, Article II, Section 3.

10. Transcript of Record (prepared for the appeal to the U.S. Supreme Court), p. 56, in the possession of the author.

11. Ibid., pp. 54-58.

12. Stanley Pieza, "School Religion Trial Opens at Urbana," Chicago *Herald American*, September 10, 1945, pp. 1, 4; Gentry, "Suit to Bar Religion from Schools Opens," Chicago *Tribune*, September 11, 1945, pp. 1-2, MA II, p. 4a.

13. Ed Borman, "Religious Beliefs Being Scrutinized As McCollum Suit Opens – Proselytizing of Children Seen by Chapman," *News-Gazette*, September 10, 1945, p. 3, MA II, p. 3.

14. Stanley Pieza, Ibid., 12, *Herald American*, September 10, 1945, pp. 1 & 4.

15. Ibid., 12,

16. Ed Borman, Ibid., 13, News-Gazette, September 10, 1945, p. 3.

17. Ibid., 13.

18. "Religion Hearing Before 3 Judges," *Courier*, September 10, 1945, p. 3, MA II, p. 4.

19. Stanley Pieza, "'Bible' Trial To Hear Boy," *Herald American*, September 11, 1945, pp. 1 & 4, MA II, pp. 7 & 8.

20. Alfred Prowitt, "Grill Champaign Teacher On Religion in Schools," Chicago *Daily News*, September 11, 1945, p. 1, MA II, p. 6.

21. Ed Borman, Ibid., 13, *News-Gazette*, September 10, 1945, p. 3.

22. Jean Lamkey, "Charge Religious Training Impairs Secular in Hearing Of McCollum vs. School Board.," *Daily Illini*, September 11, 1945, p. 1, MA II, p. 19.

23. Ibid., 18; *Courier*, September 10, 1945, p. 3.

24. Fletcher Wilson, "Missionary Tells Of Work in Classes," Chicago *Sun*, September 11, 1945, p. 1, MA II, p. 9c.

25. Fletcher Wilson, "School Bible Teaching Suit Goes To Trial," Chicago *Sun*, September 11, 1945, pp. 1 & 7, MA II, pp. 9a & 9b.

26. Dorothy Anderson, interview with author.

27. Reconstruction of the testimony was drawn from the Transcript of Record, Supreme Court of the United States, October Term, 1947, No. 90, and the following news accounts: Ibid., 1, Ibid., 12, Ibid., 13, Ibid., 18, Ibid., 20, and Ibid., 22.

28. Ibid., 18, *Courier*, September 10, 1945, p. 3.

29. Alfred Prowitt, Ibid., 5, Chicago *Daily News*, September 11, 1945, p 1.

30. Jean Lamkey, Ibid., 22, *Daily Illini*, September 11, 1945, p 1.

31. Bruce Taylor, "Girl, 13, Asks To Continue Bible Study," Chicago *Times*, September 11, 1945, MA II, p. 10.

32. *People ex rel. Ring vs. Board Of Education*, 245 Ill. 334.

33. McCollum, *One Woman's Fight*, p. 61.

34. Stanley Pieza, "Boy To Testify In Suit On School Religion," *Herald American*, MA II, p. 9.

35. Fletcher Wilson, Ibid., 24, Chicago *Sun*, September 11, 1945, p. 1.

36. Ibid., 18, *Courier*, September 10, 1945, p. 3.

37. Stanley Pieza, Ibid., 19, *Herald American*, September 11, 1945, pp. 1 & 4.

38. Francis Weeks, as related to the author. Weeks was one of two members of the Society of Friends called to testify as to the beliefs of their sect. Though he did not testify, he was present with his colleague, Edwin Reeder who did testify. It was Weeks who overheard the priest's comment.

39. Ed Borman, "McCollum Child 'Didn't Fit' Into Class Group, Teacher Testifies In Court," *News-Gazette*, September 11, 1945, p. 7, MA II, p. 17.

40. Ibid.

41. "Child Takes Stand To Ask Religious Class Continuence, McCollum Child Criticized In Testimony By Teacher," *Courier*, September 11, 1945, p. 3, MA II, p. 14.

42. Ed Borman, Ibid., 39, *News-Gazette*, September 11, 1945, p. 7. This would have referred only to the religious classes at the junior high level where the classes were offered as an elective.

43. McCollum, *One Woman's Fight*, pp. 59 & 60.

44. Ibid., p. 60.

45. Ed Borman, Ibid., 39, *News-Gazette*, September 11, 1945, p. 7.

46. Ed Borman, "McCollum Counsel Lays Foundation; Asks Witness To Illustrate Biblical Story," *News-Gazette*, September 11, 1945, pp. 3 & 7, MA II, pp. 16 and 17.

47. Ibid., 41, *Courier*, September 11, 1945, p. 3.

48. McCollum, *One Woman's Fight*, pp. 66 & 67.

49. Bruce Taylor, Ibid., 31, Chicago *Times*, September 11, 1945, MA II, p. 10.

50. Fletcher Wilson, Ibid., 25, Chicago *Sun*, September 11, 1945, pp. 1 & 7.

Chapter 6

1. Alfred Prowitt, "Hit Climax in Religion Trial Today," Chicago *Daily News*, September 12, 1945, p. 1, MA II, p. 20.

2. "10-Year Old Terry McCollum 'Likes' Religious Education; Grandfather Assails Clergy," *Daily Illini*, September 12, 1945, p. 1, MA II, p. 35.

3. Stanley Pieza, "Anti-Bible Mother on Stand Today," Chicago *Herald American*, September 12, 1945, p. 4, MA II, p. 22b.

4. Ed Borman, "McCollum Counsel Lays Foundation," *News-Gazette*, September 11, 1945, p. 3, MA II, p. 15.

5. Alfred Prowitt, "Atheist's Son Wins Urbana Court Fans," Chicago *Daily News*, September 12, 1945, p. 3, MA II, p. 21.

6. Guy Gentry, "Denies Bible Class Conflict with Any Sect," Chicago *Tribune*, September 12, 1945, MA II, p. 27a.

7. Fletcher Wilson, "10-Year-Old Testifies in Religion Trial," Chicago *Sun*, September 12, 1945, p. 1, MA II, p. 24a.

8. Prowitt, Ibid., 5, Chicago *Daily News*, September 12, 1945, p. 3, MA II, p. 21'.

9. Borman, Ibid., 4, *News-Gazette*, September 11, 1945, p. 3.

10. Transcript of Record, pp. 137-46. The testimony has been reconstructed from the Transcript of Record, pp. 137-185, and from the following press reports (including multiple editions of Chicago newspapers): Alfred Prowitt, "Hit Climax in Religion Trial Today," Chicago *Daily News*, September 12, 1945, pp. 1, 10; Prowitt, "Atheist's Son Wins Trial Fans," *Daily News*, September 12, 1945, pp. 1, 3; Stanley Pieza, "Anti-Bible Mother on Stand Today," Chicago *Herald American*, September 12, 1945, pp. 1, 4; Fletcher Wilson, "Atheism Has Its Day at Religion Trial," Chicago *Sun*, September 12, 1945, pp. 1, 7; Wilson, "10-Year-Old Testifies in Religion Trial," *Sun*, September 12, 1945, pp. 1, 3; "Atheist's Son, 10, Willing to Learn of God," Chicago *Times*, September 12, 1945 (McCollum Archive, v. 2, p. 26); *Times*, September 12, 1945, pp. 1, 3; Guy Gentry, "Bible Class Foe's Son on Stand at Trial," Chicago *Tribune*, September 12, 1945, p. 1; Gentry, "Denies Bible Class Conflict with Any Sect," *Tribune*, Sept 12, 1945 (McCollum Archive, v. 2, p. 27a); "Child Takes Stand to Ask Religion Class Continuance," *Courier*, September 11, 1945, p. 3; Ed Borman, "McCollum Counsel Lays Foundation," *News-Gazette*, September 11, 1945, p. 3.

11. Wilson, "Atheism Has Its Day," Chicago *Sun*, September 12, 1945, p. 7, MA II, p. 24.

12. Prowitt, "Atheist's Son Wins Trial Fans," Chicago *Daily News*, September 12, 1945, p. 3. Mrs. Jorgensen's quote is taken directly from the Transcript of Record, which, of course failed to report the laughter. p. 143.

13. McCollum, *One Woman's Fight*, rev. ed. (1951; Boston: Beacon, 1961), 68.

14. Prowitt, Ibid., 8, Chicago *Daily News*, September 12, 1945, p. 3, MA II, p 21.

15. Wilson, Ibid., 11, *Chicago Sun*, September 12, 1945, p. 7, MA II, p. 24a & b.

16. Wilson, "10-Year-Old Testifies in Religion Trial," *Chicago Sun*, September 12, 1945, p. 8.

17. Borman, "Mrs. M'Collum Takes Stand to Tell Fight Against Religious Education," *News-Gazette*, September 12, 1945, p. 13, pp. 3 & 7, MA II, p. 33

18. "Terry Tells His Views, *Courier*," September 12, 1945, p. 3, MA II, p. 29.

19. "Children Go on Stand in Religion Trial—Terry Tells His Views," *Courier*, September 12, 1945, p. 3, MA II, pp. 29 & 30.

20. Bruce Taylor, "Girl, 13, asks to continue Bible study," Chicago *Times*, September 11, 1945; MA II, p. 10.

21. All correspondence, originals and copies are in possession of the author.

22. Chapman to Cromwell, September 4, 1945, letter in possession of the author.

23. McCollum, *One Woman's Fight*, 62.

24. Cromwell to Chapman, September 6, 1945, in possession of the author.

25. Chapman to Cromwell, September 7, 1945, in possession of the author.

26. Borman, "Father Gives Introduction to Atheism," *News-Gazette*, September 12, 1945, p. 3, MA II, p. 34.

27. "10-Year-Old Terry McCollum 'Likes' Religious Education; Grandfather Assails Clergy," *Daily Illini*, September 12, 1945, p. 1, MA II, P. 35.

28. Prowitt, " Chicago *Daily News*, Ibid., 1, September 12, 1945, p. 1 & 10, MA II, p. 20.

29. Pieza, "Mother Tells Atheist Stand," *Herald American*, September 13, 1945, pp. 1 & 2, MA II, p. 45.

30. Ibid., 29.

31. Pieza, "Anti-Bible Mother on Stand Today," Chicago *Herald American*, September 12, 1945, p. 4, MA II, p. 22.

32. Bruce Taylor, "Atheist's son, 10, willing to learn of God," Chicago *Times*, September 12, 1945, MA II, p. 26.

33. Borman, Ibid., 26, *News-Gazette*, September 12, 1945, p. 3, MA II, p. 34.

34. Ibid., 33.

35. Prowitt, Ibid., 1, Chicago *Daily News*, September 12, 1945, p. 10, MA II, p. 20.

36. Borman, Ibid., 9, *News-Gazette*, September 11, 1945, p. 3.

37. Ibid., 19, *Courier*, September 12, 1945, p. 3, MA II, 29 & 30.

38. Wilson, Ibid.,. 11. Chicago *Sun*, September 12, 1945. p. 7, MA II, p. 24, *see also* p. 24b.

39. Cromwell to Fletcher Wilson, September 29, 1945, copy in possession of author.

40. Ibid., 33, *News-Gazette*, September 12, 1945, p. 3, MA II, p. 34.

41. *Daily Illini*, September 12, 1945, Ibid., 2, MA II, p. 35.

42. Ibid., 41

43. McCollum, *One Woman's Fight*, p. 63.

44. Ibid., 43.

45. Cromwell, interview with author, February, 21, 1980.

46. Ibid., 2, *Daily Illini*, September 12, 1945, p. 1, MA II, p. 35.

47. Ibid., 18, *Courier*, September 12, 1945, p. 3, MA II, p. 29.

48. Pieza, "Boy Denies Diety In Bible Trial," *Herald American*, September 12, 1945, p. 1, MA II, p. 22c.

49. Ibid., 2, *Daily Illini*, September 12, 1945, p. 1, MA II, p. 35.

50. Prowitt, "Hit Climax in Religion Trial Today," *Daily News*, September 12, 1945, pp. 1 & 10, MA II, p. 20.

51. "Rev. Cartlidge Given Vigorous Examination," *News-Gazette*, September 12, 1945, p. 13, MA II, p. 32.

52. Gentry, "Bible Class Foe's Son On Stand At Trial," Chicago *Tribune*, September 12, 1945, p. 1, MA II, p. 27.

53. Alfred Prowitt, Ibid., 1, *Daily News*, September 12, 1945, pp. 1 & 10, MA II, p. 20.

54. Ibid., 53.

55. Ibid., 53.

56. Ed Borman, "Mrs. McCollum Takes Stand To Tell Fight," *News-Gazette*, September 12, 1945, p. 13. (need MA II ?)

57. Ibid., 56.

58. Alfred Prowitt, Ibid., 50, Chicago *Daily News*, September 12, 1945, p. 10, MA II p. 20.

59. Ibid., 58.

60. Guy Gentry, Ibid., 52, Chicago Tribune, MA II, 27

61. Stanley Pieza, "Boy Denies Deity in Bible Trial," Chicago *Herald American*, September, 12, 1945, p. 1.

62. Afred Prowitt, Ibid., 5, Chicago *Daily News*, September 12, 1945, p. 1, MA II, p. 21.

63. Ibid. 5.

64. Ibid., 37, *Courier*, September 12, 1945, p. 3 MA II, p. 29.

65. Fletcher Wilson, "Atheist Testifies in Test of Religion in Schools," *P.M. Daily*, September 12, 1945; MA II,, p. 25a.

66. Bruce Taylor, "Atheist Tells Trial 'I Won't Be Hypocrite'," Chicago *Times*, September 12, 1945, p. 3, MA II, p. 26a.

67. McCollum, *One Woman's Fight*, 63."

68. Fletcher Wilson, "Religious Education Issue Faces Court Test Today," Chicago *Sun*, September 10, 1945, 1 & back page, MA II, p. 4b.

69. McCollum, *One Woman's Fight*, p. 64.

70. Ibid., 68.

71. Ibid., p. 72.

72. Fletcher Wilson, "School Bible Teaching Suit Is Brought To Trial," Chicago *Sun*, September 11, 1945, p. 7, MA II, p. 9b.

Chapter 7

1. Ted Duffield, "Mrs. McCollum Explains Stand," *Courier*, September 12, 1945, p. 3, MA II, p. 28.

2. McCollum, *One Woman's Fight*, rev. ed. (1951; Boston: Beacon, 1961), 64.

3. Ted Duffield, Ibid., 1, *Courier*, September 12, 1945, p. 3, MA II, p. 28.

4. Fletcher Wilson, "Not Sure I'm an Atheist, Mother Testifies at Trial," Chicago *Sun*, September 13, 1945, p. 13, MA II, p. 46a.

5. Ed Borman, "Mrs. M'Collum Takes Stand to Tell Fight Against Religious Education," *News-Gazette*, September 12, 1945, p. 3, MA II, p. 31.

6. Ted Duffield, Ibid., 1, *Courier*, September 12, 1945, p. 3, MA II, p. 28.

7. Jean Hurt, "James Terry Denies that God Exists," *Daily Illini*, September 13, 1945, p. 1, MA II, p. 58.

8. The testimony this day was reconstructed from the Transcript of Record, pp. 185-222; "Bible Tales 'Folk Lore;' Defense Calls Witnesses," *Courier*, September 13, 1945, p. 3; Ed Borman, "Mrs. M'Collum Takes Stand to Tell Fight Against Religious Education," *News-Gazette*, September 12, 1945, pp. 3, 13; "Witnesses Deny Truth of Bible," *Daily Illini*, September 13, 1945, pp. 1-2; Alfred Prowitt, "Explains Fight on Religion in School," Chicago *Daily News*, September 13, 1945, pp. 1, 3 (state ed.); "Mothers Clash at Bible Trial," *Daily News*, September 13, 1945, pp. 1, 4 (final ed.); Stanley Pieza, "Mother Tells Atheist Stand," Chicago *Herald American*, September 13, 1945, pp. 1-2, 6; Wilson, "Not Sure I'm an Atheist, Mother Testifies at Trial," Chicago *Sun*, September 13, 1945, pp. 1, 13; Bruce Taylor, "Religion foe rests case in 'Bible trial'," Chicago *Times*, September 13, 1945 (McCollum Archives, v. 2, p. 46c); Guy Gentry, "Religion Study Foe Says Ideal Led to Her Suit," Chicago *Tribune*, September 13, 1945, pp. 1, 8.

9. Alfred Prowitt, "Explains Fight on Religion in School," Chicago *Daily News*, September 13, 1945, pp. 1 & 3, MA II p. 42.

10. Ibid., 9.

11. Ed Borman, Ibid., 5, *News-Gazette*, September 12, 1945, p. 3, MA II, p. 32.

12. Ibid., 5.

13. McCollum, *One Woman's Fight*, 71.

14. Bruce Taylor, "Boy, 10, tells fight over Bible," Chicago *Times*, September 12, 1945, pp. 1 & 3, MA II, p. 26a; Stanley Pieza, "Mother Tells Atheist Stand," Chicago *Herald American*, September 13, 1945, pp. 1 & 2, MA II, p. 45.

15. Stanley Pieza, "Mother Tells Atheist Stand," Chicago *Herald American*, September 13, 1945, p. 2, MA II, p. 45.

16. McCollum, *One Woman's Fight*, 65.

17. Ibid., p. 65

18. Alfred Prowitt, Ibid., 9, Chicago *Daily News*, September 13, 1945, p. 1, MA II, p. 42.

19. Guy Gentry, "Religion Study Foe Says Ideal Led to Her Suit," Chicago *Tribune*, September 13, 1945, p. 1, MA II, p. 47.

20. Alfred Prowitt, Ibid., 9, Chicago *Daily News*, September 13, 1945, p. 1, MA II, p. 42.

21. Fletcher Wilson, Ibid., 4, Chicago *Sun*, September 13, 1945, p. 1, MA II, p. 46a.

22. Stanley Pieza, "School Religion Trial Opens at Urbana," Chicago *Herald American*, September 10, 1945, p. 1, MA II, p. 4a.

23. Fletcher Wilson, "School Bible Teaching Trial Opens," Chicago *Sun*, September 11, 1945, pp. 1 & 7, MA II, p. 9a.

24. McCollum, *One Woman's Fight*, 73-4.

25. Fletcher Wilson, Ibid., 4, Chicago *Sun*, September 13, 1945, p. 13, MA II, p. 46a.

26. McCollum, *One Woman's Fight*, 74.

27. Stanley Pieza, Ibid., 15, Chicago *Herald American*, September 13, 1945, p. 1, MA II, pp. 44 & 45.

28. McCollum, *One Woman's Fight*, 75.

29. Conversations with Vashti McCollum and Ruth and Steven Tager.

30. McCollum, *One Woman's Fight*, 74.

31. Ed Borman, "Children Aided by Religious Instructor," *News-Gazette*, September 13, 1945, pp. 3 & 6, MA II, p. 55.

32. Ibid., 31.

33. Ed Borman, "Schug Calls Santa Claus, Christ 'Folk Tales'," *News-Gazette*, September 13, 1945, p. 3, MA II, p. 54.

34. Ibid., 33.

35. Ted Duffield, "Bible Tales 'Folk Lore;' Defense Calls Witnesses," *Courier*, September 13, 1945, p. 3, MA II, p. 51.

36. Mary Ellen Brown, "Separation of Church, State Upheld by Mrs. McCollum in Religious Test Case," *Daily Illini*, September 13, 1945, p. 2, MA II, pp. 57 & 58.

37. Ted Duffield, Ibid., 35, *Courier*, September 13, 1945, p. 3, MA II, p. 51.

Chapter 8

1. Ed Borman, "Children Aided By Religious Instructor," *News-Gazette*, September 13, 1945, p. 3, MA II, p. 55.

2. Testimony for this day was reconstructed from the Transcript of Record, pp. 222-267; *News*, State Ed., September 14, 1945, pp. 1 & 3; *News*, 3 Star Ed., September 14, 1945, p. 5; *Herald American*, Sept 13, 1945, Turf Ed., M.A., Vol. II, p. 63; *Herald American*, September 14, 1945, pp. 1 & 3; *Herald American*, September 14, 1945, M.A., Vol. II, P. 62; News, September 15, 1945, p. 3; *Sun*, Sept, 14, 1945, pp. 1 & 10, M.A. Vol. II, p. 64; *Sun*, September 14, 1945, 1 & 10 (different edition) M.A. Vol. II, p. 64a; *Times*, September 13, 1945, M.A. Vol. II, p. 73; *Times*, September 14, 1945, M.A. Vol. II, p. 64b; *Tribune*, September 14, 1945, pp. 1 & 8; *Courier*, September 14, 1945, pp. 3 & 8; *News-Gazette*, September 14, 1945, p. 3.

3. Alfred Prowitt, "Religious Mother Disputes Atheist," *News*, State Ed. September 14, 1945, p. 3, MA II, p. 60.

4. McCollum, *One Woman's Fight*, p. 52.

5. Fletcher Wilson, "Fourteen Children Testify In Bible-Teaching Trial," *Sun*, September 14, 1945, p. 10, MA II, p. 64.

6. Alfred Prowitt, "One Says Religion Aids Child," News, State Ed., September. 14, 1945, p. 1, MA II, p. 59.

7. Prowitt, Ibid., 6.

8. Guy Gentry, "Children Deny Religion Study Bred Dissension," *Tribune*, September 14, 1945, p. 8, MA II, p. 8.

9. Gentry, Ibid., 8.

10. "Classmates Deny Youth Embarrassed," *News-Gazette*, September 14, 1945, p. 3, MA II, p. 70.

11. Fletcher Wilson, Pupils Tell Of Attending Bible Classes," *Sun*, September 14, 1945, p. 1, MA II, p. 64.

12. McCollum, One Woman's Fight, p. 68.

13. Jean Hurt, "Religious Education Teachers Compared to Peanut Vendors By Mrs. McCollum's Counsel," *Daily Illini*, September 15, 1945, p. 1, MA II, p. 87.

14. "Religion Work Is Voluntary, Rall Asserts," *Courier*, September 14, 1945, p. 3, MA II, p. 66.

15 Stanley Pieza, "Scents Fascism In Bible Classes," *Herald American*, September 14, 1945, MA II, p. 62.

16. Alfred Prowitt, "Religion Trial Closes In Burst Of Oratory," *News*, September 14, 1945, MA II, p. 60a.

17. Jean Hurt, Ibid., 13, *Daily Illini*, September 15, 1945, p. 3, MA II, p. 88.

18. Ibid., 14, *Courier*, September 14, 1945, p. 3, MA II, p. 66.

19. Ed Borman, "Churches 'Feed At Trough:' Chapman." *News-Gazette*, September 14, 1945, p. 3, MA II, p. 69.

20 Ibid., 19.

21. Ibid., 14, *Courier*, September 14, 1945, p. 3, MA II, p. 66.

22. Ibid., 19, *News-Gazette*, September 14, 1945, p. 3, MA II, p. 69.

23. Ibid., 19.

24. Ibid., 19.

25. Ibid., 19.

26. Ibid., 16, *News*, September 14, 1945, MA II, p. 60a.

27. Guy Gentry, "Religion Trial Ends; Decision Due By Nov. 29," *Tribune*, September 15, 1945, MA II, p. 82.

28. Ed Borman, Ibid., 19, *News-Gazette*, September 14, 1945, p. 3, MA II, p. 69.

29. Ibid., p 19.

30. Ibid., p. 19.

31. "3 Judges Study Suit On Religion," *News*, September 15, 1945, MA II, p. 63.

32. Ed Borman, Ibid., 19, *News-Gazette*, September 14, 1945, p. 3, MA II, p. 69.

33. Ibid., 31, *News*, September 15, MA II, p. 63.

34. Jean Hurt, Ibid., 13, *Daily Illini*, September 15, 1945, p. 1, MA II, p. 87.

35. Fletcher Wilson, "Religion Trial Comes To End," *Sun*, September 15, 1945, MA II p. 81.

36. Ibid., 14, *Courier*, September 14, 1945, p. 3, MA II, p. 66.

37. Ibid., 14.

38. Guy Gentry, Ibid., 27, *Tribune*, September 15, 1945, MA II, p. 82.

39. Ibid., 27.

40. Ibid., 31, *News*, September 15, 1945, MA II, p. 63.

41. Jean Hurt, Ibid., 13, *Daily Illini*, September 15, 1945, p. 3, MA II, p. 88.

42. Ed Borman, "Fate of Religious Education Classes Up To 3 Judges," *News-Gazette*, September 15, 1945, p. 3, MA II, p. 83.

43. Jean Hurt, *Daily Illini*, September 15, 945, p. 3, MA II, p. 88.

44. Ed Borman, Ibid., 42, *News-Gazette*, September 15, 1945, p. 3, MA II, p. 83.

45. Ibid., 44.

46. Jean Hurt, Ibid., 13, *Daily Illini*, September 15, 1945, p. 3, MA II, p. 88.

47. Ibid., 44, *News-Gazette*, September 15, 1945, p. 3, MA II, p. 83; Tribune, September 15, 1945, M.A. . 82, respectively.

48. Ed Borman, Ibid., 42, *News-Gazette*, September 15, 1945, p. 3, MA II, p. 84.

49. Fletcher Wilson, Ibid., 35, *Sun*, September 1945 MA II, p. 81.

50. Ed Borman, Ibid., 42, *News-Gazette*, September 15, 1945, p 3, MA II, p. 84.

51. Fletcher Wilson, Ibid., 35, *Sun*, September 15, 1945, MA II, p. 81.

52. Ed Borman, Ibid., 42, *News-Gazette*, September 15, 1945, p 3, MA II, p. 84.

53. Ibid., 31, *News*, September 15, 1945, MA II, p. 63.

54. Ed Borman, Ibid,, 42, *News-Gazette*, September 15, p. 3, MA II, p 83.

55. Guy Gentry, Ibid., 27, *Tribune*, September 15, 1945, MA II, p. 82.

56. Ibid., 27.

57. Ibid., 27.

58. Ibid., 27.

59. Jean Hurt, Ibid., 13, *Daily Illini*, September 15, 1945, p. 1, MA II, p. 87.

60. Ed Borman, Ibid., 42, *News-Gazette*, September 15, 1945, p. 3, MA II, p. 83.

61. Guy Gentry, Ibid., 27, *Tribune*, September 15, 1945, MA II, p. 82.

62. Ed Borman, Ibid., 42, *News-Gazette*, September 15, 1945, p. 3, MA II, p 84.

63. Ibid., 44, MA II, p. 83.

64. Ibid., 44, MA II, p. 84.

65. Jean Hurt, Ibid., 13, Daily Illini, September 15, 1945, p. 1, MA II, p. 87.

66. Ibid. pp. 1 & 3, MA II, pp. 87 & 88.

67. Ed Borman, Ibid., 42, *News-Gazette*, September 15, 1945, p. 3, MA II, p. 83.

68. Ibid., 44.

69. McCollum, One Woman's Fight, pp. 76-77.

70. "Religion Case Ruling Due By Late November," *Courier*, September 16, 1945, p. 9, MA II, p/ 85.

71. Ed Borman, Ibid., 19, *News-Gazette*, September 14, 1945, p. 3, MA II, p. 69.

72. Bruce Taylor, "Bible Trial Closes; Judges Wait Briefs," *Times*, September 15, 1945, M.A. Vol. II, p. 81b.

Chapter 9

1. Ruth Cromwell, letter to McCollums, September 13, 1945, in possession of the author.
2. "Cromwell Rejoices At Role of Grandson At Bible Trial" *Times-Union*, September 18, 1945, MA II p. 92.
3. "Cromwell Reports Grandson Did Well At Religion Ban Trial." *Democrat and Chronicle*, September 19, 1945, MA II, p 92.
4. Ibid., 3.
5. "Theist Wants Religion Kept Out Of Schools," *Times-Union*, September 20, 1945, MA II, p. 93.
6. "Religious Class Equality Asked By Rev. Pierce," *Courier*, September 12, 1945, p. 3, MA II, p. 30.
7. James O. Supple, "Sharply Divided Stand Among City's Pastors Found In Services," *Sun*, September 17, 1945, MA II, p. 91.
8. Ibid., 7.
9. Ibid., 7.
10. Stanley Pieza, "Study Boy's Atheist Ideas," *Herald-American*, September 15, 1945, MA II, p. 80a.
11. Rev. John Evans, "Fascism Seen If Court Closes Schools To God," *Tribune*, September 14, 1945, MA II p. 60.
12. Lloyd Hippensteele, "Disciples Of Christ End 95th Annual Convention," *News-Gazette*, September 20, 1945, p. 3, MA II, p. 94.
13. (Editorial) "The Issues At Urbana," *Courier*, September 14, 1945, p. 4, MA II, P. 68.
14. George Sokolsky, "God On Trial In Champaign Case," *News-Gazette*, September 25, 1945, p. 4, MA II, p. 97.
15. Sokolsky, "Cites Real Issue In Champaign Case," *News-Gazette*, Sept. 27, 1945, p. 4, MA II, p. 97.
16. Ibid., 15.
17. Sokolsky, "Champaign Case Is Attack On God," *News-Gazette*, September 28, 1945, p. 4, MA II, p. 98).
18. "Rev. Schug Answers Sokolsky," *News-Gazette*, September 30, 1945, p. 4, MA II, p. 98). Ruth Cromwell, reading the Book of Esther as did Schug, chose the name "Vashti" for her daughter as a statement of what the status of women ought to be—an explanation offered to the author on more than one occasion.
19. Elsie Robinson, "Listen World," Milwaukee *Sentinal*, October 16, 1945, MC-UI, Book 2, p. 3.
20. Elsa Maxwell, "Party Lie," Pittsburgh *Post-Gazette*, October 8, 1945, MC-UI, Book 2, p. 2.
21. *Saturday Evening Post*, October 6, 1945, p. 124.
22. Cromwell, letter to the *Post*, October. 5, 1945, copy in possession of the author.
23. Nelson, letter to Cromwell, October 1945, in possession of the author.
24. Nelson, letter to Cromwell, March 26, 1946, in possession of the author.
25. "Little Boy, Big Issue," Rockford (no other identification on the clip), September 13, 1945, MA II, p. 37.
26. "Schools And Religion," *Daily News*, September 13, 1945, MA II, p. ?.
27. "The Issue At Urbana," *Sun*, September 16, 1945, MA II, p. ?.
28. McCollum, *One Woman's Fight*, p. 81.
29. Ibid., p. 82.
30. Ibid., p. 82.
31. "Halloweeners' Activities Keep Police Jumping," *News-Gazette*, November 1, 1945, p. 25.
32. "Halloween Pranks Unchanged," *Courier*, November. 1, 1945, p. 3.
33. McCollum, *One Woman's Fight*, p. 83.
34. Ibid., p. 83.
35. Ibid., pp. 95-96.
36. McCollum, letter dated October 1945, copy in possession of the author.
37. Ibid., 36.
38. McCollum, *One Woman's Fight*, pp. 95-112.

39. Ibid., pp. 95-112.

40. Ibid. p. 95.

41. " M'Collum Suit Shows Need For Legislation," News-Gazette, October 21, 1945, p 3.

42. Ibid.

43. Ibid.

44. McCollum, *One Woman's Fight*, p. 122.

45. C.A.C. appeal letter, in possession of the author.

46. C.C.L.C. appeal, in possession of the author.

47. Letter, Chapman to Cromwell, September 24, 1945, in possession of the author.

48. "Religion Suit Ruling Delayed," *Courier*, October, 7, 1945, p. 3.

49. Letter, McCollum to Cromwell, October, 15, 1945, in possession of the author.

50. Ibid.

51. Letter, McCollum to Cromwell, undated, in possession of the author.

52. This letter, as some of the other letters Chapman sent to Cromwell, has not survived. In all probability, Cromwell shared these lost letters with his daughter and she failed to return them. Again, Cromwell saved everything; his daughter was just the opposite, saving little.

53 Letter, Cromwell to Chapman, October 24,1945, in possession of the author.

54. "Attorneys for Mrs. McCollum File Brief," *News-Gazette*, October 25, 1945, p. 3.

55. Letter, Cromwell to Chapman, November 4, 1945, in possession of the author.

56. Ibid., 55.

57. "Schools Are Sued To Halt Release For Church Study," *Sun*, October 27, 1945, MC-UI, Book 2, p. 8.

58. McCollum, *One Woman's Fight*, p. 123.

59. "Membership Meets November 6," *Civil Liberties News*, October 19, 1945.

60. "CCLC Opens Fight On 'Released Time' In Chicago Schools," *Civil Liberties News*, November 2, 1945.

61. McCollum, *One Woman's Fight*, p. 123.

62. Ibid., p. 123

63. "Religion Declared Needed In School," *Courier*, November 20, 1945, p. 3, and Ed Borman, "'Pagan, Atheistic' Schools Decision Up To Judges," *News-Gazette*, November 20, 1945, p. 3.

64. "Religion Suit Brief Delayed By Strike," *Courier*, November. 11, 1945, p. 10.

65. "About Town," *Courier*, November 20, 1945, p. 3.

66. "Leonard Given Chicago Ruling," *Courier*, November 25, 1945, p. 22.

67. Letter, Cromwell to Chapman, November 25, 1945, in possession of the author.

68. Letter, Cromwell to Chapman, December 2, 1945, in possession of the author.

69. Letter, Chapman to Cromwell, December 4, 1945, in possession of the author.

70. Letter, McCollum to Cromwell, December 1945, in possession of the author.

71. McCollum, *One Woman's Fight*, p. 122.

72. "Religion Fund Here Hits Total Of $3,421 Cash," *Courier*, October. 11, 1945, p. 3.

73. McCollum, *One Woman's Fight*, p. 123.

74. Letter, McCollum to Cromwell, undated, in possession of the author.

75. "Religion Suit Reply Is Filed," *Courier*, December 7, 1945, p. 3.

76. "Chapman To Debate Pastor In Danville," *Courier*, January 4, 1946, p. 3.

77. "Chapman To Demand Miracle," *Courier*, January 16, 1946, January 16, 1946, p. 3.

78. "Miracle Reply Goes Unused," *Courier*, January 18, 1946, p. 3. (Bible miracle of his own choosing not raised by Chapman in the debate.)

79. Ibid., 78.

80. "Hollis Accepts Challenge By Chapman," *News-Gazette*, January 25, 1946, p. 7.

81. No mention of a debate was reported in the local papers which surely have been covered had it occurred.

Chapter 10

1. "Stoddard's Views Assailed By Bishop Of Springfield," *Courier*, October 1, 1945, p. 3.

2. Rev. John Evans, "Bishop Griffin Raps Stoddard, New U or I Head," *News-Gazette*, October 1, 1945, p. 3.

3. "Bishop James Griffin Denounces Religious Views Of UI President, Elect," *News-Gazette*, October 1, 1945. p. 3.

4. Ibid., 1, *Courier*, October 1, 1945, p. 3. The words in parenthesis from the latter two paragraphs apparently were omitted by Griffin.

5. Ibid., 4.

6. Ibid., 3, *News-Gazette*, October 1, 1945, p. 3.

7. Ibid., 3.

8. Ibid., 3.

9. "Stoddard Charges Distortion By Bishop," *News-Gazette*, October 1, 1945, p. 3.

10. "Stoddard Surprised, Says He Is Friendly To Religion," *Courier*, October 1, 1945, p. 3.

11. Ibid., 10.

12. Ibid., 10.

13. Ibid., 10.

14. "'Profession Of Faith' From Stoddard Asked By Bishop Griffin," *News-Gazette*, October 2, 1945, p. 3.

15. "Bishop's Attack Centers On These Words By Stoddard," *News-Gazette*, October 2, 1945, p.3.

16. "Park Livingston Says Board 'Satisfied'," *News-Gazette*, October 2, 1945, p. 3.

17. "Schug To Speak On Stoddard Controversy," *News-Gazette*, October 6, 1945, p. 3.

18. Philip Schug, *The Religious Modern*, October, 1945.

19. "Public Education Is Called Target, Unitarian Pastor Replies To Attack Upon Stoddard," *Courier*, October 8, 1945, p. 3.

20. Ibid.

21. "School System Under Attack By Catholics," *News-Gazette*, October 8, 1945, p. 3.

22. Ibid., 19, *Courier*, October 8, 1945, p. 3.

23. Ibid., 21, *News-Gazette*, October 8, 1945, p. 3.

24. Ibid., 19, *Courier*, October 8, 1945, p. 3.

25. Ibid., 21, *News-Gazette*, October 8, 1945, p. 3.

26. Ibid., 19, *Courier*, October 8, 1945, p. 3.

27. Ibid., 19.

28. Ibid., 19.

29. Ibid., 19

30. Ibid., 19.

31, Ibid., 19.

32. "'Red Herring' Chancery Reports," *Courier*, October 8, 1945, p. 3; "Rev. Schug 'In Wrong Ball Park,'" *News-Gazette*, October 8, 1945, p. 3.

33. "Let's Stick To Issues In Religious Teaching," *Pantagraph*, October 3, 1945, p. 4.

34. "By The Public—No Connection In Urbana, Stoddard Cases," *Pantagraph*, October 15, 1945, p. 4.

35. "Catholic Paper Describes 'Pandora's Box' At UI," *News-Gazette*, October 11, 1945, p. 3.

36. Ibid., 55, and "Bishop Asserts Sect Not Issue In U.I. Dispute," *Courier*, October 11, 1945, p. 3.

37. Ibid., 36.

38. Ibid., 36.

39. Ibid., 36.

40. Ibid., 36.

41, Ibid., 36.

42. "Bishop Asserts Sect Not Issue In U.I. Dispute," *Courier*, October 11, 1945, p. 3.

43. See both references in footnote 36.

44. Ibid., 36.

45. Ibid., 42, *Courier*, October 11, 1945, p. 3.

46. *University of Illinois Board of Trustees 43rd Report*, 1944-1946, p. 856.

47. Fran Myers, "Dr. Stoddard Pledges Trustees He Will Uphold Religious Freedom; New President Wins Support of UI Board," *News-Gazette*, October 18, 1945, p. 3.

48. *Board of Trustees 43rd Report*, p. 856.

49. "Dr. Stoddard's Statement Appeases Bishop Griffin," *News-Gazette*, October 19, 1945, p. 3, and "Bishop Accepts U.I. Statements As Satisfactory," *Courier*, October 19, 1945, p. 3.

50. Stoddard, *The Pursuit of Education*, Vantage Press, New York, 1981, pp. 79-82 and p. 99.

51. Ibid., pp. 61-65.

Chapter 11

1. "Released Time Religion Study Upheld; Appeal Sure," *Courier*, January 27, 1946, p. 3.
2. Ibid., 1.
3. McCollum, *One Woman's Fight*, p. 113.
4. Schug, letter to author, August 13, 1960.
5. Transcript of Record, p. 63.
6. Ibid. 3; *One Woman's Fight*, p. 64
7. McCollum, Ibid. 3, p. 115.
8. Ibid. p. 64.
9. Ibid. p. 116.
10. Transcript of Record, p. 65.
11. Ibid., pp. 66-67.
12. Ibid., p. 68.
13. Ibid.
14. McCollum, *One Woman's Fight*, p. 117.
15. Transcript of Record, p. 70.
16. 319 U.S. 624, 63 Sup. Ct. 1178.
17. Transcript of Record, p. 77.
18. Ibid. p. 72.
19. 245 Ill. 334.
20. Transcript of Record, p. 85.
21. Ibid.
22. Ibid., pp. 84-85.
23. Ibid., p. 86.
24. Ibid., pp. 86-87.
25. Ibid., pp. 88-89.
26. McCollum, One Woman's Fight, pp. 118-119.
27. Ed Borman, "American Law Protects Voluntary Religion, Three Circuit Judges Tell Atheist Mother," *News-Gazette*, January 27, 1946, p. 3.
28. "Released Time Religion Study Upheld; Appeal Sure," *Courier*, January 27, 1946, p. 3.
29. McCollum, *One Woman's Fight*, p. 118.
30. Ibid.
31. Ibid, 28, *Courier*, January 27, 1946, p. 3.
32. Ibid., 28.
33. "Loser Plans To Appeal In Religion Suit," *Democrat & Chronicle*, January 27, 1946, MC-UI, Book 2, p. 31.
34. "Court Upholds Teaching Of Religion In Schools," *Sun*, January 27, 1946, p. 6.
35. "Religion In Public Schools," *Tribune*, January 29, 1946, MC-UI, Book 2, p. 30.
36. "The Issue At Champaign," *Sun*, January 31, 1946, MC-UI, Book 2, p. 30.
37. "Infant Damnation," Toledo *Blade* (no date), MC-UI, Book 2, p. 30.

Chapter 12

1. McCollum, *One Woman's Fight*, p. 121.
2. Schug, *The Religious Modern*, July, 1945.
3. Schug, *The Religious Modern*, October, 1945.
4. McCollum, interview, May 24, 1985.
5. Ibid.
6. McCollum, *One Woman's Fight*, pp. 126-127.
7. Ibid. p. 127.
8. Ibid.
9. "Name Lawyer For Appeal Of Religious Suit," *Courier*, March 19, 1946, p. 3.
10. McCollum, *One Woman's Fight*, p. 127.

11. Ibid., pp. 127-128.

12. Ibid.

13. Ibid., p. 124.

14. "Chapman Declines Comment on Suit Replacement," *News-Gazette*, March, 22, 1946, p. 3.

15. McCollum, interview, May 25, 1985.

16. "To Drop Atheism In Religious Suit Appeal," *News-Gazette*, March 20, 1946, p 3.

17. Ibid., 16.

18. Ibid., 16.

19. "Appleman Acts In County For Mrs. M'Collum: Franklin Won't Allow Atheism 'Whitewash,'" *News-Gazette*, March 21, 1946, p. 3.

20. "Judge Leonard Stricken With Heart Attack," *News-Gazette*, March 18, 1946. p. 3.

21. "Supreme Court Argues Case On Religion," *News-Gazette*, March 21, 1946, p. 2.

22. "Mrs. M'Collum Files Appeal For Review," *News-Gazette*, March 23, 1946, p. 3.

23. McCollum, *One Woman's Fight*, p. 123.

24. Ibid., 21, *News-Gazette*, March 21, 1946, p. 3.

25. Ibid., 19, *News-Gazette*, May, 21,1946, p. 3.

26. McCollum, interview, May 24, 1985.

27. "Religion Suit Appeal Ready By Fall Term," *Courier*, April 2, 1946, p. 3.

28. McCollum, *One Woman's Fight*, p. 141.

29. Ibid., p. 123.

30. "Fellowship Opposes Religious Classes Plan," *Courier*, April 2, 1946, p. 8, and "'Released-Time Study Of Religion Opposed," New York *Times*, March 24, 1946, MC-UI, Book 2, p. 34.

31. "Religion Suit's Appeal Backed," *Courier*, April 14, 1946, p. 5.

32. "Religious Suit Figure To Talk," *Democrat & Chronicle*, April 26, 1946, MC-UI, Book 2, p. 34.

33. "Liberal Parley Calls Leader," *Times-Union*, April 24, 1946, MC-UI, Book 2, p. 35.

34. Letter, Cromwell to McCollum, March 1, 1946, copy in possession of the author.

35. Ibid., 34.

36. "Religion Foe Tells Of Suit," *Democrat & Chronicle*, May 1, 1946, MC-UI, Book 2, p. 34.

37. "Court Test Seen In Religious Study," *Democrat & Chronicle*, March 17, 1946, MC-UI, Book 2, p. 33.

38. "Church To Aid Religion Suit," *Courier*, March 21, 1946, p. 14.

39. "Religion Appeal Funds Ready," *Courier*, February 1, 1946, p. 3.

40. McCollum, *One Woman's Fight*, p. 124.

41. Ibid., p 125.

42. McCollum, interview, May 24, 1985.

43. "Court Upholds Release Of Students For Religious Education Classes: Seen As End To M'Collum Contention," *News-Gazette*, May 21, 1946, p. 34.

44. "Plan Appeal On Religious Case Rule," *News-Gazette*, May 22, 1946, p. 8.

45. "Court Refuses Religion Case Rehearing," *News-Gazette*, September 13, 1946, p. 11.

46. McCollum, *One Woman's Fight*, pp. 125-126.

47. "Two Religious Education Cases," *Courier*, May 23, 1946, p. 6 .

48. Appellant's Brief To Illinois Supreme Court, September 1946.

49. Appellant's Brief, p. 5.

50. Ibid.

51. Ibid., p. 16.

52. Ibid., p. 17.

53. Ibid., p 13.

54. Ibid., p. 16.

55. Ibid., p. 18.

56. Ibid., p 24.

57. Ibid., p. 29.

58. Ibid., p. 32.

59. Ibid., 38.

60. McCollum, *One Woman's Fight*, p. 144.
61. Appellees' Brief, p. 22.
62. Ibid., p. 23.
63. Ibid., p. 24.
64. Ibid., p. 19.
65. Ibid., p. 21.
66. Ibid., p. 47.
67. Ibid., p. 66.
68. Ibid., pp. 35-36.
69. Appellant's Reply Brief, p. 2.
70. Ibid., p. 10.
71. Ibid., p. 11.
72. Ibid., p. 2.
73. Ibid., pp. 5, 6.
74. Leonard obit.
75. "Registration In Religious Classes Gain," *News-Gazette*, September 29, 1946, p. 19.
76. "M'Collum Case Argued Before State Court," *News-Gazette*, November 20, 1946, p. 3.
77. Ibid., 76.
78. McCollum, *One Woman's Fight*, p. 145.
79. Schug, Letter to author.
80. Franklin, interview, May 26; Rall, interview, September 12, 1984.
81. Decision, Illinois Supreme Court, p. 6, filed January 22, 1947.
82. Ibid., pp. 6-7.
83. Ibid.,, p. 9.
84. Ibid., p. 11.
85. Ibid., pp. 12-13.
86. Ibid., pp. 14-15.
87. Ibid., p. 16.
88. Pete Blatti, "Mrs McCollum Will Appeal To U.S. High Court," *News-Gazette*, January 22, 1947, p. 3.
89. Ibid., 88.
90. Ibid., 88.
91. "Religious Education Upheld; Appeal To Final Court Seen: Plaintiff's Attorney Heads Case For U.S. Supreme Court," *Courier*, January 22, 1947, p. 1.
92. "Religion In Public Schools Issue Headed To U.S. Court," Chicago *Times*, January 26, 1947, p. 16.
93. Ibid., 92.
94. "Attorneys Prepare Appeal In Religious Teaching Case," *Daily Illini*, January 24, 1947.
95. Ibid., 94.
96. "Mrs. M'Mcollum Attorneys Draft U.S. Court Appeal," *News-Gazette*, January 23, 1947, p. 3.
97. Ibid., 96.
98." Religion and Schools," *Daily News*, January 23, 1947, MC-UI, Book 2, p. 44.
99. Ibid., 98.
100. "Church And State Shouldn't Mix," Chicago *Tribune*, February 5, 1947, MC-UI, Book 2, p. 47.
101. By the Judge's Cousin," *Courier*, March 5, 1947, p. 6.
102. "Camel's Nose?" *Time* Magazine, February 10, 1947, MC-UI, Book 2, p. 47.

Chapter 13

1. *Everson v. Board of Education of Ewing Tp. et al.* No. 52, 67, 504.
2. "Local Religious Education Suit Before U.S. Court," *News-Gazette*, October. 6, 1947, p. 3.
3. "New Jersey's Religion Case Studied Here," *Courier*, February 19, 1947, p. 7.
4. Ibid., 2, *News-Gazette*, October 6, 1947. p. 3.
5. Franklin interview, May 26, 1980.

6. Ibid., 3, *Courier*, February 19, 1947, p. 7.

7. Ibid. 2, *News-Gazette*, October. 6, 1947, p. 3.

8. McCollum, *One Woman's Fight*, p. 154.

9. *Everson v. Board of Education of Ewing Tp. et al.* 330 US 1, pp. 511-512; McCollum, *One Woman's Fight*, p. 456.

10. *Everson v. Board of Education*, 330 US 1, p. 517.

11. "State And Church In America," Chicago *Tribune*, February 13, 1947.

12. "When State Pays Church," Toledo *Blade*, February 1947.

13. McCollum, *One Woman's Fight*, pp. 155-159.

14. "Post Scripts: Terry McCollum," *News-Gazette*, February 18, 1947, p. 3.

15. McCollum. *One Woman's Fight*, p. 158.

16. Ibid.

17. "Boy Transfers To School Here to Escape 'Atheist' Taunts," *Times-Union*, February 19, 1947.

18. McCollum, letter to Cromwell, received May 5, 1947, in possession of the author.

19. Cromwell letter to McCollum, May 9, 1947, copy in possession of the author.

20. McCollum, letter to Cromwell, probably received May 9, 1947, in possession of the author.

21. McCollum, letter to Cromwell, May 9, 1947, in possession of the author.

22. Cromwell, letter to McCollum, May 9, 1947, copy in possession of the author.

23. McCollum papers in possession of the author.

24. Cromwell, letter to Theodore Bear, May 14, 1947, copy in possession of the author.

25. "Lawyer's Brief Hits Sectarian School Classes; Franklin to Argue Case In Washington," *Courier*, June 2, 1947, p., 1.

26. McCollum, *One Woman's Fight*, p. 161.

27. "McCollum Case Will Be Heard Late In 1947," *News-Gazette*, June 6, 1947, p. 3.

28. McCollum, *One Woman's Fight*, p. 162.

29. "'School Bond Issues Voted," *Courier*, June 8, 1947.

30. McCollum, *One Woman's Fight*, p. 163.

31. Ibid.

32. "Jewish Groups Enter Brief In Religion Case," *Courier*, October 27, 1947, p. 3.

33. Cromwell, letter to McCollum, November 1, 1947, copy in possession of the author.

34. McCollum, *One Woman's Fight*, p. 163.

35. Ibid.

36. Ibid., p. 164.

37. Ibid.

38. "Religion Groups May join With Mrs. McCollum," *Courier*, November 13, 1947, p.3.

39. "Mrs. McCollum May Get Aid From Baptists," *News-Gazette*, November 10, 1947, p. 3.

40. "Local Baptists Deny Help For Mrs. M'Collum," *News-Gazette*, November 11, 1947, p. 3.

41. Ibid., 40.

42. "Baptists Can't Bind Members, Attorney Says," *Courier*, November 12, 1947, p. 3.

43. Ibid., 42.

44. McCollum, *One Woman's Fight*, p. 164.

45. "Baptist Attorney Files Brief Opposing Religious Classes," *News-Gazette*, November 16, 1947, p. 3.

46. "Bishop Calls Meet On Religion Issue," *Courier*, November 17, 1947, p. 3.

47. Ibid., 46.

48. "Oxnam's Group Not Intervening In Local Suit," *Courier*, November 20, 1947, p. 3.

49. Ibid., 48.

50. "Unitarians Aid Mrs. McCollum," *Courier*, November 25, 1947, p. 2.

51. Hazel Franklin Lewis, amicus curiae brief.

52. Franklin interview, May 26, 1980.

53. "Court Delays Religion Suit Until Dec. 8," *Courier*, November 18, 1947, p. 3.

54. Ibid. 46. *Courier*, November 17, 1947, p. 3.

55. "Barrett May File Brief In Religion Suit," *Courier*, November 13, 1947, p. 2.

56. "Barrett Enters Religion Case; To Aid School," *Courier*, December 4, 1947, p. 3.

57. "Religion Case Heard Nov. 10," *Courier*, October 14, 1947, p. 3.

58. "Schug Accepts Lincoln, Neb., Church Offer," *Courier*, October 27, 1947, p. 3.

59. Ibid., 58.

60. Ibid., 58.

61. "Dinner Monday Honors Schug," *Courier*, November 21, 1947, p. 3.

62. "Voluntary Religious Training Contested," *Daily Oregonian*, November 2, 1947, M.A.. p. 62.

63. "The Embarrassment of Terry McCollum," identified as "Catholic Boston Paper," M.A., p. 62.

64. "An Atheist's Fight," Charlotte (NC) *Observer*, December. 10, 1947, M.A., p. 77.

65. "Church And State Precedent," *Courier*, December. 16, 1947, p. 6.

66. "Church, State and Schools," *Courier*, December. 1947, MC-UI, Book 2, p. 76.

67. Fifi Nella, "The Rabin'—Religion in Schools," *The Churchman*, August. 1947, M.A. p. 57.

68. "For Religious Freedom," *Post Dispatch*, December. 7, 1947, M.A., p. 67.

69. "Church And School," Washington *Post*, December. 8, 1947, MC-UI, Book 2, p. 68.

Chapter 14

1. Appellant's Brief, p. 34.

2. Appellee's Brief, p. 165.

3. Ibid., p. 166.

4. Ibid.

5. Ibid., pp. 166 & 167.

6. Brief, Illinois Secretary of State (Barrett), p. 2.

7. Ibid., 6.

8. McCollum, *One Woman's Fight*, p. 166.

9. Brief, Protestant Council of the City of New York, p. 7.

10. Greenawalt, letter to McCollum, January 29, 1948.

11. Brief, A.C.L.U., pp. 41-72.

12. Brief, Joint Committee on Public Relations (Baptists).

13. Brief, Jewish, pp. 2 & 3.

14. Brief, American Ethical Union.

15. Brief, Seventh-day Adventists, p. 31.

16. Brief, American Unitarian Association, p. 5.

17. Brief, Hazel Franklin Lewis, pp. 1 & 2.

18. Ibid., 17, p. 6.

19. Ibid., 17, pp. 11 & 12.

20. McCollum, *One Woman's Fight*, p. 170.

21. Ibid., pp. 169 & 170.

22. Ed Borman, "M'Collum Case Set Monday In Highest Court," *News-Gazette*, December 7, 1947, p. 3.

23. McCollum, *One Woman's Fight*, p. 170.

24. Ed Borman, Ibid., 22, *News-Gazette*, December 7, 1947, p. 3.

25. McCollum, *One Woman's Fight*, pp. 170 & 171.

26. Ed Borman, Ibid., 22, *News-Gazette*, December 7, 1947, p. 3.

27. McCollum, *One Woman's Fight*, pp. 172 & 173.

28. Sam Tucker, "Justices Questions Pelt Religion Case Attorneys," *Courier*, December 8, 1947, p. 3.

29. Joseph Hanlon, "Appeal To Bar Religious Classes Gives High Court Hard Problems," Washington, D.C. *Evening Star*, December 9, 1947, MC-UI, Book 2, p. 72.

30. Sam Tucker, Ibid., 28, *Courier*, December 8, 1947, p. 3.

31. Ibid., 28.

32. Joseph Hanlon, Ibid., 29, *Evening Star*, December 9,1947.

33. "Religion In Schools Tested On Legality," New York *Times*, December 8 or 9, 1947, MC-UI, Book 2, p. 69.

34. Sam Tucker, Ibid., 28, *Courier*, December 8, 1947, p. 3.

35. Ed Borman, "Don't Strike Interest in Religion Franklin Urges Supreme Court: 'Talks Back' At Final Hearing In M'Collum Case," *News-Gazette*, December 9,1947, p. 3.

36. Sam Tucker, Ibid., 28, *Courier*, December 8, 1947, p.3.

37. Ibid., 28.

38. Ibid., 28.

39. Ed Borman, Ibid., 35, *News-Gazette*, December 9, 1947, p. 3.

40. Ibid,, 35.

41. Ibid., 35.

42. "Supreme Court Hears Arguments On Legality Religious Education In The Public Schools," Washington, D.C. *Times-Herald*, December 9, 1947, MC-UI, Book 2, p. 75.

43. Ibid., 42.

44. Joseph Hanlon, Ibid., 29, *Evening Star*, December 9, 1947.

45. Ed Borman, " Schools Try To Establish A Religion; M'Collum Attorney Tells Court: Justices Fire Questions On Tiny Details," *News-Gazette*, December 8, 1947, p 3.

46. Ed Borman, Ibid., 35, *News-Gazette*, December 9, 1947, p. 3.

47. Ed Borman, Ibid., 45, *News-Gazette*, December 8,. 1947, p. 3.

48. Sam Tucker, Ibid., 28, *Courier*, December 8, 1947,p. 3.

49. Rall, interview with author, September 12, 1984.

50. Franklin, interview with author, May 26, 1980.

51. Sam Tucker, Ibid., 28, *Courier*, December 8, 1947, p 3.

52. Ed Borman, Ibid., 45, *News-Gazette*, Dec. 8, 1947, p. 3.

53. Ibid., 45.

54. Rall, interview with author, September 12, 1984.

55. Sam Tucker, Ibid., 28, *Courier*, December 8, 1947, p. 3.

56. Ed Borman, Ibid., 35, *News-Gazette*, December 9, 1947, p. 34.

57. Sam Tucker, Ibid., 28, *Courier*, December 8, 1947, p. 3.

58. Ibid., 33, New York *Times*, December 8 or 9, 1947.

59. Ed Borman, Ibid., 45, *News-Gazette*, December 8, 1947, p. 3.

60. Joseph Hanlon, Ibid., 29, *Evening Star*, December 9, 1947.

61. Ed Borman, Ibid., 35, *News-Gazette*, Dec. 9, 1947,p. 3.

62. Ibid., 35.

63. Ibid., 35.

64. Ibid., 35.

65. Ibid., 35.

66. Joseph Hanlon, Ibid., 29, *Evening Star*, December 9, 1947.

67. Ibid., 29.

68. Lynn Ruester, "The Nervousness Didn't Last," *Courier*, December 11, 1947, p. 3.

69. Joseph Hanlon, Ibid., 29; *Evening Star*, December 9, 1947.

70. Appellee's Brief, pp. 70 & 71.

71. Lynn Ruester, Ibid., 68; *Courier*, December 11, 1947, p. 3.

72. Ibid., 68.

73. Ibid., 42, *Times Herald*, December 9, 1947.

74. Dillard Stokes, "Church And State Issue: Supreme Court Urged To Ban Public School Bible Classes," Washington *Post*, December 9, 1947, p. 3.

75. Sam Tucker, "Debate Finished In Religion Case," *Courier*, December 9, 1947, p. 3.

76. Lynn Ruester, Ibid., 68; *Courier*, December 11, 1947, p. 3.

77. Ibid., 68.

78. Rall, interview with author, September 12, 1984.

79. Sam Tucker, Ibid., 75, Courier, December 9, 1947, p. 3.

80. Ed Borman, Ibid., 35, *News-Gazette*, December 9,1947,p. 3.

81. Sam Tucker, Ibid., 75, *Courier*, December 9, 1947, p. 3.

82, Franklin, interview with author, May 26, 1980.

83. Rall, interview with author, September 12, 1984.

84. Sam Tucker, Ibid., 75, *Courier*, December 9, 1947, p. 3.

85. Ed Borman, Ibid., 35, *News-Gazette*, December 9, 1947, p. 3.

86. "Profound Effect On Schools Seen," *Courier*, December 8, 1947, p. 3.

87. Lynn Ruester, "The Nervousness Didn't Last," *Courier*, December 11, 1947, p.3.

88. "Mrs. McCollum Awaits Ruling," *Courier*, December 12, 1947,p. 3.

89. Ibid., 88.

90. "Franklin Files Religion Brief," *Courier*, December 12, 1947, p. 3.

91. Appellant's supplemental brief, pp. 15 & 16.

92. "Religion Basis For War, Other Human Friction...Mrs. McCollum," *News-Gazette*, December 19, 1947, p. 3

Chapter 15

1. McCollum, *One Woman's Fight*, pp. 180 & 181.

2. "Decision Of Court Leaves Mrs. M'Collum Speechless," *Courier*, March 8, 1948, p. 3.

3. McCollum, *One Woman's Fight*, p. 181.

4. Ibid., 2, *Courier*, March 8, 1948, p. 3.

5. Ed Borman, "All Efforts Of Church, State Open To Fire," *News-Gazette*, March 9, 1948, pp. 1 & 3.

6. "Mrs. McCollum's Parents, Her Son Here, Hail Decision," *Democrat & Chronicle*, March 9, 1948, p. 1.

7. Ed Borman, Ibid, 5, *News-Gazette*, March 9, 1948, pp. 1 & 3.

8. Ibid., 7.

9. Ibid., 7.

10. Ibid., 7.

11. Ibid., 2, *Courier*, March 8, 1948, p. 3.

12. Ibid., 2, *Courier*, March 8, 1948, p. 3.

13. Ibid., 2.

14. Nathon Udisky, "Court Favors Minorities: Franklin," *Daily Illini*, March 9, 1948, p. 1.

15. Ibid., 14.

16. Ed Borman, Ibid., 5, *News-Gazette*, March 9, 1948, pp. 1 & 3.

17. "Religion Class Backers Study Alternative Plans," *Courier*, March 10, 1948, p. 3.

18. Ed Borman, "Mrs. McCollum Gives Warning of Any Abuses," *News-Gazette*, March 8, 1948, p. 3.

19. "School Religion Classes to End Before Easter," *Courier*, March 11, 1948, p. 3.

20. Ibid., 2, *Courier*, March 8, 1948, p. 3.

21. "Church-State Separation Fortified," *News-Gazette*, March 8, 1948, p. 1.

22. Ibid., 2, *Courier*, March 10, 1948 p 3.

23. Ibid. 17, *Courier*, March 10, 1948, p. 3.

24. "Clergy's Views Vary On Effect of Decision," *News-Gazette*, March 9, 1948, p. 3.

25. "School Religion Classes to End Before Easter," *Courier*, March 11, 1948, p. 3.

26. Ibid. 24, *News-Gazette*, March 9, 1948, p. 3.

27. "Religion Class Backers Study Alternate Plans," *Courier*, March 10, 1948, p. 3.

28. Ibid., 21, *News-Gazette*, March 8, 1948, p. 1.

29. Ibid., 21.

30. Ibid., 21.

31. Ibid., 2, *Courier*, March 8, 1948, p. 3.

32. Ibid., 2.

33. Ibid., 5, *News-Gazette*, March 9, 1948, p. 3.

34. Ibid., 5.

35. Ibid., 5.

36. "Released Time Faces Fight Here." New York *Times*, March 9, 1948, MC-UI, Book 2, p. 103.

37. "Religious Schooling To Continue Here Despite Court Blow," Rochester *Times-Union*, March 9, 1948, p. 1.

38. "Religious Teaching In School Forbidden By Supreme Court," *Christian Science Monitor*, March 9, 1948, MC-UI, Book 2, p. 108.

39. "Religion Ruling Draws Protest," *Courier*, March 26, 1948, p. 3.

40. Ibid., 6, Rochester *Democrat & Chronicle*, March 9, 1948, p. 1.

41. ""Supreme Court Ruling To Halt Montgomery Religious Classes," Washington *Post*, March 10, 1948, MC-UI, Book 2, p. 117.

42. Ibid., 41.

43. "Religion Ban Assailed By Catholics," *Herald Tribune*, March 10, 1948, MC-UI, Book 2, p. 121.

44. "High Court's Decision On Religious Teaching Just Adds Confusion," Springfield *Leader-Press*, p. 20, MC-UI, Book 2, p. 125.

45. Ed Borman, Ibid. 18, *News-Gazette*, March 10, 1948, p. 3.

46. "Court Has Safeguard Our School System Mrs. McCollum Says. Church-State System Fortified," *News-Gazette*, March 8, 1948, p. 1.

47. Ed Borman, "All Efforts of Church, State Open to Fire," *News-Gazette*, March 9, 1948, p. 1.

48. Ibid. 25, *Courier*, March 11, 1948, p. 3.

49. Willard Hanson, "Religious Education Council To Study New Class Plans," *News-Gazette*, March 11, 1948, p. 3.

50. Ibid., 25, *Courier*, March 11, 1948, p. 3.

51. Ibid., 25.

52. Ibid., 25.

53. Ibid., 25.

54. "Religion Class Teaching Ends In Urbana," *News-Gazette*, March 11, 1948, p. 3.

55. "March 24 Date School Religion Classes To End," *Courier*, March 14, 1948, p. 3.

56. Ibid., 55.

57. Minutes of the Champaign Board Of Education, March 12, 1948.

58. "Religious Class Plan Drawn By Rev. Cartlidge," *News-Gazette*, March 16, 1948, p. 3.

59. Ibid., 58.

60. "M'Collum Rule Reversed By State Court," *News-Gazette*, May 19, 1948, p. 3.

61. "Mrs. McCollum Attorney Asks Broad Ruling," *News-Gazette*, July 23, 1948, p. 3.

62. "Arguments In School Religion Case Presented By McCollum, Franklin," *Daily Illini*, August 5, 1948, p. MC-UI, Book 3, p. 58.

63. Ed Borman, "Watson Faces 'Tough' Rule In Religious Suit," *News-Gazette*, July 25, 1948, p. 3.

64. Ibid., 63.

65. Ibid., 63.

66. "School District Change Delays Religion Action," *Courier*, July 23, 1948, p. 3.

67. Ibid. 61, *News-Gazette*, p. 3

68. "Appeal Expected In Religious Case," *Courier*, August 13, 1948, p. 3.

69. Ibid., 68.

70. Ibid., 68.

71. Ibid., 68.

72. Ibid. 68.

73. "Watson Ruling May Suffice Dodd Declares," *Courier*, August 24, 1948, p. 3.

74. Vashti McCollum, interview with the author.

75. "Watson Signs Order Ending Bible Classes," *News-Gazette*, September 25, 1948, p. 3.

76. Ibid., 75.

77. "Watson Issues Last Order On Religion Case," *Courier*, September 26, 1948, p 3.

78. Ibid., 77.

79. Ibid., 75, *News-Gazette*, September 25, 1948, p. 3.

80. "Final Victory For Mrs. McCollum," St. Louis *Post-Dispatch*, September, 1948, MC-UI, Book 3, p. 82.

Chapter 16

1. "New Law Is Created, Hostile To Religion," *News-Gazette*, March 11, 1948, p. 4.

2. "Why Oppose Bible In School? (Marked "Oklahoma," *Daily Oklahoman* (no date), MC-UI, Book 3, p. 18. (Note: Many of the citations of the original sources are incomplete because many of the clips that were sent to Vashti McCollum often were without proper identification. She kept them and pasted them in her scrapbooks and are offered here as flavor of the debate which followed the decision in her case.)

3. "But Religion Goes On," Buffalo *Courier-Journal*, March 10, 1948, MC-UI, Book 2, p. 126.

4. "May 'In God We Trust' Be Retained?" (marked "Mansfield, Ohio"), MC-UI, Book 2, p.

121.

5. "Religion In School," Salisbury *Post*, MC-UI, Book ?, p. 119.

6. "Religion And Constitution," Scranton *Times*, March 9, 1948, MC-UI, Book 2, p. 113.

7. Frank Waldrop, "Church and State," Washington, D.C. *Times-Herald*, March 14, 1948, MC-UI, Book 2, p. 132

8. "Church And State," MC-UI, Washington *Star*, Book 2, p. 143.

9. "The Supreme Court Endorses Communism," (source not identified), dated March 9,1948, MC-UI, Book 2, p 107.

10. "Office Memo," *The Progressive*, April 1948, p. 2.

11. Milton Mayer, "Come All Ye Faithless," *The Progressive*, April 1948, pp. 34 & 35.

12. Cromwell, letter to the editor of *The Progressive*, April 20, 1948. Cromwell's letter arrived too late to be included in a special section of the May issue, which featured a response to Mayer by Professor Max C. Otto, along with letters pro and con. For Harry Truman's defense of his daughter, see: Merle Miller, *Plain Speaking, An Oral Biography of Harry S. Truman*, Berkley Publishing Corp, 1973, pp. 87-89.

13. "What Price Victory?" *The Indiana Catholic and Record*, March 12, 1948, MC-UI, Book 2, p. 136.

14. "In Favor of Mrs. McCollum," St. Louis *Lutheran*, March 20, 1948, MC-UI, Book 2, p. 139.

15. "The Wall Between Church And State," Richmond *Times-Dispatch*, MC-UI, Book 2, p. 123.

16. "A Victory For Freedom," St. Louis *Post-Dispatch*, March 10, 1948, MC-UI, Book 2, p. 126.

17. "St. Louis And The McCollum Decision," *Post-Dispatch*, March 11, 1948, MC-UI, Book 2, p. 126.

18. "The School Boards Duty," *Post-Dispatch*, March 14, 1948, MC-UI, Book 2, p. 132.

19. "Mrs. Vashti McCollum's Victory," *Jewish News*, March 13, MC-UI, Book 2, p. 122.

20. "Religion in Schools," Washington *Post*, March 13, 1948, MC-UI, Book 2, p. 132.

21. Mrs. Walter Ferguson, "A Woman's View: Parents Find One Job Tossed Back to Them," Tulsa *Tribune*, MA-UI, Book 2, p. 120.

22. "The Case Of One Small Boy," St. Petersburg *Times*, March 10, 1948, MC-UI, Book 2, p. 124.

23. "Religion In The Schools," Tampa *Tribune*, March 10, 1948, MC-UI, Book 2, p. 97.

24. "Public School Religion Vetoed," Rockford *Argus*, MC-UI, Book 2, p. 100.

25. Clarissa Start, "Today Magazine," *Post-Dispatch*, March 14, 1948, p. 1.

26. "The Atheists' Child," Chicago *Herald American*, American Weekly Section, December 26, 1948, MC-UI, Book 3, p. 103.

Chapter 17

1. McCollum, *One Woman's Fight*, Doubleday & Co. Garden City, N.Y., 1951.

2. McCollum, interview with author.

3. Jean Bickmore, "A Courageous Young Woman Fought For Her Beliefs Against a Community," Salt Lake City *Tribune*, April 8, 1951, p. 7, MC-UI, Book 5, p. 7.

4. R. Magat, "Mrs. McCollum Recounts Her Battle For Religious Freedom," the Dayton *Daily News*, May 6, 1951, MC-UI, Book 5, p. 13.

5. *New Yorker* Magazine, May 5, 1951, MC-UI, Book 5, p. 23.

6. Nash K. Burger, "Churches And Schools," New York *Times*, no date, MC-UI, Book 5, p. 21.

7. James G. Noth, "Personal Story Of Mrs. McCollum," *Books on Trial*, June, 1951, MC-UI, Book 5, p. 23.

8. E. B Long, "Literary Guidepost," Woonsocket, R.I., *Independent*, May 3, 1951 MC-UI, Book 5, p. 16.

9. Alfred C. Ames, "Re: Fight On Religious Instruction In Schools," Chicago *Tribune*, April 29, 1951, MC-UI, Book 5, p. 5.

10. "One Woman's Fight—For All," St. Louis *Post-Dispatch*, March 26, 1951, MC-UI Book 5, p. 8.

11. "One Woman's Fight," Louisville *Courier-Journal*, May 20, 1951, MC-UI, Book, 5, p.

19.

12. McCollum, interview with the author.

13. Bruce Taylor, "Vashti McCollum's Book Gives Inside Version of Religious Education Suit," *Courier*, April, 1951, p. 20.

14. V.T. Thayer of *The Saturday Review*, June 30, 1951, MC-UI, Book 5, p 26.

15. "Mrs. M'Collum's Book Tells Of Religious Teaching Fight," *News-Gazette*, April 25, 1951, pp. 3 & 33.

16. Rev. John S. Kennedy, "Balancing The Books: Vashti McCollum's Atheism," *Catholic Courier-Journal*, p. 5, April 27, 1951, MC-UI, Book 5, p. 14.

17. Marcus Duffield, "Woman Of Principle, Fighter For Her Cause," N.Y. *Herald-Tribune*, March 25, 1951, MC-UI, Book 5, p. 22.

18. McCollum, *One Woman's Fight*, Beacon Press, Boston, 1952.

19. McCollum, *One Woman's Fight*, Beacon Press, Boston, 1961.

20. McCollum, *One Woman's Fight*, Freedom From Religion Foundation, Madison WI, 1993

Chapter 18

1. Owen Rall, interview with the author, September 12, 1984.

2. John Franklin, interview with the author, May 26, 1980.

3. Ibid., 2.

4. Eugene Mellon, interview with the author, May 20, 1980.

5. Ibid., 4.

6. McCollum, script in possession of the author.

7. Clarissa Start, "A Woman Of Strong Convictions" *Post-Dispatch*, March 14, 1948, MC-UI, Book 2, p. 134.

8. Edna Ruth Johnson, "Vashti McCollum Has Convictions," *The Churchman*, January 1, 1949, MC-UI, Book 3, p. 105.

9. Maxine Lowry, "Mrs. McCollum Continues Fight," Louisville *Courier-Journal*, February 11, 1961, Book 5, p. 123.

10. 'Loretta Lambroussis, Houston *Post*, March 23, 1962, Section 2, p. 4.

11. Richard Icen, "She'd File Famed Suit Again, Vashti Says 20 Years After," *Courier*, September 5, 1965, p. 38.

12. Michael Hirsley, "Is God Going Back To School?," Chicago *Tribune*, Midwest Edition, September 19, 1976, pp. 1 & 12.

13. Marlene Fritz, "Vashti McCollum Recalls Battle With Local Schools," *Courier*, March 8, 1978, p. 3.

14. Ibid., 13.

15. Beth Bosch, "Church, State Ruling 30 Years Ago," *News-Gazette*, March 8, 1978, p. A-3.

16. Abe Aamidor, "Schools And Religion," *News-Gazette*, March 23, 1986, pp. C-1 & 5.

17. Letter from William Sholem to David Sholem.

18. Melissa Merlie, "Champaign Woman Recalls Landmark Lawsuit," *News-Gazette*, June 18, 1995, pp. A-1 & 10.

19. Melissa Merlie, "McCollum Case Still A Landmark 50 Years Later," *News-Gazette*, March 8, 1998 pp. A-1 & 12.

A Brief Biography of Vashti McCollum

Vashti Cromwell McCollum was born in Lyons, New York, on November 6, 1912, the second daughter of Arthur Gifford and Ruth Clausz Cromwell. The family lived in Lyons until the early 1920s, when they moved to Rochester. There were two reasons for the move—Arthur had health problems related to military service during World War I that required treatment in Rochester, and Ruth was determined that her girls were going to have a good education, which she felt was not possible in so provincial a place as Lyons.

In Rochester, Arthur was trained as an architect as part of his rehabilitation. One of his early projects was the restoration of a very old home that they purchased in the old Third Ward—a home that during its lengthy life has had at least three different addresses without ever moving. Vashti and her older sister, Helen, graduated from West High as top students. Helen went on to the University of Rochester. Two years later, Vashti headed off to Cornell on a scholarship. She was there for two years, time enough to get in three years of credits. Unfortunately, as the Great Depression deepened, her scholarship failed to produce sufficient funds to keep her in school and she had to leave.

After laying out of school for a year, she resumed her university studies at the University of Illinois where she had also been accepted when she had applied to Cornell. There, the costs were more affordable. She entered law school there as a senior, but completed only one year. She was short of credits for graduation when she met and married a young Ph.D., also from Cornell, John Paschal McCollum. She had to stay completion of her undergraduate education when her husband was transferred to DesPlaines, Illinois, to head up the agricultural experiment station there.

Three children soon followed: James Terry (1934), Dannel (1937), and Errol Cromwell (1940). By the time Dannel arrived, John McCollum had been transferred back to the Champaign-Urbana campus as an assistant professor in the College of Agriculture. Vashti was then able to return to her undergraduate studies and complete her degree in political science (1944). Her Masters degree followed years later in 1957.

The years between the two degrees were ones of challenge, stress, and notoriety. In 1940, the Champaign Board of Education had allowed a program of released time religious education to be inserted into the junior high school. In subsequent years the program was moved into the elementary schools, first the sixth grade, then the fifth and then the fourth, where it encountered young James Terry in the fall of 1944.

It must be noted that Vashti was no passive plaintiff as is so often the case in such civil liberties and civil rights test cases. She was the major player from start to finish. Whether it was grunt work chasing down witnesses during the trial, speaking to groups around the country to raise money, or participating in all major strategic and legal decisions, Vashti was not only at the table, she was at the head of the table; at the same time, she was a shrewd team player. The objective was to win her case; there was credit enough for all.

Her husband, John, was careful to avoid the limelight during the law case and thereafter. But he quietly shared the views of his father-in-law and his wife. Growing up in the rural South with a surfeit of hellfire and damnation in the local churches, he had had enough. He simply had no use for organized religion.

Vashti was 35 years old when her case was decided. She lived on for another 57 years. She was the last adult alive who was associated with the case; gone were Cartlidge, Northcott, Nickell and Mellon, the three trial judges, attorneys Franklinson, Rall, Chapman, Dodd, and earnest supporters Schug, Raynor and all the other members of the Chicago Action Council, and all nine members of the United States Supreme Court.

Her suit had been the first civil liberties case where the high court decided that what local authorities were doing constituted an "establishment of religion," and thus under the ban of the First Amendment as applied to the states by the Fourteenth Amendment. She had never felt comfortable with the atheist label, preferring "rationalist" and "humanist."

She remained interested in public school issues. Hearing about schools in the Effingham, Illinois, area that were tax-supported and listed as public, but in effect operated as Catholic parochial schools, she and a small group made a field trip to the area for a firsthand check of the situation. And indeed, the schools were staffed by nuns and there were crucifixes in the classrooms. Champaign photographer Edward Dessen went along on the trip to document what was going on. While the others were inside one of the schools, Dessen wandered around the playground. He happened upon a youngster of whom he inquired if all the children in the school were Catholic. "No," the child responded, "but they soon will be."

Vashti enjoyed her status as a minor celebrity and continued serving the cause of freedom by writing and speaking on her case and the problem of the Catholic Legion of Decency censorship of films. She received awards from the Humanists, American Rationalists and the Chicago chapter of the American Civil Liberties Union. Looking for organizations that suited her causes and philosophy, Vashti became associated with Protestants and Other Americans United for Separation of Church and State (POAU), now Americans United for Separation of Church and State, and the American Humanist Association (AHA). On lecture tours, she shared the podiums with such notables as Sir Julian Huxley, Corliss Lamot and Nobel laureate geneticist Herman Muller. For two years in the early 1950s, she served as president of the American Humanist Association.

When Madalyn Murray (later O'Hair) filed her case many years after the decision in the *McCollum* case, she wrote to Vashti, who did not respond. Not that she did not agree with the former's cause, but their styles were worlds apart. Madalyn was out to build a following and ultimately turn her cause into a business. Vashti, on the other hand, was content to move on.

In 1956, she attended the meetings of the International Humanist and Ethical Union in Europe. That excited an interest in travel which over the next three decades took her to six continents, often by herself, and at last count included some 160 countries. Stimulated by her husband's interest in photography, she carried a camera and took thousands of slides of her travels and adventures. In 1971, upon John McCollum's retirement from the University of Illinois, they moved to Springdale, Arkansas. During their years there, Vashti continued her travels and organized her slides into shows. She and John started the Armchair Travelers program at the local library and provided many of the shows, which were highly popular. Vashti once commented that she did not know if the appeal was due to her slides or to her famous chocolate chip cookies, which she provided. The shows continued even after her return to Champaign. Her activities were slowed considerably in 1998 when she had major heart surgery, and in 2004 she moved into a senior living facility. She died August 30, 2006, at the age of 93.

Over the years, Vashti reminisced about the law case and its effects on her life and that of her family. Clearly there were some serious negative personal impacts. But as she often said in later years, "I knew I was right." Her family would be the first to agree and, as one member somewhat tongue-in-check observed: "The experience can be character-building if you survive it."

About the Author

Dannel McCollum is the second son of John and Vashti McCollum. Born in 1937, his lifelong home has been Champaign, Illinois. He earned AB, BS, and MS degrees from the University of Illinois in, respectively, political science, secondary education, and geography. After obtaining his AB in political science he served in the U.S. Army as a reserve officer and achieved the rank of captain. He later taught in junior and senior high schools for six years in Rochester, New York, and Champaign, Illinois.

He has written widely on education, conservation, local history, and local, state and national public affairs. His books include *Your Life and Mine: Problems and Projects in Conservation; A Guide to the Big Vermilion River System* (with J.O. Smith); and *Essays on the Historical Geography of Champaign County, Illinois.*

For most of his adult life he has been active in such causes as civil rights, civil liberties, peace, and conservation. From 1983 to 1999 he served on the Champaign city council, including three consecutive terms as mayor. Declining to run for a fourth term, he ran for the State Senate at the request of local Democrats, losing by less than half of one percent. He currently serves as Champaign City Historian. His wife Jeanette has been his soulmate for over a quarter of a century. His son Dan and stepson Todd are sources of ongoing pleasure. Now retired, he spends much of his time writing and running his 200-acre "farm" bordering the Big Vermilion River in East-Central Illinois.